Clocaenog Parish
and its
People

Plwyf Clocaenog
a'r
Trigolion

Past and Present Ddoe a Heddiw

A project inspired by W.I. Pathways 2000

Editor/Golygydd
Audrey Naisby

Clocaenog Women's Institute
Millennium Committee

Clocaenog Parish and its People/Plwyf Clocaenog a'r Trigolion
Past and Present/Ddoe a Heddiw
First published in Wales
by
BRIDGE BOOKS
61 Park Avenue
Wrexham, LL12 7AW
on behalf of

**CLOCAENOG WOMEN'S INSTITUTE
MILLENNIUM COMMITTEE**

© 2006 Clocaenog Women's Institute
Millenium Committee
© 2006 Design and layout Bridge Books, Wrexham

The publication of this book has been funded by the efforts of the book committee and the encouragement and co-operation of local residents. All the travel, research, interviewing, recording, computer work, editing and publishing has been carried out on a vomuntary basis by a loyal team from Clocaenog Women's Institute.

The printing of the book has been made possible with the financial support of

**Cadwyn Clwyd
The Forestry Commission
Awards for All Wales**

All Rights Reserved
No part of this publication may be reproduced,
stored in a retrieval system, or transmitted
in any form or by any means, electronic,
mechanical, photocopying, recording or
otherwise, without the prior permission
of the Copyright holders.

A CIP entry for this book is available from the British Library

ISBN 1-84494-025-X

Cover photograph by Dennis Bailey, Clocaenog

Printed and bound by
Cromwell Press Ltd
Trowbridge

Contents

The Book Committee	5
Introduction	7
In the Beginning	13
Brief History of the Area	17
Welsh Settlements	22
Clocaenog	24
Royal Parks	26
Taming the Common Land	28
Bryn Coch — a farm on enclosure land/fferm ar tiroedd caeedig	31/33
From the Correspondence of *Archaeologia Cambrensis*	36
The Drovers	42
Relgion	45
St Foddhyd's Church	45
Rectors	51
The Yew Tree	52
The War Memorial	54
The Old Rectory	56
Church Hall	58
Glebe Land	60
Caring for the Poor	60
Clocaenog Parish in 1861 — the Rev. Hughes's diary	63
The Religious Census of 1851	68
Bethesda Wesleyan Chapel/Eglwys Fethodistaidd	69/71
Cades Calvinistic Chapel/Capel Calfinaidd	73/74
Glimpses of People	75
Parish Administration	77
Population Changes	77
Changing Occupations	80
Lost Dwellings	81
Maes Caenog	84
Water Supply	85
Education	86
History of Clocaenog School/Hanes Ysgol Clocaenog	86/92
Some of the Subscribers and their Donations	100
The Building of the New School	101
Schoolmasters	101
Some Welsh Nursery Rhymes	103
Clocaenog Families	108
The Lewis Family, Tŷ Coch	108
Beryl and Dennis Bailey, Maes Caenog	112
Glenys Williams, Maestyddyn Isaf	118/119

Eryl Wyn Williams, Maestyddyn Isaf	120
Saunders Davies, Brynffynnon	122/123
June Vlies, Tŷ Capel	124
The Stephenson Family, Tan Llan	126
Edward William Davies, Glandŵr	129
Gwyneth Roberts, Childhood Days	134/135
Roy Wilson and Edgar Moody, Min-y-dŵr	138
Irene and Bryn Lewis, Maes Caenog	141
David and Clair Craig, Cae Wgan	144
The Griffiths Family, Bryngwyn	148
Catherine Susan Black, Stryt Cottage	153
William George Roberts, Y Fron	156
Morfydd Edwards and Lilian Jones	159
Beryl and David Jones, Maes Caenog	163
Mair and John Roberts, Glan Aber	166
Audrey and Eddie Naisby, Paradwys	169
History of a House — Paradwys	175
People who have lived in Paradwys	180
Paradwys may have been a pilgrims' inn	182
Early worship and holy wells	188
Licensing of alehouses	189
Coleg Llysfasi	192
History of Llysfasi	192
Interview with Mr Cunningham, the Principal	194
Ruthin Animal Auction/Yr Ocsiwn Anifeiliaid, Rhuthun	197/198
Pool Park	201
Auction of the Pool Park Estate	202
Sale of the 'Clocaenog Estate'	204
Canolfan Cae Cymro	207
Management of Clocaenog Forest	210
The Future of Clocaenog Forest	213
Red Squirrels	215
Przewalski Horse	216
Black Grouse	217
Fauna	219
Plants of Clocaenog Parish/Planhigion Plwyf Clocaenog	220/220
A Brief History of Clocaenog W.I.	228
Memories of Clocaenog W.I.	229
Clocaenog W. I. in 2006	234
Bibliography	237
Map of Clocaenog Parish Past and Present	238-9

The Book Committee

Barbara Collins
Glenys Jones Davies
Gaenor Jones
Mary Long
Audrey Naisby
Gwyneth Roberts
Hazel Robinson
Meg Syme

Articles written by:

Martin Buxbaum	M.B.
David Craig	D.C.
Ted Davies	T.D.
Gaenor Jones	G.J.
Lilian Jones	L.J.
Rhian Jones	R.J.
Audrey Naisby	A.N.
Eddie Naisby	E.N.
Hazel Robinson	H.R.
Mary Long	M.L.
Meg Syme	M.S.

Translations by:
Gaenor Jones
Lilian Jones
Rhian Jones
Gwyneth Roberts

Interviews and their editing by:
Barbara Collins
Audrey Naisby

All other editing by:
Audrey Naisby

Mrs Audrey Naisby

Mrs Gwyneth Roberts

Mrs Mary Long

Mrs Gaenor Jones

Mrs Hazel Robinson

Mrs Barbara Collins

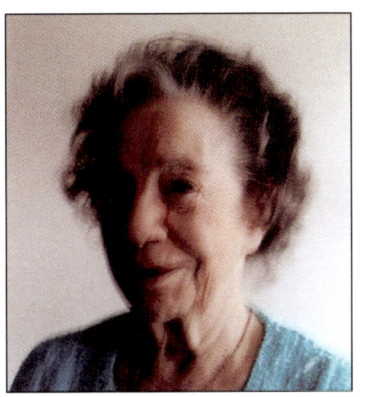
Mrs Margaret Syme

Mrs Glenys Jones Davies

Introduction
Clocaenog Women's Institute Millennium Celebrations, 2000

How we decided to celebrate with the community.

At a Women's Institute meeting in 1999 we discussed how best to join in the celebrations to mark the coming Millennium. This book is the culmination of one of those first proposals It is about a community, a very Welsh community, and also a very welcoming one, where outsiders who come to live here are accepted and whose children and grandchildren grow up here and learn to speak Welsh and become bilingual. What matters is that this place, Clocaenog, is where we, and all the rest of this community, have chosen to live for one reason or another. The fact that we are from many backgrounds adds to the interest and diversity of our input; more importantly, we accept each other and live together in harmony.

The writing of this book about Clocaenog Parish and its people has been funded by the efforts of the book committee and the encouragement and support of local inhabitants. All the travel, research, recording, computer work, editing and publishing has been carried out on a voluntary basis by a loyal team from Clocaenog Womens' Institute.

Our biggest problem has been funding. Originally we obtained a £5,000 grant from the Millennium Fund but, as the book was not completed in the required time — partly because the local archives, housed in Ruthin Gaol, were inaccessible over a two-year period while the bulding was being refurbished — we had to return the money when the Millennium Fund was wound up. You can imagine our disappointment, but we were told to re-apply to the subsequent fund. In view of the breadth and scope of the burgeoning contents, it was recognised by the book committee that the time scale for interviewing and collating material and illustrations would take much more time, though I doubt any of us realised how long.

When we neared completion we re-applied for funding but were told this could not happen in retrospect and we were turned down. As an alternative we were asked to produce a professional standard audio-visual presentation of our material for which we could have £50,000! We decided this was a totally new project and we had gone on long enough. We were encouraged by help from Cadwyn Clwyd which gave us new hope and cannot thank them enough.

We are extremely grateful to Lisa Orhan and Andrew Redfern at Cadwyn Clwyd, Greg Vickers and the Forestry Commission and, on the third attempt, Awards for All Wales for their help in financing the printing of the book. We should also like to thank Gareth Mawby and Emyr Williams from the Denbighshire Voluntary Services for their patient guidance and advice in form-filling to access the funding. I should personally like to thank Mr. Cunningham, the principal of Coleg Llysfasi, for his generous gift of time; also Mr. Levell who wrote

The Millennium Embroidery, made by Clocaenog Women's Institute.

Planting of trees and shrubs around the car park area, with villagers' support.

A break for refreshments was always welcome.

Maes Caenog car park in 2004.

Clocaenog Primary School juniors assembled with their planting tools, 2002.

Children involved in planting around the bus shelter opposite the school.

about Clocaenog Forest when he was the District Forest Planning Officer there. We are also grateful to Shakespeare Electrical Engineering Ltd and our own W.I. for their donations; Ms Fiona Gale (the archaeologist for Denbighshire, for her interesting guided walks in Clocaenog Forest); Mr Kevin Matthias and the staff of the Denbighshire Record Office, Ruthin; Mr Nick Long; Mr Joe Phillips M.Sc., Dip.F.Biol.; Mr Goronwy Wynne MSc., PhD., F.L.S. and all those who have written articles

We appreciate the help and support given throughout the project by our publisher, Alister Williams, Bridge Books, Wrexham.

I apologise that we could not include everyone in our interviews but hope you will enjoy reading those we have recorded. My grateful thanks are due to my committee, to my patient husband who had never failed to keep me going with advice or criticism, and to all those who have helped to bring this enterprise to a successful conclusion.

Anne Richards introducing Helen Prince, the representative from the Prince's Trust, who unveiled the bench.

In addition to the book the Clocaenog W.I. decided to make a picture embroidery of the village where we hold our meetings. We made it as a joint effort so that several people could participate and Pat Edwards was asked to coordinate it. Individual members each chose a house in the village, photographs were taken, and the embroideries were based on these. The finished pictures were then stitched onto a cloth. Originally intended as a wall hanging, it was decided to use it as a drape in front of the table during our W.I. meetings. Each month we are reminded of our efforts by seeing this very worthwhile compilation which shows the parish, representations of the forest, the walks in the area, the sheep and cattle of the farming community as well as the church and some of the village houses, with the title on a banner below. The embroidered hanging went on to be displayed at County and Federation level.

It was also decided to call an open meeting in the village to ask if the inhabitants would like to enhance the village environment by planting trees and shrubs. This idea was agreed to by the meeting and plans went ahead. Having chaired that meeting I continued to involve the local Community Council, and consulted the householders who might be affected by the plantings, asking for their agreement. The Community Council undertook to maintain the plantings. Permission was sought from Denbighshire Highways' Department to plant on some road verges and around the car park in Maes Caenog. Maps had to be submitted and lists of plants were drawn up. The Countryside Commission was consulted and the tree expert from Denbighshire came for an on-sight meeting. He was so thrilled to see one of the old yew trees in the churchyard because of its great antiquity and enormous girth — a specimen tree of which he had been completely unaware until then — and he judged it to be about a thousand years old. This gave us the idea to plant another yew tree to grow into the next millennium!

We had a tree planting ceremony to coincide with the church's festival in August 2000. One of our W.I. members, Mrs. Hazel Robinson, offered to donate the tree and I took her to choose it from Morrey's Nursery in Cheshire and arranged to have a plaque made. Four years on, the tree is thriving.

We were raising money to fund these activities by coffee mornings, music evenings, open gardens, whist drives and sponsored walks; some of these were better attended than others. Our treasurer, Glenys Davies, opened a bank account. We were successful in our contacts with Helen Prince, the representative of the Prince's Trust and funding was promised.

Eventually the shrubs and trees were ordered and collected — again from Morrey's — with a generous donation from them when they heard it was a millennium project, and which we acknowledged in our posters — and villagers turned out one weekend to help with the planting; stakes for the trees were donated by Mr.

The second bench, up above the village at the gateway to Fron.

Some of the villagers who gathered for the inauguration of the Village Bench, positioned in front of Old School House.

Below: Mrs. Betty Lloyd, W.I. Chairperson for Wales and Mrs. Audrey Naisby.

Bryn Lewis. The junior children from the school were involved and helped one day to plant shrubs round the bus shelter opposite.

To complete this part of our project an oak bench, which had been commissioned from Mr. Tony Collins was installed and securely bolted to a concrete base, in front of Old School House, with the approval of Mr. and Mrs. Mitchell, who overlook it, and the bench was unveiled by Helen Prince of the Prince's Trust. Also present was Mrs. Pauline Linley who was a link person in the W.I. Pathways Project and the National President, Mrs. Betty Lloyd. Another, more rugged bench, was made and placed by Eddie Naisby, at the top of the steep climb from the village to the edge of the forest, at the gateway to Fron, with the consent of Mr. W. G. Roberts (then the owner of Fron). A funding of £1,320 was received from the Princes' Trust towards the cost of planting and the two benches.

Here, at last, is our final project, the book -- and we sincerely hope there is something of interest in its pages for everyone who knows and loves this area as I do. I apologise that we could not include everyone in our interviews but hope you will enjoy reading those we have recorded. My grateful thanks go to my committee and all those who have helped to bring this enterprise to a successful conclusion.

Audrey Naisby
Editor

In the Beginning

About 15,000 years ago the last Ice Age was coming to an end, and the thousands of feet of ice which covered North Wales was beginning to melt, leaving behind a thick deposit of clay containing stones. Some of these stones and boulders, not native to this area, are unlike the local underlying Silurian shale. From fossil evidence, this shale is considered to be 350 million years old and because it is so friable it makes poor building stone. In contrast, the stones carried by the glaciers from the Arenig Mountains and other parts of Snowdonia consist of a recognisable type of granite and, although difficult to work, make good building stones and can often be found in some of the older structures. The two large boulders on the bank in front of Old School House are examples of this hard granitic matter.

Through these layers of glacial debris streams have carved out the valleys we see around us. Imagine Clocaenog without any roads, buildings or manmade features, and we see a roughly circular hollow surrounded by sheltering hills, with only one gap in the rim of this saucer shape. The river has drained this hollow by cutting an exit in the glacial deposits out towards Bontuchel. Of the six roads out of Clocaenog, this is the only route without a steep up-hill, and in later times was the main way in and out of Clocaenog

The gap in the surrounding hills where the stream runs out towards Bontuchel. The two streams flowing through Clocaenog meet near the Old Post Office to run towards Bontuchel and then on, alongside Lady Bagot's Drive, eventually becoming the Afon Clywedog before joining the Afon Clwyd just beyond Llanynys.

Archaeology in the Clocaenog area

This is a very ancient landscape and people who lived here long ago have left evidence of their lives and deaths here. Men and women who had been itinerant hunter-gatherers and using bronze tools, began to clear upland areas like this in about 3000 BC. Within the clearings they would build their homes, many of which would have been wooden, but in some instances they may have been circular stone houses built within a raised bank. Having a more permanent home meant that these first farmers were beginning to grow crops. Around 2000BC as they became more settled, living in one area; they also started to bury their dead in round shaped mounds. Later still, when people had learnt to smelt iron, they created the hill forts for which this region is famous. These were people with good organisational skills and a recognised hierarchy; their

A stone circle marking a burial cairn at Bryn Beddau.

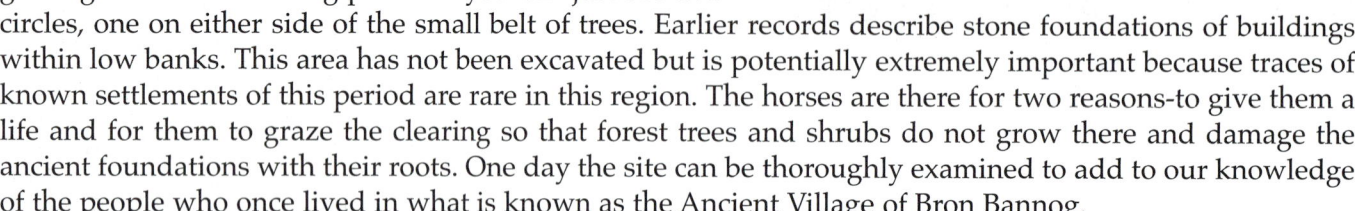

competence to live within their environment cannot be doubted and one wonders what their beliefs were when we see the effort they put into building 'ceremonial' sites such as those at Llyn Brenig.

Archaeologists have identified sites in the area probably dating from the Bronze Age in the second millennium B.C. [OS map references are given].

SJ 044 523 This is where the Przewaltski horses are grazing. From the viewing platform you can just see two circles, one on either side of the small belt of trees. Earlier records describe stone foundations of buildings within low banks. This area has not been excavated but is potentially extremely important because traces of known settlements of this period are rare in this region. The horses are there for two reasons-to give them a life and for them to graze the clearing so that forest trees and shrubs do not grow there and damage the ancient foundations with their roots. One day the site can be thoroughly examined to add to our knowledge of the people who once lived in what is known as the Ancient Village of Bron Bannog.

Maen Cred or the Stone of Faith.

SJ 020 509 Here there were two similar enclosures or 'homesteads' about 100 feet apart called the Ancient Village of Cefn Bannog. Earlier records speak of stone foundations enclosed within a low bank, but again the dating is as yet unknown. Nearby is the present house known as Cefn Bannog.

In 1991 forestry workers discovered an ancient stone lying half-buried in the forest near Cefn Bannog. It was described in the 19th century and then lost [Cf. the following article from the *Archaeologia Cambrensis*] Now it has been re-erected and a plaque placed nearby, calling it Maen Cred or Stone of Faith. In the mediaeval period it was probably a route marker for passing pilgrims to stop and pray and maybe trace the engraved cross with their finger-tips.

SJ 035 546 This site is just south of the road from Pennant Chapel towards Cerrig y drudion. It is a simple ring cairn of which some of the larger stones have been removed from the bank and at one time there was a small mound in the centre.

SJ 032 545 At the edge of the forest west of the track to Cruglas is a small stone circle with a central mound. Only three stones remain in the circle but a close examination will reveal as many as fifteen hollows where the other stones once stood. The complete circle would have been 43ft. across.

SJ 053 533 There is a small hill south-west of Maestyddyn Uchaf, known as Bryn Beddau (the Hill of Graves) which, before the

The road from Ruthin down to the village of Clocaenog.

Left: In 1960, a bulldozer clearing a swathe through the forest revealed two urns of the enlarged FV type. These were not made from local clay but were probably traded. Their design shows an Irish influence. [Denbighshire Record Office]

Below: Excavations of a grave pit in ClocaenogForest, 1960. [Denbighshire Record Office]

forestry planting, must have had a clear view all around; on the top is a stone circle, roughly 15m across, made up of 19 stones with a large boulder in the centre. It is thought to be at least 3,500 years old and dates from the Bronze Age. In this position it may have been a focal point or centre of 'ritual' for a community living round about, with many burial mounds built of earth, turves and stone, on the slopes below it, and perhaps similar in its purpose to our village churches and chapels. Some people think that these monuments may also have played a part in the lives of the early farmers by acting as a calendar and helping them to work out times of planting and reaping by 'reading' the alignments of the stones in regard to the sun, moon and stars, to define the passing seasons.

Nearby is a Bronze Age Barrow or burial mound known as Bedd Emlyn, which in 1854 was dug in the centre by the Cambrian Archaeological Association but they found no burial — the hollow is still there. An inscribed stone stood in the centre of the site until 1813 when it was removed to Pool Park; it is now in the National Museum in Cardiff. This Stone of Emlyn has an inscription in Latin and in Ogham, commemorating Similinus the Prince. This is one of the rare examples of such writing found in this area; it is more commonly found in Ireland and enabled the interpretation of Ogham, when related, as on this stone, to Latin. Ogham was an early Irish Christian alphabet of twenty characters, formed by parallel strokes on either side of a continuous line, sometimes along an edge of stone or wood.

Further excavations were carried out by Clwyd Archaeology in

Left: A sketch showing the inscription on the stone from Bedd Emlyn.

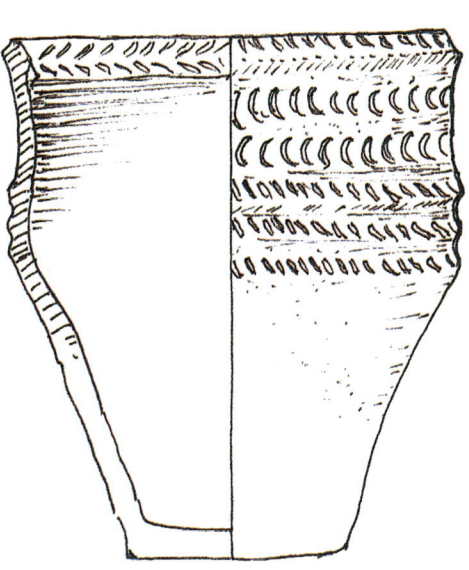

Right: A sketch of the cremation urn as shown in The Archaeology of Clwyd *and found in Clocaenog.*

1960 and remains of burial urns for cremation were found nearby, and many artefacts, which were in secondary burials within the cairn area. The clay of the Brenig urns suggests that beakers such as these had been produced elsewhere and must have been carried into the area through some trading system.

Bryn Bethau and Bedd Emlyn are scheduled ancient monuments and are being cared for under the forestry management plan.

SJ 064 552 As well as the Bagot monument on Pincyn Llys there is a cairn. A quadrilateral enclosure on the hill is called Llys y Frenhines (Queen's Court) and up there was found a stone 'seat' which may have been used to enthrone a new ruler, overlooking her domains, and this also was taken to Pool Park.

SJ 036 547 There are old accounts of a line of interesting Bronze Age monuments running across the saddle between the two valleys on the edge of the forest near Pennant Chapel (now a private house); one may have been a ring cairn but is now ploughed and gone. Those you can see at Llyn Brenig on the archaeological trail may be similar.

The Romans penetrated to most parts of Britain, and although there have been no finds in Clocaenog, not far away in Betws Gwerfil Goch a hoard of Roman coins was found, and there is evidence of Roman occupancy at the site of the Brynhyfryd estate in Ruthin. After the departure of the Romans early in the fifth century A.D. many parts of coastal Wales were visited by Viking and Irish raiders. The Ogham stone found in Clocaenog shows Irish influence, as do the pottery relating to burial urns which were probably traded.

A.N.

Fiona Gale, archaeologist for Denbighshire, speaking to a group of interested amateurs at a stone circle in the Clocaenog Forest.

Brief History of the Area

Celtic Wales
The Celtic peoples living in this part of the country before the Romans came were the Deceangli, while to the south in 'mid-Wales' were the Ordovices. (These are the Romanised names) We know that they spoke a Celtic language and that about the same time a written language appears. They had their own system of law, promulgated by Hywel Oda, a major part of which was concerned with inheritance. In effect this was of great importance when a father died, for all his sons would claim an equal share of his land and property. This was very different from many other societies of that time where the eldest son would inherit. Imagine the difference when a Welsh ruler died; under Celtic law the property, land and wealth were fragmented.

Roman Wales
The Romans certainly came to Wales and left their mark on Ruthin, as was confirmed when the Brynhyfryd estate was being built. Even if Latin dominated the secular rulers and was paramount in the church litany, the language of the ordinary people was Brithonic. Both the Christian church and the subsequent Welsh language were affected by contact with Rome. Another retained influence was the form of agriculture set up in late Roman times based on large tracts of land which contained both upland and lowland, and was settled by tenant farmers and serf labourers, and could form a more or less self-sufficient economy. These were the trefi of mixed farming and cattle raising which formed the estates of the ruling class, whether Roman or on Welsh commotes.

Throughout the Dark Age north-east Clwyd was essentially border country and fought over with tenacity. The Anglo-Saxons made many incursions and the Kingdom of Mercia certainly had designs on the flatter, fertile countryside of the Vale of Clwyd. There must have been much resistance for the construction of Offa's and Wat's dykes to be needed. Unfortunately the Welsh people were powerless to prevent all these invaders and their own fratricidal princes from devastating the land with war. Often there were Welshmen fighting on both sides in a conflict, depending on the allegiance of their leader at that time. All troops hoped for plunder and lived off the land through which they were travelling. The Welsh rarely fought as a large army but became experts at guerrilla warfare and when the Normans came they harried their supply lines and their contingents on the move.

The Norman Conquest and the Welsh Church
In 1070 William the Conqueror came to Chester and granted the county to Hugh of Avranches, ordering him to build a castle at Rhuddlan (the only recorded castle in this northern region before 1100) and it was given to Hugh's cousin, Robert, with orders to contain the Welsh. Robert was successful because the Domesday records show that he had established a church, a mint, iron mines and fisheries there by 1086.

The Welsh Church had acknowledged the supremacy of Rome even before the Normans came to Britain. After the invasion, the Welsh churches lost some of their national character and were brought into line with those in western Europe. The country was gradually divided into areas, each under the pastoral care of a bishop — in North Wales the bishops of Bangor and St. Asaph. Each bishopric was sub-divided into archdiocese, such as Dyffryn Clwyd, and then into deaneries and parishes. In each parish the tithes were collected in the tithe barn and belonged to the incumbent priest a tenth of all produce was collected from every household — the tenth calf, lamb or pig born, a tenth of eggs laid or butter made, a tenth of fish caught

Early Mediaeval Wales — ninth century

or of sheaves of corn harvested, even a tenth part of an animal slaughtered for winter food. It was a burdensome tax on peasant productivity.

The outlying places like Clocaenog — 'Clok' on some maps — would be served by a chapel under the care of a chaplain, who received a fixed stipend (Clocaenog was once a chapel under the mother church of Llanynys). If a church was established by a Norman lord, he would receive the profits of the tithe, appointing a vicar to conduct services and then paying him part of the revenue as a stipend. All the parishioners had to attend services or could suffer a fine. An incumbent who enjoyed the entire ecclesiastical revenue of a parish was termed the rector. The revenues of a bishop however came from his estates; as a great landowner, he rented out the land to tenants and in addition, he was especially privileged in being free of certain secular obligations, such as service in the army.

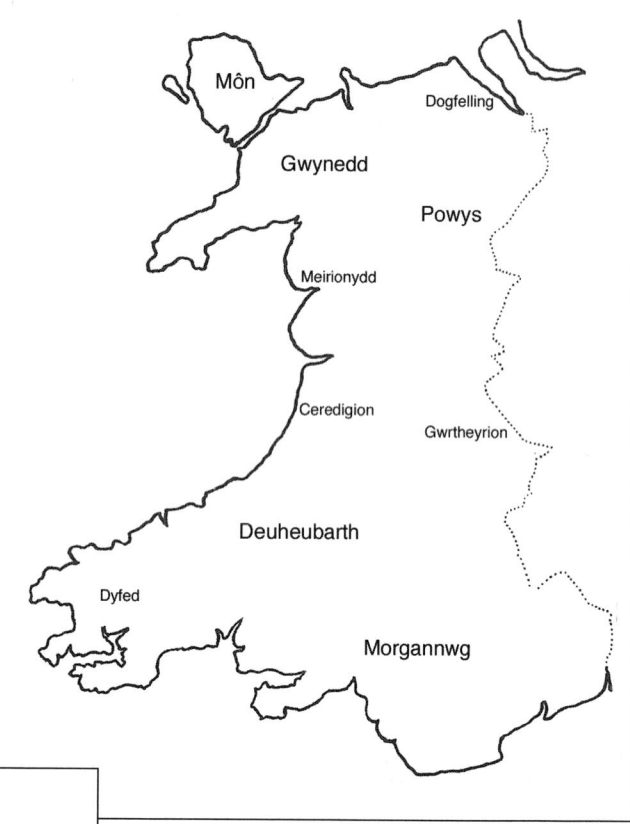

The Church and its clergy in mediaeval times were free and independent of state law, the Church having its own courts for the trials of offending clergy. These courts were also used in deciding cases concerning marriage and separation, and the proving of wills. It was the exercise of these rights which became the main bone of contention between Church and State in the Middle Ages and it was not until the Reformation that the Churches of England and Wales were made subject to the State, in the reign of Henry VIII.

Dyffryn Clwyd

In the thirteenth century the princes of Gwynedd were superior to all other Welsh princes and this was recognised by the English king. While further south had been conquered and put under the rule of various Norman lords, North Wales was still a turbulent area. Gruffydd ap Llwelyn was one of the

Welsh Administrative and Territorial Units in the Middle Ages.

The lordship of Dyffryn Clwyd was made up of the three units of Dogfeiling, Llanerch and Colyan (Colion) with the central town and castle of Ruthin as the controlling point.

The Principality of Wales at its greatest extent in 1267.

Llewelyn ap Iorwerth (Llewelyn Fawr) ruled this territory in feudal style but still had to show fealty and pay a massive sum of money to the English Crown. He married Joan, the illegitimate daughter of King John, and arranged the marriage of one of his daughters to a Mortimer (a descendant gave the Welsh strain to the present royal house). He did his best to have the succession of Dafydd (his son by Joan) recognised by the king and the pope but, after Llewelyn's death, Dafydd's half-brother Gruffydd fought him for the inheritance and once more civil war broke out in the Welsh lands.

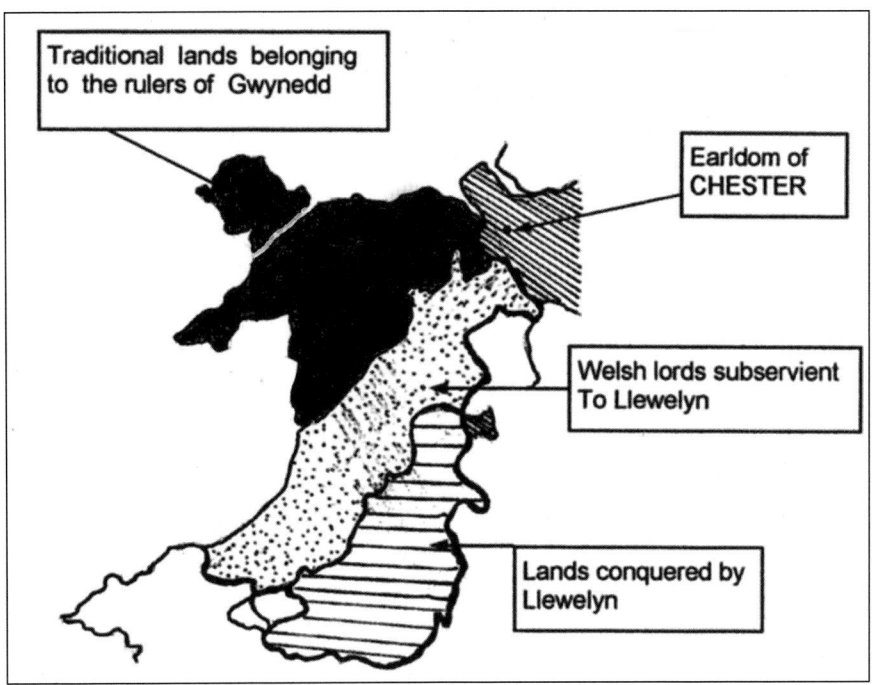

chief trouble makers over a period of 25 years. However, Prince Edward, on behalf of his father, King Henry III, decided to show his authority over this northern area by granting the lordship to a Welshman (Llewelyn), on condition that his title to the land should be conditional on his first being obliged to acknowledge the king, as his overlord. Edward obviously hoped that the Welsh would obey one of their own princes more readily.

In 1263, Dafydd (Llewelyn's brother) who changed sides several times, was given lordship over Dyffryn Clwyd, with Ruthin as its administrative centre, and Rhufoniog (where Denbigh would later be the centre of administration) but first he had to pay homage to Prince Edward, and again in 1277, when Edward had become king. It was stipulated that Dafydd's title to those lands should only remain valid until he was restored to his other lands 'beyond the Conwy'. It was in 1277 that King Edward commenced building his castles at Flint, Rhuddlan and also Denbigh and Ruthin; initially the defences would have been wooden structures and only later were master builders brought in to construct the stone castles, the remains of which are still to be seen.

After the Treaty of Conway, when Dafydd realised he would never regain his lands in Gwynedd, he foolishly rebelled against the king and attacked Hawarden Castle in March 1282 with the reluctant support of his brother, Llewelyn. They were defeated and Welsh resistance withered away after Llewelyn was killed in 1283 and his

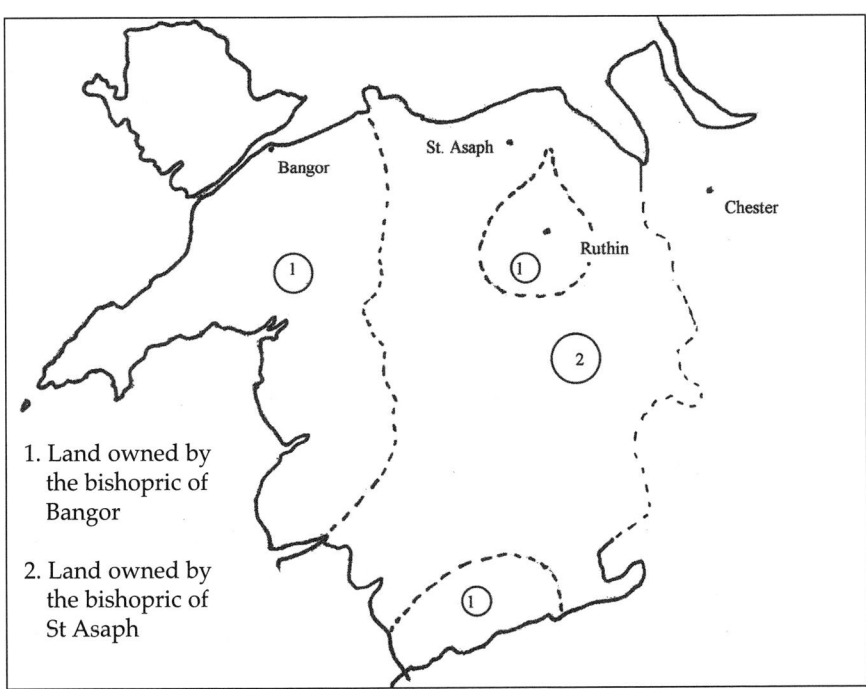

Land once owned by the Bishop of Bangor in the twelfth century *(based upon the map in* The Historical Atlas of Wales, *Plate 33, with acknowledgement to the National Library of Wales).*

head exhibited at the Tower of London; Dafydd was executed in Shrewsbury soon after. During a visit to Denbigh on 23 October 1282 Edward I granted Ruthin Castle and the commote of Dyffrynclwyd to the de Grey family, who had been leaders of the English forces retaking the area.

About one hundred years later, Owain Glyn Dŵr, a Welsh lord who had established himself in English law, training at the Inns of Court, owned a moated mansion at Sycharth. He had lordship over Glyn Dyfrydwy and Cynllaith Owain, held directly of the king, and lived as a Marcher gentleman. He had fought with honour for the English king in Scotland and was respected by all.

In 1399, Reginald de Grey, the lord of Ruthin and a friend of the new king, Henry IV, was quarrelling with Owain Glyn Dŵr over some common land which Owain said had been stolen. An insult to Owain was a very serious matter, but there must have been great rumblings of discontent of which he was aware and, with the support of the dean of St. Asaph, and other Norman-Welsh Marcher lords, he raised his banner outside Ruthin and attacked de Grey with several hundred men. No mercy was shown to the town or its people and Owain then went on to fire every town in north-east Wales. Surely men from Clocaenog must have been involved.

Wherever Owain went the Welsh rose up to fight. Henry IV marched north with a big army and the subsequent devastation in Wales was to last for twelve years. Owain held a parliament in Machynlleth and was called Prince of Wales. In 1405 there was agreement to a tripartite indenture of the realm with Mortimer to take the crown and the south, Percy the north and Glyn Dŵr himself to rule all the land from the Mersey to the Severn, covering the Marches and to include vast areas of western England. At first the revolt was amazingly successful and Owain Glyn Dŵr was never betrayed by his own people but, strange to say, nobody knows where he died and was buried. This was the last attempt to gain self-rule for the Welsh people.

Local Government

Everything revolved around the proper working of the court of the shire, to administer the local government and to mete out justice. The king ruled through the courts and the people learned of the king's will. Grievances could be heard by the appointed Anglo/Norman sheriff, with the help of token local Welsh freeholders whom he chose to sit in judgement with him. The court had to meet once a month on a fixed day and at a definite place, which in the case of Dyffryn Clwyd was Llanerch, in the Parish of Clocaenog. Tradition has it that the old barn of the farmstead of Llanerchgron (near to the present village of Pwllglas), a building 45 feet long externally, and certainly of ancient construction, was where the manorial courts of the commote were held; this court is often mentioned in the manorial records of the tenth century. They were discontinued as separate courts about 1600.

At the end of the 13th century Dyffryn Clwyd was transformed into a marcher lordship. It became part of the diocese of Bangor, despite being surrounded by the lands belonging to the diocese of St. Asaph. The crown and the church between them were the greatest landowners, and bishops not only held privileged positions in the church but also drew a substantial income from their tenants; in the case of the bishop of Bangor, he was the principal owner of land in the cantref of Dyffryn Clwyd and lord of almost the whole of the commote of Llanerch, which covered the modern parishes of Llanfair and Llanelidan.

Clocaenog Parish

Present day parishes tend to follow the old patterns of land division, with some slight modifications. Certainly parts of the parish of Clocaenog were owned by the Bishop of Bangor at one time, before being transferred to the authority of the Bishop of St Asaph. In more recent times the fields around present day Brynfedwyn were still marked on the enclosure map of 1828 as belonging to the manor of Brynfedwyn, owned by the Bishop of Bangor (manor was a unit of land consisting of a lord's demesne and lands rented out to tenants, the bishop having feudal lordship over those lands — it does not indicate a manor house).

Cefn Cloion

This was a considerable area of uncultivated land, lying at a high altitude, to the south east of the village of Clocaenog. The name 'Cloion' is thought by some to be a corruption of 'Coelion', which is said to have been one of the three Welsh commotes of Dyffryn Clwyd or Ruthinland, in which were the parishes of Efenechtyd, Derwen, Cyfylliog, Llanfwrog, Clocaenog and part of Llanynys. It is more likely that Coelion, also Colegion, were simply scribal mistakes, of which there were many. The area was enclosed in 1852 following the local Enclosure Acts.

Status

In the Middle Ages everyone knew his station in life — you were born to it — and the land owners, including those of the church, maintained the framework of social hierarchy. At the top were the gentlemen (those who could live without manual labour), with the prince at the head and the nobility, down to the squires; in the second layer were the citizens and burgesses of some 'substance' — mainly merchants in the cities, then came the affluent yeomen of the countryside; and lastly the majority, made up of labourers and craftsmen who were poor and had no voice in the government or decision-making of the state. Only 2% of the population were classed as gentlemen and they owned the land and had influence over the lives of all those socially below them.

Modern Times

Most people living in Clocaenog parish were either engaged in agriculture or craftwork. Right up to the nineteenth century farmers were tenants of the estates, latterly of the Pool Park Estate owned by Lord Bagot. Others were serving the local community and making it almost self-sufficient by working as blacksmith, shoemaker, baker or wheelright. Clocaenog is still largely an agricultural area, where sheep predominate and there are few milking herds now. Almost all farmers now own their own farm but extra land is still rented. A few people now commute to work in the cities.

At the beginning of the 19th century there was a determined effort to reshape the landscape with the enclosure of common land, new roads and the flooding of some of the marshier valleys for reservoirs, to supply the needs of the growing cities with drinking water.

There was the welcome arrival of piped water to Clocaenog village and the switch to electricity in the 1950s. Other events that deeply affected Clocaenog were the establishment of the two chapels and the building of the two schools (Old School House and later the National School) to educate the village children.

Twelve council houses were built, and in the 1980s, the six detached houses above and below Stryt Cottage and three more houses on Glyn Dŵr field behind them have been added. The bridge by the present school has been improved (2003) in the hope of preventing further flooding in this low-lying part of the village.

The sale of the Jones' farms and the development of new houses on their sites will lead to more traffic on the lanes but may also bring more young families into the community.

A.N. & E.N.

Welsh Settlements

Prior to the twelfth century there is no clear written evidence of land settlements and until the Domesday Book of 1086 it is only possible to go by archaeological field work--there is thought to be a mediaeval settlement at Bron Bannog but it has not yet been excavated. The Domesday Book provides a record of land held by Norman manors and estates and largely ignores other people — in this case the Welsh — living in scattered settlements which are not recorded. At the end of the twelfth century Gerald of Wales observed that the Welsh 'neither inhabit towns, villages nor castles'; where presumably the Norman English lived. Gerald remarks that the Welsh mostly live in scattered dwellings in the woods, made of wattle and daub, strong enough to last a year or two and costing little to construct. Despite this, on his travels, he comments on a few settlements around Welsh churches, with their villages and burial grounds, some of which had been burnt down by the invading Norman armies. Many of these settlements had English names from earlier invasions by the Mercians.

A *commote* was an administrative area with supposedly about 50 *vills*, ruled on behalf of the king or lord, from a *maerdref* (a centre containing a hall, a kitchen, a sleep-house, the stables and a privy), surrounded by a fenced enclosure. Outside the fence there would probably be a barn and a corn-drying kiln and the arable land for ploughing. An important settlement might have another building in which the king's court, or *llys*, could function. A *llys* could also be on high ground where a lord could be seated overlooking his *demesne*. At Pincyn Llys or Llys y Frenhines (Queen's Court) a chair-shaped stone was found which was removed to Pool Park in 1804. A *vill* would obviously work best if situated on good agricultural land and if possible on an important route or crossing point. The settlement would also own land elsewhere for summer grazing, often on higher ground.

The other dwellings, outside the villages, were said by the Welsh mediaeval law books to need two pathways, one to the church and the other to a watering place, as well as access to the common land of the *vill*. Each habitation would have a garden around it to grow food for the

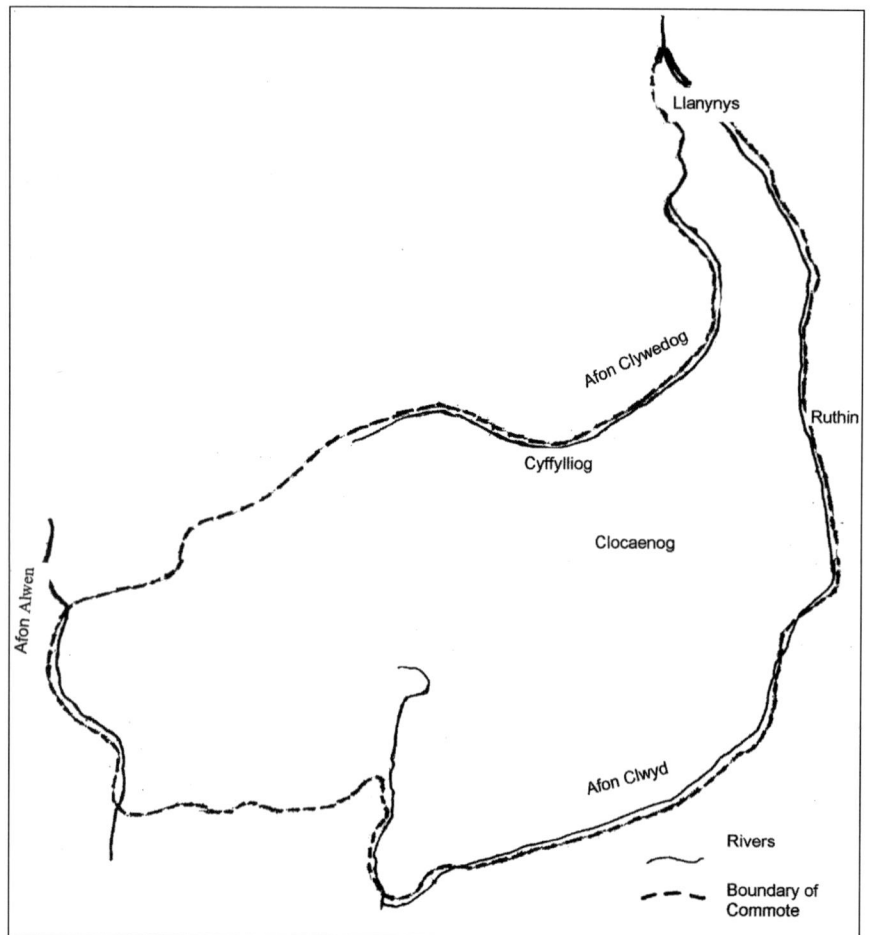

Sketch map showing the outline of the commote of Colion in the fourteenth century.

household, and the right of rough grazing on the higher land. It was only a rich free man who could own a plough and cut the furrows on his allocated strip of arable land or *quillet*. Some strip fields at Maes Isa, Llanynys, in the Vale of Clwyd, were ploughed until the mid-twentieth century and the ridge-and-furrow fields can still be seen in some places, as at Pickhill Hall, near Wrexham.

Who was 'David the Chaplain'?
David is mentioned as the Dean of Llanynys in 1254 and again in 1291 when he inherited land, shared with his brother, Gronw. Llanynys was at that time one of the richest churches in North Wales. The settlement was sited on raised well-drained land between the rivers Clwyd and Clywedog and had a *clas* or community of canons under an abbot. Of the 24 *portionaries* of the church revenue, only David the chaplain had the duty 'to cure the souls of the parishioners'. David and Gronw, his brother, held two messuages and half a carucate (ploughland) at Llanynys, as well as a messuage in Cyfylliog, together with other hectares here and there; these lands would be let to bonded tenants. The whole community of Llanynys shared land on Cefn Moor above Cyffylliog. David also inherited the chaplaincy of the church of Saint Ffoddhyd, Clocaenog, from his father (name unknown).

It was this fragmentation through the right of several sons to inherit in Celtic law that led to property being divided up into uneconomic parcels of land — and led to family feuds and many of the battles of the Welsh princes.

A.N.

Quillet = small garden. Dates back to the long narrow strips of allocated arable land lying outside the *'llan'* (village/parish).
Vill = feudal township usually associated with a manor, estate or church, generally in the lowland.
Messuage = A dwelling house with outbuildings and land assigned to its use.
Manor = can be the house of the lord of the manor, but can be a unit of land consisting of a lord's demesne and lands rented out to tenants. e.g. Manor of Brynfedwyn, Clocaenog, was rented land belonging to the Bishop of Bangor, and consisted of the church and all the land within three miles radius.
Demesne = a domain; land belonging to an estate and often worked by bonded tenants; only a freeholder owned his own land and house.
Bondsman = a form of slavery dating back to Norman times, when a peasant was in thrall to his lord and tied to the land he lived on. Even a lord was bonded to his king and received protection in return for service, usually in the form of being required to bring armed men to defend king or country whenever called upon to do so.

Clocaenog

A parish in the hundred of Ruthin, county of Denbigh; 3½ miles (SW) from Ruthin This parish is situated in a mountainous district, and the village is almost surrounded by unproductive and widely extended heaths: in the vicinity are some excellent quarries of stone, among which is that peculiar kind used for hones.

A Topographical Dictionary of Wales, 1833 & 1849, by Samuel Lewis

View of the village of Clocaenog.

Hones — various stones were used as hones or whetstones, to give a razorsharp edge to tools such as scythes or sickles, and even ploughshares all of which were the essential implements of the farmer for centuries. In the case of Clocaenog most of the local stone is soft shale which makes poor building stone as it is so friable and easily split by frost — and is certainly not hard enough for sharpening tools.

The ancient parish of Clocaenog comprised the townships of Bryngwrgi, Llanerchgron, Maen-ar-ei-gilydd, Maestyddyn, Clocaenog Uchaf and Clocaenog Isaf. Townships in this sense were simply small clusters of dwellings not villages. The names Clocaenog, Maestyddyn, Bryngwrgi, and Llanerchgron are still in use. The Old Barn of the Farmstead of *Llanerch* was used for courts manorial. The courts of this manor appear regularly in the rolls of the lordship of Dyffryn Clwyd. They were discontinued as separate courts about 1600.

Maen-ar-ei-gilydd — has been impossible to definitely identify but, just below Craig Bron-Bannog, and marked on the Ordinance Survey map at SJ 021516, as 'Pile of Stones' is a widespread heap of hard dark gritstone, mostly hidden by growth; a forestry track cuts across, but the stones are distinctly different from

Above: Bryngwrgi today. A much older cottage stood on the left of the picture but has now been demolished.

Left: The lane still winds round a cluster of buildings.

On the OS map there is a site just below Craig Bron-bannog marked 'Pile of Stones'. These are hard, black gritstones and are suitable for making hone stones. Could this be the place where there was a township for quarry workers to live and known as Maen-ar-ei-gilydd? Could this settlement have included Cefnbannog, Lodge Uchaf, Lodge Isaf and Brynhyfryd or perhaps the ancient homesteads also marked on the map?

those in the more modern quarry nearby. Could this 'heap' be the reason for the naming of the township of Maen-ar-ei-gilydd, and given rise to a cluster of miners' houses near to the unusual but useful 'Pile of stones'? Maen-ar-ei-gilydd can be translated as 'stones on each other'. Are these the hone stones for which Clocaenog was once known?

Maen-ar-ei-gilydd was considered of value and so was mentioned in a marriage settlement of December 1718, between

1. Thomas Puleston of Emrall, Co. Flint, esq.

2. Sir Roger Mostyn of Mostyn, Co. Flint Bart. and George Shakerly of Gwersitt, cc. Denbigh, esq.

3. Mary Thelwell of Nantclwyd, Co. Denbigh, spinster.

1 and 3 grant 2 upon trusts (specified) capital messuage called Emrall with its parks and demesne lands, 2 water mills and the messuages called Maen-ar-ei-gilydd, Ty yn y Kelyn, Llanerch Gron in Clocaenog.

A.N.

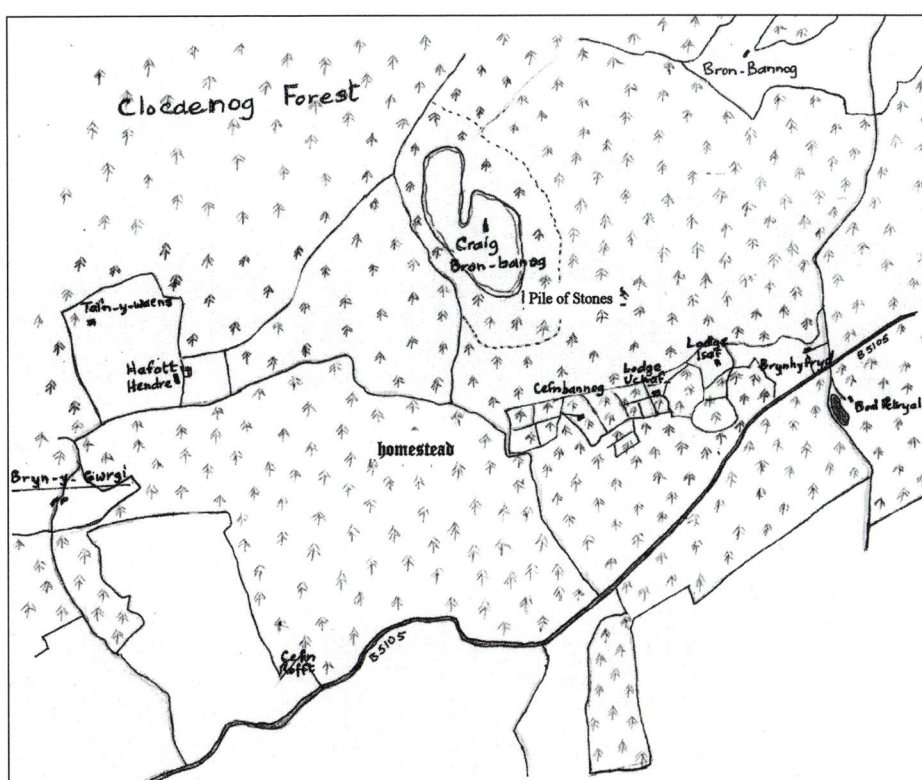

Sketch map to show the possible position of Maen-ar-ei-gilydd, below Craig Bron-banog

Royal Parks

Clocaenog and Pool Park

In mediaeval times, Ruthin, with its castle, was the administrative centre of Dyffryn Clwyd. Much attention has been given to the history of castles, but also of importance was the use of the surrounding areas, and how the land supported the castle administration with game, hunting and revenue.

To the south of Ruthin the early Welsh princes laid out the Royal Parks of GLYMPOLVA (Pool Park) and CLOK (Clocaenog), together with the forest of BROUNBANNOCK (Bron-banog). Eventually, in 1282 Dyffryn Clwyd came under the rule of the English Crown, and Edward I granted the area to Reginald de Grey. He probably inherited this already established network of parks, forests and reserved woodland which also included the forest of DERWEN, and the park of BATHARFAN (to the north of Ruthin), about which there is a lot of written evidence available.

Mediaeval forest was not an area all planted with trees, but was land subject to forest laws, not necessarily wooded; such an area was used as a covert for deer and wild boar, and might have included settlements. Forests were carved out of waste-land. Parks, on the other hand, were formally enclosed, with a ditch on the inside and a bank on the outside topped by a wooden fence. Foresters were encouraged to oversee these parks and would rent farms within the area. The forests and parks of Dyffryn Clwyd were protected by at least ten 'foresters' and seven 'parkers'. A link to the present day is seen in the farms, cottages and woods named 'Park' or 'Lodge'. Sometimes *parks* and *forests* lay adjacent to one another, e.g. Brounbannok forest and Clok park, the latter being a secure breeding area for restocking the forest with beasts for the chase.

Apart from the lord's utilisation of the forest for hunting, it was a useful source of income, the timber being used for roof shingles, weapons, wood for the slaking of lime to make mortar, charcoal for iron forges, fuel wood, fodder for cattle and bark for tanning. Reginald de Grey, for example, granted burgesses of Ruthin the right of housebote and haybote (the right to take timber for house building and hedge construction respectively). Eventually the revenue collected from rents, grazing, fines for trespass, and the sale of timber, became more important than the use of the land as hunting preserves.

This state of affairs existed throughout the thirteenth and fourteenth centuries. During the fifteenth century land within the parks and forests was being leased and sold, particularly in the reigns of Elizabeth I and James I. Batharfan Park had been sold to John Thelwall by 1592. In

The mediaeval park boundary is still quite high in places.

The old boundary can be seen in the centre of this photograph with Clocaenog Forest on the left and pasture falling away to the valley on the right. A section of the bank has been cleared to allow access.

Below: The Clok Royal Park boundary under snow.

1630 the parks of Clocaynog and Pool combined were sold for £400.

In the case of Clocaenog much of the park and forest remained as common land until 1860 when it was formally fenced under the Enclosure Acts. In the nineteenth century, the park was owned by Lord Bagot and many acres were planted with oak forest, which later again were planted by the Forestry Commission, and some parts of the original boundary ditch were obscured. However, about 50% of the boundary can still be identified, particularly along the ridge to the north-east of Maes-tyddyn-isaf. Documentary sources, with place-name evidence, suggest that the park and forest enclosed about 2,500 acres and included Cyffylliog and Bontuchal.

A more detailed account of the parks and forests of Dyffryn Clwyd can be found in the *Transactions* of the Denbighshire Historical Society (1994) as researched by André O. Berry.

E.N.

Taming the Common Land

In 1800, about a quarter of the land in Wales was classified as Common Land, that is, waste or unenclosed land. This Common Land was invaluable, and even indispensable to the small farmers and cottagers who used it as summer pasture, without them having to pay rent or tithes.

There had been always been a gradual reclamation of this land, usually the work of squatters who built small dwellings and cleared patches of ground to grow food; this had actually been encouraged by the authorities, as it kept the poor off the rates. By 1795, a report by the Board of Agriculture estimated that in Denbighshire there were still 102,000 acres of common and waste land. By 1829 half the parish of Clocaenog was common land. In *A Topographical Dictionary of Wales*, 1833 & 1849, Samuel Lewis describes how 'This parish [Clocaenog]is situated in a mountainous district, and the village is almost surrounded by unproductive and widely extended heaths'.

During the reign of George III the mania for enclosure took hold and this involved the fencing in of common land, in order to bring new areas under cultivation and to allocate them to individual owners who could pay for that land. It was hoped that this would lead to more efficient agricultural regimes, such as rotational planting which would include nitrogenous crops like clover. Each area was dealt with by a separate Enclosure Act of Parliament, generally promoted by the landed gentry who were the proprietors and owners of other property within a parish; in the case of Clocaenog Parish, it was Lord Bagot.

The Act involving the Clocaenog Common Land was included in the Enclosure Act for Ruthin of 1852 and it comprised the allocation of 5,600 acres. Fields in this area dating back to earlier times, and near to villages, tend to have irregular shapes and were usually small in size; by contrast the Enclosure Commissioners marked out rectangular fields, each of about three or four acres. Approaching Clawddnewydd from Ruthin, there are examples of such fields on each side of the main road, carved from an area known as Cefn Collion Common. These new fields are numbered on the Enclosure map in Ruthin Record Office and the accompanying document shows the allottee and how much was paid for each field; for instance a field near Bryn-y- Ffynnon,OS 094537, of roughly four acres, was sold for £3.10s in 1852.

There were three principal allottees:

- Lord Bagot purchased 1,272 acres.

- Frederick Richard West purchased 529 acres.

- Sir Watkin Williams Wyn purchased 310 acres.

In most cases it was the cottagers who suffered, with no compensation or allotment provided for them, and often the ejected people were forced to move to the towns, even to America, or the men into the army or navy, leaving their dependants to live on the scanty allowance of the parish. Generally those who did not own any land came off badly with the loss of communal grazing rights. Their reaction was understandably hostile and there were disturbances in Caernarfonshire in 1809, 1810 and again in 1812; surprisingly few considering the enormity of what was being done to the population of Britain at that time.

However, in our area, some land was set aside for the poor of Clocaenog, and squatters who had occupied their patches of land for 20 years or longer were allowed to keep it; if less than 20years they had the first option to buy — if they had the capital!

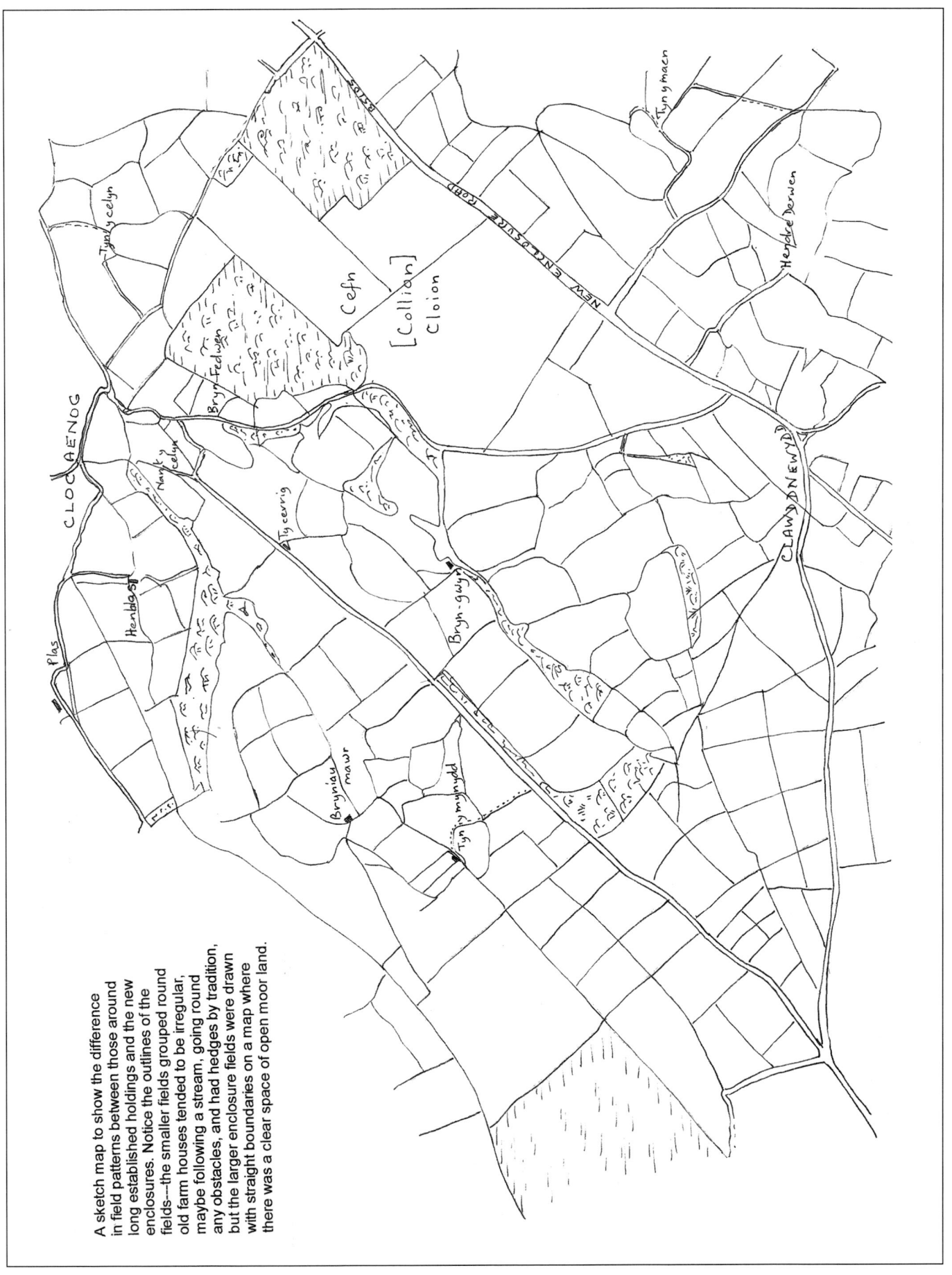

A sketch map to show the difference in field patterns between those around long established holdings and the new enclosures. Notice the outlines of the fields—the smaller fields grouped round old farm houses tended to be irregular, maybe following a stream, going round any obstacles, and had hedges by tradition, but the larger enclosure fields were drawn with straight boundaries on a map where there was a clear space of open moor land.

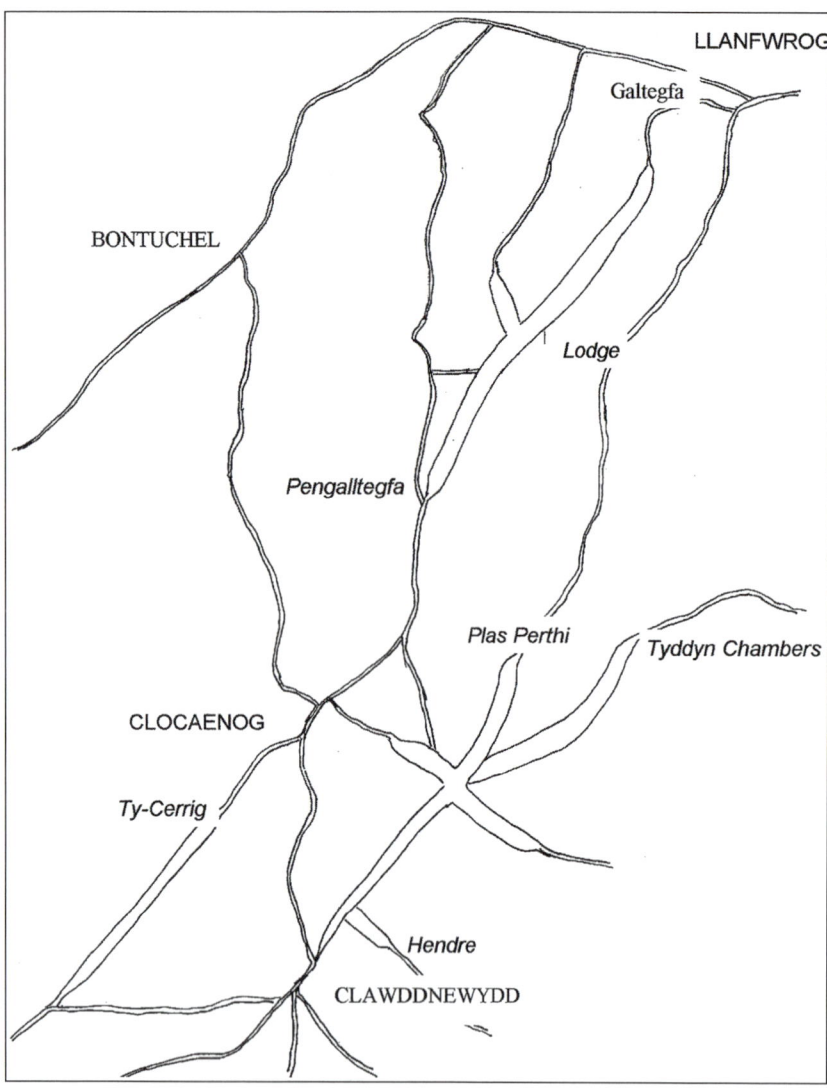

The wider enclosure roads near Clocaenog.

We are now accustomed to seeing our landscape as a view of neat fields with very little of thegorse and bracken-covered ground so prevalent 150 years ago. Equally we take our main roads and tarmacked lanes for granted. Part of the work of the Enclosure Commissioners in 1852 was to lay out new roads and to improve or replace the existing labyrinth of winding lanes and tracks. The Commission stipulated that the new roads on what had been common land should be between 15 and 25 feet in width and 'shall forever hereafter be maintained and repaired by the Owner of the said farm' which those roads crossed. A width of 25 feet is not always necessary nowadays, but before the advent of tarmacadamed surfaces on the roads it allowed carriages and carts to negotiate to the side of the deepest ruts and potholes. So, as we travel away from Clocaenog, we find wider roads with grass verges set well back to the 25 feet limit; the exceptions being the already established old road to Bontuchel and the accompanying map shows these new roads which were laid out in the 1852 Enclosure Award. Parts of the B5105 have these 'new' characteristics in the stretch between Bryn-y-Ffynnon and Clawddnewydd.

To conclude, the Enclosure Award closed off the common land, created new fields and made travel much easier.

E. N.

Tollborth *(Toll Gate) at the junction of the old lane from Clocaenog, where it meets the 'new' B5105.*

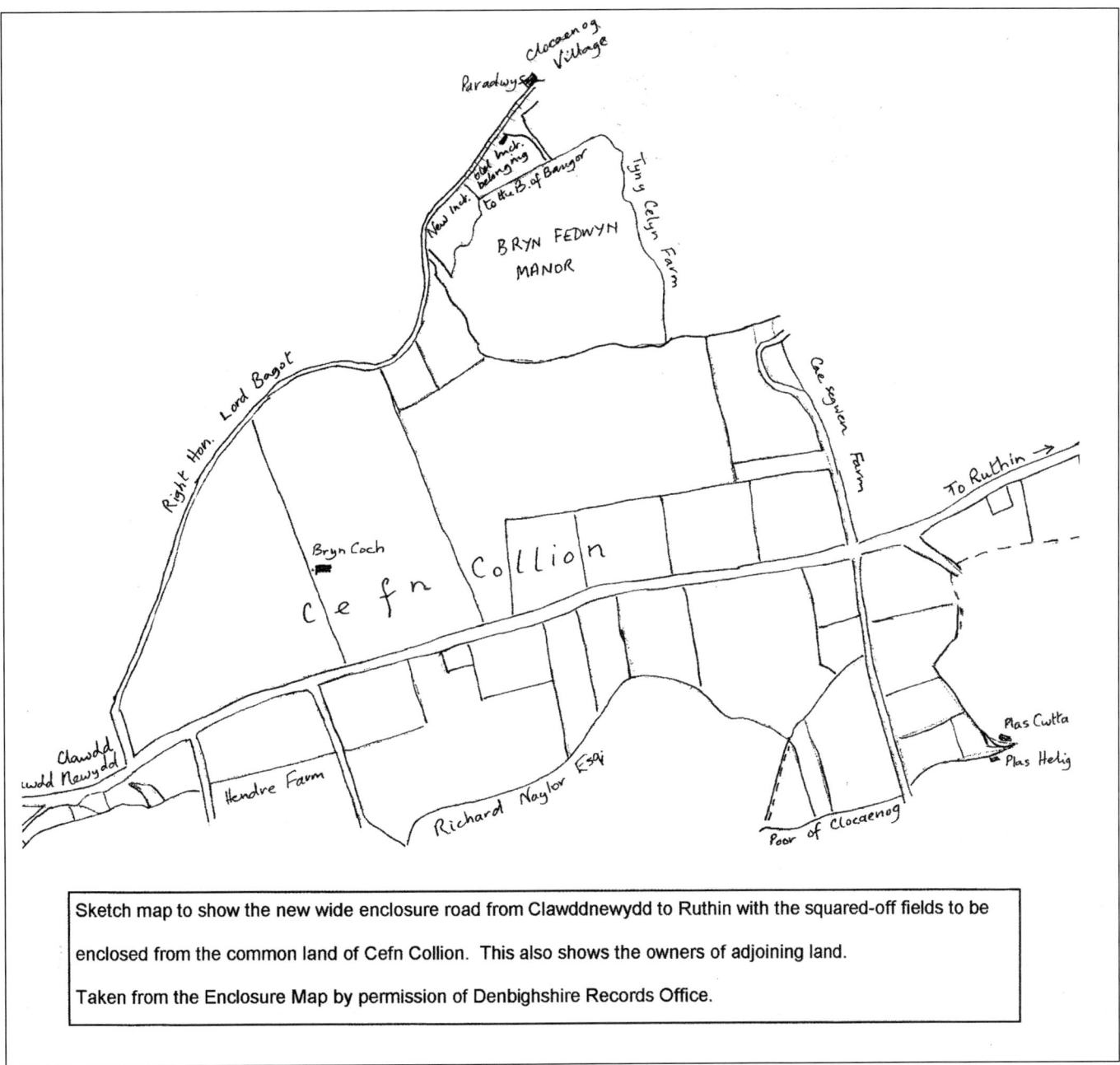

Sketch map to show the new wide enclosure road from Clawddnewydd to Ruthin with the squared-off fields to be enclosed from the common land of Cefn Collion. This also shows the owners of adjoining land.
Taken from the Enclosure Map by permission of Denbighshire Records Office.

Bryn Coch — a farm on enclosure land

The Jones Family

Einir: Bryn Coch is a farm built on land enclosed from the common and bought by Lord Bagot. It is probable that red bricks were made from clay found on the land and hence the farm being named 'Red Hill' (Bryn Coch). There are grooves to be seen in some of the fields today where the clay may have been extracted. The farm house and out-buildings must have been built sometime after 1852. The house was modernised in 1984. The holding consists of around 80 acres and was originally part of the Lord Bagot Estate.

According to the 1881 census Margaret Williams and her family were living at Bryn Coch, but by 1891 it was David Davies. The first people from my family to live there moved to the farm about the turn of the century; they were my great grandparents, James and Maggie Jones. James Jones' family came from Llangwm. His father's name was Morris Jones but his father was called John Morris — this indicates some clerical error in the register. Anyway, at one period Morris Jones and his family were living in Berthen Gron, Llanfwrog, and then later in Mwrog Street, Ruthin.

James Jones, my great grandfather, was born at Berthen Gron. He married Maggie Hughes, who was born in Liverpool but whose family also came from Llangwm originally. After they came to Bryn Coch their first son, David William (my grandfather) was born on 24th May 1900. So my family have lived here for over a century.

Shire horses were used on the farm and my father remembers two of them in particular called Polly and Bess, kept here in the 1940s. During the Second World War the 'War Ag' ploughed up some of the fields, getting rid of the gorse and bracken (remember it had been moorland); every inch of land was needed for the war effort. Because my grandfather did not own a tractor the Ministry of Agriculture provided tractors to carry out the work. The first tractor we bought in 1947 was a Ferguson and it ran on petrol. A plough and a transport box were purchased at the same time and so one of the horses had to go. The other horse was kept until the 1950s.

My grandfather, David William, was the tractor driver, whilst my uncle, John Henry, stuck with the horse. I remember John Henry well as he lived into his eighties, but I never saw him on a tractor or driving a car! During the war there were milking cows at Bryn Coch and they all needed milking by hand, until a Fullwood milking machine was bought in 1948.

There were a lot of changes in the 1950s. In 1953 the first car was bought, a Morris 10 — JC9081. Electricity came in 1959 and with it a black and white television. Before this, gas was used to light the lamps and the family would spend their spare time playing darts or cards, as well as listening to the radio. Another popular pastime was catching rabbits and a man from Connah's Quay came round regularly to buy them. Everyone had a ferret to help catch the rabbits. A shearing machine was bought in 1960; before this, all the shearing was done with hand shears. All the farmers would help each other out at shearing time, and with the haymaking and the threshing.

Although Bryn Coch is in the parish of Clocaenog our family has always attended the Calvinistic Methodist Chapel in Clawddnewydd. John Henry Jones was a deacon there for many years. All the children have attended Clocaenog School and my father, Wynne, and now my brother, Dylan, have been community councillors.

James and Maggie Jones, my great grandparents, had eleven children. Here is some information about them:

John Henry Jones.

• Hugh Morris, the eldest, married Mary Edwards and they lived in Rhuddlan for years. They had two children, Trefor and Glenys — sadly Glenys died at the age of six.

• John Henry, the second child, lived at Bryn Coch all his life and never married.

• Susannah Elisabeth (Siwsi) married William Lloyd and they lived at Groesffordd, Prion with their four children, Margaret, Olwen, Emyr and Ceinwen.

• The fourth child was David William my grandfather. He married Kate Jones from Maentrwrog and they had two children, Margaret (Meg) Jane and Wynne my father.

- Mary Catherine (Kate) married John Roberts and they lived in Cae Wgan, Clawddnewydd; their daughters were Bessie and Morfudd. Bessie married Llew Roberts who kept a garage in Cae Wgan and later on, for many years had a garage and petrol pumps on the main road in Clawddnewydd. They had twins called Carol and Erfyl.

- Edith Anne was the seventh child. She was a maid in Blaen Ddol, Corwen for many years before marrying Robert Williams and going to live in Cwm Pennant.

- Robert Owen (Bob) married Sally and lived in Bryn Meibion, Clawddnewydd. They had four children, Rhiannon, Beryl, Eric and Margareta (Gret).

- The ninth and tenth children were twins, Edward Herbert married Margaret, and David William married her sister, Kate. Edward and Margaret had two sons, Brian and Keith, while David and Kate had a son, Thomas Trefor who died, a young man of eighteen.

- James Elwyn was the eleventh child. He married Dorothy Davies and had three sons, John Eyton, Gareth and Arwel. They moved to live in Anglesey in the 1950s.

Kate Jones with her children, Wynne and Megan.

Today, Wynne Jones, son of David William Jones, lives with his family in Bryn Coch. He married Gaenor Pritchard in 1962 and they have three children, Sharon, Einir (me) and Dylan. My brother, Dylan, now farms at Bryn Coch and is the fourth generation to do so.

E.W.J.

Wynne and Gaenor Jones.

Bryn Coch — fferm ar tiroedd caeedig

Y Fferm a'r Teulu

Yn wreiddiol adeiladau yn unig oedd ym Mryn Coch. Y son yw fod y brics coch a ddefnyddiwyd i adeiladu'r lle wedi cael eu gwneud ar dir y fferm allan o'r clai coch a ddaeth o'r caeau. Dyma sut y cafodd y lle ei enw, ac y mae pantiau i weld yng nghaeau Cae Caewgan a'r Ffridd hyd heddiw lle y credir y turiwyd am y clai. Fe gafodd un adeilad ei drawsnewid yn dŷ oddeutu 1870 ac fe gafodd y tŷ ei adnewyddu a'i ddiweddaru eto yn 1984. Mae'r fferm oddeutu 80 acer o faint.

Yn ol Senssws 1881, teulu Margaret Williams oedd yn byw ym Mryn Coch, ac yna David Davies yn 1891. Symudodd ein teulu ni, sef James a Maggie Jones, yno ar droad y ganrif ym 1900. Roedd teulu James Jones

David William a John Henry ar gefn un o'r ceffylau gwedd.

yn wreiddiol o Langwm. Morris Jones oedd enw ei dad, a John Morris oedd ei dad yntau. Newidwyd cyfenw y teulu o Morris i Jones yn y cyfnod yma. Mae'n debyg mai Morris, mab John, oedd fy hen daid a newidwyd hwn i Morris Jones. Bu Morris Jones a'i deulu yn byw yn Berthen Gron, Llanfwrog, ac yna ar Stryd Mwrog. Cafodd James Jones ei eni ym Merthen Gron. Er fod gwraig James Jones, sef Maggie Hughes, wedi cael ei geni yn Lerpwl, roedd ei theulu hithau o Langwm. Y plentyn cyntaf i gael ei eni ym Mryn Coch oedd David William Jones — sef Taid — ar y 24 ain o Fâi 1900, ac y mae'r teulu yn byw yno ers dros ganrif bellach. R'oedd Bryn Coch yn ran o stâd Lord Bagot yn wreiddiol, ac fe'i prynwyd gan David William a John Henry Jones yn 1930 am £600.

Ceffylau gwedd oedd yn cael eu defnyddio i wneud llawer o waith y fferm ar y cychwyn. Mae Dad yn cofio dwy yn arbennig oedd ar y fferm yn y 40au, sef 'Poll' a 'Bell'. Yn ystod y rhyfel bu'r 'War-Ag' yn trin rhai o'r caeau, gan eu bod yn llawn rhedyn ac eithin. Wrth gwrs, yn y cyfnod yma roedd angen pob modfedd o dîr i'w weithio, a gan nad oedd gan fy nhaid ag ewyrth dractor, roedd rhaid i'r Gwasanaeth Amaethyddol ddod a tharactorau i mewn i wneud y gwaith. Prynwyd y tractor cyntaf i'r fferm yn 1947 sef Ffyrgi Bach petrol. Cafwyd aradr dau gwys a 'transport box' ar yr un adeg. Cawsant ymadael ag un ceffyl, ond cadwyd y llall tan y 50au. Taid, sef David William, oedd yn dreifio'r tractor, tra bo yncl, sef John Henry, yn cadw at y ceffyl. Yn wahanol i heddiw, roedd gwartheg godro ar y fferm yn ystod y rhyfel. Godro gyda llaw oeddynt hyd nes y prynwyd peiriant godro 'Fullwood' yn 1948.

Yn ystod y 50au cafwyd tipyn o newid ar fyd. Yn 1953 prynwyd y car cyntaf, sef Morris 10 — JC 9081. Daeth trydan i'r fferm yn 1959 a hefyd teledu du a gwyn. Cyn hyn roedd nwy ar gael i olau lampau, a treuliwyd oriau gyda'r nos yn chwarae darts a cardiau, yn ogystal a gwrando ar y radio. Hela cwningod oedd yn mynd a bryd bobl bryd hynny hefyd, a daethai Jones Connah's Quay o gwmpas i brynnu'r cwningod. Roedd rhaid cadw fferet wrth gwrs, i helpu dal y cwningod. Cafwyd peiriant cneifio yn 1960 — cyn hyn roedd rhaid cneifio gyda gwellau. Roedd y ffermwyr i gyd yn gymdogol iawn ac yn helpu eu gilydd yn ystod tymor y cynhaeaf gwair, cneifio a dyrnu.

Er fod Bryn Coch ym mhlwy Clocaenog, y mae'r teulu wedi mynychu Capel MC Clawddnewydd erioed. Roedd John Henry Jones yn flaenor yno am flynyddoedd maith. Aeth y plant i gyd i Ysgol Clocaenog, ac roedd Yncl John Henry, Dad, a rwan Dylan, fy mrawd, yn aelodau o'r cyngor plwyf.

Magodd James a Maggie Jones, sef fy hen daid a nain, un-ar-ddeg o blant ar aelwyd Bryn Coch. Dyma hanes byr amdanynt.

- Hugh Moms oedd y plentyn hynaf. Priododd Mary Edwards a buont yn byw yn Rhuddlan am flynyddoedd. Cawsant ddau o blant, sef Trefor a Glenys, ond bu farw Glenys pan yn blentyn chwech oed.

- Yr ail blentyn oedd John Henry. Bu'n byw ym Mryn Coch y rhan fwyaf o'i oes, ac roedd yn ddi-briod.

- Y trydydd plentyn oedd Susannah Elisabeth (Siwsi). Priododd William Lloyd a roeddynt yn byw yn Groesffordd, Prion. Cawsant bedwar o blant, sef Margaret, Olwen, Emyr a Ceinwen.

- Y pedwerydd plentyn oedd David William, sef fy nhaid. Priododd Kate Jones o Faentwrog a cawsant ddau o blant sef Margaret Jane (Megan) a Wynne — fy nhad.

- Y pumed plentyn oedd Mary Catherine (Kate). Priododd John Roberts, a buont yn byw yn Penstryt,

Llanfwrog am flynyddoedd. Roedd ganddynt un mab, sef Trefor.

- Y chweched plentyn oedd Margaret Alice. Priododd Robert Owens, a buont yn byw yng Nghae Wgan, Clawddnewydd. Cawsant ddwy ferch, sef Bessie a Morfudd. Priododd Bessie a Llew Roberts a buont yn cadw garej yng Nghae Wgan, ac yna yng Nghlawddnewydd am flynyddoedd. Cawsant efeilliaid, sef Carol ac Erfyl.

- Y seithfed plentyn oedd Edith Anne. Bu'n forwyn ym Mlaen Ddol, Corwen am flynyddoedd ac yna priododd Robert Williams ac aeth i fyw i Gwm Pennant.

- Yr wythfed plentyn oedd Robert Owen (Bob). Priododd Sally, a buont yn byw ym Mryn Meibion, Clawddnewydd. Roedd ganddynt bedwar o blant sef Rhiannon, Beryl, Eric a Margareta (Gret).

- Efeilliaid oedd y nawfed a degfed plentyn, sef Edward Herbert a Thomas Trefor. Priododd Herbert a Margaret, oedd yn chwaer i Kate, gwraig David William. Buont yn byw yn Hendre Waelod, Glan Conwy am flynyddoedd. Roedd ganddynt ddau fab, sef Brian a Keith. Bu farw Trefor yn ddyn ifanc deunaw oed.

- Y plentyn ieuengaf oedd James Elwyn. Priododd Dorothy Davies a cawsant dri mab, sef John Eyton, Gareth ac Arwel. Symudodd y teulu i Sir Fôn yn y 1950au.

O'r chwith ir dde — John Henry, Siwsi, Kate, David William, Bob. Herb, Alice. Blaen — Elwyn a Edith.

Erbyn heddiw Wynne, mab David William, ai deulu sy'n byw ym Mryn Coch. Priododd Gaenor Pritchard ym 1962 ac y mae ganddynt dri o blant, sef Sharon, Einir (fi) a Dylan. Dylan sy'n ffermio ar hyn o bryd, sef y pedwerydd cenhedlaeth o'r teulu i wneud hynny.

E.J.

From the Correspondence of *Archaeologia Cambrensis*

Lost Churches in Wales 1864

Before the present generation of old men and women are removed, it would be as well to obtain from them such information as they may be able to furnish concerning the small churches which once existed in various parts of Wales. The following information I have been enabled to obtain from a resident in the village of Clocaenog (Mr. Robert Pierce), who at my request kindly undertook to make some inquiries, the result of which I now give you.

John Williams of Glan Llyn, near Clawddnewydd, sixty-eight years of age, and son of a former parish clerk, remembered his father pointing out the ruins of the church to him. The walls at that time were two or three feet above the ground. His father at the same time pointed out a spot near the corner of the present plantation of Cefn Mawr, which he described as a sanctuary for criminals, charged with lesser offences, who were free from arrest as long as they remained within the limits. The sanctuary belonged to the old church.

David Roberts of Tyn-y-Coed, Clocaenog, seventy-one years of age [Ty'n-y-Coed has gone completely now — the cottage stood on the right of the lane going up to Plas and opposite the lane leading to Henblas]. I knew the church for some years as standing near Cefn-fynydd. His grandfather and great-grandfather had lived in the neighbourhood, and he had heard them say (for he remembered his great-grandfather) that a small village stood near the church. He also confirmed John Williams' statement about the sanctuary. The mountain is now enclosed, and the walls removed; but the foundations may still be traced.

Rambles over the Denbighshire Hills 1885

The writer had arranged with Mr. Robert Roberts, Clocaenog, to accompany him on a ramble over the hills to the west of Ruthin; but the day fixed upon, August 27th turned out to be a wet day. Still the journey was undertaken, and much curious information, or folk-lore was collected; and in this letter I will relate what we saw and heard.

My companion is a native of Bala; but his vocation has made him

Glan Llyn, Clawddnewydd, on the left of the picture.

Glan Llyn, Clawddnewydd in 2004.

This is where the writer of the letter met Robert Roberts of Clocaenog before setting out on their walk.

acquainted with other people and places than those that were or are in the neighbourhood of the place of his birth. He has walked over most of the hills in West Denbigh-shire, and he has visited most of the farmers that live along those hills; and he is well known for many miles around the village of Clocaenog, which is about four miles distant from Ruthin. He has read Welsh poetry, and the literature of his native country he is not ignorant of, nor is he an unbeliever in the traditions of the people. He has mastered English, and the few books that he has in this language he has carefully read. Such was my agreeable fellow traveller.' Could this have been the Robert Roberts who was the innkeeper of Paradwys at this time? If so, his wife, daughter of the schoolmaster, must have taught him to read and write because he could only put his mark when he married.

We were to meet each other, at 9.30 a.m., at a hamlet called Clawddnewydd, or the New Dike … we proceeded for about three miles along the road that leads to Cerrigydrudion from Ruthin, until we came to a bridge called Pont Petrual, which spans the river Clwyd.… We leave the bridge and go to a house called Bodrual, a small farm reclaimed from the mountain, and here trap and pony are left.

As the day continued to be wet and no out-door work could be done, everyone sat round the fire and talked. John Roberts of Pentre, near Felin y Wig, told a story about a Corpse-Candle. He said he was 'in the habit of sitting up after his family had retired to rest, to smoke a quiet pipe; and the last thing he did, before going to bed, was to take a peep into the night to ascertain the state of the weather. One night, while peering about, he saw in the far distance a light in a place where no house was, and upon observing it intently he ascertained that the light was moving slowly along the road leading from Bettws G.G. to Felin y Wig. It was so late and so unusual … that John Roberts continued watching with considerable curiosity.… It passed Felin y Wig, and took the road towards Botrual … turned towards Pentre, Jones' abode, and came slowly along, and evidently its destination was John Robert's house. Jones could not hear footsteps … nor could he detect anyone carrying the light; he therefore, in considerable fear, entered the house, closed the door, and seated himself with much dread by the fire … To his horror, the light passed through the shut door, then gradually approached the place occupied by Jones, and then it ascended to the floor above the kitchen, and after quivering in a certain spot awhile it vanished.

Bod Petrual (Betrual).

The small lake below Bod Petrual

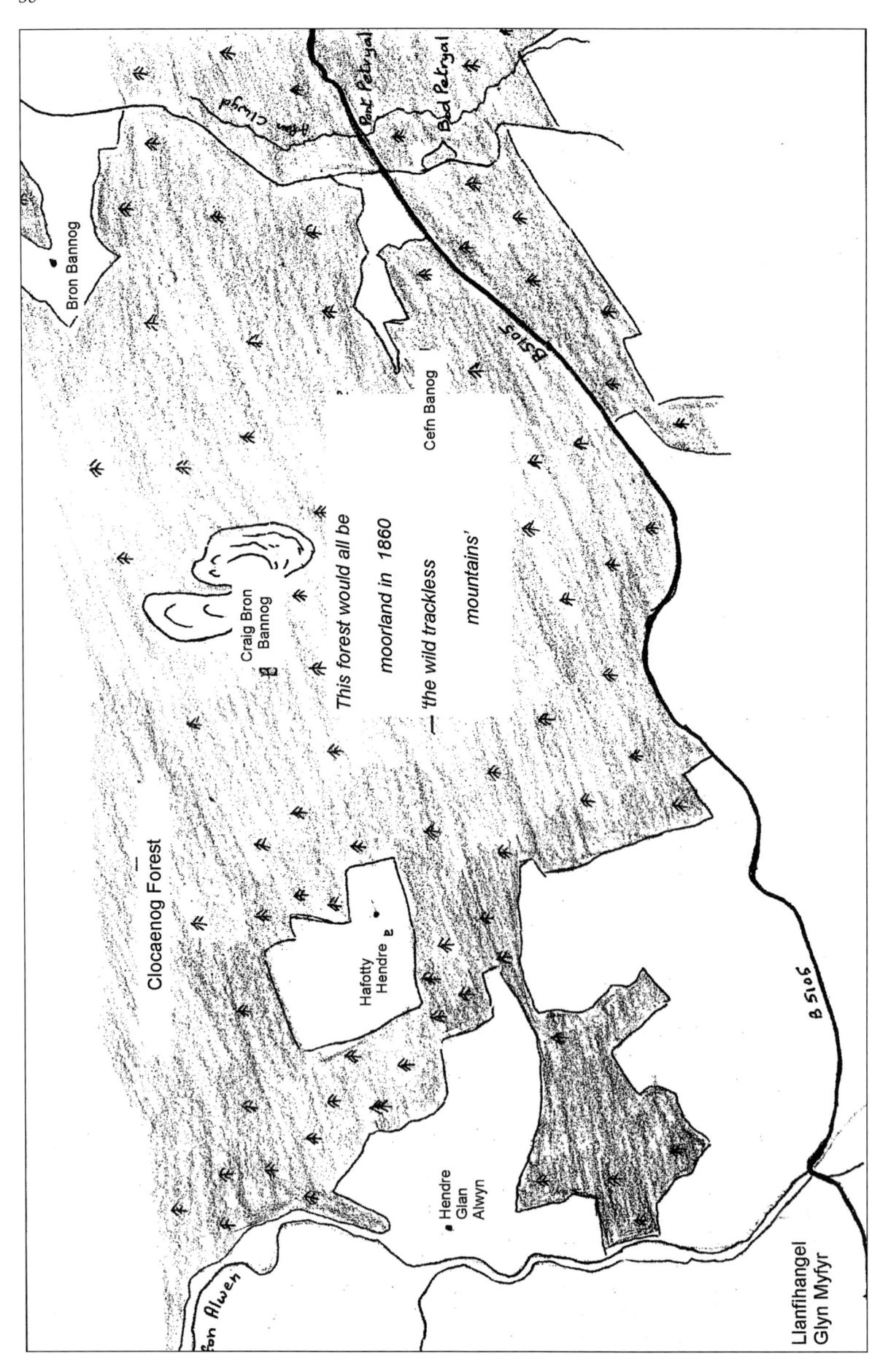

This forest would all be moorland in 1860 — "the wild trackless mountains"

Pentre Farm, Melin y Wig.

Sketch map to show the location of Pentre, Melin y Wig.

Jones, when he recovered the use of his limbs, retired to rest for the night; but, singularly enough, the servant-man was found dead in his bed, which was over the very spot where the light had disappeared.

An Apparition. Another story told by Jones was to the effect that two men went to visit two girls, who lived over a spur of the Arenig Mountains. When they were returning in the early morning, each made his own way home, but one did not arrive. All the neighbours searched for him for several days, but to no avail. The following the night the mother of the missing man saw her truant son looking through the window at her. She immediately remonstrated with him for playing tricks with them, and bade him come at once to supper. But there was no response to her words. She now went to the door, expecting to see her son; but no he was not to be seen; but turning her head towards the mountain, the poor woman observed a strong light resting on a certain spot on the Arenig Mountains, and she was convinced that there her son was to be found. The neighbours, the following day, proceeded to that spot which the mother indicated, and there they discovered the body of the young man, who evidently had lost his way, and having fallen over a precipice was killed.

The Speckled Cow's Well. This is about a wonderful well in the neighbourhood of Bodrual.

The well stands in a ffridd, by a wall, and it is in a very neglected state. A few stones surround it, but it is overgrown with grass, and presents the appearance of a simple mountain spring. However, tradition says that in remote times a wonderful cow quenched her thirst in this now forsaken well, and gave her name to it, for it is called after her, Ffynnon y Fuwch Frech.

Thomas Jones (Cefn Bannog) who occupies a small mountain farm close to the well, gave me the following particulars concerning this cow. She gave milk willingly and copiously to every one who milked her, and this she continued doing until she was milked into a riddle, when she immediately left the country, and her offspring also followed her. Two of her children made for a lake, Thomas Jones said, called after them Llyn dau Ychain (the lake of the two oxen), in the parish of Cerrigydrudion; and it is related of these *dau eidion Bannog* as Jones called them, that they went one on either side of the lake, and, bellowing as if the one was calling the other, they entered the lake and disappeared.

This famous cow was the mother, Jones said, of all the ychain Bannog; and it is certain that after her the places on the hill-side were called by the names they still retain. Thus there is a pathway (now unused) that led from the well to the Preseb y Fuwch Frech, of which traces are left to this day. It was along this path the cow went from her crib when she wanted water. The road or pathway is about a hundred yards from the cowhouse. Here, again,

Looking west towards Craig Bron Bannog (302m), the highest point of Clocaenog Forest, with the Lookout.

there is another pathway from the cowhouse to the pasture of the cow, called Gwal Erw y Fuwch Frech, and the side of the hill is called Cefn Bannog.

All these names give the tradition a reality for the people; similar stories are told in otherplaces, like Shropshire and Derbyshire.

Bwlch y Forwyn Pillar-Stone 1886

The Stone stands right at the top of the pass, or *bwlch*. It is about 5 feet high, and about 1^1/$_2$ feet broad. On one side is the date 1630, and underneath these figures are the initials H.R. On the other side, cut into the stone, is a small St. Andrew's cross. At one time there were a series of these stones to be seen along this hill, but they have been removed, and utilised. Thomas Jones, Ceth Bannog, removed one of them and it at present forms a gatepost near his house — and besides it has another date, 1863, and other initials, J.R.S., cut into it. These modern letters and date were engraved on the stone (T. Jones told me) by John Roberts, a saddler, Pontuchal.

These pillar-stones were placed on the hill (the wild, trackless mountains) to direct the traveller to the Hendre, or, as it is called in full, Hendre Glan Alwyn, where a bed, supper and breakfast awaited him. The initials HR stood (Jones informed me) for Hugh Reynallt, who held the Hendre in 1630 on the condition that he should supply all travellers …. The occupier of the Hendre paid no other rent for his farm than that now stated. The farm belonged to the Salesbury family. There were many such places in various parts of Wales, and such hospitium would be indeed welcome to a weary traveller in winter. Pilgrims and travellers alike were entitled to hospitality in these places. At present the Hendre is an ordinary farmhouse. [i.e. Hendre Glan Alwyn]

As the weather continued unpropitious, [sic] we returned to Cefn Bannog, and we were glad to find ourselves sitting around a good, blazing fire. In the house I noticed a

Above: Imagine 'the wild, trackless moor' with no roads and no forest. Here the B5105 curves near Craig Ddu.

Left: Hendre Glan Alwyn, Llanfihangel.

Hafodty Hendre — on sale in 2005.

settle with the date 1639, and the initials E.F.M.M. underneath. These initials, the occupants of the house told me, stood for Edward Ffoulk and Mary Morris, relatives of the present owner of the settle; the woman, Mary Morris, according to a Welsh custom, retaining after marriage her maiden name.

The pillar stone carved with the initials was removed in the twentieth century.

A.N.

The Drovers

For hundreds of years the Welsh farmers depended on selling meat to the rich markets in England. They sold cattle and sheep to pay their rent and tithes, and lived on a subsistence diet. Most farmers in Britain were poor, and only the rich could afford to eat meat — other than rabbit. Much of the land of Wales is hilly and wheat is difficult to grow on high, rough terrain, with thin soil, so in order to buy flour to make bread they needed to sell meat. Apart from their woollen cloth and hand-knitted woollen socks (made by the men as well as the women in the long winter evenings — Bala was famous for its socks) the main produce of the Welsh farmers was their black cattle and sweet tasting, mountain pastured sheep, their pigs and flocks of geese. Without refrigeration the only way to get fresh meat to market was to walk it there 'on the hoof'.

It took about three weeks to walk the herds, at two miles an hour, all the way to London or, even further, the 250 miles to Kent, which for centuries was the main trading centre for north Wales. The cattle had to be shod, the pigs had small boots made and even the geese were driven through a mixture of tar and sand to harden on their webbed feet for the long journey. The men would generally be riding Welsh ponies, with two drovers at the front of the herd to lead the way and the rest behind to make sure that none escaped or got left behind. The noise of the men shouting, and the animals bellowing and bleating, could be heard long before they came into view. Wise farmers would hurry to shut up their creatures so that they would not be swept up in the drove.

Farmers who wished to sell cattle could take them to their nearest local market and offer them for sale or give them directly to the drovers as they passed. The drovers were men of repute who were trusted to strike a good bargain and return with the money and pay the farmer on the journey home. By the early 1600s, the drovers, because of their responsible position, had to be licensed at the quarter sessions to ply their trade like any craftsman. They had to be aged over 30 and a married householder, before they could be granted a licence which would discriminate them from casual vagabonds or cattle thieves, and, of course, they became well known as they travelled each year to the markets. Often they were farmers themselves, who drove the cattle as an extra income in the summer months. The drovers were mostly law-abiding men who enjoyed the change and liked to travel despite the hardships; they were important people in the community who could be trusted to sell the beasts and bring back the sale price — less the drovers' share, of course.

The animals were well fed and watered or they would not fetch a good price on arrival. It needed skill and experience to strike the right balance between speed and good husbandry, to reach the markets on certain fair days when the buyers gathered. Life on the journey could be precarious because of thieves and brigands as drovers were known to carry large sums of money. During the Civil Wars an added hazard were the teams of soldiers, from both sides, who were on the look out for meat to feed the troops.

At other times, the drovers were welcomed because of the news they collected and told as they journeyed, and they were reliable in bringing facts back from London or in spreading new ideas. When they stopped at an inn, it often brought out the fiddlers to entertain, or locals came to try their strength in a bout of wrestling or boxing.

There were few roads until the toll roads were developed and in any case the herds were best driven away from the cultivated land, over the moors and as directly as possible, only pausing to let the animals graze and sleep, and time for the men to eat and rest. No drover wanted to have to pay the tolls imposed on all beasts on the main roads by the eighteenth century and avoided using them. The tolls were greatly resented by small farmers and landowners alike, but especially hard hit were the poor farmers who could lose all their profit in paying tolls on the way to market. This gave rise to the Rebecca Riots in the nineteenth century

Y Gro, Betws Gwerfil Goch, an old drovers' inn.

Old drovers' road, Betws Gwerfil Goch.

when, at night, men broke down the gates set across the roads. We still have the house called Toll Bar on the B5105.

Only when it came to nightfall did the drovers make for the villages where there was the chance of an inn, with ale for all, and a bed for the head drovers; many of the men would sleep with the animals to guard them. A few inns were up on the moors and were often marked in Wales by Scots pine trees which could grow at a high altitude, and could also be seen from a long distance away and helped to mark the route and announce where there was accommodation to be found, with food and home brew. One local drovers' inn was at Gro Farm in Betws Gwerfil Goch where there were holding-pens and a ford across the Afon Alwen and on to Wrexham. Another was, of course, the Drovers' Arms in Rhewl coming in to Ruthin. Whereas the pilgrims were travelling north–south, the drovers were travelling west–east, via Wrexham, until they crossed the border into England. From here the main droves headed for Shrewsbury before turning south.

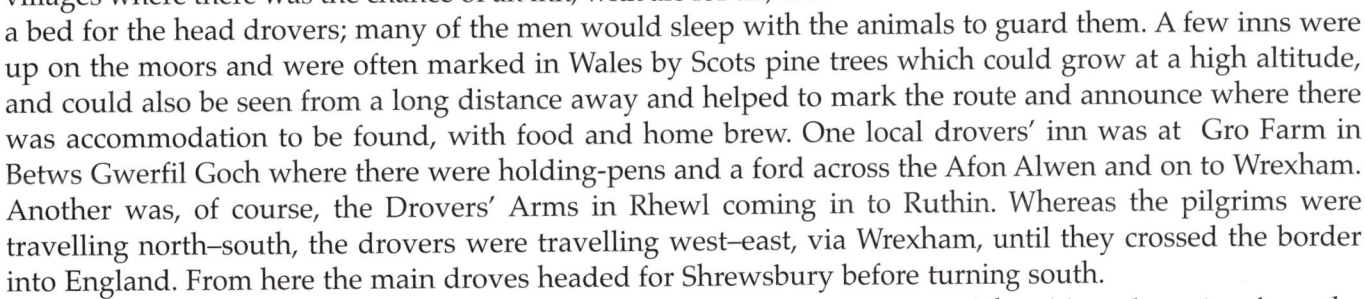

If you look for drovers' roads here in Clocaenog there is the possibility of the old road coming from the direction of Cerrigydrudion and crossing Craig Bron-banog, over the waste land to the south of Maestyddyn, and onto the old track (now a footpath) and sunken way down past Henblas and so to the village and a night spent at the inns of Tŷ Coch or Paradwys, where there would be ample holding ground, before an early start next day to the market in Ruthin.

Possibly an old drovers' road near Henblas.

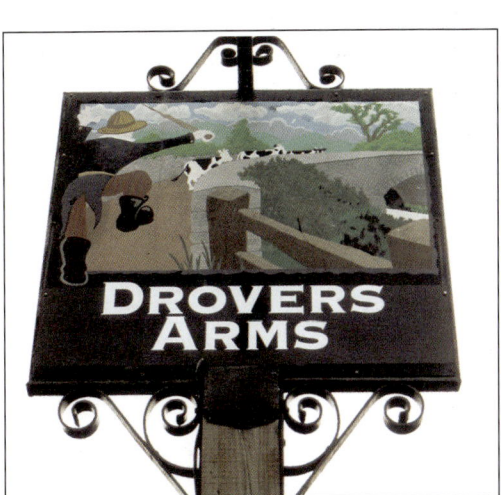

The modern sign outside the Drovers' Arms, Rhewl.

In the Denbighshire Historical Society *Transactions* of 1960 there is a quote from the Council Book of Ruthin:

> Be it remembered that Ruthin Fayre is always to be kept ye 28 day of July and the 29th except it falls to be on a Sunday … This fayre was kept before some fourscore yearns agone as is remembered by some alive this present and our charters do mencon yt neare upon 400 yeares agow the warres and troubles forced us to forget ourselves. There were likewise beastes to be sould every munday and come market every mundays and Frydayes which customs wee hope the town will encourage and keep up as formerly wch will be for all peoples forever.

Sunday had to be observed and no one was allowed to move the drove until after midnight on the Sabbath when everyone worked hard to be ready to move at dawn.

Ruthin was a gathering place for the drovers; Corwen was another such market town. As well as being trusted to sell the beasts in the English markets, the drovers often acted as couriers for individuals, or in later times for the banks which were set up to facilitate trade. In 1636 the Denbighshire drovers were entrusted with the county's ship tax money to be carried to the government in London.

To show that the English inn-keepers were used to hosting the Welsh drovers, an inn at Stockbridge keeps an early advertisement well painted on the side of the house, which says, GWAIR TIMHERUS – PORFA FLASUS – CWRW DA – A CWAL CYSURUS meaning, 'Worthwhile grass – pleasant pasture – good beer – and a comfortable shelter'.

The drovers were an important part of the structure of society, both socially and economically. Maybe the tolls and the improvements to the roads and the development of better transport was the beginning of the end for that way of life which the drovers had enriched in many ways.

B.J. & A.N.

Religion

St Foddhyd's Church

The church is thought to have been founded as early as the ninth or tenth century but the first documented evidence to be found is in the Norwich Taxation of 1254; the first recorded priest was 'David the Chaplain' in 1282. During archival research in the Records Office at Ruthin, the following unsigned note was found:

> S. MEDDWID, or MED WIDA, Virgin'.
> 'A festival, entered against Aug. 27 as 'Gúy! Feddwid', occurs in the Calendars in Peniarth MSS.187 and 219, the Iolo MSS., and the Prymers of 1618 and 1633 (the last as Foddwid). The name is a mutated form, and can only stand for either Beddwid or Meddwid. In a will, dated 1530, a cleric of Bangor Diocese directs his body to be buried '*in eclesia Sancte Medwide Virginis*' which is identified with the parish church of Clocaenog in Denbighshire. Down to 1859, it was in the Diocese of Bangor, but is now in that of St. Asaph. Browne Willis gives the church as dedicated to St. Vodhyd, with a festival on August 27, and other spellings of the name are: Foddyd and Foddhyd.
> Sometimes the church is said to be dedicated to an imaginary St. Caenog, and also to St. Trillo, but it is perfectly clear that its real patron is Medwida, Meddwid, or Meddwyd.

The church, surrounded on all sides by a well-kept graveyard, is set on rising ground above the village of Clocaenog. Access to the churchyard is through an unusual square lychgate (dated 1691) with masonry walls and a slated pyramidal roof — the gate is of timber topped by a spiked metal rail. From there, a pathway leads between laurel shrubs to a timber-framed porch (dated 1682) on the south wall of the church. Although the principal entrance is through the south porch, there is also a doorway on the north side. The roof is clad in Welsh slate and is supported internally by nine bays of trusses, arch-braced with cusped struts above the collar, and there are cusped windbraces (a similar fine carved example can be seen in Llangollen's church, proving the skill of local woodworkers). The entrance porch and main aisles are paved with slate slabs but the chancel is paved with black and red quarry tiles; carpet runners were added in 1990.

Built of stone, the church has a west bellcote and is a rectangular, single chamber. The most interesting window, in Perpendicular style, is set in the east wall of the church and consists of five lights containing fragments of mediaeval stained glass (including some heads of men and angels). The following entry in the oldest church register states: 'Upon the east window of Clocaenog Church this inscription if left (though somewhat defaced) 'Jesu Christ of might is most have matre on them that made this cost a'o D'ni MCCCCCXXXVIII'. The north window is a two-light in Decorated

St. Foddhyd's Church, Clocaenog.
Eglwys y Santes Foddhyd, Clocaenog.

The east window from outside.

Entrance porch to the church.

The bell and weather-cock above the west end of the church.

Detail on the entrance door.

style, and the south window, made by Holland of Warwick (commemorated in 1865) is a memorial to Mary, wife of T. Hughes, M.A., Rector.

The church is divided into a nave and chancel by a handsome rood screen which is ornamented with open work and running bands of wheat-ear and vine leaf (alluding to the sacramental elements). The rood-screen is a good example of a Welsh type, with continuous middle rails between the end standards: heavily moulded uprights and bressumer, and two stages of trailing ivy berries on the west side and one on the east — the trade-mark of local craftsmen who made the screens here at Clocaenog and also in the churches at Llanelidan and Llanrhudd. There are traceried heads to the openings and pierced tracery in the wainscot panelling. Many of these screens were destroyed during the troubles in the Reformation period, and Derwen Church is a rare example, complete with its rood loft, where musicians would have played during services. Secured to the rood screen is an oak lectern, with open carving, which bears a brass plate inscribed 'in the Reverence of God and for His Service This Lectern The Gift of Mrs. Henry Perkins of Leeds was Here Placed AD. 1882'. There is also a vestry screen which was installed during the Victorian era.

The altar is a simple, four-legged oak table on a solid base and the seventeenth/eighteenth century altar rail is of fret-cut oak which may have come from the original rood screen.

Detail of the rood screen.
Manlyn o'r groglen.

The fifth century stone font, standing at the back of the church, is octagonal and unlined, with some roll moulding; it has a jointed wooden cover with a raised square platform topped by a simple cross. There is a stainless steel baptismal bowl and a mother-of-pearl scoop with a silver handle in the form of a cross, purchased by Mrs. C. Roberts in 1985 in memory of her husband, Mr. W. Roberts, who was, for many years, church organist.

The six sided Jacobean oak pulpit is reached by two wooden steps and contains a simple corner bench seat — the front of the pulpit is carved 'WR:IH 1695'. Above the aisle hangs an unusual, elaborately carved Georgian chandelier of white painted wood, dated 1725 with 20 candle holders which are still used on festive occasions.

Other furnishings include: an oak Bishop's chair of 1796 with I.H.S. carved on the back; two sanctuary litany-desks from St. John's Church, Hightown, Wrexham, acquired in 1986; two matching prayer desks in the chancel; one portable light oak lectern originally given to Pool Park Hospital Chapel by Clocaenog W.I.

Interior of the church.
Tu mewn i'r eglwys.

The roof timbers.

*Chandelier
Canhwyllyr*

*The font.
Y bedyddfan.*

*Old oak chest.
Hen gist pren.*

and subsequently presented by the W.I. to St. Foddhyd's Church in 1991 when the hospital closed; two modern oak flower pedestals donated in 1992 in memory of Aurial Eve Donne Horsley of Bontuchel; the church pews are Victorian and made of pitch pine; a double cross-stitched wedding kneeler donated in 1990 by Anwen Davies in memory of her father, Emrys Jones.

There is a massive early mediaeval churchwarden's chest, hollowed out from a single oak trunk, with beaten metal strap hinges and a hasp with a lock. This chest is used to store various old Bibles (in Welsh and English), New Testaments, current church records and copies of old records dating from 1813 to 1933- the originals of which are kept in Denbighshire Record Office.

The Cason Patent Single Manual Pipe Organ, with 414 octaves, was made by the Positive Organ Company of London and was installed in February 1924; an electric organ blower was added in June 1970. In 1985, the organ was moved to the back of the church when a Johannus 2 Manual Electronic Organ was purchased from Rushworth & Drapers, Chester, and positioned in front of the rood screen.

There are various memorial plaques around the church, some of which are mounted on the walls and others leaning on the walls at ground level (for safety reasons). The oldest memorial, to Evan Lloyd ap Rice of Derwen Hall, is dated A.D. 1597. Other plaques include: a Benefaction Board above the west wall of the vestry containing the names of Griffith Thomas ap Evan and others and is dated 1788; a memorial inscribed

Memorial plaque

'Sacred to the memory of the Reverend Thomas Roberts A.M. Chief Master of Ruthin School. Rector of this parish who died 11 March MDCCXCVI age XXXIII'; a Hanoverian coat of arms above the bell tower door commemorating a donation by the Society for Building Churches; a pink plaque in memory of Edward Meredith Griffiths, Rector of the parish, dated 1908; a brass plate on the south wall in memory of Joseph Roberts 1908–1981 commemorating the renovation of the church and the purchase of the new organ in 1985; a framed list of saints (in the porch) to whom the church may be dedicated.

It is only comparatively recent restoration work that has been recorded: in 1856/7 work was done by Kennedy; in 1882 further work by Perkin & Bulmer of Leeds, when the south porch was added but wall paintings found on the east wall were not preserved; the rood screen and chandelier were restored in 2001.

There is an interesting anecdote in *Country Churchyards in Wales* by Donald Gregory: '… in Clocaenog, in Clwyd, fives were generally played after service on Sunday morning. Fives was very popular, probably because the external walls of the tower and the north wall of the church, along with its buttresses, lent themselves to this particular ball game!' Fives is a game in which a ball is hit with a gloved hand, or a bat, against the walls of a court with three walls (Eton fives) or four walls (Rugby fives).

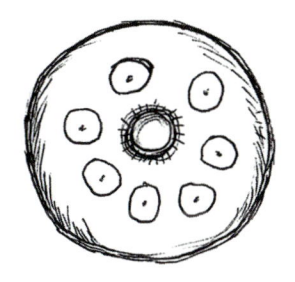

A spindle whorl of clay, ornamented with small circles, said to have been found in the churchyard of Clocaenog, was exhibited at the temporary museum in connection with the annual meeting of the Cambrian Archaeological Association at Carmarthen in 1875. Its present location is unknown.

A spindle whorl of clay.

A similar one found at Nilig, Cyffylliog, 'appears to be made of sandstone' and looked like this drawing.

Sunday services and religious festivals are still celebrated in St. Foddyd's Church, led by the present incumbent, the Reverend John B. Davies; the bell is still tolled for all services.

B. J.

Modern memorial plaque.

50

Window in the north wall.

Stained glass in the east window.

The window in the north wall dedicated to Mary, the wife of T. Hughes, M.A., Rector.

Rectors of St. Foddhyd's Church, Clocaenog

- 1282   DAVID, the Chaplain.
- 1517   Dns. HENRICUS ap Ieuan ap Hugh (resigned).
- 152?   JOANNES ap Holl Llud (Lloyd) [will proved 1530].
- 1530   SALISBURY, Ffoulke, of Maes Cadarn, (3rd son of Piers Salisbury of Bachymbyd).
- 1561   GALFRID ap John, Dns., "declareth God's word sincerely to his knowledge —".
- 15??   JONES, Griffith.
- 1581   JOHN ap Price, A. M. (brother of Sir ThomasPrice, Parson of Llangar & Newtown).
- 1582   THEOLAL (Thelwall), Tubal (Eubal), A. M.
- 1594   GWYN, David, A. M., Rector of Llanychan, 1603.
- 1633   LLOYD, Richard, A.M., Jesus College, Oxford, (son of Sir John Lloyd, Knt., of Llanrhaiadr), Rector of Llanychan, 1633.
- 1672   JONES, Thomas, Burgess & Lecturer, St. Hilary's, Denbigh, 1675.
- 1705   SALUSBURY, Robert, B. C. L., Jesus College, Oxford, (son of Revd. Wm. Salusbury, of Llanrwst), Rector of Ffestiniog, 1700; Vicar of Llanrwst, 1709; Canon of Bangor, 1710.
- 1714   WILLIAMS, John A.M., Head Master of Ruthin School, 1705–14.
- 1763   SUTTON, William, AM., All Souls College, Oxford, (son of Edward Sutton of Holywell), Vicar of Llanynys, 1759–63; Rector of Llanychan, 1789–94.
- 1794   ROBERTS, Thomas, A.M., Head Master of Ruthin School, 1789–96; Rector of Efynechtyd, 1789–90; Rector of Llangwyfan, 1790–94; Chaplain to Archbishop Moore.
- 1796   WILLIAMS, Hugh, M.A., Rector of Llanelidan, 1780–96.
- 1807   REYNOLDS, Owen, M.A., Vicar of Conway, 1802; Rector of Aber, 1819.
- 1829   NEWCOMBE, Richard, M.A., Vicar of Llanrhaiadr; Archdeacon of Merioneth.
- 1834   PARRY, John, M.A., Jesus College, Oxford,(son of Edward Parry of Llanelidan, gent.).
- 1846   HUGHES, Thomas, M.A., Jesus College, Oxford, (son of David Hughes, Head Master of Ruthin School), Lecturer at St. Peters, Ruthin, 1830–40; Perpetual Curate of Llandyrnog, 1840–46; wrote *Communion Tracts* for his parishioners.
- 1874   JONES, William H., Curate of Llantrisant, Glam., 1861–64; Curate of Cymmer, 1865–73.
- 1886   GRIFFITHS, Edward Meredith, Queen's College, Birmingham; Rector of Llanwyddelan, 1876–86.
- 1908   JONES, William Hopkins, L.Th.; Curate of Llantilio, Pertholey, 1889–91 Curate of Aberaman, 1891–1902; Curate of Abertillery,1902–08.
- 1932   DAVIES, J Thomas.
- 1942   DAVIES, W. A., Rector of Llansannon, 1951.
- 1951   THOMAS, Hugh
- 1979   WILLIAMS, Cyril
- 1984   JONES, Godfrey C., Curate of Ruthin & Llanrhydd, 1983; Vicar of Ruabon, 1993.
- 1993   DAVIES, John B., Dip. Th., Curate of Rhosllanerchrugog, 1971–5; Rector of Llanbedr-y-Cennin & Trefriw, 1975; Vicar of Betws-y-Coed & Penmachno, 1986.

Researched, and hung in the church for the Celebrations in the Millennium Year by the church-warden, Michael Hewer.

The Yew Tree (*Taxus Baccata*)

As part of the Clocaenog Women's Institute Project, a young yew tree was planted in the churchyard of St. Foddyd's Church on Saturday 19th August 2000 to commemorate the beginning of the second millennium. The tree was donated by W.I. member, Hazel Robinson, in memory of her husband, Peter Robinson (born 7.2.28, died 7.10.91). Both were members of the Parish and Peter's ashes are buried in the churchyard of St. Foddyd's Church. Sadly, Hazel died in July 2004, aged 76.

In a recent article, David Bellamy stated: 'Every parish, village or town in the country should plant a yew tree for the millennium — ideally in a churchyard — as a living symbol of sustainable growth, of creative evolution, and of renewed faith in God's part in Creation'.

Traditionally grown in churchyards, yew trees have a capacity for reaching a great age and, throughout Britain, there are examples which have survived for well over a thousand years. About twenty of these trees are now over 2,000 years old and the tree's reputation for a long life is due to the unique way in which the tree grows: its branches grow down into the ground to form new stems, which then rise up around the old central growth as separate, but linked, trunks. So the yew has always been a symbol of death and rebirth, the new that springs out of the old.

Yew wood is hard, fine-grained and heavy, with white or creamy sapwood and amber to brown heartwood; the lumber was once popular for cabinetwork and making implements, and was also used to construct the longbows of old. The yew is unpopular with farmers as its seeds contain a poisonous alkaloid that is often fatal to livestock.

Yew trees had high status in Irish mythology and, in the bardic schools of the druids; poets used staves of yew to help them memorize long incantations. Veneration of yews continued into Christian times when they became associated with churches and, on the mainland of Scotland, St.Ninian, a priest in Roman Britain, planted numerous yews in churchyards, including the famous Fortingale Yew in Perthshire, while the remains of Anglo-Saxon churches suggest that the early English planted yews in a circle around the church, usually built upon a central mound. The Fortingale Yew is the remnant of a stupendous tree that stood in the corner of the churchyard where worship has been known since at least pre-Reformation times. In 1769 its girth was 52 feet but it was already a hollow ring of wooden pillars, like a wood-henge, and funeral processions would pass through the trunk. Nearby there are a group of ancient, possibly druidical, stones.

After the Norman Conquest, a spate of church building led to the planting of numerous churchyard yews, many of which still thrive today. The trees were generally planted in a deliberate manner: one beside the path leading from the funeral gateway to the main door of the church, the other beside the path leading to the lesser doorway and, in early times, the priest and clerks would gather under the first yew to await the corpse-bearers --- this has led, latterly, to yew trees being associated with sadness.

William Shakespeare wrote of the 'dismal yew' and his witches bore 'slips of yew silvered in the moon's eclipse', while the 19th century naturalist, Gilbert White, described the trees as an emblem of mortality by their funereal appearance'.

Traditionally, it thought that Christ's cross was made from yew, and the famous yew trees of Nevern (Nyfer), Pembrokeshire, are said to bleed a red substance every year in sympathy with Christ. Branches of yew have been used traditionally in many churches to decorate the altar on Easter Day and, in some parishes,

The old yew tree in Clocaenog churchyard, probably growing here for a thousand years.

Right: Hazel Robinson, assisted by Eddie Naisby, planting the yew tree, watched by her daughter, Lois, and Reverend John Davies.

Below: The Reverend John Davies held a short service of blessing after the planting.

villagers used to gather beneath the churchyard yew to see in the New Year.

The yew's capacity for great age has enriched its symbolic value and both Druids, with their belief in reincarnation, and the later Christians, with their teaching of the resurrection, have always regarded it as a natural emblem of everlasting life.

The largest of the yew trees in St. Foddyd's churchyard (Clocaenog) has a girth of 27 feet and so is estimated to be over 1,000 years old. We thought it would be a good idea to plant another yew tree to be still growing in the year 3000 and this is what we did during our Church Festival in August 2000.

A.N.

Yew trees, old and new, in the churchyard.

The new yew tree and plaque which reads: 'Planted Aug. 2000 by Clocaenog W.I. "Millennium Project". Donated by Hazel Robinson in memory of her Husband Peter.'

The War Memorial

Gnr. Evan Edwards, 60461, 108th Siege Battery, Royal Garrison Artillery, who died, aged 23, on 8th April 1918. His parents, David and Eleanor Edwards, lived at Lodge Uchaf, Cynfal, Corwen, Merionethshire. Evan must have been working in Clocaenog before he joined the army. He is buried in the Etâples Military Cemetery, Pas-de Calais.

Pte. Edward William Jones, 59271, (Tyneside Irish) Battalion, Northumberland Fusiliers, died aged 28 on 11th April 1918. He was the son of Mr. and Mrs. T.O. Jones of Penparc, Bryn, Corwen. Edward must have been working on the Pool Park Estate or in the forestry. No known grave. He is remembered at Ploegsteert Memorial, Ypres.

Pte. Hugh Edward Davies, 266955, 13th Battalion, Welsh Regiment who died on 21 August 1917. He lived at Brynffynnon. No known grave. He is remembered at the Tyne Cot Memorial, Passchendaele.

The War Memorial in the churchyard.

Pte. William Jones, 54792, 15th Battalion, Royal Welsh Fusiliers, who died on 27th July 1917, aged 22, was the son of Mrs. Elizabeth Ann Jones of Gweithdy, Bontuchal. He was living at Tŷ-isa-Cefn, Clocaenog. He must have died in the intense fighting at Ypres and is remembered on the Menin Gate Memorial to the Missing.

Pte. Robert Thomas Roberts, 2784, 1st Battalion, Welsh Guards, who died on 11th October 1918, aged 40. He was a native of Telpin, Rhewl, was the son of John and Martha Roberts and husband of Ellen Gould (formerly Roberts) of Bryn Awel, Clawddnewydd. Thomas is recorded as being a worker for Pool Park. He is buried in the Saint Vaast Communal Cemetery Extension, near Cambrai.

Pte. John Henry Lovesay, 134551, 67th General Hospital, Royal Army Medical Corps, who died on 11th December 1918, aged 26. He was the son of John and Harriet Lovesay of Great Barrow, Chester, but John Henry was working at Pool Park. He is buried in the Mikra British Cemetery, Kalamaria, in Greece.

Pte. John William Addis, 21064, 14th Battalion, Royal Welsh Fusiliers, who died aged 36 on 7th July 1916, is buried at Corbie Communal Cemetery Extension, Somme. He was the son of William and Sarah Addis of Llan. His father, a gamekeeper for Pool Park, was born in Mainstone, Shropshire, and his mother in Chilgrove, Sussex. They had two daughters, Gertrude Helena and Dilys, who were born here. Dilys is remembered going to Clocaenog School.

The Lewis family, Tŷ Coch/Cloion tavern, John and Jane Lewis. The men seated on the right was Mr Addis, the father of John Addis, killed in 1916. The man with the gun is Jim Crumpton who married John's niece.

Pte. Henry Barguss, 12210, 9th Battalion, Royal Welsh Fusiliers who died on September 1915, has no known grave and is remembered on the Loos Memorial, Dud Corner Cemetery, Pas-de-Calais. He was working at Pool Park.

Pte. J. Askey, 8780, 4th Battalion Royal Welsh Fusiliers, who died on 24th November 1916 and is buried in the Lijssenthoek Military Cemetery, Poperinge, West-Vlaanderen. He lived at Llan, Clocaenog.

Pte. William Williams, 200419, 4th Battalion, Royal Welsh Fusiliers, who died on 6th April 1918, aged 23. He was living at Tŷ-isa-Cefn, Clocaenog, but was the son of Mary Williams of 31, Park Road, Ruthin, and the late Richard Williams. William has no known grave but is remembered on the Pozieres Memorial, Somme.

Pte. Eben Morris, M.M., 200614, 1st/4th Battalion, Royal Welsh Fusiliers, who died on the same day as William Williams (above), 6th April 1918, aged 22. He was the son of John and Jane Ann Morris, living at Parc, Clocaenog. Eben is buried at Martinsart British Cemetery, Somme.

Fusilier Elwyn Edwards was fostered at the age of seven from the children's home in Llanelwy, by Jane Hughes of Plas Newydd, Clocaenog, following the death from a brain tumour of her own son, David John Hughes, when he was 19. He was taken to London but died before they could operate. Unfortunately, her husband, John Hughes, died shortly afterwards and she was left alone. Having adopted Elwyn she had hoped that, as he grew up, he would be interested in the farm but he showed no aptitude for the life and so, two years later, she adopted another boy, Herbert Jones. She brought both boys up together as her sons. Herbert is still living locally at Denbigh Green.

Elwyn wanted a different life and, as soon as he was old enough, joined the regular army in the Royal Welch Fusiliers; this was before the war broke out. Sometime after the Dunkirk withdrawal of 1940, he volunteered for special duties and became a member of the newly formed Army Commandos (not the same as the modern-day Royal Marine Commandos), which had been the brainchild of Winston Churchill, who wanted to see units which could act as guerilla forces, similar to those he had seen in the Boer War. Elwyn was sent up to Irvine in Scotland, on the coast north of Prestwick, where the Commandos were trained. Even then, there was a further selection process before anyone could be accepted into a Commando unit. Elwyn was successful and joined No 1 Commando.

The youthful Elwyn Edwards, the only local man killed in the Second World War.

In 1941, under the command of Lieutenant Hemmings, Elwyn and his comrades were taken across the Channel in darkness aboard HMS *Leopold*, an adapted Belgian ferryboat. It was a moonless night and the sea was calm; Operation Chopper had begun. When they were about 30 kms off-shore, the Commandos were transferred to landing craft, forming two parties which were intended to land simultaneously at two different points on the French coast. Elwyn's group, aboard two landing craft, were escorted by an MTB (motor torpedo boat). Delayed by the currents, they encountered rough water and the craft began to fill with water, making them difficult to handle. To make matters worse, the MTB broke down and had to be repaired before they could continue towards the shore. By now they were behind schedule and, as the other group had already successfully reached the shore, killed some Germans and withdrawn with a prisoner, the enemy were on the alert. Elwyn's group had intended to come ashore at St Aubin but, unfortunately, the current had carried them along the coast and they came ashore on a long sloping Normandy beach, right in front of the German command headquarters.

Firing broke out almost immediately and Elwyn and his friend Cyril Evans (a former South Wales Borderer from Ebbw Vale) were killed and others wounded. The soldiers withdrew to their landing craft and headed back to HMS *Leopold*, taking with them their wounded.

The German officer ordered coffins to be made and, draped in Union Flags, the two Welshmen were buried with full military honours in Luc-sur-mer churchyard.

For some years, the fate of the two soldiers was unknown to their relatives, but the villagers of Luc-sur-mer tended their graves and held an annual service of remembrance on 29 September. It was eventually realised that the commando unit had landed at Luc-sur-mer rather than St Aubin and the British authorities identified the graves. Fifty years later, a memorial service was held at Luc-sur-mer, attended by some of the original commandos and their officer, and the relatives of Elwyn Edwards and Cyril Evans.

After his death in 1994, in accordance with his wishes, Lt Hemming's ashes were taken to Luc-sur-mer by his widow and interred alongside his soldiers.

Elwyn Edwards is the only man from the Second World War to be commemorated on the Clocaenog War Memorial.

Above information given to me by J. Iorwerth Davies and Wynne and Robert Hughes, the grandsons of Jane Hughes.

A. N.

A memorial card of Fusilier Elwyn Edwards.

The Old Rectory

Information about churches is found in ecclesiastical and other church records, such as terriers (inventories). Although many private houses have deeds which trace ownership, rectories and vicarages owned by the church have no formal documents until sold by the church. Information about these buildings, and any account of their origins and development, relies on passing references in terriers and reports following an archdeacon's visitation or that of a rural dean.

A fascinating snapshot of life and social attitudes in the mid-nineteenth century is provided by the diary of the Rev. Thomas Hughes, M.A., incumbent of Clocaenog Parish 1846–74.

The old straw thatched Glebe House stood pretty nearly upon the site now occupied by the present one which was erected in 1832 during the incumbency of Rev. Richard Newcome Warden of Ruthin, & Rector of Llanfwrog (Who, in two years afterwards resigned his Living for the Archdeaconry of Merioneth, vacant by the lamented death of the Venerable John Jones, Archdeacon thereof, & Rector of Llanbedr D.C.. Mr. Newcome, being a non resident Rector took care that this house should not be built larger than curate dimensions, i.e. he built it for his Curate the Rev. John Parry who in 1834 succeeded him as Incumbent of the living & was my immediate predecessor. The building mortgage laid on by the Governors of Queen Anne's Bounty was for £497. Had the sum been £100 more it would have been better. The house would have been larger. It was no better than a good sized cottage consisting of two parlours, (one very small) a large kitchen — 4 bedrooms & 2 or 3 closets. The bedrooms are low — the windows small- the roof too flat. The chimneys badly constructed & smoked badly, so badly at times that not only the room door but the outer or house door had to be left open, or we were enveloped in smoke. This nuisance, after sundry attempts & considerable expense, I have at last tolerably succeeded in remedying. The cellars are good, being (singularly enough for a Country place) constructed for offices -Washhouse, Dairy &c., Inconsistent with the small upstair accommodation, — but it renders the floors drier. Granted — still I maintain that had less been extended upon underground apartments, stone window mouldings &c., there would have been more means left for more headroom beneath the roof, instead of making the sleeping-apartments little better than attics. The architect who planned the house, was Mr. T. Cash, formerly of Liverpool. When the mortgage expired in 1657, I was in better heart to make improvements.

I wanted an additional room or two — I applied to Mr. Christopher Hodgson of the Bounty Office for a small mortgage grant to enable me to build the addition. His reply was that nothing less than the amount of the one year's net income of the living could be advanced. This was more than I wanted to lay out. Therefore, I looked to my own resources & set about getting the work done with as little expense as possible. And built a new small kitchen (without even a room over it) on the back yard and altered the former kitchen into a well sized parlour our present dining room. The outlay altogether amounted to about £50 of which sum more than half was at my own cost The bedrooms being too few one of them has been divided in two by a wooden partition. So contrived to extend across the wall to the middle of the window-frame. Thereby allotting one half of the light to each apartment. These little rooms being sufficient size for servants, they added to the accommodation. These trivial details have been mentioned for the purpose of shewing the effect of recent internal arrangements. The Glebe House, which previously consisted of 2 parlours, a kitchen & 4 bedrooms only — has 3 parlours, a (new) kitchen, & 5 bedrooms — a gain of two rooms And this has been done without laying any additional burden or mortgage upon the Living.

An extract from a typed copy of the Rev. Thomas Hughes's hand-written diary.

The rectory continued to be used by succeeding incumbents until the Rev. Hugh Thomas retired in 1979, after 28 years service in the parish of Clocaenog. Subsequent amalgamation of the parishes resulted in the rectory being sold to private buyers in 1982. The new owners, Irene and Mike Chamberlain, carried out many alterations and additions, including a new bathroom, a double garage/workshop and a utility room. They had most of the roof re-slated, some windows replaced, partial central heating installed, and a conservatory erected with access from the kitchen to the cellar steps; they also converted three cellars to three bedrooms and a shower room. Sadly, Irene died after being thrown from a horse and Mike sold the house to the Taylor family who eventually sold it to the present owners, Martin and Gillian Buxbaum, who have further improved and extended the property.

Central heating has been extended to all areas, including the basement; the kitchen has been modernised; a back door relocated and protected against the prevailing wind by a second conservatory. Upstairs, there are now three double sized bedrooms, two of which have en-suite shower/bathrooms. A studio has been added onto the north east corner of the house and a storage shed/workshop has been built on the western boundary of the rectory grounds.

The Rev. Richard Newcome, obviously conscious that he had built the house for a curate, modestly left an indelible reminder of his efforts by inserting an engraved stone above the lintel of the back door, now an archway leading from the kitchen:

RICHd. NEWCOME
RECTOR
MDCCCXXXII

Despite 'improvements' inflicted by a succession of incumbents and owners, the house retains many original features: some of the chimney pots with stacks in good condition; the upper windows, with the exception of those above the garage (most of the lower windows have been replaced); the front door, with its lock intact; two servants' bells on the hall wall. At one time, there were a dozen coat hooks as evidence of numerous visitors,

The Old rectory, Clocaenog; probably built on the site of a much older 'straw thatched Glebe House'.

and the old pantry (now a cubbyhole and passage) still has eight wrought-iron hooks in the ceiling, for hanging hams, bacon and game in times past.

The Old Rectory is a large, comfortable home and now has regular and welcome visitors including our own family, bed and breakfast guests (who provide income for upkeep) and our most regular summer visitors are bats — harmless and fascinating, they are no trouble and there are several roosts in the main roofspace. The limited space between insulation and slates of the pitched roof and studio ceiling appears to have been adopted as the bats' maternity ward; when the youngsters mature, they migrate to the main roof space. The majority of these are Pipistrelle bats.

Anyone who has read the diary of the Reverend Thomas Hughes will realise he was a man of strong views, and his comments about the size of the rectory would have been linked to his sense of the clergy's status in the community. To our eyes, the property is large, particularly when compared to some modern houses, and whatever the Rev. Hughes' opinion in the 1880s, the Rectory must have been one of the largest houses in the parish.

In the nineteenth and early twentieth centuries, substantial outbuildings provided stables, storage and probably a coach house while three acres of glebe land, close to the house, provided grazing and fodder for the horses — so necessary for the incumbent to minister to his large scattered parish.

M.B.

Clocaenog Church Hall.

Church Hall

In 1933, the Rectory outbuildings underwent a change of use when the local community raised sufficient funding to convert them to provide a hall and kitchen for use as a social centre. Until 2002, school dinners were cooked in the kitchen and served to pupils in the hall, and generations of children remember walking in crocodile from the school, shepherded by members of staff.

The *Church Magazine* for November 1933 reported that:

The New Church Hall shall be opened by Lady Tate, Galltfaenon, Thursday December 7th, 3p.m. Following the opening of the hall, there will be a bazaar which will be opened by Lady Naylor Leyland, Nantclwyd Hall. Entrance Bazaar 3d. Tea Adults 1/- Children 6d. Whist drive in the evening 8p.m.

When the Old Rectory was sold in 1982, the converted outbuildings were retained by the Church in Wales and continue to be administered by the Parochial Church Council. The County Education Authority paid a small rent, fitted out and maintained the kitchen and provided facilities in the hall for dining until, for various reasons, this came to an end in 2000.

At the beginning of the new millennium, the hall appeared to be structurally sound but needed more work to bring the facilities up to modern standards. The County Education Authority had fitted out and maintained the kitchen for their exclusive use and improved the Hall to ensure adequate facilities for dining, paying a small rent to the church. The Parochial Church Council now have to fund all improvements.

In 1998, sufficient money was raised to begin modernising the hall and to improve the heating system, with a total spending of about £5,600. Since then, other improvements have been completed: the drive has been

*Village Drama Group, 1946.
Back L–R: Robert Jones, Maes Gwyn; Mr Williams, Siop Isaf, Clawddnewydd; Joe Roberts, male nurse at Pool Park (came from Bryn Glas, Trefnant, brother of Mrs Jones, Brynfedwyn); Hywel Williams; Idwal Evans, Tan Llan; Saunders Davies, Bryn-y-ffynnon.
Front L–R: Mrs Williams, Llidiadau; Mrs A. M. Jones, wife of Robert Jones (above); Mr Emlyn Jones, Tŷ Capel; Mrs Hilda Jones, wife of Emlyn Jones; Mrs H. F. Jones, Henblas, wife of schoolmaster. Rehearsals and performances were always in the Church Hall.*

widened and resurfaced (land donated by M. and G. Buxbaum); a stone retaining wall which borders the drive has been rebuilt; the entrance porch has been demolished and the building extended to make a much-needed toilet area, including facilities for the disabled.

Substantial funds will still be needed to complete the modernisation and there are plans to replace all the windows and doors, to insulate and reslate the roof and to supply new interior furnishings including kitchen equipment.

The conversion of the Church Hall was funded by local residents in the early 1930s and, hopefully, it will continue as a community hall for present and future generations living in Clocaenog.

By March 2004, the cost of completed work amounted to about £67,000. Sources of funding towards these improvements include: Denbighshire County Council Community Project; Welsh Assembly

Above: Meeting of the Cloion Club, January 2004. Standing: Sandra Waldcote (visiting speaker from Clawddnewydd), Diane Ballard and Beryl Edwards. Seated: Alec Burnett, Beryl Jones, Gerald White, Ceinwen Roberts and Hazel Robinson.

Above right: The Cloion Club took part in the 1991 WRVS Quiz Finals and were runners-up. L–R: Mrs Stephenson, Mr & Mrs White, Hazel Robinson. Standing one of the WRVS organisers.

Right: The Church Hall is used by the Cloion Club, the Youth Club, the W.I. and for church social evenings and occassionally by the village school.. Here it is used for the 2004 W.I. Sports Day tea party.

grants; Wales Council for Voluntary Action (Community Buildings Grant Scheme); Garfield Weston Foundation; Awards For All (via National Lottery); Hartsheath Trust; Small Grants Lottery Scheme; private and other donations.

Today, the Church Hall is used by the Cloion Club for over 60s, the Youth Club, the Women's Institute, the children's sports day party, and whenever the Church Committee hold a special community event such as the summer barbecue.

M.B.

Glebe Land

Glebe land (those areas which were owned by the church) served as part of the clergyman's benefice--a living and especially the property (the Glebe House) and land attached — which formed the income for a rector or vicar.

This income was for a long time enhanced by the collection of tithes which were one tenth of the annual produce or labour, formally taken as a tax for the support of the Church and its clergy. This tax became a source of much resentment throughout Britain, especially when individuals chose to attend a different form of worship in chapels, rather than in church, and were obliged to fund ministers in both, out of their very meagre earnings. In rural areas particularly the tithes were paid in kind, that is one tenth of a field of hay or corn (hence the need for the tithe barn), one tenth of any animal slaughtered or one tenth of eggs collected. Many ministers were poor because their parishioners were so impoverished and their produce so limited that there was no possibility of extracting the tithes.

In Clocaenog in the year 1832 the ancient yard and garden of the Rectory were enlarged by the following additions, namely:

1. A small piece of land containing by estimation about the quarter of an acre which was given by the kindness of the Right Honourable William, Second Lord Bagot, and which now forms a part of the pleasure ground and the farm yard; a map of which is lodged in the Bishop's Registry at Bangor.

2. A small piece of land adjoining the highway leading from the common, called Bryniau Mawr, to the town of Ruthin, procured from John Roberts and Richard Roberts, gentlemen, the owners of Paradwys, in exchange for a small quillet called Erw yr Eglwys, which adjoins Cae Ysgybor, now in the possession of Mrs. Roberts; a map of which has also been transmitted to the Bishop's Registry at Bangor.

3. One little quillet or patch of ground adjoining to the lands of the late David Powell called Erw'r Person estimated to be worth 5s. per annum. And exchanged by the consent of the ordinary, when Dr. Eyrton was Bishop of Bangor, for an equal quantity of land adjoining to the Glebe House.

4. One field now in two called Cae'r Eglwys adjoining to the churchyard to east, to Richard Roberts and Lord Bagot's lands to west and north, and to the highway leading to the church on the south, containing about three acres of land.'

The west end of the churchyard adjoining the glebe land was in the upkeep of the Rector.

A.N.

Caring for the Poor

For a long period the poor could get help from the monasteries; in the cities the trade guilds also provided assistance for those in need, but, after the Reformation, local parish councils and justices of the peace took over relief for those families who were poverty stricken. In 1552, a statute was passed in Parliament ordering parishes to register their poor and which made each area responsible. This Elizabethan 'poor law' was introduced to reduce beggars and to try to keep a check on those who were forced to resort to crime in order to eat and live.

The early Poor Law was to be locally administered and locally funded by a tax on property — the state and the government were hardly involved. The deserving poor were offered relief and the justices of the peace could institute compulsory work for the able-bodied and those considered undeserving could be punished for malingering. The parish was to administer relief from the rates, according to the local resources available.

A major problem before you could even claim benefit was that you had to have a place to live. If you had no work and could not pay the rent, you could be turned out of the house. It was no wonder that some families resorted to seizing a small plot on the common land to live on and grow a few crops.

People had to work until they were physically incapable, and so, more and more, the Poor Law relief was being paid to the elderly. This remuneration was only paid to you as long as you remained in that parish and the result was that it curtailed movement even to find work elsewhere.

The old Poor Law could vary remarkably from parish to parish depending on how the local administrators assessed need and how they made their moral judgements in individual cases. The funding also varied according to the intrinsic wealth of that region and the ability of the landowners to pay their taxes and whether they could offer the necessary support in times of economic depression. In some areas there were few 'gentlemen' and, inevitably, the poor remained destitute.

The old Poor Law was initiated between 1597 and 1601 to deal with the increasing numbers of vagrants roaming the country who had no fixed abode, no permanent work, probably no particular skill, and therefore could only resort to begging or crime. The idea of the new law was to distinguish between the deserving and the undeserving poor and who better to judge than the parish where they were born or where they resided.

Until the twentieth century many people would walk the boundaries of their parish to establish precisely where those boundaries were. Anyone caught in a criminal act could be marched to the boundary and cast out of that parish; in this way a community was not forced to offer help to that person — they were someone else's problem!

The Poor Law remained in force (though with changes) until 1834 and was administered by churchwardens and overseers of the poor, the latter being appointed annually by the local justices, under penalty of fine, to work alongside the churchwardens. They were unpaid for their efforts, all of which were centred on the people in need within their parish boundary.

Sources of the Clocaenog Poor Law Fund

Hendre-ddu
Humphrey Salisbury of Clokaenog, gentleman, who died in the year 1633, did lay out a sume of money for lands called Hendre-ddu in the Parish of Derwen, wch he left charged with fourty and eight shillings p. annum towards the relief of the Poore of Clokaenog; John Jones, Rector of De,wen, being Tenant to the said lands for abt 40 years together did duely pay the rent above sd to the Poor of Clokaenog until his death wch happened in the year 1672. At wch time John Hughes of Voel in the Parish of Deiwen laid claime to the Poore's tenement of Hendre-ddu & by veftue of an old entaile from some one of his Ancestors (who sold the said Hedre-ddu to the above mentioned Humphrey Salisbury) was ready to evict the Poor from enjoying their annual pensions out of the said tenement.

Court case heard by Mr. Thelwall of Nant Clwyd, Esq., vice-chancellor of Chester.

Subsequently the money from the land was 'let out at interest', and also added to by gifts from Mr. Thelwall, the Rector (£5), and Lady Bagot (£3).

Old Wills relating to this Parish
Griffith Thomas ap Evan of Llanfwrog left by Will the Overplus of a certain Rent of a Tenement in Llangynhafel called Llidiart fawr lydau to the use of the Poor of this Parish for ever, the Overplus being in value 10s. and now £16 0s. 0d.

Hugh Thomas of Llangower in the County of Merioneth left by Will a Tenement in the Township of Llanerchgron called Graig Wan to the use of the Poor of this Parish for ever, now in the Holding of Thomas Moms, its present Rent £250.0

A tenement in the parish of Llanfwrog called Frith agored purchased by the minister and church wardens for the use of the Poor of this Parish for ever, its present Rent is £14.0.0.

Dy' Gwyl Domos (Dydd Gwyl Domos)

1687: On the saint's day of St. Thomas, 21 December, just before the celebration of Christmas, charity in the form of coal and groceries was given to many of those in the parish in need. An original source of the funding came from some of the above sources. This charity was administered by the rector and the churchwardens of Clocaenog parish in the succeeding years; sometimes responsible local people were co-opted onto the committee to help in deciding who was to be given aid and in what form. Many parishioners must have been very thankful for the help given. In the time of the Rev. Thomas Davies the charity was given out at the Cloion Inn but the women of the parish complained that their husbands spent half of it before they went home! Perhaps this is why they started to deliver goods to the houses. Eventually the land was sold and the money invested, so that only the interest was distributed. Graigwen was bought by the Jones family for £800 and Ffrithagored was also sold for £800.

By 1936, grants in kind were distributed twice a year, in June and December; 42 households benefitted, with the amounts ranging from five shillings to three pounds. Mostly it was coal that was delivered and people were told when to go to the Rectory for the distribution of vouchers for groceries. Medical aid was offered and when people had to be admitted to hospital the committee would negotiate a contribution towards funding with the hospital concerned — there was no National Health Service then. Parishioners could also be given new boots or shoes, or helped to buy clothes or bedding; these might be *ad hoc* payments at any time of the year, when the need arose.

When parish boundaries were altered the poor living in an area given over to another parish created the need for adjustments to be made and an allowance handed over to the other parish. In the past some people had been known to claim from the charities of both parishes. The boundary changes in this area concerned Llanfwrog, Pwllglas, Llangynhafel and Cyffylliog with Clocaenog.

Another complication was the ever-rising price of coal. In 1939, for instance, 188 cwts. cost £19 11s. 8d. but by 1946 181 cwts. cost £31 13s. 6d. Also in 1939 the groceries distributed cost £23 7s. 6d. and actual money given out was £6.5.0d. and the total amount distributed was £49 4s. 2d., with an additional £2 for the clerk's expenses for the year. In the year 1944 the total expenditure was £75 18s. including a grant towards the cost of an invalid chair.*

Gradually needs changed and it was decided that fewer people were actually in need, but those who were, needed more help, and as a result larger sums could be spent on fewer people. Also one reads in the accounts of a film projector for the use of the village children or a special pair of spectacles to help one pensioner. The charity was seen to be satisfying different needs.

The capital had been invested in various government stock and only the interest was used each year. It was a registered 'Custodian Charity' and the books had to be balanced and audited; the Charity Commission had suggested an apportionment of stock to meet the annual payments. Through all the years the charity has continued to function here in Clocaenog. In 1996 it was decided that there were no longer any poor in the parish who could not access other sources of monetary help; instead Dy' Gwyl Domos should be given to those families in the community who had the burden of a person with special needs, whether permanently handicapped or temporarily seriously ill. This is the way the charity is administered to this day.

Graig Wen (Cf second old will above.)

During the early twentieth century the Jones family lived at Graig Wen Farm and their fields adjoined those

---

* The magazine *History Today*, reported in May 2006 that a pub in Ipswich has been told it must pay an annual fine of £2 as a penalty for a murder that took place there more than 300 years ago. This was because the gift of money was to be paid in perpetuity. The money was to be distributed in kind on St. Thomas's Day, before Christmas.

of the 'Poore of Clocaenog' on what had been Hendre Ddu land. It seems that they entered into an indenture or contract on 8th December 1919. This agreement was between:

1. George Chivers Bower
2. Rev. William Hopkins Jones and his church council, John Hughes, Richard Morris, William Winder Christopherson, John Jones, Edwin Roberts, Richard Francis and John Williams.
3. Roger Jones and Elizabeth Elenaeor Jones, his wife, regarding the field No. 546 which had no physical boundary between it and the field *'for which there is no paper Title'*.

As the current accounts for the Dy' Gwyl Domos Charity only date from 1936, I cannot be sure if the deed referred to above, concerning Graig Wen, dates the time when the fields were sold and the money invested. Graig Wen was auctioned recently, in 2002, as part of the Jones' family estate but has again been sold in 2004.

Here in the Parish of Clocaenog the payments were made out of the rents from properties bequeathed to the Poor Law Fund; initially the three fields of Hendre Ddu, and later the properties of Graigwen and Frithagored were added. Later still, after these properties had been sold on the advice of the Charity Commissioners, only the interest from bank investments was used. As interest could fluctuate and costs rose (e.g. coal) the money for distribution was finite and was given to fewer people.

It was not until 1946 that the state took over responsibility, under the post-war Labour government, with the National Insurance Act and the National Health Service Act to provide 'a shield for every man, woman and child … against the ravages of poverty and adversity.' The old Poor Law of 1601, and the 1834 Poor Law with its Boards of Guardians had gone, and were replaced by the National Assistance Act of 1948 which was to be financed out of taxes, not local rates. The great hope was that 'the poor would no longer be with us.'

The needs of the poor lessened after state pensions were introduced. The idea of retirement is a very recent innovation and is already being questioned as to whether it is affordable, when the balance of the age structure in society is changing.

A.N.

Clocaenog Parish in 1861 — the Rev. Hughes's diary

Clocaenog, 'a Parish in the County of Denbigh in the Diocese of St. Asaph — in the Archdeaconry of St. Asaph and the Deanery of Dyffryn Clwyd'. This is in the opening sequence in the diary of the Rev. Thomas Hughes in 1861. 'The living is a Rectory — the gross Value or Rent Charge in lieu of Tithes (commuted in 1839) is Three hundred and forty-two pounds, 14/-'.

The Rectory built in 1832, was said to be a 'Mansion House' of bricks and slated, and erected during the incumbency of the Rev. Richard Newcombe, rector of this parish, but also warden of Ruthin. The rooms are described as 'including a passage way with a parlour to the right, a smaller parlour to the left, an inner room, a kitchen and two pantries; four bedrooms with two dressing rooms, and in the cellar a small room called the Wine Cellar, a Beer cellar, a Brewhouse and a Dairy'. The outbuildings, erected the previous year in 1831, contain 'a Stable, a Cowhouse, a Threshing Floor and a Bay'.

Small plots of land were exchanged to enlarge the garden and glebe land to make it a better unit. (see Glebe Lands below). In the 'true Note and Terrier' written by the minister, Rev. Parry, in 1834, he listed all the glebe land and buildings belonging to the church together with books, vestments and silver, and the income from the various sources for which he is responsible.

He goes on to describe the parish of Clocaenog: 'The parish reaches from the River Ciwyd in the East to the River Aiwen in the West- a distance of about 7 miles. It is extremely hilly -but not rugged or rocky. It contains 6,337 acres (statute measure). Total quantity subject to Tithes 6,134 acres — leaving 203 acres not subject to Tithes — Common (or waste) land, subiect to Tithes 3,167 acres — Glebe Lands 3 acres.' Thus it appears that one half of the parish was common land but, in the previous seven years, the 'Inclosure' Commissioners had sold or allotted several hundred acres and, although stated to be subject to tithes, the rector found that no rent was being paid by the tenants in lieu of their tithes — as such, tithes had ceased after an Act of Parliament passed in 1836.* Tithes were explained as being 'the Tenth of all Corn and Hay, Wool and Lambs; also the Tithes of Pigs and Geese, Honey together with all Lactuals and Easter Dues which are due to the Rector throughout the Parish'. Now he could only attempt to collect rent due, and that was with great difficulty. An old Welsh saying goes: *'Degfed rhan o gnwd y maes, i gadw gwas y Diawl'* [One tenth of the produce of the fields to keep the servant of the Devil.] This hated tax on their efforts was greatly resented by the farmers and smallholders, in addition to which they did not attend church because so many of them were dissenters and belonged to the various Nonconformist chapels. The rector goes on to say that, as the common land is coming under cultivation and the people are building their houses and farms on their new plots, there will be an increase in population 'and of course increase in proportion the Labour and Responsibilty of the Pastoral (Spiritual) Charge'. Actually there is little difference in population according to the Census Returns

1801	437	1831	461
1811	421	1841	457
1821	462	1851	421

The church at that time was the Church of England (not the Church in Wales as it is now) and was one more symbol of English sovereignty. Tithes were resented at that time throughout Britain, and had become a great source of unrest, and in Wales, people were expected to pay to the Church of England, when most of them attended chapel. Locally the most famous instance of what came to be called the 'Tithe Wars', arose when the people of Llangwm refused to pay and took up implements to drive away the agent: the militia was brought out and some men were killed and others wounded, though this is disputed.

The minister faced an uphill battle and was not very subtle in the way he approached his parishioners and so was often flatly refused. He had great difficulty collecting in his dues. When he came to the parish sixteen years previously he had found 'the minds of the people pre-occupied by prejudice and suspicion' and little changed for him during his stay, and he felt that, although he came intending to do good, he had misgivings that his efforts had been in vain and felt that he had done very inadequately to the hopes at first indulged in'.

In 1856/57 he supervised the re-roofing and re-furbishing of the church and acted as Treasurer for the fund-raising to the sum of £400, a little from inside the parish but mostly donations from wealthier well-wishers outside. The Bishop of Bangor gave £30 and £10 was given by the Rt. Hon. F. R. West of Ruthin Castle. This was when the gallery was dismantled. The Rev. Hughes objected to it because '3 or 4 singing men and singing women, boys and girls … all well concealing their rude and irreverent conduct children playing marbles, pelting each other etc. … perhaps 3 or 4 steadier old people at the other end, shaking their heads at them, or lugging their ears' could be screened from sight up there, and he wanted to put a stop to such 'indecent behaviour in church'.

Also he wished to replace the 'low, narrow oak benches or planks without backs' for the congregation. There were three or four large square pews, one at either end of the communion rails, blocking the sides, and another in the middle of the aisle, blocking off a view of the massive stone font. This pew was owned by a 'rigid dissenter' who lived 2½ miles away and who never came to church; but he maintained that it stood over the burial place of his family. When the pew was moved to the side against the wall, he objected but the Rev. Hughes told him the space could be marked and he was satisfied.

The reading desk stood in the pew on the south end of the communion rail and the previous minister had paid the owner a shilling a year 'for the accommodation'. Rev. Hughes soon had the desk moved to a more

---

* Tithe Maps: In 1836 an Act of Parliament was passed to end the practice of paying Tithes in kind to the church, and Tithes were commuted for a rent-charge on land. This meant that it was necessary to make accurate maps on a large scale showing every field and building, roads, paths, rights of way and other details in order to levy taxes. Landowners and Occupiers of properties were also shown. This was done with such thoroughness that it constituted a Victorian Domesday Book and has been recognised ever since as an accurate source of information for all those doing any historical research.

central place near the pulpit, outside the chancel. He bought a new crimson alter cloth and bought a stove to heat the church in cold weather, but it 'smoked badly at times and was more an eyesore than ornament'. As the roof no longer leaked and the floor was dry, people would have to wear extra clothing when the winter was cold.

In 1857 the minister reckons the attendances at the various places of worship were as follows:

>Church of England about 20 people
>Methodist (Wesleyan) about 70 people
>Anabaptists about 15 people
>Scotch Kirk about 5 people
>Methodists (Calvinists) about 300 people

Two Methodist preachers lived in the parish; the Calvinist one had purchased land and was a freeholder. He became very influential and useful to his sect, 'performing marriages and burials, and would on request pray and preach at the house before the funeral procession set out on foot for a church burial'. Sometimes both the minister and the preacher would be present at the home at the same time. The Rev. Hughes said he had known 100 people to be present, and tells how the old custom of 'offering' was kept up in the village here. 'Farmers generally offer 6d. (pence) and even the preachers conform to it'.

Rev. Hughes did attempt to visit the people whom he thought of as being in his pastoral care. On one occasion he went to see a family living near the river Alwen on the outskirts of the parish, where he found the woman lying in bed, ill and very weak. The family remarked that it was a novelty to have a visit from the minister and it had never been known before and so they showed him great hospitality, offering him oatcakes and buttermilk as refreshment. However when he went a second time and took wine with him, intending to offer her the sacrament, he was surprised when she refused as she said she had already received it from the preacher. Rev. Hughes did not wish to give in to her 'bigoted prejudices' and continued to urge her, until her husband told him to stop troubling her. Sadly she died soon afterwards — and was not brought to the church to be buried.

As you read the diary the minister seems stiff and pedantic but you cannot help but feel that he was up against insuperable odds. He showed genuine concern for the education of the village children, and although he wanted them to be taught through the medium of English, he sincerely believed that it would benefit them when they went to seek work in service or as apprentices in England. This was the time of 'Welsh not' when all children were forbidden to speak Welsh in school or the playground.

In the beginning School was held in the church — not a very suitable choice thought the minister — and so it was decided to build a schoolroom and accommodation for the schoolmaster, on land adjacent to the churchyard boundary. This building is now one dwelling and known as Old School House. John Jones is the first to be called schoolmaster in the church baptismal records in 1751. Later there is Rhys Evans in about 1814. He was succeeded by Mr. John Price, who was educated at Ruthin Grammar School. Under him the village school at first flourished and the number of pupils rose to nearly 70, so that bigger premises were needed.

The present school was built by public subscription on waste ground, at the bottom of the village, donated by Lord Bagot, where there was sufficient land for the children to have a playground. Mr. Price taught until 1845 when he died at the age of 64.

Soon after Rev. Hughes came to the parish the teacher was Mr. Pierce who allowed Welsh to be spoken and even spoke it himself to his pupils! Parents complained about his behaviour and when tackled he admitted he could be 'hasty and hot tempered' and he was not always as sober as he might be outside school — his behaviour was well known! Rev. Hughes decided to dismiss him. But then the parishioners called a meeting and re-instated him, despite the fact that the minister had engaged a new teacher from England. Other than totally antagonising them, the minister had to give in to the wishes of the villagers.

He had been warned by a university friend that he would be dealing with the 'Aegean stables' when he came to the parish but he had never imagined he would have so little influence and he admits somewhat sadly he is no 'Hercules' to be able to cope with such indifference to his presumed authority. The schoolmaster himself had left the church and joined the Wesleyan Chapel congregation and had much support in the village. The Vestry held a meeting in 1847 at which they passed a resolution that no one should hold the position of schoolmaster 'who is not conversant with the Welsh language'. Mr. Pierce was to be allowed a further three months (in fact he stayed another 10 years) and only be discharged if any charges were brought against his moral character. The minister then withdrew from all responsibility for the school and cancelled the appointment of the new teacher he had engaged. In other words he retired, defeated by the situation in which he found himself. He and his family must have felt very isolated. He had come to a parish 'where dissent is so universally prevalent …' and '… the Calvinists being so numerous, encourage each other with more determination in opposing us' and he could make no progress. He noted in his diary that 'the Wesleyans consider themselves the rulers of the parish and its affair …' and '… are located in or near the village and consist mostly of poor labourers and Cottagers', but are nevertheless not as antagonistic to the church as the Calvinists. He did not ask from them when he was collecting for the Church so that he could justify refusing them when they asked him to give to 'The Bible Society' etc. 'Let there be conciliation but no compromise on my part', he remarked in his comments in his diary.

Rev. Hughes said that the school 'continued to languish' and he was powerless to change the situation. Eventually even the parishioners could not turn a blind eye and wished to do something about the poor teaching. This was after another 10 years remember, and they came to the minister to ask for his help to remove the schoolmaster and appoint a new one. He made the most of the opportunity and blamed them for the 'ruinous state' of the school. Mr. Price had 'kept school in Clocaenog for nearly 30 years. He had a good reputation at one time with 60 or 70 pupils, some coming from Ruthin and boarding with him or in the neighbourhood 'so popular did he become in the conduct of his school. Tho' latterly he fell off through intemperate habits and ill health' so that numbers and attendance decreased — also he joined the Wesleyan Methodists' Society but 'found no panacea for all evils' commented the minister.

The salary was inadequate — about £16 a year in subscriptions towards a salary which the minister managed to raise to £20. This was still not enough for a Certificated man and they could not get any grants, so the school had to make do with untrained schoolmasters. Some of the better off farmers sent their older children 'say about 12' to some superior school such as the British School in Ruthin.* The minister could not help but admire them for doing their duty to their children but this also entailed them in paying for board and lodging in Ruthin. He felt that if they had together augmented the teacher's salary they could have kept their children at home and had a better teacher for the younger ones too.

The old school came to be divided into two cottages and the rent (about £5 a year) was added to the school funding to improve the master's salary. As the schoolmaster could let the cottages, he then qualified to be on the Register of Voters, 'being assessed to the poor's rate'. He could live in one of the cottages if he wished or opt to have lodgers. Rev. Hughes suggested that for a single man he would arrange for the school room to be partitioned and create two small rooms with a grate, and the teacher lived there for several years but found the place very damp at the confluence of the two streams and he was 'afflicted by Rheumatism and other similar complaints'. One inspector suggested he exchange with one of his tenants in the Old School House but the tenants would not agree!

When he first came to Clocaenog the Rev. Hughes struggled to create a Sunday School. Both the Wesleyans and the Calvinists met on Sundays in the schoolroom but at different hours. The minister visited one Sunday and found 30 or 40 persons of all ages present 'busy reading and spelling'. He applauded their work but insisted that he wished the Catechism to be taught. He was shown a small catechism book but the minister said it was inadequate as it was not that of the Church. One of the men stood up and said, 'This, Sir, is the catechism we are used to teach here — the Catechism of Mr. Charles.'† Soon after starting his own Sunday

---

* The British School was in the building now known as Borthyn Primary School.

† Thomas Charles, an ordained priest of the established Church, quarrelled with his bishop, left the church to join the dissenters and was then based in Bala. He became an ardent Methodist and founded both the Sunday school movement in Wales and the British & Foreign Bible Society. He was keen to improve the education of the poor and to enable them to read the Bible in the Welsh vernacular.

school in the church Rev. Hughes discovered that the schoolroom had been vacated — the Methodists now held theirs in a room in a farmhouse and the Wesleyans went to their own chapel. The minister found that some families coming to his Sunday school also attended the chapel Sunday school.

Not understanding 'this want of religious stability' he did not enquire further for fear of losing them. He held two sessions in the morning and in the evening, and he thought they were better occupied whichever Sunday schools they chose to attend. He allowed Welsh to be taught so that the people could read the Bible in the vernacular but, 'One day in the week is quite enough,' he said, 'which will ere long most probably become a dead language … Until English, all conquering English, shall come to be the uniform language of Great Britain.' How wrong he was.

In 1852 the minister started a Clothing Club, called at first a Penny Club, as that was what the members aimed to save each week. There was an initial starting fund with a capital of £6 raised by the minister, and his wife £3, Lord and Lady Bagot £2 and James Maurice of Ruthin £1. It soon became the custom to collect monthly and the minister's wife kept the accounts. At the end of each year the members received a ticket for the sum of their deposits plus an additional bonus of two or three shillings to take to the shop of their choice to spend on clothing or bedding. Mostly they went to one of the two shops in Clawddnewydd. The purchases were returned to Mrs. Hughes for inspection before the bills were paid. Rev. Hughes claimed that over the years the villagers were less raggedly clothed than when he came. By 1862 they had 40 members in the savings club.

Charities and bequests in the parish amounted to £56 — a considerable sum in those days, the 'equivalent to the produce of the present rents of 3 tenements' — of this £6 was given to the poor in other parishes. It was collected and administered by the two church wardens. The minister was very aggrieved that he had no say in the affairs of the charity even though he was the principal trustee. Parishioners could come and request assistance at any time in the year but most of the money was given out in the winter to buy coal. This was at the Feast of St. Thomas on December 21st known as '*Dy' gwyl Domas*'. Some 50 or 60 families were given help during the year. 'They labour hard to support their families, and abstain from being burdensome on the parish.' He stressed these were the 'poor' and not the 'paupers' who were even worse off, being destitute. Most of his parishioners were small farmers and crafts people, such as carpenter, wheelwright, or blacksmith.

There were three manors in the parish,

- Part of the extensive Lordship of Ruthin belonging to the Middletons of Ruthin Castle.

- Pool Park belonging to the Right Honourable Lord Bagot.

- The small manor of Brynfedwyn belonging to the Right Reverend, the Lord Bishop of Bangor.

'This little Manor (about three miles in circumference) contains within its bounds the Church of Clocaenog, the Village, Parsonage, Glebe, Parts of some half a dozen Farms; two small tenements, formally paying chief-rent, but now a (moderate) rack-rent to the Bishop; a small common by a late arrangement come into the possession of Lord Bagot; and the waste situated at the junction of the two streams and three roads and on which stands the parish school.'

The minister was advised by the Bishop's agent to pay 2/6 (2 shillings and sixpence) annual chief rent on this wasteland as it stood at his entrance gate and then he could deny encroachment upon it. In fact he planted a few trees and allowed the school children to play there, but would not allow a man who had been deprived of his cottage to build there.

His diary does not continue. What more could he have said? He was not a happy man living here in the mid 19th century.

A.N.

The Religious Census of 1851, Volume II

Perhaps this will explain why the Rev. Hughes was so disappointed in his ministry.

CLOCAENOG PARISH, consisting of Isa Division and Uclia Division

Area: 6,671 acres
Population: Isa   62 males   62 females   Total 124
             Ucha 156 males   141 females Total 297

Clocaenog Parish Church Diocese of Bangor.
Endowed: Tithe £240   Glebe 3$\frac{1}{2}$ acres   Other sources £3
Space free. 24 benches; other 5 or 6 pews.
Present   Average: morning 25   afternoon 12–20
Remarks.   The Church is (I suppose) about 400 years old. The few sittings in it (mostly old-fashioned oak benches) are almost all appropriated. The attendance at Church is very fluctuating and uncertain, and difficult to take an average of In consequence of the evil and unjust effects of Free Trade Iam at the moment suffering from a decrease of Income to the amount of 10p. cent

Thomas Hughes.   Rector.

Rectory rated at £12: patron, the Bp. Tithes commuted for £342 10s.: glebe-house.
2 services in Welsh taken by the incumbent.
Incumbent resident.

Now compare with the following, taken from the Welsh Church Commission for the County of Denbigh:

Bethesda (Wesleyan Methodists)
Erected: 1836
Space: Free 250; other 15
Present: Morn. 30; aft. 48 scholars; even. 36
Average: Morn. 40 + 27 scholars: aft. 52 + 34 scholars; even. 70.
Remarks: In consequence of the minister's absence on March 30, 1851, the general congregation was much less than usual.
John Jones.
Superintendent of Sunday School. Brynfedwen

Clawddnewydd Chapel (Calvinistic Methodists)
Erected: 1827.
Space: Free 72; other 150; standing 72.
Present: Morn. 68; aft 124 scholars + 17 teachers; even. 172.
Average: Morn. 126 + 112 scholars; aft. 20 + 132 scholars; even. 190.
Remarks: As the Chapel is situated near the boundary of the parish, [Derwen] part of the congregation are residents of the parish of Clocaenog.
No. 7   The Chapel inside measures 32ft. by 26ft. and contains 26 seats Let, and about 30 sq. ft. common floor on which benches are provided.
No. 8   The 'general congregation' is understood to include the Sunday Scholars & teachers, as it is generally attended by all ages and held either morning or afternoon as one district service.

Owen Williams.   Elder.   Pentre Derwen.

The two services in the Parish Church had an average attendance of 20–25, the three services in the Wesleyan Methodist Chapel had between 67 and 86, and the Calvinistic Methodists drew as many as 190 people at an evening service.

An early view of Clawddnewydd, showing the Chapel on the left, opposite the lane to Melin-y-Wig.

The Statistics of the Nonconformist Churches for 1905.

Cades Chapel	Calvanistic Methodists	No. of 'adherents' 67
Bethesda Chapel	Wesleyans	No. of 'adherents' 40

Today (2004) both the chapels in Clocaenog have closed; Bethesda Chapel has been sold to the adjoining house and has yet to be developed, while Cades Chapel has been partially dismantled and lowered to be used as a garage for Tŷ Capel. Clawddnewydd Chapel is comparatively flourishing.

A.N.

Bethesda Wesleyan Chapel, Clocaenog

These are the words on the tablet located on the chapel wall

Bethesda
Wesleyan Chapel
Renovated 1835
Renewed 1913

In 1805, Robert Lewis, a carpenter, who resided at Hen Dŷ (site unknown), succeeded in persuading Wesleyan friends, mainly from Ruthin, to attend prayer meetings and very soon sermons were regularly preached. Meetings were held for twenty years at his home, Hen Dŷ, and he was the first deacon to be appointed.

Robert Lewis was grandfather to John Jones (Johannes) and a great grandfather to the Rev. T. Isfryn Hughes who was raised at this chapel. Robert Lewis was a faithful member all his life. In 1821 there were 14 regular members in the congregation. Later, Mr. John Bonner, the Rev. R. Bonner's brother came to live in the neighbourhood and he was hardworking and conscientious in the chapel and was also a lay preacher.

Hen Dŷ became too small for the congregation and the meetings were then held in the school. During this period John Hughes, the grandfather of Isfryn Hughes, paid a visit to the district and preached at School House and his sermon on the subject 'The day has come for the Lord's vengeance' was well received and successful. This meeting became very influential and many returned rejoicing and were faithful members all their lives.

John Hughes married Robert Lewis's daughter and came to live in the area. It is said that he made the most effort to establish a chapel here; land was secured from Lord Bagot on a 99 year lease — on the understanding that the parson had no objection. At a meeting in Bangor on 12th May 1835, an application to

Bethesda Chapel, with the old Post Office adjoining.

construct a chapel was presented, at an approximate cost of £120, to seat 35 members and 150 listeners; the chapel was built during that year. Archdean R. Newcome and curate Rev J. Parry contributed £2 each towards the fund and presented a Bible for the pulpit with the following inscription 'Gift from Rev J. Parry and Archdean R. Newcome to Clocaenog Wesleyan Chapel'. Because of poor workmanship, the chapel soon needed renovation and after completion of the work the chapel was re-opened on 13–14th December 1864, officiated by Rev. O. Williams and John Evans, Eglwysbach.

After John Hughes, John Jones (Johannes) took responsibility; he was the grandson of Robert Lewis the first nominated deacon. John Jones was a keen reader, able writer, a first class poet and a cultured and acceptable preacher and it is noted that he preached 1,701 times and travelled 13,832 miles for the benefit of man and glory to God. He died in 1883 aged 62 years. He was succeeded by William Jones, an excellent teacher, and a forester in the employment of Lord Bagot. Then came John Hughes, son of John Hughes previously mentioned, and the father of Rev. T. Isfryn Hughes and for many years he welcomed missionary workers to his home. He was a faithful deacon, a well liked preacher, a man of high principal and a great reader with a brilliant personality. He died in 1904. The Rev. Caenog Jones also became a minister and his family were very active within the chapel. Although Bethesda was only a small chapel, several famous preachers were raised here. Edwin Hughes, the youngest brother of John Hughes, started preaching and at about the same time. Ellis Roberts started preaching and became a candidate for the ministry and chose to undertake missionary work. When questioned whether it would be better for him to stay in his own country during his lifetime he replied, 'work beckons me overseas'. When he was in failing health he came back to the Vale of Clwyd and had his wish when he died to be buried in Clocaenog cemetery alongside Edwin Hughes.

Thomas Isfryn Hughes, a prominent minister brought up in Bethesda, and son of John Hughes, Tŷ Capel, was an apprentice tailor with his father. In 1887 he started preaching and attended Handsworth College where he received tuition to become a Wesleyan minister. His name was listed in the Welsh Biographies 1941–50. His sister Sarah and her husband were the first residents to live in the bungalow erected in the 1930s in the village and she named it 'Isfryn' after her brother and this property is known by this name today.

Another minister raised at the chapel was Rev. Alec Jones who was a conscientious worker in his community before applying for the ministry. He was ordained at St Paul's Church, Abergele, in May 1964 and he became minister at Bethesda, Caernarfonshire and it was there that he met his wife, Dilys, and they later became missionary workers in Ghana. They returned a few years later, and he became a minister in the Corwen Circuit and then the Ruthin Circuit, becoming minister of the chapel where he was brought up. He returned to Ghana where he remained until his retirement in 1996 when he settled in Shrewsbury, only to die a year later, following all his hard work.

Richard Francis was a native of Coedpoeth and worked in the coal mines before deciding to apply for the ministry. Whilst he attended colleges at Didsbury, Manchester, and Handsworth, his health started failing. He became assistant minister at Clocaenog, Llanelidan, Graigfechan and Hirwaen. He died suddenly in September 1933 aged 55 years.

Cadwaladr T. Roberts spent his childhood in Bethesda and then resided in Clocaenog at Ffrith Agored and was a nephew of Robert Roberts, Plas Cwta. The family moved to Cynwyd in 1930 and he became a lay preacher and occasionally preached at Bethesda. He read his scriptures by braille due to an impairment of his sight and many will remember him with his white stick.

We had a great number of ministers at this chapel and at one period they were moved to a new district every three years; later they stayed for five-year periods. We were part of the Ruthin Circuit and the minister resided at Bathafarn House in Ruthin. Sunday School was held at 10.00 a.m., a sermon at 2.00 p.m and a prayer meeting at 6.00 p.m

Deacons elected from the late 1930s and thereafter:
Dafydd Hughes, Bryn Fedwen, Robert Roberts, Plas Cwta,
Gabriel Thomas Edwards, Haulfryn, Francis Lloyd Jones, Bod Idris,
Robert Davies, Bryn Teg, Robert R. Evans, Llug Fynydd, and
Gwyn Atkinson, 10 Maes Caenog.

Organists:
Mrs Francis, Post Office, Mrs Gwyneth Francis Jones, Post Office,
Mrs B.M. Hughes, Hafod, and Miss M. M. Edwards, Haulfryn.

Musical Conductor:
Mr Robert Roberts, Plas Cwta.

Tŷ Capel:
Mr. and Mrs. Richard Francis lived in Tŷ Capel for many years, where they also ran a post office and shop. Following them, Mr. and Mrs. J. W. Jones became tenants, until Mr. M. Moneypenny came to live there; he now owns the house and the chapel.

The last meeting at the chapel was on Sunday 23 May 1993. There remains only one place of worship at present in the village compared to three in the past.

L. J.

Bethesda, Yr Eglwys Fethodistaidd, Clocaenog

Dyma'r geiriau sydd ar dabled ar fur y capel:
Bethesda
Capel y Wesleyaid
1835
Adgyweiriwyd 1864
Adnewydd 1913

Tua'r flwyddyn 1805 llwyddodd Robert Lewis a drigai yn yr Hen Dŷ, i gael cyfeillion Wesleyaidd o Rhuthun yn bennaf i ddyfod i Glocaenog i gynnal cyfarfodydd gweddio ac yn fuan cafwyd pregethu rheolaidd.

Cynheilid y moddion am ugain mlynedd yn ei gartref, yr Hen Dŷ, ac ef oedd y blaenor cyntaf benodwyd. Yr oedd ef yn daid i John Jones (Johannes), ac yn hen daid i'r Parch T. Isfryn Hughes (un o blant yr eglwys hon) a ochr ei dad. Bu Robert Lewis yn ffyddlon gyda'r achos ar hyd ei oes. Yn 1821, dywedir fod 14 o aelodau yn y cyfarfod yn gyson. Daeth John Banner, brawd y Parchedig R. Banner i drigo yn yr ardal, a bu'n selog a defnyddiol gyda'r achos ac yr oedd yn bregethwr cynorthwyol. Aeth yr Hen Dŷ yn rhy fychan i'r cynulliadau, a sicrhawyd yr ysgoldy i gynnal y moddion.

Yn y cyfnod hwn, ymwelwyd a'r ardal gan John Hughes, taid Isfryn Hughes. Pregethodd yn yr ysgoldy a chafodd oedfa lewyrchus iawn. Ei destun oedd 'Canys daeth dydd mawr ei ddicter ef'. Dychwelodd amryw ac aeth yn orfoledd cyffredinol a bu'r dychweledigion hyn yn ffyddlon ar hyd eu hoes. Arhosodd dylanwad yr oedfa ar yr ardal am flynyddoedd.

Priododd John Hughes a merch Robert Lewis a daeth i fyw i'r ardal a dywedir mae ef wnaeth yr ymdrech fwyaf i gael capel. Cafwyd tir gan Arglwydd Bagot ar bridles am 99 mlynedd, ar ôl deall nad oedd y person yn erbyn. Yng Ngyfarfod Taliethol Bangor gynhaliwyd l2fed Mai 1835, daeth cais i adeiladu capel; amcangyfrif y draul oedd £120. Cyfrifid yr aelodau yn 35 a'r gwrandwyr yn 150. Cafodd y capel ei adeiladu y flwyddyn honno. Cyfrannodd yr Archddeon Newcome a'r cured, y Parch J. Parry, £2 yr un tuag ato, gan roddi Beibl ar y pulpud, ac ysgrifennu ynddo, 'Rhodd y Parch J. Parry a'r Archddeon R. Newcome i gapel y Wesleyaid yn Clocaenog'. Oherwydd adeiladwaith gwael, bu'n rhaid ei atgyweirio ac, wedi cwblhau y gwaith, ail-agorwyd y capel Rhagfyr 13–14, 1864 trwy weinyddiad y Parch O. Williams a John Evans, Eglwysbach.

Ar ol dyddiau John Hughes, daeth y gofal yn bennaf ar John Jones (Johannes). Yr oedd yn ŵyr i Robert Lewis, y blaenor cyntaf, ac yr oedd yn ddarllenwr mawr, yn llenor medrus ac yn fardd gwych. Dechreuodd bregethu ac yr oedd yn bregethwr doeth a chymeradwy. Bu farw yn 1883 yn 62 mlwydd oed. Dywedir iddo bregethu 1,701 o weithiau, a theithio 13,832 militir er lles dyn a gogoniant Duw. Dilynwyd ef gan William Jones, coediwr o dan Arglwydd Bagot ac athro rhagorol.

Yna, daeth John Hughes, mab y John Hughes a enwyd, ef oedd tad y Parch T. Isfryn Hughes. Bu ei ddrws yn agored i groesawu cenhadon hedd am flynyddoedd. Blaenor ffyddlon, pregethwr cymeradwy, dyn o egwyddorion pur, darllenwr mawr a chymeriad disglair ganddo oedd y John Hughes hwn. Bu farw yn 1904. Un arall aeth yn weinidog oedd y Parch. Caenog Jones a bu ei deulu yn amlwg gyda'r achos.

Er mai eglwys fechan yw hon, magodd bregethwyr enwog. Dechreuodd Edwin Hughes bregethu, brawd ieuengaf John Hughes. Tua'r un adeg cychwynodd Ellis Roberts bregethu, a daeth yn ymgeisydd am y weinidogaeth a dewisodd fynd yn genhadwr. Yr oedd ei galon yn ei waith cenhadol, a phan ofynwyd iddo onid gwell fuasai iddo aros yn y wlad hon weddill ei oes, ei ateb oedd 'na, mae cloch y gwaith yn galw'. Pan dorrodd ei iechyd daeth trosodd i Ddyffryn Clwyd a chafodd ei ddymuniad i gael gorwedd wrth ochr Edwin Hughes yn mynwent y llan.

Un o blant Bethesda oedd y gwenidog amlwg Thomas Isfryn Hughes, sef mab John Hughes Tŷ Capel a bu'n brentis teiliwr gyda'i dad. Yn 1887 dechreuodd bregethu ac aeth i goleg Handsworth oedd yn hyfforddi gweinidogion Wesleyaidd. Cafodd ei enw ei gynnwys yn y Bywgraffiadau Cymreig 1941–50. Ei chwaer Sarah a'i gwr oedd y cyntaf i fyw yn y byngalo godwyd yn y tridegau yn y llan ac fe roddwyd yr enw Isfryn arno ar ol ei brawd; a dyna'r enw sydd arno hyd y dydd hwn.

Un arall o blant yr eglwys hon oedd y Parch. Alec Jones a bu yn weithgar yn y gymdeithas cyn mynd yn ymgeisydd am y weinidogaeth. Cafodd ei ordeinio yn Eglwys Sant Paul, Abergele, fis Mai 1964 ac aeth yn weinidog i Bethesda, Arfon. Yno y cyfarfu a'i wraig, Dilys, ac aeth oddiyno yn genhadwr i Ghana. Dychwelodd am ychydig flynyddoedd a bu'n weinidog yng nghylchdaith Corwen ac yna cylchdaith Rhuthun gan ddod yn weinidog ar yr eglwys a'i magodd. Dychwelodd i Ghana a bu yno hyd nes iddo ymddeol a daeth i'r Amwythig i fyw, ond bu farw'n ddisymwth yn 1997 ac ni chafodd ond blwyddyn o ymddeoliad wedi llafur caled.

Brodor o Goedpoeth oedd Richard Francis, Tŷ Capel, a bu'n gweithio yn y pyllau glo cyn penderfynu mynd yn weinidog. Bu'n ngholeg Didsbury, Manceinion, a choleg Handsworth, ac yna tarrodd ei iechyd. Bu'n ail weinidog ar Clocaenog, Llanelidan, Graigfechan a Hirwaen ond bu farw'n ddisymwth fis Medi 1933 yn 55 mlwydd oed.

Treuliodd Cadwaladr T. Roberts ei blentyndod yn Methesda. Trigai yn Ffrith Agored ac yr oedd Robert Roberts, Plas Cwta, yn ewythr iddo. Aeth y teulu i fyw i Gynwyd tua'r flwydd 1930. Daeth ef yn bregethwr cynorthwyol a deuai i Bethesda i bregethu yn achlysurol. Darllenai o'r ysgrythyr gyda chymorth braille a ddysgodd oherwydd nam ar ei olwg a chofir amdano gyda'i ffon wen.

Cawsom nifer fawr o weinidogion ar yr eglwys hon gan y byddent ar un cyfnod yn symud bob tair blynedd, ac yna arhosent am bum mlynedd. Yr oeddem yn rhan o gylchdaith Rhuthun a'n gweinidog yn byw yn Nhŷ Bathafarn, Rhuthun. Cynhaliwyd Ysgol Sul am ddeg y bore, oedfa am ddau y prynhawn, a chyfarfod gweddi yn yr hwyr am chwech.

Blaenoriaid gofir a ddiwedd y tridegau ymlaen:
>   Mr Dafydd Hughes, Bryn Fedwen
>   Mr Robert Roberts, Plas Cwta
>   Mr Gabriel Thomas Edwards, Haulfryn
>   Mr Francis Lloyd Jones, Bod Idris
>   Mr Robert Davies, Bryn Teg
>   Mr Robert R. Evans, Llug Fynydd
>   Mr Gwyn Atkinson, 10 Maes Caenog.

Organyddion:
>   Mrs Francis, Post Office
>   Mrs Gwyneth Francis Jones, Post Office
>   Mrs B. M. Hughes, Hafod
>   Miss M. M. Edwards, Haulfryn

Arweinydd y gan:
>   Mr Robert Roberts, Plas Cwta

Tŷ Capel: Mr a Mrs Richard Francis fu'n y Tŷ Capel am flynyddoedd ac yr oedd yn siop a swyddfa'r post yn ogystal. Daeth Mr a Mrs J. W. Jones yn denantiaid i'w dilyn ac yna daeth Mr M. Moneypenny. But oedfa olaf yn y capel dydd Sul 23ain o Fai 1993. Nid oes yn awr ond un man addoli lle cynt y bu tri.

L. J.

Cades Calvinistic Chapel, 1872–1974

Cades Calvinistic Chapel was opened in Clocaenog in 1872, but a Sunday School had been in existence since 1810, when the first meetings were held in the house of Robert Jones, cobbler. Subsequently, meetings were moved to the barn at Tan Llan for the summer months (until harvest time) and to the barn at Y Plas for the winter. Eventually, meetings were all held at Henblas — in the barn during the summer and in the parlour for the winter months — and, during those years, the 80–100 members of the Sunday School collected £18 towards building a chapel.

The first application for land on which to build the new chapel was initiated by Hugh Hughes, Y Plas, and made to Thomas Turner, Pool Park, the manager of Lord Bagot's Welsh estate. However, no reply was received after the application, and it was generally believed that it had been opposed by the rector, but there is no evidence for this assumption. After Thomas died, Michael Turner, his brother, took over as manager of the estate. During a visit by Michael to Ty'n-y-Celyn, the tenant, John Roberts, told him that the majority of people in the area were Noncomformists and were in need of a chapel; Michael promised to do his best for them but, again, nothing materialized. Despite these setbacks, the Methodist faith remained strong in the district and, in 1871, an application was made to the monthly meeting of the Presbytery concerning the building of a Calvinistic chapel in Clocaenog.

Huw Jones, Tŷ Coch, promised the elders a piece of land which did not belong to Lord Bagot and was situated just outside the curtilage of the village. Robert Evans of London Road, Liverpool (born and bred in Y Plas Farm, Clocaenog) had promised £100 towards the project, and other donations amounting to £120 had been received. Trustees were appointed, the local people being: Thomas Jones (Rhewl Bach), Ivor Jones, (Y Parc), and Henry Davies (Bryn Gwyn) and the land was purchased prior to Cades Chapel and Tŷ Capel being built.

The chapel closed in 1974 and the building was partially dismantled; the upper half was removed, a new, lower roof installed and the building then became a workshop and garage for Tŷ Capel.

Members of Cades Chapel on the 100th anniversary in 1972.

Capel Calfiniaidd Cades 1872–1974

Agorwyd Capel Calfinaidd Cades yn 1872 and yr oedd Ysgol Sul yn bodoli ers 1810 pan gynhaliwyd y cyfarfodydd cyntaf yng nghartref Robert Jones, y crydd. Yna symudwyd i ysgubor Tanllan yn ystod misoedd yr haf (tan dymor y cynhaeaf) ac yna i ysgubor Y Plas am y gaeaf. Yn ddiweddarach cynhaliwyd yr holl gyfarfodydd yn Henblas, yn yr ysgubor yn yr haf a symud i'r parlwr am y gaeaf, ac yn ystod y blynyddoedd yma casglodd 80–100 aelodau yr Ysgol Sul £18 tuag at adeiladu capel.

Hugh Hughes, Y Plas, weithredodd y cais cyntaf am dir i adeiladu capel newydd, ac anfonwyd y cais i Thomas Turner, Pool Parc, rheolwr stâd Gymreig yr Arglwydd Bagot. Ni chafwyd ateb, a credir fod y rheithor wedi gwrthwynebu y cais, er nad oes tystiolaeth i'r tybiaeth yma. Wedi marwolaeth Thomas, cymerodd Michael Turner, ei frawd, reolaeth y stâd. Yn ystod ymweliad Michael a Ty'nycelyn dywedodd John Roberts y tenant wrtho fod y mwyafrif o boblogaeth yr ardal yn Anghydffurfwyr ac angen capel ac addawodd Michael Turner wneud ei orau iddynt, ond eto ni chafwyd ymateb.

Er yr holl drafferthion yr oedd y gred Fethodistaidd yn gryf yn yr ardal, ac yn 1871 gwnaed cais i'r

Cades Sunday School, 1924/5
Back row L–R: Sarah Ellen (Sally) Davies, Pentre, sister of Ted Davies – became Mrs S. E. Jones; Nelly Williams, Glan Aber (mother of Mair Roberts); Madge Jones, Nant y Celyn (became Mrs Roberts); two sisters, Laura and Sydney Griffiths, Bryngwyn (step-sisters of Ifor Griffiths). Front row L–R: Mary edwards (aunt of William George Roberts); Thomas Davies, Cae Segwyn; Mary Catherine Williams (sister of Nelly Williams, above, became Mrs Chapman).

cyfarfod misol Presbyteraidd i gael adeiladu Capel Calfinaidd yn Clocaenog.

Addawodd Hugh Jones, Tŷ Coch i'r blaenoriaid y buasai yn rhoi darn o dir nepell o'r pentref, nad oedd yn eiddo i'r Arglwydd Bagot. Addawodd Robert Evans, Ffordd Llundain, Lerpwl (wedi cael ei eni a'i fagu yn Y Plas), £100 tuag at y cynllun, a chafwyd rhoddion eraill o £120. Penodwyd ymddiriedalwyr a'r rhai lleol oedd Thomas Jones (Rhewl Bach), Ivor Jones (Y Parc), a Henry Davies (Bryn Gwyn) a cwbwlhawyd y pryniant cyn adeiladu Capel Cades a'r Tŷ Capel.

Caewyd y Capel yn 1974, a datgymalwyd y rhan uchaf o'r adeilad a gostwng y tô er mwyn ei addasu yn fodurdy a gweithdy.

G. R.

Glimpses of people

From the Parish Burial Registers

Grace Lloyd, a widow who died in 1677 and left a will, which is fairly unusual for a woman in that period.

Jane Wynne, died 1678 and was the first in this parish to be buried 'in woollen cloak'. [In 1667 an Act had been passed for everyone to be buried in a woollen cloak, the idea being to enhance the woollen trade. The act was only strictly enforced after 1679 and was only repealed in 1814.]

Evan John Tudor, who was buried in 1678 and was said to have been 'a good and tranquil man'.

Margaret Lloyd, poor soul, who 'died out of her senses and was buried' in 1687.

The Rector was generally an absentee and the parish would have been looked after by his clerk (this explains why a small cottage was sufficient, and a rectory was only built when the minister actually came to live here).

Jane, wife of Thomas Jones, Rector of Clocaenog, 'died at her house, Tŷ Gwyn, in Llanychan on Thursday at five of ye clock in the morning Nov. 24th 1687 and was buried on Tuesday following in the Church of Llandyrnog. *Requiescat in pace sempiterna.*'

Hugh Salisbury, a servant at Clocaenog Park, who died in 1689.

John Cadwalader, from Park Clokaenog died in 1690 — 'live in eternal peace.'

Thomas Jones, Rector of Clocaenog, died in 1705 in Llanychan parish and was buried at Llanychan Church.

Robert Salusbury, Rector of Clocaenog, 1715 'died at his home, Plas isa in the Parish of Llanrwst where he was temporary Vicar.' He was buried at Llanrwst.

On September 3, 1729, a traveller whose name was not known, but who lived in Chester, 'who no sooner than he had come into the parish than death took him off and he was buried next day.'

Cadwalader Roberts, Park, died in 1729 — 'a man of the greatest integrity without an oath in his speech, of a mild disposition, always most charitable.'

In the 1899 register of christenings are three girls, christened as adults: **Sarah Anne Kempson** and **Sarah Elfin Clough**, who came from Stockport Industrial School, and **Agnes Goodwin**, from the Industrial School, Sale. Agnes worked at the Rectory, and the other two were servants, one at Tŷ

Isa Cefn and the other at Llanerch-gron. Later still another girl came from the Stockport Girls' Industrial School to work at the Rectory — **Lily Shaw** — who is also recorded as being christened as an adult.

A 'Robin Hood' of Clocaenog

By chance, there is some correspondence preserved from June 1400, soon after Henry IV came to the throne, concerning a troublesome Welshman, namely Gryffydd ap Dafydd ap Gryffydd; apparently he came from Cynllaith or somewhere in the Ceiriog Valley. This incident took place only a few weeks before the uprising of Owain Glyn Dwr. Some relatives of Gryffydd, cousins who worked in Chirkland, which was Arundel property, were trying to get him a job in the forestry there but a very unfriendly witness described him as the 'strengest thiefe of Wales'.

He was presented to various people but it was thought that a trouble-maker like him would best be employed fighting for the king abroad. His cousin, at a cost of 'twenty marks', fitted him out for the journey and, with two retainers, he presented himself in his new outfit in Oswestry, ready to go on foreign service. Then he was passed on again and told to report to Sir Richard Lacon. Gryffydd began to suspect a plot against him and wisely made his escape. He next appears to have established himself, with a crowd of followers, as another Robin Hood in the lordship of Ruthin, in the Earl de Grey's park of Bryn Cyfo. Here he was caught with two horses belonging to Earl de Grey and was brought to court — probably at Llanerchgron. He was tried for theft and said in his own defence, 'I have no living worth anything and no work, so must take my livelihood as God may ordain it'.

We are not told how he was punished but it was likely to be severe.

Acknowledgements to *Archaeologica Cambrensis*, 1923.

Other more recent people of Clocaenog

H. Turner-Evans lived at Plas Helig, went to the village school and then to Denbigh Grammar School for Boys. He worked as a librarian in Ruthin and then became County Librarian of Carmarthenshire. He wrote *A Bibliography of Welsh Hymnology* and in 1975 was elected a member of the Gorsedd of Bards for his services to Welsh culture. His bardic name was *Clwydwas*.

J. Iorwerth Davies, also a librarian, who lived at Craigwen. He later became County Librarian of Montgomeryshire and then of Mid Glamorgan. This gentleman has been a great help in tracing Elwyn Edwards and his story (see page 55).

Edward Charles, 1760–1828, of Clocaenog, wrote *Siames o Wynedd* and *Sierlyn Fardd*.

Rev. J. Thomas Davies here in Clocaenog from 1932–42. Wrote 'Forgiveness' — a hymn?

Thomas Roberts of Clocaenog, remembered in the E. Whittington Jones (Memorial) and in *Eurgrawn Wesleyaidd* 1931 (Wesleyan magazine).

The last three are mentioned in Parker's *Bibliography of Denbighshire*, under 'Famous People'.

A. N.

Parish Administration

Population Changes

1811 Census Returns

	Male	Female
ClocaenogUcha	141	161
Clocaenog Isa	63	65
	208	213

Total Population　　　　　421

1831 Census Returns

	Male	Female
ClocaenogUcha	159	174
Clocaenog Isa	63	65
	222	239

Total Population　　　　　461

The view from the Fron bench on a winter's day.

Employed in Agricultur — 25 out of 26 families

1st Class Tenants = Occupiers of land who constantly employed and paid one or more than one labourer or farm servant in husbandry. (14 families)
2 Class Tenants = Occupiers of land who employ no labourer other than their own family. (8 families)

Male servants 20+	13	Female servants 20+	22
Male servants under 20	12	Female servants under 20	8

Census returns compared

Year	Total Population						
1801	437	Area of parish = 6,671 acres					
1811	421						
1821	462						
1831	461						
1841	457						
1851	421						
1861	439						
		Houses inhabited	91	uninhabited	3	building	3
1871	477		94		0		0
1881	421	Area of parish = 7,182 acres	88		4		9
1891	356		81		6		1
1901	373		83		4		0
1911	372		80		-		-
1921	339	Area of parish = 5,952 acres					
1931	303						
1941	No census						
1951	274	No of households	73				
1961	229		73				
1971	213	Area of parish = 2,409 acres	65				
1981	Not available						
1991	223		77				

1991 Census Return

	Totals	Male	Female
Usually resident	223	118	105
Total households	77		
Total dwellings	83		
Owner occupied	67		
Privately rented	5		
Local authority rented	5		
Welsh speakers	132		
Born in Wales	136		
In-migrants 1990–91	15		

Occupations		
	16+ years of age and working	118
	Unemployed	4
	Professional	0
	Managerial	16
	Skilled	2
	Partly skilled	4
	Unskilled	3
	Agriculture & forestry	8
	Transport	2
	Banking & finance	3

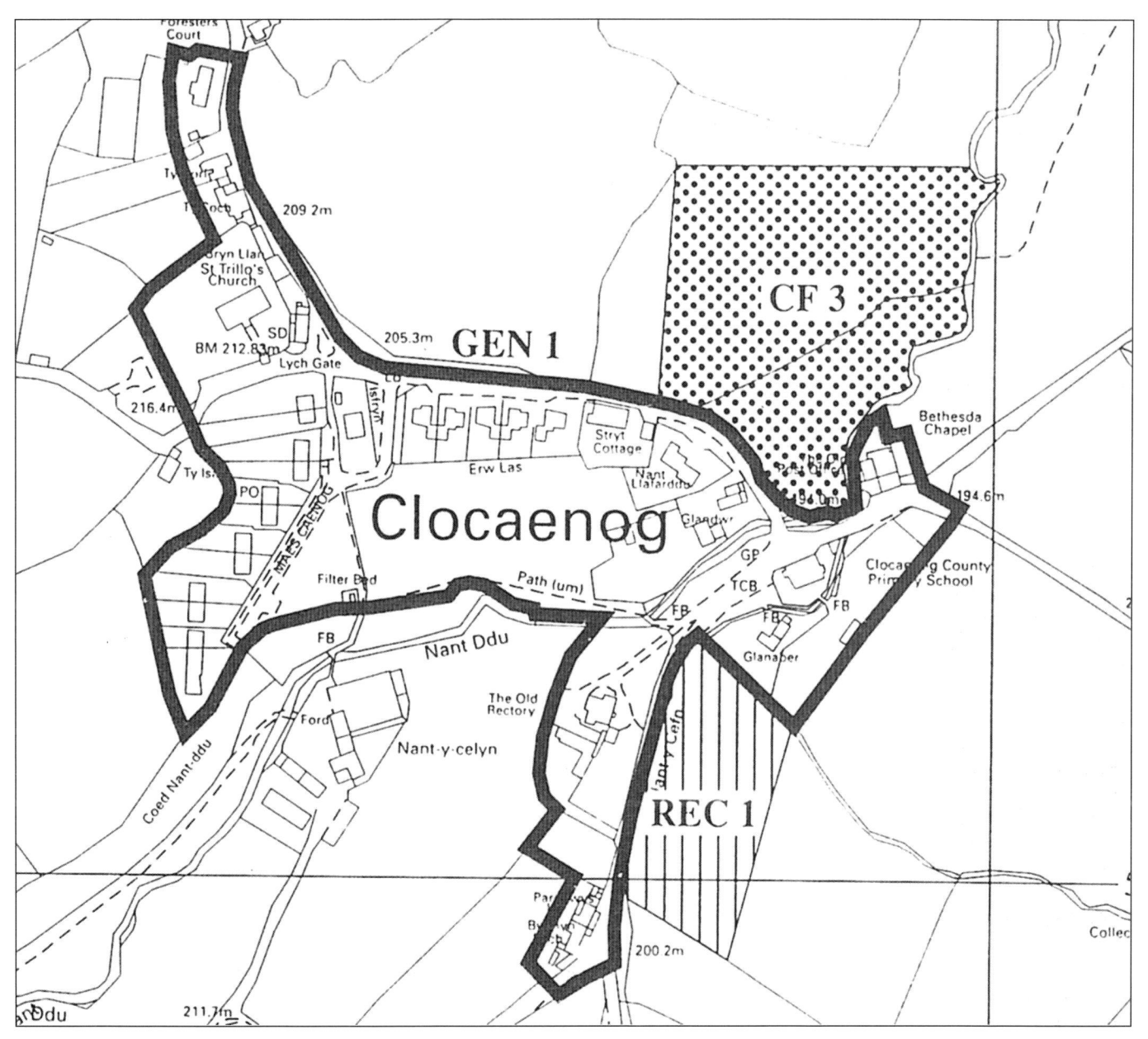

Map showing the curtilage of the present village of Clocaenog.

Other services	5
Economically inactive	54
Pensioners living alone	7
Single parents	1
No car	3
1 car	18
2+ cars	52
Lacking or sharing bath/ shower/inside WC	1
No central heating	20

From Government Census Returns

There has been only a slow decline in population through the years of the census returns, except when there have been parish boundary changes. The farms are still scattered, and since agriculture has been mechanised, fewer people are employed on the farms. Much of the parish lies at a high altitude and is unsuitable for food cultivation, so much of the moor land and rough grazing have been replaced on two occasions by forestry, which is to be retained and developed, not only for timber but ecologically and as an area for recreation.

Clocaenog was never a nucleated village, and there has been space for it to grow within its own curtilage, when Maes Caenog was built, and later, the five houses of Erw Las. Then Nant Llafarddu was built, initially for the son of a local builder to live in, and another house has been built on the field behind Erw Las and a house and a bungalow are in the process of being built on the same field. All these are houses for people with relatives living in the vicinity.

This is not an area with potential for industrial development and remains extremely rural. Land has been bought adjacent to the village but outside the present curtilage, with the possibility of erecting further housing. More cars on the narrow lanes would be a major problem and another factor would be the lack of flow in the small stream, during hot summers, to remove the sewage effluent of more houses (the present sewage treatment plant is higher and is already inadequate and natural drainage is insufficient).

Clocaenog Village has few amenities; there is no shop and no pub, but there is one of each in the next village, Clawddnewydd. The parish encompasses a varied and beautiful landscape, and despite the fact that employment has diversified and many people have to travel outside the area to work, there is still the feel of a country community.

A.N.

Changing Occupations

The Clocaenog Parish area has always been basically agricultural, but it is interesting to note the gradual introduction of new occupations. In the 1831 census 25 out of 26 families were employed in agriculture; the one family not so employed was probably the Rector's. Many of the smallholders used their skills and doubled as weavers, shoemakers, bakers and brewers — a village had to be fairly self-sufficient. Just occasionally someone of note lived here —

1617	Thomas Needham, High Sheriff of Denbighshire from Clocaenog (residence is not given).
1672	Rector
1681	Butcher
1683	Copper worker
1684	Smith and weaver
1686	Sexton
1689	Taylor and a servant at Clocaenog Park
1694	High Sheriff of Denbighshire lived at Bryngwyn Hall, by name, Humphrey Kynaston Esq.
1698	Clerk and curate
1714	Yeoman (Tre'r Llan)
1750	Publicans (x 3) — the earliest licences issued for Clocaenog
1751	Schoolmaster
1752	Copper miner
1768	Drover and joiner
1782	Freeholder and shoemaker
1797	Sawyer
1799	Wheelwright

Here is a list of some old and some new occupations in the nineteenth century, mainly taken from the parish records.

1836	Barber (from Manchester)
1837	Discharged soldier
1840	Stonemason
1846	Carpenter, horse-breaker and gardener
1847	Dressmaker at Lligfynydd
1848	Turnpike gatekeeper

1851	Broom maker (Stryt No. 2)
1854	Husbandman and sempstress
1855	Clerk in Holy Orders
1856	Blacksmith and turner
1861	A thatcher lived at Cyfsegwyn and a nursemaid is recorded
1864	Drainer, woman tolltaker and horse dealer
1865	Groom and coachman living at Tŷ isa, and a gentleman at Llanerchgron Isa
1866	Clogger
1867	A pauper died in the village
1869	Butcher and a carter from Pool Park
1871	Shepherd
1872	Victualler and farmer (Tŷ Coch), woodman and a cowman and a vallet from Pool Park Lodge
1874	Mason at the Toll Bar
1875	Timber merchant (from Glyndyfrdwy)
1876	Station master (Ty'n y Mynydd)
1883	Cook (Ty'n y Mynydd)
1884	Platelayer
1896	Merchant
1911	Clerk of works at Nant Clwyd Estate
1915	Police constable — retired — from Stockton Heath, Warrington
1916	Private R.W.F. [Royal Welch Fusiliers]
1917	Travelling licensed hawker
1921	Engineer and roadman
1922	Farm bailiff at Pool Park Farm
1923	Water pipe tract inspector and a bootmaker
1929	Hairdresser
1930	Gentleman farmer (Derwen Hall), a roadman and a smith
1931	Forestry manager (Foel Fach) and a gamekeeper
1933	Timber feller (Paradwys Isa)
1935	Quarryman (Glandŵr) and an auctioneer's clerk (Tŷ Cerrig)
1938	Housekeeper (Tŷ Gwyn) and a lorry driver
1939	Sawyer and an engineer
1941	Produce merchant (from Birmingham) and a driver
1942	Bricklayer

I believe there must have been teachers and shop assistants, forestry workers and bank clerks, electricians and plumbers, and now I know of an air-hostess and a professor, a social worker and a post-mistress; and all the time the continuing succession of farmers. A very varied community lives here in Clocaenog.

A. N.

Lost Dwellings

1. **Ty'n y Llan** — (sometimes known as Llan, Glandŵr) was situated in the corner of Glandŵr field which, at one time, was a garden rented by R. Francis of the Old Post Office, from the Lord Bagot Estate.

2. **Glandŵr Cottages** — five houses of a

Mrs William Roberts, Cefn Isa, which was later uninhabited for over 40 years. It is still standing in front of a bungalow called Braeburn

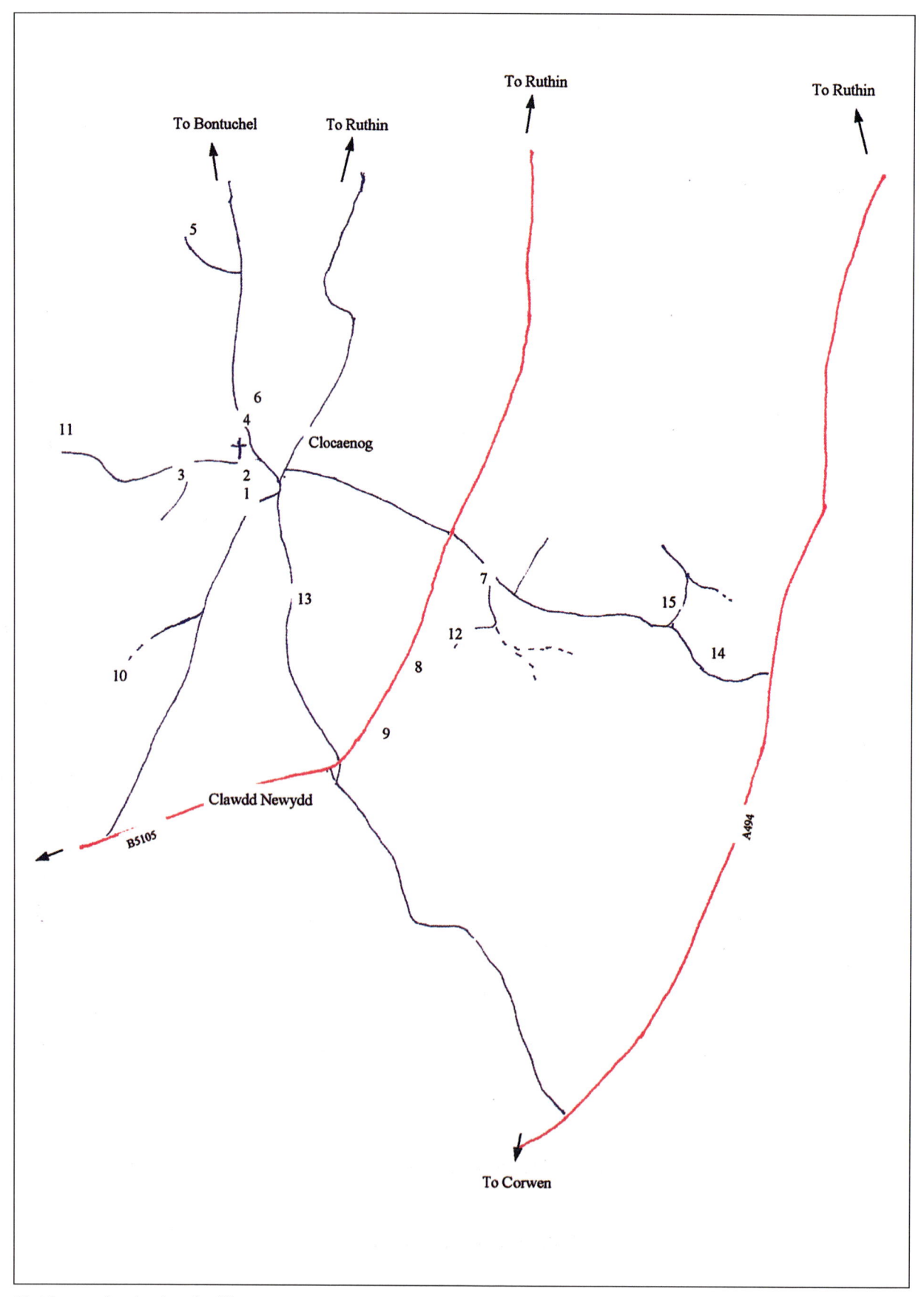

Sketch map showing lost dwellings.

Mrs Roberts, Ty Cerrig. These two cottages are now one dwelling. They used to be owened by Bryngwyn Farm for their workers.

row of eight, three of which survive and are known today as Stryt Cottage, now one dwelling. Nant Llafarddu stands where the five cottages once stood.

3. **Ty'n y Coed** — a small cottage opposite the lane leading to Henblas, which stood on a piece of land adjoining the glebe land and one of Plas fields.

4. **Tan Llan Bach** — a cottage lower down the road from Tŷ Capel and on the other side of the entrance to Tŷ Coch fields, the cottage garden area now belonging to Tŷ Capel. Large stones at the roadside are all that remain.

5. **Pentre Bach** — a cottage on the side of the old lane leading to Pentre Farm. A plum tree denotes the garden and large stones in the hedge are the remains of the dwelling.

6. **Fron-y-gof Isaf** — a small holding of about 40 acres, now part of Cil Llwyn, and situated near to Tan Llan field, now also part of Cil Llwyn. Last inhabited by the Roberts Family, before they moved to Pentre Farm in 1873. Traces almost completely disappeared.

7. **Cefn Eithin** — a farmstead demolished by Sir Vivian Naylor Leyland, Nantclwyd Hall, in the 1960s. Situated on the right along a lane off the B5105 at Brynffynon. Last inhabited by the Davies family.

8. **Bryn Golau** — a smallholding beside the main Rhuthun to Clawddnewydd road on the left side after Brynffynon is passed which suffered the same fate as Cefn Eithin at the hands of the Nantclwyd Estate.

9. **Ty'n y Maen** — a well-built farm house and outbuildings, off the B5105, down a lane almost opposite that of Bryn Coch, which was also demolished by the Nantclwyd Estate. Last tenanted in the 1960s by Vernon Kellet.

10. **Bryniau Mawr** — situated in Nant y Celyn land towards Ty'n y Mynydd. In the nineteenth century it was a farm in its own right. In the 1970s the farm house had gone but there were still good outbuildings in use.

11. **Clwt** — a cottage with garden on the right of the track going up to the forest, past Fron, and on the edge of Coed y Fron. No trace now, but shown on the 1879 map.

12. **Cefn** — in the 1811 census and on the 1879 map, situated behind Bryn Goleu.

13. **Cefn Isaf** — the small, old cottage in the garden below Braeburn, on the left of the road from Clocaenog to Clawddnewydd, but not inhabited.

14. **Drylliad** — a cruck cottage demolished by Sir Vivian Naylor Leyland.

15. **Tŷ Isa'r Cefn Uchaf** — demolished, it was located near Ty'n y caeau and Gwalia, and, of course, Tŷ Isa'r Cefn Isaf which is still inhabited.

Information mainly from Ted Davies and William George Roberts.

Maes Caenog

In February 1929, Clocaenog Parish Council was asked by the Ruthin Rural District Council if there was a need for 'workers' houses' in the village and the April 1933 meeting of the Parish Council was informed that two houses would be built during that summer. The site chosen for the houses was near School Cottage (now Old School House) on land belonging to Mr. and Mrs. Evans, Glandŵr.

In February 1934, the Parish Council was asked to suggest two tenants for the houses and, after much discussion, a vote was taken and the tenancies were offered to: Mr. and Mrs. Jones, Tŷ Cerrig, No. 1 (Gwynfryn) and Mr. Gabriel Edwards, No. 2 (Haulfryn) where they all lived for many years. After the deaths of Mr. and Mrs. Jones, the tenancy of Gwynfryn was transferred to their son, David and his wife, and eventually the tenancy of Haulfryn went to Gabriel's granddaughter, Morfydd, who still lives there.

The Parish Council meeting of 3rd April 1944 decided that the village was in need of more houses and asked for four dwellings '2 parlour type' and '2 non-parlour type'. They decided the best site would be on the field, directly in front of School Cottage, which belonged to Mr. Roger Jones (Ty'n y Celyn).

The war ended and, in February 1946, the Parish Council asked the District Council to speed up the building plans and again, in May 1947, the Parish Council reiterated that there was still a great need for more houses in the village. However, nothing had been done by October 1947 and a letter was received from the District Council to say that Mr. Roger Jones had refused to sell the land and that another site would need to be chosen. The Parish Council was dissatisfied with the lack of progress and selected four alternative sites in the village:

- The corner of Tan Llan field (by Tan Llan Bach)

- Tŷ Coch field (by Derlwyn)

- Henblas field (by Tŷ Isa)

- Glan yr Afon field

Henblas field, owned by Mr. and Mrs. Evans, Glan Dwr, was the final choice but, as their smallholding consisted of only three fields, they refused to sell. The District Council, however, issued a Compulsory Purchase Order on the land and, in 1949, the Parish Council was informed that work on the first four houses would soon begin. The parish quota was for ten houses; the Parish Council decided to ask for the full quota and, by February 1951, work was well in hand. The Parish Council's suggestion of Caenog Estate as a name for the new development was later changed to Maes Caenog.

The first tenants started to move into the new houses in July 1951 and they were:

- No. 3 — Mr. Williams, headmaster of Clocaenog School

- No. 4 — Mr. and Mrs. Thomas

Maes Caenog.

- No. 5 — Mr. E. Jones, retired forestry worker, and his wife

- No. 6 — Mr. R. Roberts, forestry worker, his wife, and their sons, Dennis and Glyn

- No. 7 — Mrs. E. Jones and family

- No. 8 — Mr. K. Lewis, forestry worker, his wife and son, Keith

- No. 9 — Mr. D Jones, farm worker (at Gerallt) and his wife, Beryl

- No. 10 — Mr. David Downy, Ministry of Agriculture advisor, wife Helen and son, John.

- No. 11 — Mr. Craft who worked in the County Offices, his wife and children, Ian, Gail and Adrian

- No. 12 — Mr. and Mrs. Tarry and daughter, Anthea.

Of these, only Mr. David Jones and his wife, Beryl, are still living in Maes Caenog (now in No. 7).

B. J.

Water Supply

1925   It was decided to apply for a supply of mains water from the water main at Brynffynnon for the school and the houses in the village — one mile of pipe track. Decision taken to move forward with the matter and seek any grants available. Total estimated cost £352 16s. 3d.

1927   Denbighshire County Council ready to contribute £160 0s. 0d. towards the cost. Decided to ask the Ruthin Rural District Council to proceed at once with the work.

1928   October: Ruthin Rural District Council have completed the work on the supply of mains water in Clocaenog to the school and most of the village houses. The work was carried out in a very satisfactory way and everybody is happy.

T.D.

Education

A History of Clocaenog School

A day school was held in the village church during the latter half of the eighteenth century and eventually, in 1814, a schoolroom and accommodation for the teacher was built on waste ground, adjoining the churchyard (Old School House). When the building became too small for the growing numbers of pupils, a new school was funded by parishioners' donations, varying from one shilling to fifty pounds, and the school was completed in 1824 at a final cost of £103 3s. 4d (the old school had cost £76).

Old School House, in front of the Church.

The outside bell rang to summon the children to their lessons, held in one large rectangular room heated by two large open fires; initially, all age groups were taught together but later, the infants were separated and taught in a smaller classroom. Although all the children were Welsh speaking, English was the language used in the church school, but those who attended the Wesleyan and Methodist Sunday schools learned to read and write in Welsh.

The first log books relating to Clocaenog Church School are deposited in the County Record Office in Ruthin and are most interesting. The first entry was written by John Maurice Roberts, headmaster from 1876–79, followed by Lewis Owen 1879–82 and William Roberts 1882–98. By reading these reports, one realises how answerable the headmasters were to the School Board. Exact records were kept of the lessons taught and there were frequent tests for reading, spelling and arithmetic to establish the progress of each pupil. Members of the Board visited the school regularly to check the register, collect monies from the children, check their progress and inspect the building; a review of headmaster, staff and pupils' progress took place annually. Headteachers were keen for their school to achieve good results during the annual visit by Her Majesty's Inspector because extra monies were available if the standard of education qualified for an Excellent Merit Grant — awarded in 1884 and 1890, when William Roberts was headmaster. However, in 1881, a percentage of the grant had been withdrawn because the report condemned the state of the building as follows:

> The closets and urinals should be kept at all times in a proper state. A skirting of wood for the walls is advisable. On the day of the examination of the school, the closets and the urinal were in a filthy state but upon a subsequent visit it was found that they had been whitewashed and put into proper order except that lime had not been thrown into the pits.

William Roberts was very concerned about absenteeism and wrote in the log book that it was impossible to get good results when pupils were absent for periods of weeks and, sometimes, months. In the log book for November 15 1889, he writes: 'Several of those that were absent through the summer months have

Clocaenog school pupils, c.1905.

Clocaenog School pupils c. 1918.

Pupils lined up outside Clocaenog School during an inspection, probably c.1920. The poor condition of the buildings is clearly evident.

returned'. A week later he writes: 'Some more of the irregulars returned — one of which had been absent since last year, the others almost through the summer'. In January 1892 he wrote: 'I find it very difficult to get the children ready for examination, more so than any other year; many have been at home most of the time since the last exam; some of them incessantly ill; average weekly attendance for the month of January is 24.5.' However, the inspector's report in the following June started as follows: 'This is a good school', and the only criticism was: 'Drawing has not been taught at school but endeavours should be made to teach it in the future.' Reading, writing, spelling, arithmetic, poetry reciting and geography were the main subjects, but music and needlework were also taught. During this period, prizes were awarded to the children at annual tea parties and mention is made regarding the award of certificates, books and oranges to pupils who did well and attended regularly. There was also an evening concert to raise funds.

Attendance at school varied considerably due to such things as: weather conditions, assistance required on the family farms or illnesses such as scarlet fever and whooping cough. There were few instances of closing the school for any of the above reasons towards the end of the nineteenth century compared to those in the first half of the twentieth century. Headteachers had discretionary authority to close the school for one day (or half a day) for important events such as Ruthin Fair Day; official school holidays were much shorter than today, with no mention of Easter or summer holidays but, during September, the school closed while crops were being harvested.

Qualified teachers were in short supply, so it was essential for the headteacher to be proficient and pupil teachers were trained by the Clocaenog headmaster from 7a.m. to 8a.m. and 1 p.m. to 1.30 p.m. In 1877, John Maurice Roberts had only two pupil teachers to help him with 120 pupils.

School records show that sad news, regarding the death of a pupil, was a regular occurrence and, in July 1890, Emily Roberts, from Clawddnewydd, a former monitor at the school, died at an early age. A moving tribute by the headmaster is given in the log book and he describes the schoolchildren, each carrying a posy of flowers, walking in front of the coffin from Clawddnewydd to the cemetery at Clocaenog Church.

At the end of 1890 it is noted that the number of pupils on the school register had decreased and, by May 1895, only 63 pupils were on the register compared to 120 a few years previously. In 1898, William Roberts, the headteacher, wrote in the log book: 'It is the saddest news I ever received, all grant is lost' and he resigned from Clocaenog School at the end of September that year after over fifteen years in the post.

The new headmaster was Mr. Jenkins and it is recorded that he closed the school for a fortnight for the Christmas holidays. Details of the lessons taught were not recorded (as was done by his predecessor) but he wrote at length about the weather and attendance. In 1899, a poor report was given by the inspector, but things improved the following year, possibly because Mr. Jenkins opened the school on some Saturdays to make up for poor attendances due to bad weather. Shortly after he arrived, Mr. Jenkins installed a glass window in the door between the two classrooms to enable him to keep an eye on things and, for the first time, photographs of the pupils were taken by Mr. Lettsome of Llangollen. On 22 June 1900, the headmaster and the children walked to Pincyn Llys (perhaps Mr. Jenkins was the first teacher to take his class on a nature walk).

Children commencing school for the first time in April 1901 were named as: Nelly Williams (Glan Aber), Martha Ann Evans (Plas Helyg) and Sydney Griffiths (Bryn Gwyn). I remember Nelly Williams still living in Glan Aber during my attendance at Clocaenog School in the 1950s and I feel certain that Sydney Griffiths was closely related to the family living at Bryn Gwyn today.

As mentioned above, the school was rarely closed due to illness or weather conditions

Clocaenog, 1909, showing the two school buildings.

Interior view Clocaenog School, 1920s.

during the nineteenth century, but it happened frequently while Mr. Jenkins was headmaster. For instance, in 1901, the school was closed for the summer holidays from 15 August to 10 September but had to remain closed until the beginning of October because several children were suffering from whooping cough; however, a good report was given the following May. In October 1902, Mr. Jenkins left the school and was replaced by Mr. Robert Wyn Evans.

Every new headmaster made changes. Mr. Evans introduced a token system, whereby every pupil attending the school for a whole week was given a token and, for every 48 tokens received, they were awarded a book prize. In January 1904, the first pupils to be given books were Emily Pierce, Winifred May Jones, Tommy Roberts, William David Evans and Nellie Williams (the mother of Mair Roberts, who still lives in Glan Aber). Mr. Evans also started a savings bank scheme and the sum of six shillings and five pence was deposited at the Post Office on 3 April 1903.

There were 90 pupils in the school by May 1903, and a new teacher was needed because assistant teacher, Miss Ruth A. Jones, had left. Until Miss E. E. Davies was appointed as teacher for the infants' class in January 1904, Mr. Evans from Nantglyn helped out for one month, and Robert F. Watkins, Glandŵr, acted as a monitor for a short period. In 1905, a third teacher, Miss Mary Jean Chepstow, was appointed.

On 1 June 1904, the Church School (Ysgol Eglwys) was taken over by Denbighshire County Council and, from that date, was known as Clocaenog School (Ysgol Clocaenog). The following year, a report stated 'Welsh is used as a medium of instruction throughout the school'.

Some head teachers wrote more interesting records than others, and in 1904 R. W. Evans wrote 'Nearly all the 95 present today were in their places by 9 o'clock — a very creditable thing when the great distance some of them have to walk is considered'. He managed to get the children to attend school more regularly than his predecessors had done, and on 9 May 1905 wrote '100 on books of which 98 were present'. He complains, however, that Ruthin Fair affected school attendance due to the fact that farmers' sons were required to walk the cattle to market. As a reward for regular attendance, the headteacher would close the school for a whole day, or take the pupils for an outing, and this seemed to be quite effective because, at the end of the school year 1904/5, the average attendance was 91.6% — 'the highest percentage ever attained at the school'. Mr. Lettsome (from Llangollen) came to the school on 29 May 1905 to take photographs of the five pupils who had never missed a school day throughout the previous year — they are named as: Tommy Roberts, (Llanerchgron), Robert Owen (Plas Newydd), Winifred Watkins (Glandŵr), Nellie and Mary Catherine Williams (Glan Aber).

Two meetings of a sub-committee, appointed to discuss a new house for the headteacher, took place during May and June 1906, but no further reference to this is made in the minutes. In His Majesty's Report in 1907, the school was required to modernize its approach to education, including the need to supply reading books which were more suitable for children. Another requirement was that English language had to be taught to enable the children to write and converse adequately (in English) without the need to teach complicated grammatical structures. The report praised the headmaster for teaching outdoor activities, such as football and cricket, and the infant teacher for the high standard of her needlework lessons.

It was a great loss to the school when R. W. Evans left in May 1907, and it was not until February 1909 that a new headmaster, J. H. Richards, was appointed to the permanent post. By then, term times were similar to those of today with holidays at Christmas, Easter, Whitsun and summer. The inspector's report in 1910 suggested that a new school was required 'It would be well for the Education Authority to consider the advisability of erecting a new school rather than spending more money in repairing an old one'. During the next few years, several meetings took place to discuss this suggestion and, in 1913, the Education Authority decided the new school should be built on land belonging to Pen y Maes (not far from the present school). Nothing came of this and it looks as if we will have to wait for another 100 years for this to take place!

Like his predecessor, Mr. Richards wanted the children to attend school regularly and he complained that the local chapels held their Harvest Thanksgiving services on different dates. In the Log Book, he wrote

> Wesleyan harvest festival — half-day holiday given. It is a great pity that an arrangement cannot be come to when all harvest festivals in the district could be held on the same day. Clocaenog School is seriously affected by Rhiw, Clawddnewydd, Clocaenog Wesleyan, ditto C.M and ditto C of E. holding their thanksgiving services purposely on different days, several of them necessitating the granting of a holiday.

At the end of 1919, Mr. Roberts left the school and Mr. Llewelyn Roberts was appointed headmaster (many local people living today will remember him). The following year, Miss Annie Mary Davies (later Mrs. A. M. Jones, Maesgwyn) was appointed as an unlicensed teacher, continuing at the school until her marriage in 1929; Mr. Llewellyn retired in 1937. It is only whilst these two members of staff were at the school that the first reference is made to reports on the progress of each child, being sent to parents at the end of the Christmas, Easter and summer terms. During this time, the school was often closed for long periods due to infectious illness e.g. 15 November 1924 – 12 January 1925 (measles), 15 February 1929 – 14 March 1929 (scarlatina). Towards the end of 1927 there was a mumps epidemic and in 1928, one pupil, M. Louisa Roberts (Fron), died of scarlet fever. In 1929, after the death of another pupil, Alun Roberts (Tŷ Gwyn), the schoolchildren were taken to place wreaths on their friend's grave.

For many years, Sir Ernest Tate and family, Pool Park, gave a Christmas feast for the school children; however, from 1931 onwards (after the sale of Pool Park in 1928) the Clocaenog Womens' Institute, who held their meetings at the school, prepared a Christmas tea and distributed oranges, apples and cakes. During this period, the W.I. also began to provide tea at the annual sports day in July (which they continue doing to this day).

The Wesleyans held an annual concert at the school and, on several occasions, Mr. Llewelyn Roberts expressed his sadness regarding the state of the building at the end of the evening. On 5 February 1932, he wrote:

> School in an awful state in the morning after the concert by Wesleyans; window, and glass on cotton sampler, broken; walls under windows marked with footmarks of those sitting on the windowsills and some of the desks covered with dirt after people standing on them the previous evening. Called Mr. Francis' attention to it - showed the state of room to him.

By the 1930s, a dental service was available for the children and the dentist visited to do fillings and extract teeth; occasionally, the visits lasted for three days as from 6 – 8 December 1932. During 1933, there were two new improvements in the school — a piano, and a stove to heat the largest classroom. Mr. R. Francis, a school governor, had raised a substantial sum of money to purchase the piano but, unfortunately, he died a fortnight before it was delivered. The new stove smoked and was not a great success so, in 1935, it was replaced by a more efficient heating system, keeping one grate to provide boiling water for use at dinner times.

At the end of February 1937, deep snow covered the ground so the school had to be closed and, on 25 March, the headteacher stated that attendance had been very low for seven weeks and the term's work had not been completed. By July 1937, pupils on the register had decreased to 58 due to some 11 year-old children going on to grammar schools — boys to Denbigh and girls to Ruthin. One of the first Clocaenog pupils to attend Denbigh Grammar School was Ifor Griffiths from Bryn Gwyn (where he still lives today). Despite the decrease in numbers, three teachers still remained at the school. Jennie Blodwen Evans (later Mrs. Jim Davies, Pool Park) started as an unlicensed teacher in October 1937, and, after the retirement of Mr. Llewelyn Roberts in December, Mr. H. F. Jones was appointed headteacher in March 1938. During his first year, gardening lessons were introduced for the boys and, for the first time, the children were vaccinated against diphtheria by Dr. Bright of Ruthin.

In 1939, two references were made to the Church Hall: during April, children and staff were moved there whilst a new partition was erected to divide the largest classroom into two; from September, the hall was used as a school for wartime evacuees. During this year, Horlicks drinks were provided for all the children and reference is made to the war — women knitting socks and jumpers to send to the armed forces, gas masks introduced and several pounds of rosehips collected. As in other winters, problems arose when the outside toilets froze and the school had to close because there were no lavatories available. The original lavatories were in the school yard and it was the caretaker's duty to empty the filled buckets; new lavatories were built in the school playing field in 1937 (the present ones were installed in 1968).

In 1940, the old system of summer holidays was changed when the school was closed for a fortnight in July, to harvest the hay crop, and for a fortnight in September for the corn harvest. At this time, there were four teachers at the school: H. F. Jones, Miss Jean Telford, Mrs. J. B. Davies and a student teacher, Miss Ceinwen Roberts.

After 13 years at the school, Miss Jean Telford left in 1944 to marry and Miss Ceinwen Roberts was appointed as a permanent member of the staff, remaining there until her retirement 34 years later in 1978 when she was presented with a silver tea service.

The first Welsh language entry in the Log Book, dated 1 March 1945, was;

> Dathlwyd gwyl ein Nawsddant heddiw'r bore drwy gynnal raglen amrywiaethol o ganeuon gwerin, canu penillion, adroddiadau a dramau cymwys i'r dydd. Llunildd y plant fathodyn bach a faner Cymru — y Ddraig Goch a ddyry gychwyn — ac anerchwyd hwy gan Y Prifathro ar arwyddocad y faner. Agorwyd y cyfarfod gyda gwasanaeth crefyddol. Hanner diwrnod o wyl y prynhawn. *[St. David's Day was celebrated this morning with a varied programme of folk songs, penillion singing, recitations and drama suitable to be performed on this day. The children designed a banner with the Welsh Dragon and the teacher explained to them the significance of the banner.]*

School dinners were first served in February 1945 and, in October, it was recorded that the 44 children on the register all had a school dinner. Both Mr. H. F. Jones and Mrs. Blodwen Davies left the school in 1946 and Mr. E. O. Roberts was appointed as headmaster. In 1947, the school hours were set out as follows: morning session 9.30 a.m. to 12.30 p.m; dinner period 12.30 p.m. to 1.45 p.m. and the afternoon session from 1.45 p.m. to 4.15 p. m.

The whole of the spring term in 1947 was disrupted by extreme weather conditions — heavy falls of snow blocked all roads and, once again, the school lavatories were frozen. In addition, there was an epidemic of whooping cough and some children had not attended school since early December. During this period there were several changes of staff until, in 1951, Mr. Gwyn Williams was appointed as headmaster remaining until 1977.

Although over fifty years have now elapsed, many of us have memories of the school during this time: Dr Peggy and Nurse Beech came to school to check our health; bottles of milk replaced the Horlicks drinks consumed during the morning breaks; happy years spent by many children in the infants' class with Mrs. Mair Jones, a kind and caring teacher. Our memories are not so sweet of the 11+ examination and the pressure placed upon us to work hard to achieve good results.

Great changes were made to the education system in the 1950s when Ysgol Brynhyfryd became a Comprehensive School and all children over 11-years of age automatically transferred to Brynhyfryd — Clocaenog School was designated as a Junior Council School and was left with only 59 pupils on the register. Prior to this, children who did not pass the 11+ examination would remain in the village school until they were 15 years of age.

Many of us over 50 remember Gabriel Edwards, the school caretaker for many years (as was his father before him). In 1955, Mr. Gwyn Williams wrote that 'Mr. Gabriel Edwards passed away at the age of 75. He took a great interest in his work and kept the school spotlessly clean'. The connection between the Edwards family and the school continues to the present day Gabriel's daughter, Morfydd, was the school cook for many years and her grandchildren still attend the school.

The teachers, Ceinwen Roberts and Mair Jones both married in the 1950s and, to mark the occasion, were presented with barometers by three of the school governors: Mr. Gwilym Roberts (Pen y Gaer), Mr. Saunder

Davies (Bryn Ffynnon) and Mr. John Henry Jones (Bryn Coch). When Mrs. Edwards (Stryd Cottages) retired as school cook, she was presented with a clothes iron by the Reverend Hugh Thomas.

At the beginning of the school year in September 1965, the headmaster, Gwyn Williams, wrote in the log book: 'The number on the role is 32, the lowest number I have known in this school. Rural depopulation is having its effect on school numbers. It has become the pattern for vacant homes to be bought and then used as weekend or holiday homes' — but the number soon increased again and, by the end of 1977, there were 47 pupils.

During the 1960s many improvements were made to the school: electricity had been installed in 1959; a hot water heater in 1961; a telephone in 1967; a new central heating system in 1968; a television in 1969. Flooding from the nearby stream had been a regular event for many years and, finally, in the late 1960s, a low wall was built round the school yard.

When Mr. Williams was headmaster, there was a close connection between Clocaenog School and the local branch of the Forestry Commission and he took every opportunity to extend the children's knowledge of their environment. In December 1972 when a group of children visited the forest to see Christmas trees being felled and trimmed, they were filmed for the Welsh television series, *Cant a Mil*.

In the mid 1970s, the connection between Clocaenog School and three of the staff was broken — Mrs. Edith Watson (Clawddnewydd), retired in 1974, after 10 years as school cook; Mrs. Dilys Jones retired in 1975, after 23 years as school caretaker; and Mr. Gwyn Williams retired in 1977, after 26 years as a firm, fair and very effective headmaster. Although he was a quiet and private person, he was very highly thought of, and those of us who were his pupils owe him a great deal as he was a gifted and conscientious teacher.

Since Mr. Williams retired, the headteachers have been Rhian Wyn Jones, Nesta Kaye, John Kerfoot Jones, Gwynant Hughes and the current headmaster, Geraint Davies, who was appointed in 2001. During this period there have been many changes in the educational system — the greatest being the introduction of the National Curriculum which has given teachers strict guidelines in relation to subjects taught. School inspections have become more rigorous and frequent, and the detailed recording of every pupil's work and progress has led to increased pressure on all teachers. However, the extra work and time involved has also brought benefits.to the children. An innovation has been the introduction of computers to all schools.

These days, lack of funding for many schools, particularly for small country schools like Clocaenog, causes problems. Parents and friends of our village school now have to raise funds to augment the public money provided. But we must not be down-hearted as the school is still here, and the children are taught through the medium of Welsh. The current teachers, Gwenda Evans, Nan Lloyd and the headmaster, Geraint Davies, are industrious and kind and the children are happy. Long may it last!

R. J.

Crynodeb o Hanes Ysgol Clocaenog

Cynhaliwyd yr ysgol ddyddiol gyntaf yng Nglocaenog yn 1811 a hynny mae'n debyg yn yr Eglwys. Yn 1814 codwyd ysgol ar safle School Cottage ond sylweddolwyd yn fuan fod yr adeilad yn rhy fach ac yn 1824 dechreuwyd ar y gwaith o adeiladu ysgol newydd ar y safle presennol. Cafwyd cyfraniadau yn amrywio o swllt i hanner cant o bunnoedd gan amryw o'r plwyfolion tuag at adeiladu'r ysgol ac mae cofnod yn dangos mai'r gost o'i hadeiladu oedd £103 3s. 4^{1}/₂c.

Saesneg oedd iaith yr ysgol ar y dechrau ond cyn hir deuai'r plant i'r ysgol ar y Sul i ddysgu darllen a sillafu yn Gymraeg, yn yr ysgol Sul a gynhaliai'r Wesleiaid a'r Methodist Calfinaidd yno.

Uwchben un porth i'r ysgol crogai cloch a genid i alw'r plant at eu gwersi. Oddi mewn roedd un ystafell hir lle derbyniai'r disgyblion i gyd eu haddysg ar y dechrau. Yn ddiweddarach gwahanwyd y babanod a'u dysgu yn yr ystafell fechan. Roedd grât fawr agored yn y ddwy ystafell dosbarth a'r gwres o'r tân ynddynt a gynhesai'r adeilad. Safai'r tai bach gwreiddiol ar fuarth yr ysgol a gellir eu gweld mewn amryw o'r hen luniau cynnar. Rhai gyda bwcedi ynddynt oedd rhain a byddai'n rhaid i'r gofalwr druan eu gwagu. (Yn 1937 yr adeiladwyd y toiledau yng nghae'r ysgol ac yn 1968 ychwanegwyd y toiledau presennol at yr ysgol).

Clocaenog School pupils 1951.

Mrs Nesta Kaye, Mrs Rhian Jones (Headmistress, 2nd from the left) and Mrs Nan Lloyd (far right) with the pupils of 1979.

Clocaenog School pupils, 1986.

Mae'r 'Log Books' cyntaf sydd wedi eu cadw o Ysgol Clocaenog yn Archifdy Rhuthun ac maent yn werth eu darllen. Y cofnodwr cyntaf oedd John Maurice Roberts, prifathro yr ysgol rhwng 1876 a 1879 ac fe'i dilynwyd ef gan Lewis Owen (1879–82) a William Roberts (1882–98).

Un o'r pethau diddorol a sylwir arno wrth ddarllen cofnodion y prifathrawon yma yw mor atebol oeddynt i'r 'Board' a redai yr ysgol. Cadwent nodiadau manwl o'r gwersi a gyflwynent i'r plant a byddent yn asesu datblygiad eu disgyblion yn fynych iawn trwy roi profion darllen, mathemateg, sillafu a.y.y.b. Ymwelai aelodau'r 'Board' âr ysgol yn rheolaidd i arolygu'r cofrestri a chasglu arian y plant, yn ogystal a chadw golwg gyffredinol ar bethau. Roedd arolwg allanol o'r prifathro ai staff, yr adeilad, a safon gwaith y plant yn digwydd yn flynyddol.

Yr oedd yn naturiol ers talwm i rifau presenoldeb y plant amrywio yn ddirfawr o wythnos i wythnos, a hynny oherwydd y tywydd, galwadau'r cartref ar feibion ffermydd ac hefyd afiechydon fel y 'scarlet fever' a'r 'whooping cough'. Ond, yn wahanol i hanner cyntaf yr ugeinfed ganrif, prin iawn fu'r achosion o gau'r ysgol am yr un o'r rhesymau uchod at ddiwedd y bedwared ganrif a'r bymtheg. Wedi dweud hynny, rhaid ychwanegu fod gan y prifathrawon cynnar yr hawl i gau'r ysgol am ddiwrnod, neu hanner diwrnod, yn ol eu mympwy mwy neu lai e.e. ar ddiwrnod ffair Rhuthun. Roedd gwyliau swyddogol yr ysgol yn llawer byrrach nag ydynt heddiw; ni sonir am wyliau Pasg na Haf yn y cofnodion cynnar ond caewyd yr ysgol am fis ym Medi dros y cynhaeaf ŷd.

Mae'n ymddangos fod rhaid i'r prifathrawon cynnar fod yn ddisgyblwyr o fri oherwydd prinder athrawon a nifer y disgyblion dan eu gofal. Nid oedd gan J. M. Roberts ond dau 'bupil teacher' i'w helpu yn 1877, er bod 120 o biant yn bresennol ar Ebrill 11eg y flwyddyn honno. Byddai'r prifathro yn hyfforddi'r 'pupil teachers' rhwng saith a wyth y bore, a rhwng un a hanner awr wedi un y prynhawn.

Roedd y prifathrawon yn awyddus iawn i'r plant wneud yn dda yn yr Arolwg Blynyddol gan Arolygwyr ei Mawrhydi, yn rhannol am fod mwy o arian i'w gael os oedd yr addysg a gaent yn yr ysgol yn haeddu 'Excellent Merit Grant'. Derbyniwyd hwnnw yn 1884 ac yn 1890 dan brifathrawiaeth Mr William Roberts. Yn 1881 fodd bynnag, roedd adroddiad yr arolygwyr wedi bod yn hallt iawn, yn enwedig am safon yr adeiladau. Dyfynnir:

> The closets and urinals should at all times be kept in a proper state. A skirting of wood for the walls is advisable. On the day of the examination of the school the closets and the urinals were in a filthy state but upon a subsequent visit it was found that they had been white washed and put into proper order except that lime had not been thrown into the pits.

Fe ellid cadw peth o'r grant yn ôl pe bai'r arolygwyr yn anhapus gyda unrhyw agwedd o waith neu adeiladau yr ysgol.

Fel y crybyllwyd, cafwyd yr 'Excellent Merit Grant' i'r ysgol o leiaf dwywaith pan oedd Mr William Roberts yn brifathro. Fe boenai ef yn ddirfawr am absenoldeb plant gan ysgrifennu yn aml yn y 'log book' ei bod bron yn amhosib cael canlyniadau da i'r ysgol pan oedd rhai disgyblion yn absennol am wythnosau, neu hyd yn oed fisoedd, ar y tro. Dyma ddyfyniad o'r 'log book' yn 1889; Tachwedd 15fed — 'Several of those that were absent through the

Clocaenog Primary School

Clocaenog School, 1991

summer months have returned. November 22' — some more of the irregulars returned — one of which had been absent since last year, the others almost through the summer'.

Eto yn Ionawr 1892 ysgrifennodd 'I find it very difficult work to get the children ready for examination, more so than any other year, many have been at home most of the time since the last exam; some of them incessantly ill; average weekly attendance for the month of January -24.4, 24.1, 25.2 and 24.4.'

Er hyn, mae adroddiad yr arolygwyr ym mis Mehefin y flwyddyn honno yn un da gan ddechrau gyda'r geiriau 'This is a good school'. Yr unig feirniadaeth a gaed yn yr adroddiad oedd 'Drawing has not been taught at school; but endeavours should be made to teach it in the future'.

Yn y cyfnod yma y dechreuwyd yr arferiad o wobrwyo plant. Cyn hyn sonir amdanynt yn cael té parti blynyddol yn yr hâf gyda chyngerdd yn dilyn gyda'r nos i godi arian. Ond yn awr mae son am gyflwyno tystysgrifau, llyfrau ac orennau i blant oedd yn llwyddo yn dda yn eu gwaith ac yn mynychu'r ysgol yn rheolaidd. Darllen, ysgrifennu, sillafu, arithmetic, adrodd, barddoniaeth a daearyddiaeth oedd y pynciau pwysig ond yr oedd canu a phwytho yn cael eu dysgu hefyd.

Ceir y newyddion trist am farwolaeth un o'r disgyblion yn weddol rheolaidd yng nghofnodion yr ysgol. Ym mis Gorffennaf 1890 bu farw cyn fonitor yr ysgol, sef Emily Roberts o Glawddnewydd, 'Yng ngwanwyn ei dyddiau'. Ceir teyrnged teimladwy gan y prifathro yn y 'log book' a disgrifia sut bu i'r plant ysgol gerdded o flaen ei harch o Glawddnewydd i fynwent Eglwys Clocaenog yn cario tusw o flodau bob un.

Sylwir fod rhifau'r disgyblion ar gofrestr yr ysgol wedi disgyn tua diwedd y 1890au a gellir tybio bod hyn yn gysylltiedig ag ambell adroddiad gwael iawn gan Arolygwyr ei Mawrhydi am safonnau'r ysgol. Ym Mai 1895 chwe-deg tri o enwau oedd ar y cofrestri o'i gymharu a cant dau-ddeg ychydig o flynyddoedd ynghynt. Fe all mai absenoldeb mynych llawer o'r plant oedd yn gyfrifol am ganlyniadau gwael mewn arholiadau — roedd hyn yn poeni'r prifathro yn ddirfawr. Ysgrifenna William Roberts yn y 'log Book' yn 1898 yn dilyn adroddiad gwael 'It is the saddest news I ever received, all grant is lost', ac ar ddiwedd Medi y flwyddyn honno gadawodd ysgol Clocaenog.

Dilynwyd Mr William Roberts fel prifathro gan Mr Jenkins a sylwir yn syth ei fod ef yn cau'r ysgol am bythefnos dros y Nadolig. Ni cheir manylion am gynnwys y gwersi gan y prifathro hwn fel a gaed gan ei ragflaenydd ond mae yntau yn ysgrifennu llawer am y tywydd a phresenoldeb y plant. Cafwyd adroddiad gwael iawn gan yr arolygwyr eto yn 1899 ond erbyn y flwyddyn ganlynol roeddent wedi gwella yn enfawr — tybed oedd gan hyn rhywbeth i'w wneud a'r ffaith fod Mr Jenkins yn agor yr ysgol weithiau ar ddydd Sadwrn 'to make up for poor attendances recently due to very bad weather'.

Yn ystod misoedd cynnar Mr Jenkins yn yr ysgol, rhoddwyd gwydr yn y drws rhwng ystafell y prifathro ac ystafell y babanod er mwyn iddo gael cadw golwg ar beth oedd yn mynd ymlaen yno! Yn ystod y cyfnod yma hefyd y mae son am y plant yn cael tynnu eu lluniau yn yr ysgol am y tro cyntaf, a hynny gan Mr Lettesome o Llangollen. Tybed ai Mr Jenkins oedd y cyntaf i fynd a'r plant am daith natur? A'r Fehefin 22ain 1900 cerddodd ef a'r plant am dro i ben Pincyn Llys.

Roedd Mr Jenkins weithiau yn enwi'r plant oedd yn cychwyn yr ysgol am y tro cyntaf ac yn Ebrill 1901 mae'n enwi Nelly Williams (Glan Aber), Martha Ann Evans (Plas Helyg) a Sydney Griffiths (Bryn Gwyn). Nelly Williams yw'r disgybl cyntaf a enwir i mi ei chofio yn byw yn Nglan Aber yn ystod fy nghyfnod yn

Clocaenog School, 2003

yr ysgol yn y 1950au, ac mae'n siwr fod Sydney Jane Griffiths yn perthyn yn agos i deulu'r Bryngwyn heddiw.

Fel y crybyllwyd ar ddechrau'r nodiadau hyn ni chaewyd yr ysgol rhyw lawer oherwydd y tywydd nag afiechydion yn ystod y ganrif flaenorol ond digwyddai hyn yn fynych yn ystod prifathrawiaeth Mr Jenkins e.e. bu'r ysgol ar gau o Awst 15fed hyd Fedi'r 10fed dros wyliau'r haf yn 1901 ac yna, oherwydd fod amryw or plant yn dioddef o'r y pas ar ddechrau'r tymor newydd fe'i caewyd wedyn tan ddechrau mis Hydref. Er hyn, cafwyd adroddiad arbennig o dda gan Arolygwyr ei Mawrhydi yn y mis Mai canlynol. Dechrau Hydref 1902 gadawodd Mr Jenkins yr ysgol a cymerwyd ei le gan Mr Robert Wyn Evans.

Roedd bob prifathro newydd yn gwneud newidiadau ac yn cyflwyno pethau newydd i'r ysgol. Dau o'r pethau cyntaf wnaeth Mr Evans oedd cychwyn system docynnau h.y. roedd pob disgybl oedd yn bresennol am wythnos gyfan yn derbyn tocyn a phan fyddent wedi ennill 48 o docynnau fe gaent lyfr yn wobr. Y rhai cyntaf i dderbyn llyfr o ganlyniad i'r system yma oedd Emily Pierce, Winifred May Jones, Tommy Roberts, William David Evans a Nellie Williams a hynny yn Ionawr 1904. Nellie Williams oedd, wrth gwrs, mam Mair Roberts (Glanaber) heddiw.

Yr ail beth a gychwynwyd gan Robert Wyn Evans oedd banc cynilo ar swm cyntaf a roddwyd yn y cyfrif yn y Swyddfa Bost ar Ebrill 3ydd 1903 oedd chwe swllt a phump ceiniog.

Yn ystod mis Mai 1903 roedd rhifau'r disgyblion wedi codi i naw deg un ac argymhellwyd gan yr arolygwyr fod trydydd athro yn cael ei apwyntio i'r ysgol, ond ni ddigwyddodd hynny ar unwaith. Yn wir gadawodd yr unig athrawes gynorthwyol, sef Miss Ruth A. Jones, am Ysgol Treuddyn yn mis Awst ac ni phenodwyd athrawes barhaol yn ei lle tan mis Ionawr 1904. Yn y cyfamser cafwyd cynorthwy Mr Evans o Nantglyn am un mis, a bu Robert F. Watkins (Glandŵr) yn monitor am gyfnod hefyd. Miss E. E. Davies o Ysgol Bryn Coed Ifor oedd yr athrawes newydd ddaeth i ddysgu'r babanod.

Roedd Mehefin y cyntaf 1904 yn ddiwrnod tyngedfennol yn hanes Ysgol Clocaenog gan mai dyma'r diwrnod y cymerwyd hi drosodd gan y Cyngor Sir ac o hynny ymlaen fe'i galwyd yn 'Clocaenog Council School'. Yn adroddiad yr arolygwyr y flwyddyn ganlynol ceir y dyfyniad canlynol 'Welsh is used as a medium of instruction throughout the school' ond ni wn os oedd cysylltiad rhwng y ddwy ffaith uchod. Penodwyd trydydd athrawes i'r ysgol ym Mawrth 1905 a hi oedd Miss Mary Jean Jones o Chepstow.

Mae ambell brifathro yn ysgrifennu'n fwy diddorol na'i gilydd ac mae Mr Robert Wyn Evans yn un felly. Ym Mehefin 1904 ysgrifenna 'Nearly all the 95 present today were in their places by 9 o'clock — a very creditable thing when the great distance some of them have to walk is considered'. Llwyddodd ef i gael plant i fynychu'r ysgol yn llawer mwy rheolaidd na'i ragflaenwyr fel y gwelir yn Mai 9fed 1905 — '100 on books of which 98 were present', ond mae yntau'n cwyno weithiau fod ffair Rhuthun yn cael effaith dychrynllyd ar y rhifau presenoldeb. Roedd hyn yn rhannol, wrth gwrs, am fod angen y meibion ffermydd i gerdded gwarlheg i'r ffair. Fel gwobr am fynychu'r ysgol yn rheolaidd yn y cyfnod hwnnw fe fyddai y prifathro yn cau'r ysgol am ddiwrnod bob hyn a hyn, neu yn mynd ar plant allan o'r ysgol am dro. Roedd y disgyblion yn ymateb yn dda i hyn ac yn dod i'r ysgol yn rheolaidd iawn. Ar ddiwedd y flwyddyn ysgol 1904–5 roedd y cyfartaledd presenoldeb yn 91.6 — 'the highest percentage ever attained at the school'. Daeth Mr Lettsome o Langollen i'r ysgol ar Fai 29ain 1905 i dynnu llun 5 o blant na chollasant ddiwrnod o ysgol yn ystod y flwyddyn flaenorol a'u henwau oedd: Tommy Roberts (Llanerchgron), Robert Owen (Plas Newydd), Winifred Watkins (Glandŵr), Nellie Williams a Mary Catherine Williams (Glan Aber).

Ym Mai a Mehefin 1906 cynhaliwyd dau gyfarfod o is-bwyllgor a sefydlwyd i drafod adeiladu tŷ newydd i'r prifathro — ond ni cheir cyfeiriad pellach at hyn yn y cofnodion.

Erbyn 1907 mae adroddiad Arolygwyr ei Mawrhydi yn cynnwys argymhellhion i foderneiddio addysg y plant e.e dywedir fod angen newid y llyfrau darllen a fod yna rhai oedolion am lyfrau mwy addas i blant. Argymhellir hefyd mai dysgu Saesneg a fydd o ddeunydd i blant sgwrsio ac ysgrifennu a ddylid yn hytrach na dysgu 'technical expressions such as participal and prepositional phrases' i blant mewn ysgol wledig fel hyn. Canmolir y prifathro am roi gwersi pêl droed a chriced i'r bechgyn ac athrawes y babanod am safon ei gwersi gwnio. Credaf i'r ysgol gael cryn golled pan adawodd y prifathro R. Wyn Evans ym Mai 1907 ac ni chafwyd prifathro parhaol nes J. H. Richards ymgymeryd a'r swydd ar Chwefror 15fed 1909. Erbyn hynny roedd y flwyddyn ysgol yn llawer tebycach i heddiw o ran tymhorau, gyda gwyliau bob blwyddyn dros y Nadolig, Y Pasg, Y Sulgwyn a'r Haf.

Yn adroddiad blynyddol yr arolygwyr yn 1910 y crybwyllir gyntaf fod angen ysgol newydd yng Nglocaenog — 'It would be well for the local Education Authority to consider the advisibility of erecting a new school rather than spending more money in repairing an old one'. Mae'n beryg mai dal i aros y byddwn ni gan mlynedd yn ddiweddarach, er bod ambell i gyfarfod wedi cymeryd lle dros y ddwy neu dair mlynedd ar ôl yr argymhelliad gwreiddiol a bod yr Awdurdod Addysg wedi penderfynu ar safle ar un o gaeau Penymaes, heb fod ymhell o'r ysgol bresennol, i adeiladu un newydd yn 1913.

Roedd Hydref 29ain 1913 yn ddiwrnod mawr yn hanes yr ysgol gan i Mr T. H.Parry Williams M.A., B.Litt., Ph.D ymweld ar ysgol gyda cyfaill iddo ar y diwrnod hwnnw. Ond efallai fod dydd Nadolig y flwyddyn cynt wedi bod yn un pwysicach gan y plant gan iddynt gael gwahoddiad gan Mr a Mrs Tate i fynd i Pool Park am 'Grand tea party and Christmas Tree'.

Roedd Mr Richards, fel ei ragflaenydd, yn awyddus iawn i'r plant bresenoli eu hunain yn yr ysgol yn rheolaidd a chwynai ef fod y gwahanol gapeli yn yr ardal yn cynnal eu Cyfarfodydd Diolchgarwch ar ddyddiau gwahanol. Ysgrifenna ar Hydref l7eg:

> Wesleyan harvest festival — half day holiday given. It is a great pity that an arrangement cannot be come to where by all harvest festivals in the district should be held on the same day. Clocaenog school is seriously affected by Rhiw, Clawddnewydd, Clocaenog Wesleyan, ditto C.M. and ditto C. of E. holding their thanksgiving services purposely on different days, several of them necessitating the granting of a holiday.

Yn dilyn ymadawiad Mr Richards ar ddiwedd 1919 penodwyd Mr Llewelyn Roberts i gymeryd ei le ac mae amryw o'r trigolion lleol heddiw yn ei gofio. Y flwyddyn ganlynol dechreuodd Miss Annie Mary Davies — Mrs A. M. Jones (Maesgwyn) yn ddiweddarach — ar gyfnod fel athrawes annhrwyddedig yn ysgol Clocaenog. Bu Mr Roberts yma tan 1938 a Mrs A. M. Jones tan ei phriodas yn 1928. Yn ystod eu cyfnod hwy yn yr ysgol y ceir y cyfeiriadau cyntaf at anfon adroddiadau i rieni am ganlyniadau'r ysgol a hynny ar ddiwedd bob tymor, y Nadolig, y Pasg a'r Haf. Parhai afiechydon i fod yn achos cau'r ysgol am gyfnodau hir weithiau. Bu ar gau o Dachwedd 15fed 1924 hyd Ionawr 12fed 1925 gan fod amryw o'r plant yn dioddef o'r frech goch. Fe restrodd Mr Llewelyn Roberts enwau'r plant oedd yn gadael yr ysgol am yr ysgol ramadeg bob blwyddyn. Y cyntaf a enwir i mi ei adnabod yw Ifor Griffiths, a aeth i Ysgol Dinbych ym mis Medi 1927, ac a oedd yn fab y Bryngwyn ar y pryd, ac sydd yn daid y Bryngwyn heddiw. Ar ôl hyn, cyfeirir at amryw yr ydym yn eu hadnabod yn llwyddo yn yr arholiadau i fynd i'r ysgol ramadeg ond nid af ati i'w henwi i gyd yma.

Bu Sir Ernest Tate, Pool Park, a'i deulu, yn paratoi gwledd ar gyfer plant yr ysgol bob Nadolig am flynyddoedd ond erbyn 1931 Sefydliad y Merched Clocaenog oedd yn rhoi té parti iddynt ac yn rhannu orennau, afalau a chacennau iddynt fynd adref. Roedd y Sefydliad y pryd hwnnw yn cynnal eu cyfarfodydd yn yr ysgol. Cychwynnodd yr arferiad o roi parti i'r plant ar ddiwedd mabolgampau'r ysgol ym mis Gorffennaf yn y cyfnod yma hefyd.

Cynhaliai'r Wesleaid gyngerdd blynyddol yn yr ysgol a mwy nag unwaith cofnoda Llewelyn Roberts ei dristwch ynglyn a'r stad y gadawyd yr adeilad ynddo ar ddiwedd y noson. Ysgrifenna ar Chwefror 5ed 1932

> School in an awful state in the morning after the concert by Wesleyans; window and glass on cotton sample broken; walls under windows marked with foot marks of those sitting on the window sills and some of the desks covered with dirt after people standing on them the previous evening. Called Mr Francis' attention to it — showed the state of the room to him.

Erbyn tri degau'r ganrif ddiwethaf roedd gwasanaeth deintyddol ar gael i blant yr ysgol. Deuai'r deintydd i'r ysgol i lenwi a thynnu dannedd fel bo'r angen ac weithiau byddai yno am dridiau fel y bu rhwng Rhagfyr 6ed a'r 8fed yn 1932.

Yn 1933 cafwyd dau ychwanewgiad newydd i'r ysgol sef stôf i gynhesu'r ystafell fawr, a phiano. Roedd Mr R. Francis, un o lywodraethwyr yr ysgol, wedi codi llawer o arian i brynu y piano, ond yn anffodus bu farw tua pythefnos cyn iddi gyrraedd yr ysgol. Ni weithiai'r stôf newydd yn arbennig o dda, ond yn 1935 cafwyd offer gwresogi llawer mwy effeithiol a gwell. Er hyn cadwyd un grât i ferwi dwr ar gyfer cinio'r disgyblion.

Cafwyd eira mawr ar ddechrau 1937 a bu'n rhaid cau'r ysgol o'i herwydd. Ar Fawrth 25ain ysgrifenna'r prifathro fod y rhifau presennol yn isel ers saith wythnos a bod gwaith y tymor heb ei gwblhau. Roedd nifer y disgyblion ar y cofrestri wedi disgyn yn arw erbyn hyn — 58 o enwau oedd arno yng Ngorffennaf 1937 a hyn yn rhannol gan fod rhai o'r plant yn gadael am Ysgol Ramadeg y Bechgyn yn Ninbych neu Ysgol Ramadeg y Merched yn Rhuthun wedi iddynt gyrraedd un ar ddeg oed. Er fod y rhifau wedi disgyn cymaint roedd yn dal i fod yn ysgol tri athro, cychwynnodd Miss Jennie Blodwen Evans (Mrs Jim Davies, Pool Park yn ddiweddarach) ar ei swydd fel athrawes didrwydded yno ym mis Hydref 1937.

Yn dilyn ymadawiad Mr Llewelyn Roberts ar ddiwedd 1937, daeth Mr H. F. Jones i lenwi swydd y prifathro ym Mawrth 1938. Ceir amryw o gyfeiriadau at arddu gyda'r bechgyn yn ei gofnodion ef ac yn ystod ei flwyddyn gyntaf yng Nglocaenog y cyferir at frechu'r plant am y tro cyntaf rhag 'diptheria' gan Dr Bright o Rhuthun.

Er bod toiledau newydd yng ngae'r ysgol erbyn hyn nid oeddynt heb eu problemau. Trwy holl flynyddoedd eu defnyddioldeb ceir cyfeiriadau mynych iawn atynt yn rhewi yn ystod y gaeaf ac weithiau byddai'n rhaid cau'r ysgol gan nad oedd cyfleusterau ar gael at ddefnydd y plant.

Cyfeirir ddwywaith yn 1939 at Neuadd yr Eglwys Clocaenog. Ym mis Ebrill symudwyd yr ysgol gyfan yno tra roedd 'partition' yn cael ei osod yn yr ysgol i rannu yr ystafell fawr yn ddwy. Yna, ym mis Medi, cychwynwyd defnyddio'r Neuadd i addysgu'r plant a symudwyd i'r ardal yn ystod y rhyfel, yr 'evacuees'. Dyma'r flwyddyn hefyd y dechreuwyd paratoi Horlicks i'r plant yn yr ysgol.

Aethpwyd yn ôl i'r hen drefn o wyliau haf yn 1940, pan gaewyd yr ysgol am bythefnos ym mis Gorffennaf dros y cynhaeaf gwair, ac am bythefnos arall mis Medi dros y cynhaeaf ŷd. Ym mis Hydref dechreuodd Miss Ceinwen Roberts ar ei gwaith fel 'Student Teacher' yng Nglocaenog ac, fel y gwyddom, rhoddodd hithau flynyddoedd o wasanaeth cydwybodol iawn i'r ysgol. Felly yn 1940 roedd pedwar o athrawon — H. F. Jones, Miss Jean Telford, Miss J. B. Evans a Miss Ceinwen Roberts.

Yn ystod y blynyddoedd 1939–44 ceir amryw o gyfeiriadau at y rhyfel e.e y merched yn gwau sanau, siwmperi a.y.y.b i'w hanfon i'r lluoedd arfog a'r angen i brofi 'gas masks' a chasglu pwysi o 'rose hips'.

Ym mis Mai 1944, priododd Miss Jean Telford a gadawodd ei swydd yng Nglocaenog a dyma pryd y daeth Ceinwen Roberts yn aelod parhaol o'r staff. Y flwyddyn ganlynol paratowyd cinio ysgol i'r plant am y tro cyntaf ac mae'n siwr fod hyn yn ddarpariaeth derbyniol iawn gan y plant a'u rhieni. Ar Hydref 23ain roedd 44 o blant ar gofrestr yr ysgol a chymerodd bob un ohonynt ginio ysgol. Mae'n ddiddorol sylwi mai ar Fawrth 1af 1945 y ceir y cyfnod cyntaf yn yr iaith Gymraeg yn yr 'log book'

> Dathlwyd gwyl ein Nawddsant heddiw'r bore drwy gynnal rhagleni amrywiaethol o ganeuon gwerin, canu penillion, adroddiadau a drama cymwys i'r dydd -Lluniodd y plant fathodyn o faner Cymru — y Ddraig Goch a ddyry gychwyn — ac anerchwyd hwy gan y prifathro ar arwyddocad y faner.

Ffarwelwyd a'r prifathro a Mrs Blodwen Davies yn 1946 a chymerwyd lle Mr H. F. Jones gan Mr E. O. Roberts, a lle Mrs Blodwen Davies gan nifer o wahanol athrawon nes i Miss Dilys S. Jones gaei ei phenodi yn 1949. Yn ystod 1947 newidiwyd oriau'r ysgol dros gyfnod i'r canlynol: bore 9.30–12.30; cinio 12.30–1.45 a'r pnawn 1.45–4.15. Digwyddodd hyn yn union wedi'r eira mawr ar ddechrau'r flwyddyn, ond ni wn a oedd cysylltiad rhwng y ddau beth. Dim ond pedair blynedd a wariodd Mr E. O. Roberts yng Nglocaenog ac, yn dilyn cyfnod byr dan ofal Mr Elwyn Wilson Jones, penodwyd Mr Gwyn Williams yn brifathro yn 1951. Er bod hyn bron hanner can mlynedd yn ôl bellach, mae gan amryw ohonom a fagwyd yn lleol ein atgofion ein hunain am yr ysgol yn ystod y cyfnod diweddarach yma.

Cofiwn Dr Peggy a Nyrs Beech yn ymweld ar ysgol i arolygu ein hiechyd. Cofiwn y poteli llaeth a gymerodd lle y diod Horlicks, ac a yfwyd yn ystod amser chwarae'r bore. Cofiwn ddyfodiad Miss Mair Jones fel athrawes garedig y babanod a'r blynyddoedd hapus a dreuliodd llawer o blant bach yn ei dosbarth. Nid mor felys yw'r atgofion am arholiadau 11+ a'r pwysau oedd arnom i weithio'n galed er mwyn llwyddo ynddynt. Roedd oddeutu 70 o blant yn yr ysgol ar ddechrau y 50au ond disgynodd i tua 55 yn 1954 pan agorwyd ffrwd yn Ysgol Brynhyfryd i blant unarddeg a throsodd oedd heb lwyddo y 11+. Cyn hynny, wrth gwrs, byddai'r plant hyn wedi aros yng Nglocaenog nes cyrraedd 15 oed.

Fe gofia amryw ohonom sydd dros ein hanner cant am Mr Gabriel Edwards a fu'n ofalwr yr ysgol am nifer fawr o flynyddoedd, fel ei dad o'i flaen. Pan fu farw Mr Edwards yn Rhagfyr 1955, ysgrifennodd Gwyn Williams 'Mr Gabriel Edwards passed away at the age of 75. He took a great interest in his work and kept the school spotlessly clean'. Felly roedd cyflwr glendid anfoddhaol yr ysgol drosodd er pan fu Gabriel Edwards yn ei glanhau. Parhaodd y cysylitiad rhwng y teulu yma a gofalu am yr ysgol hyd yn weddol ddiweddar, a bu Morfydd Edwards yn gogyddes yr ysgol am sbel hefyd.

Priodwyd y ddwy athrawes Ceinwen Roberts a Mair Jones tua diwedd y 50au a daeth tri o reolwyr yr ysgol i'w anrhegu a 'barometer' ar yr achlysuron. Y tri rheolwr oedd Mr Gwilym Roberts (Pengaer), Mr Saunders Davies (Bryn Ffynnon) a Mr John Henry Jones (Bryn Coch). Pan ymddeolodd Mrs Edwards, Stryt fel cogyddes yr ysgol yn 1959, cafodd anrheg o haearn smwddio a gyflwynwyd iddi gan y Rheithor, Y Parch Hugh Thomas.

Mae Sefydliad y Merched lleol wedi cyfrannu té parti i blant yr ysgol ar ddiwrnod eu mabolgampau dros hanner can mlynedd. Yn anffodus nis cafwyd yn 1961 oherwydd bod gymaint o blant yn dioddef o'r frech goch. Cawsant fag o fferins bob un yn lle parti y flwyddyn honno. Arferai Sefydliad y Merched Clawddnewydd roi parti Nadolig i blant yr ysgol am gyfnod hir.

Yn tydi'n rhyfeddol fel mae'r gaeafau wedi newid yn ystod y blynyddoedd diwethaf yma. Y mae'n anarferol iawn i ni gael cawodydd trwm iawn o eira erbyn hyn and hyd yn oed yn 60au'r ganrif ddiwethaf roedd y ffyrdd i'r ysgol ar gau yn weddol aml yn y gaeaf.

Ym mis Medi 1965, roedd nifer y plant ar gofrestri yr ysgol i lawr i dri deg dau; ysgrifenna Gwyn Williams 'The number on the roll is 32, the lowest number I have known in this school. Rural de-population is having its effect on school numbers. It has become the pattern for vacant homes to be bought and then used as weekend or holiday homes'. Roedd hyn yn sicr yn wir, ond fe gynyddodd y rhifau eto ac erbyn 1977 roedd pedwar deg saith o blant yma.

Yn ystod y 60au hefyd adeiladwyd wal o gwmpas buarth yr ysgol i rwystro'r afon rhag gorlifo drosti. Bu'r broblem o ddŵr a mwd ar y buarth yn un drafferthus iawn dros y blynyddoedd. Gwnaed bywyd ysgol yr athrawon a'r plant yn esmwythach hefyd pan adeiladwyd toiledau newydd ynglwm ar ysgol yn 1968 ac chafwyd system wresogi newydd hefyd.

Roedd cysylltiad agos rhwng Ysgol Clocaenog a'r goedwig leol yng ngyfnod prifathrawiaeth Mr Williams. Cymerodd fantais o bob cyfle i ymhelaethu gwybodaeth y plant am eu hamgylchedd trwy fynd a hwy i ymweld a gwahanol safleoedd yn y goedwig. Cawsant dynnu eu lluniau ar gyfer y *Free Press* a buont ar raglen deledu *Cant a Mil* yn mis Rhagfyr 1972, yn gwylio coed Nadolig lleol yn cael eu torri a'i trin.

Ynghanol y 70au torrwyd cysylltiad rhwng Ysgol Clocaenog a thri aelod o'i staff, sef Mrs Edith Watson (Clawddnewydd) a ymddeolodd fel cogyddes yn 1974 ar ôl deg mlynedd yn y swydd; Mrs Dilys Jones a ymddeolodd yn 1975 ar ôl dau ddeg tri o flynyddoedd fel glanhauwraig yr ysgol a Mr Gwyn

Mr Gwyn Williams.

Williams a ymddeolodd yng Ngorffennaf 1977 ar ol dau ddeg chwech o flynyddoedd fel prifathro. Gŵr tawel a phreifat oedd Mr Williams ond roedd yn brifathro cadarn, teg ac effeithiol dros ben. Roedd yn uchel iawn ei barch ac mae dyled pawb ohonom a fu'n ddisgyblion iddo yn enfawr gan ei fod yn addysgwr cydwybodol a thrylwyr.

Wedi cyfnod Mr Williams deuwn i adeg mwy diweddar a modern yn hanes Ysgol Clocaenog. Y prifathrawon a'i dilynodd oedd Rhian Wyn Jones, Nesta Kaye, John Kerfoot Jones, Gwynant Hughes a'r prifathro presennol Geraint Davies. Bu'r cyfnod diweddar yma yn un chwyldroadol yn hanes addysg yn gyffredinol, yn arbennig oherwydd y Cwricwlwm Cenhedlaethol. Golyga hyn fod gan athrawon ganllawiau pendant sy'n rheoli beth, a sut y maent yn cyflwyno addysg i blant. Golyga hefyd eu bod yn atebol iawn i'r llywodraeth a'i arolygwyr a bod arolygiad rheolaidd yn cymeryd lle ym mhob ysgol. Daeth toraeth o waith papur i fodolaeth gyda dyfodiad y cwricilwm a hyn yn golygu oriau ychwanegol o waith i athrawon arwahan i baratoi gwersi a marcio gwaith y plant. Ond er y gwaith a'r pwysau ychwanegol a ddaeth yn ddiweddar, mae amryw o bethau derbyniol wedi eu cyflwyno hefyd. Mae cyfrifaduron yn bethau cyffredin ac mae plant yr oes hon yn cael hyfforddiant technegol yn gynnar yn eu gyrfa haddysgol sydd yn ei gwneud yn hawdd iddynt addasu i'r byd sydd ohoni yn nes ymlaen.

Y trueni mwyaf efallali 'y dyddiau hyn' yw'r prinder arian sydd ar gael i ysgolion. Mae amryw o ysgolion bach gwledig fel Clocaenog yn gorfod ymdopi heb y nifer delfrydol o athrawon oherwydd hyn, ac mae rhieni a chyfeillion ysgolion yn gorfod helpu i godi arian i brynu adnoddau angenrheidiol iddynt. Ond rhaid peidio terfynnu ar nodyn digalon. Mae'r ysgol 'yma o hyd' ac mae'r iaith Gymraeg yn gyfrwng dysgu yma. Mae'r athrawon presennol Gwenda Evans, Nan Lloyd a'r prifathro Geraint Davies, yn weithgar a charedig, ac mae'r plant wrth eu bodd. Hir y parhaed pethau felly.

R. W. J.

Some of the Subscribers and their Donations towards Erecting the New School

	£	s.	d.
The Rt. Hon. Lord Bagot	50		
Rev. Dr. Hughes, Bryngwyn	15		
Rev. Mr. Parry, Curate	3		
Mr. Robert Williams, Bryngwyn	2		
Mr. Robert White, Pentre	1		
John Price, Schoolmaster	1		
Mr. John Evans, Plas	1		
Mr. John Jones, Maestyddyn	1		
Mr. Edward Williams, Bryngwyn		15	0
Mr. John Parry, Tyn y Celyn	10	0	
Mr. John Evens, Fron		10	0
Mr. Gabriel Jones, Ty'n Celyn		10	0
Mr. David Roberts, Grocer	5	0	
Mrs. Catherine Morris, Nant y Celyn	2	6	
Edward Lewis, Ty Coch		2	6
Robert Roberts, Paradis		2	6
John Jones, Ty'n Celyn		2	6

Everyone gave according to what they could afford and the final total was an amazing £106 7s. 6d.

The Building of the New School

The land was donated by Lord Bagot of Pool Parc on a 99-year lease from 29th August 1822. It was waste land at the confluence of the two streams at the lowest point of the village, and was to cause trouble for years to come as it was subject to flooding and the accommodation was very damp.

Some of the expenses incurred in building contrast markedly with prices today.

	£	s.	d.
To Masoning, 195 yds. 5ft. @ 10d.per yd.	8	2	11
To 8 days altering and taking down @ 2/6 per day	1	0	0
To 7 Arches @ 1/6 each		10	6
To raising 183 yds. of Stone @ 5d. per yd.	3	16	3
To fetching timber from Pentre		1	0
To 4000 slates and Gates	3	5	4
Paid carriage for timber from Llanfwrog		15	0
To one day cutting the foundations		1	6
Robert Roberts, Mason, received	9	13	5
Merideth Roberts, Slater, received	8	5	1$^{1}/_{2}$
William Roberts, Sawyer, received	4	2	1$^{1}/_{2}$
William Jones, Stone Cutter, received	5	0	0
Robert Lewis, Carpenter, received	14	9	7

The total cost of building the school was £103-3s.-4$^{1}/_{2}$d

Headteachers

The first mention I have found of anyone in the village acting as a schoolmaster is in the parish baptismal records.

    1751 Birth of John, son of John Jones, schoolmaster, and Elizabeth.

Originally the school was held in the church, probably to teach the catechism and to prepare children for their first communion. Then it was felt that a special building was necessary, with accommodation for the teacher. The school was built on land adjoining the church yard — now called Old School House. As time went on the schoolmaster would be expected to teach the alphabet, some reading and basic numeracy. Elizabeth Jones was a widow by the 1811 census, and a little later in the records I came across:

    1813 Birth of Evan, son of Rhys Evans, schoolmaster.

Then it becomes better documented because even the school kept its own records.

1820	John Price, educated at Ruthin Grammar School. The school flourished and the number of pupils (70) made it necessary to build a bigger school and accommodation for the teacher on land adjoining the church yard (Old School House). Mr. Price helped to raise the money and served as teacher for 25 years. Tenant in Paradwys 1839.
1845-59	Robert Pierce from Chester was appointed but, as his English and his discipline were poor, the minister tried to get him dismissed, but at first he was popular in the village. See the Rev. Hughes' Diary. Resigned.

1859–60	Richard Jones took over. He had been educated in the village school and at the Ruthin British School 'as far as Vulgar Fractions'. He was very popular with the parents (he was a Dissenter) but was in poor health and did not like the damp accommodation. Because the wages were so low, he could not afford alternative accommodation but, as he was a good teacher, he soon found a better post.
1860–70	John William Jones was schoolmaster until he died aged 52.
1870–6	John E. Roberts became master although he was only 17. He lodged at Paradwys.
1876–9	John Maurice Roberts.
1879–82	Lewis Owen.
1882–98	William Roberts.
1898–1902	Edward John Jenkins.
1902–07	R. Wynne Evans.
1907	Emilia Burton, the first woman stand in.
1907–09	J. H. Williams.
1909	Evan Jenkins.
1909–19	J. H. Richards who left for 'two years service on home and active service with the colours' in 1917 and returned two years later in January 1919, only to leave finally in December. In 1918 his daughter, Nesta Elizabeth, was born in Paradwys but died aged 7 months. Mr. Richards had married the daughter of Elizabeth and John Jones who kept the shop there.
1919–37	Llewelyn Roberts.
1938–46	H. F. Jones.
1946	Edward Morris standing in for 3 months.
1946–50	E. O. Roberts.
1950–1	Elwyn Wilson Jones stood in.
1951–77	Gwyn Williams was the headmaster for 26 years and was well respected. He retired to live in Rhuthun and died in 1999.
1977–80	Rhian Jones, the first fully appointed woman headmistress. She gave up the post before Catherine was born and still lives, with her husband in our community.
1981	Nesta E. Kaye.
1981–92	John Kerfoot Jones.
1985–6	Mrs. Kaye took charge again for a short time while J. K. Jones was in America.
1993–2001	Gwynant Hughes was here for 8 years until he retired.
2001–04	Geraint Davies.
2004–	Gwennol Ellis is the present headmistress.

Some Welsh Nursery Rhymes

When interviewing some of the older residents of Clocaenog, one question which was sometimes asked was about singing games played in the school playground and almost invariably the reply would be in terms of English word games, like 'The farmers in his den'. I knew that during the period of the 'Welsh not' children were taught through the medium of English and were forbidden to even play in Welsh at school, but that time had long gone - and yet these children from Welsh-speaking homes still played English games. Asked if they were sung to in Welsh at home they said, 'Yes, of course.' This led to my searching for nursery rhymes which were handed down in the families and helped to keep the old traditional songs alive. A book I purchased was rejected as not belonging to North Wales! The ones which follow have been checked and translated for me by Gwyneth Roberts and Enid Jones; they are ones that are still sung to children today.

Gee, geffyl bach, yn carlo ni'n dau
Dros y mynydd i hel y cnau;
Dŵr yn yr afon a'r cerrig yn slic;
Cwympo ni'n dau! Wel dyna i chi dric!

Gee up little horse, carry us both
Over the mountain to collect some nuts;
Water in the stream and the pebbles are slippery,
Down we both fall! Well there's trick for you!

Croen y ddafad felen
Tu gwrthwyneb allan
Troed yn ôl
A throed ymlaen
A ph'run 'di'r ola 'rwan?

Fleece of the ewe
Turned inside out,
One foot backwards
And one foot forwards;
Now which one comes after?

Croed y ddafad felen
Tu gwrthweneb allan
Troed yn ôl
A throed ymlaen
A throed i gicio'r nenbren.

Fleece of the ewe
Turned inside out,
One foot backwards
And one foot forwards;
And a foot to kick the rafter.

Pedoli, pedoli, pedoli, bi-dinc;
Mi fynnaf pedoli pe gostiau i mi bunt;
Pedol yn ôl
A phedol ymlaen;
Pedol yn eisiau o dan y troed aswy,
Bi-dinc, bi-dinc, bidinc!

Shoe the horse with a clang! Clang!
Shoe the horse, even if it costs me a pound;
One shoe on the back,
One shoe on the front,
And one shoe on the left leg.
Clang! Clang! Clang!

Modryb Elin ennog
Os gwelwch ch'in dda ga'i grempog?
Cewch chwithau de a siwgr gwyn
A phwdin lond eich fedog
Modryb Elin ennog!
Mae 'ngheg i'n grimp am grempog;
Mae 'mam yn rhy dlawd i brynu blawd,
A Siân yn rhy ddiog i nôl y triog
A 'nhad yn rhy wael i weithio;
Os gwelwch chi'n dda ga'i grempog?

My dear Aunt Elin
Please may I have a pancake?
You shall have some tea and sugar
And a pudding in your apron
My dear Aunt Elin!
I want to taste your pancake;
My mother's too poor to buy flour,
And Siân's too lazy to fetch the treacle,
And my father is too ill to work;
Please will you give me a pancake?

Hen fenyw fach Cydweli
Yn gwerthu losin du,
Yn rhifo deg am ddime
Ond un-ar-ddeg i mi!
O dyna'r newydd gore
Daeth i mi! i mi!
Oedd rhifo deg am ddime
Ond un-ar-ddeg i mi!

The little old lady from Kidwelly
Selling black sweets
Ten for a ha'penny
But eleven for me!
That is the best news
That ever reached me!
Ten for a ha'penny
But eleven for me!

Dacw Mam yn dwad
Ar ben y gamfa wen;
Rhywbeth yn ei barclod
A phiser ar ei phen;
Y fuwch yn y beudy
Yn brefu am y llo.

A'r llo'r ochr arall
Yn chware Jim-Cro
Jim-Cro-Crystyn,
Un, dau tri!
Mochyn bach yn eistedd
 Yn ddel ar y stôl

There is Mother coming
Over the white style;
Something in her apron
And a pail on her head;
The cow is in the shippon
Lowing for the calf.

The calf is on the other side
Playing Jim-Crow;
Crusty Jim-Crow,
One, two three!
The little pig is sitting
Smartly on the stool

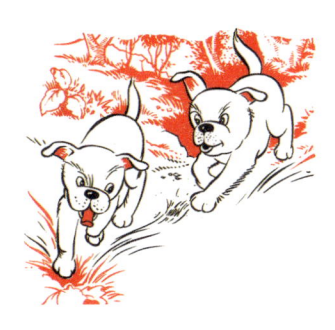

Dau gi bach yn mynd i'r coed
Dan droi'u fferau, dan droi troed;
Dwad adre hyd y pylle
Blawd ac eisin hyd eu coese.

Two little dogs are off to the woods
Kicking their heels as they go;
Coming home through the puddles
Flour and husks on their legs.

Bachgen bach o Felin-y-Wig,
Welodd o 'rioed damed o gig;
Gwelodd falwen ar y bwrdd
Cipiodd ei gap a rhedodd i ffwrdd.

A little boy from Melin-y-Wig
Had never seen a piece of meat;
Saw a snail on the table
Grabbed his cap and ran away.

Tair llygoden ddall!
Gwelwch tair yn mynd;
Yn mynd fel y gwynt ar ôl Siân Tŷ Llyn
Sy'n torri pob cynffon â'r twca mawr gwyn
A welsoch chi 'roed y fath beth â hyn,
A tair llygoden ddall?

Three blind mice!
Watch the three going;
Going like the wind, after Siân Tŷ Llyn
Who cut off every tail with a big white knife
Did you ever see such a thing,
As three blind mice?

Very similar to:

Three blind mice!
See how they run;
They all ran after the farmer's wife,
Who cut off their tails with a carving knife;
Did you ever see such a thing in your life,
As three blind mice?

I'r farchnad, i'r farchnad,
I werthu y moch,
Ffordd yma, ffordd acw,
Hysoch! Hysoch!

To market, to market
To sell a [fat] pig,
This way, that way,
Grunt! Grunt!

Si-so Jac-y-Do!
Dal y deryn dan y tô,
A mynd i Lunden i roi tro,
A dyna ddiwedd Jac-y-Do!

See-saw Jack Daw!
Catch the bird under the roof,
And go to London to turn around,
And that's the end of Jack Daw!

and

Mi welais Jac-y-Do
Yn eistedd ar ben tô,
Het wen ar ei ben,
A dwy goes bren,
Ho, ho, ho, ho, ho, ho!

I saw a Jack Daw
Sitting on a roof-top,
A white hat on his head,
And two wooden legs,
Ho, ho, ho, ho, ho, ho!

Sung to me, in Welsh, by my little grandson, aged four, who has been taught it in school.

A. N.

Clocaenog Families

The Lewis Family
Tŷ Coch (also known as the Cloion Tavern)

My name is Margaret Elizabeth Hughes (née Lewis) but I have always been known as Begw. I was born in Cerrigydrudion (where my mother came from) in 1909 and was the first of seven children — George Bonar born 1911 (at Bryn Llan, Clocaenog); Jane Elinor born 1913 (Bryn Llan); Annie Maud born 1915, Catherine born 1918 and Effie Muriel born 1920 (all at Tŷ Coch) and John Nelson born 1925 (Drovers Arms, Rhewl).

My great grandfather, Edward Lewis, was a tailor and farmer living at Tŷ Coch Farm with his wife, Ellen, who brewed ale for the Cloion Tavern which she ran in the front parlour of the house. Two of their sons, William and Robert, became tailors like their father and went to work in Chester. Another son, Edward (my grandfather), eventually married Margaret Williams, a nursemaid at Clocaenog Rectory, in 1859. When first married in 1816, Edward and Ellen lived in Paradwys which was an inn at the time, and made home brew and herb beer there — sometimes containing bog myrtle. During their marriage, they had nine children, at one point moving back to Tŷ Coch which was then the only public house left in the village as Paradwys then became a shop. They were certainly at Tŷ Coch by the time money was being collected to build the new school in 1923. Ellen, my great-grandmother, kept a small shop in the entrance hall at Tŷ Coch and would walk to Chester once a year, going over the Bwlch — the old road which goes from Llanbedr, over the shoulder of Moel Fammau, down to Tafarn y Gelyn. She would then follow the main Ruthin to Mold road and then the road to Chester, a distance of about 30 miles. She would stay overnight with one of her sons, before walking home the next day with her basket full of fancy goods — gloves, laces and ribbons for the shop.

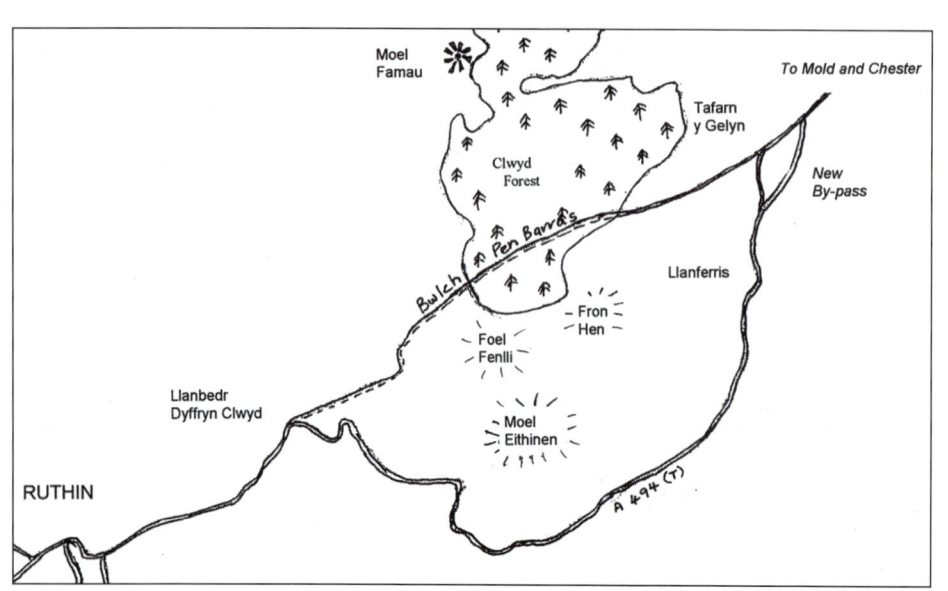

My great-grandmother was of the Baptist faith and, as there was no Baptist chapel in Clocaenog, she would walk over the mountain, crossing

Margaret Elizabeth Hughes (née Lewis).

The walk on the old road over the Bwlch on the way to Chester.

Ellen Lewis (née Jones), wife of Edward Lewis, farmer and tailor. Married 1816, died 1864, aged 73 years. Her husband died in 1867, aged 77 years. Both died at the Cloion Tavern/Tŷ Coch. This was Begw's great-grandmother, who would walk to Chester once a year.

Cefn Cloion, and down to Pandy Chapel in Llanelidan every Sunday morning to attend the service there. In one of the barns at Tŷ Coch there was an old pulpit on wheels which would occasionally be brought out, scrubbed cleaned, then wheeled into the farm kitchen which had been stripped of bills of sale and daily clutter. This was when my great-grandmother called the family to congregate at the house because a travelling Baptist preacher was coming to hold a service. I remember my father, John, telling me that when the Revival was in progress, people were on their knees, banging their heads on the floor in repentance and in fear of hellfire whilst the preacher was laying down the law — I think we could do with a bit of that now. Look at the young girls in pubs these days!

One day, my grandmother took my father and his sister on a train trip with the minister's wife, her daughter, Janet, and her son, John. They walked over the mountain to Nantclwyd Station (on the floor of the valley near the Ruthin to Corwen road) where they were joined by John's friend from Nantclwyd Rail. At that time, under 14s travelled at half price and, when the ticket collector came down the carriage to inspect their tickets, he asked about John's age. 'Twelve,' responded the minister's wife. 'Oh, no, mother, our John's fourteen,' said sister Janet. An embarrassing moment for the minister's wife but we should remember that her husband was on a low stipend with a family, a horse and carriage, a groom, living-in servants and position in society to maintain (her husband was finding it difficult to collect in rent money and in many cases vicars were the second sons who had not inherited).

Because Tŷ Coch was a small farm as well as a tavern, it had a cellar, a stable and shippon, and a barn with another stable and hay lofts above (now converted to a house — Tŷ Doli). I remember my father, John Lewis, pointing to some old wooden skates hanging in the barn and telling me that, when he was young, he used to skate on the small pond behind the Old Post Office where there is still a marshy area — in the 1880s there were some very hard winters. He also told me that when his parents were installing a new grate, they discovered a large hole behind the old fireplace and they always wondered if this could have been a 'priest hole' because it contained a piece of slate with an etched drawing of a man's head.

Tŷ Coch was inhabited by our family, as tenant farmers, for several generations, with the pub run as a sideline. In 1891, Margaret, my grandmother suffered a stroke which led to her death at the age of 54. Her son, Edward, carried on at Tŷ Coch until 1903 when his wife, also named Ellen, took over until her death in 1914. That was when my mother and father moved from Glan yr Afon and continued to run the farm and tavern at Tŷ Coch until, in 1922, when my father was offered the licence for the Drovers' Arms in Rhewl. My family moved to Rhewl in 1923 and I remember going along Lady Bagot's Drive with the furniture piled on a horse-drawn cart and driving the cattle before us. Evan Roberts took over Tŷ Coch and the licence of the Cloion Tavern. In the Bagot Estate sale of 1928, a milestone in the history of Clocaenog, Tŷ Coch was sold to Mr. Wynne, a vet from Ruthin, and it then became a private dwelling. There was no longer a public house in the village.

Amongst the regulars frequenting the inn were

Lady Bagot's Drive.

John and Jane Lewis with their children (L–R): Jane Elinor, Margaret Elizabeth (Begw), Catherine (Cassie, sitting on mother's knee), George with Annie Maud in front of Margaret. Photograph taken behind Tŷ Coch.

the gamekeepers from the Pool Park estate: Mr. Smith, bailiff, Mr. Jackson, head keeper, David Edwards, keeper, and Mr. Addis, a retired keeper. I remember the Irishmen who were working on the construction of the Alwen reservoir, enjoying a drink there. They would all come and sit in the front parlour where there was a dresser, two settles, two chairs, a wooden bench and, by the fire, a comfortable armchair. In this room, they were served with ale, brewed in a large copper cauldron built into the side of the fireplace in the back kitchen.

During the First World War (1914–18) I knew men from the village who were killed in France. One was Bob Roberts who had a large family of children who attended Clocaenog School; also James Askey whom I remember coming home on leave in uniform. My father received a post card from James before he was killed at the front. The vicar, Reverend Hopkins Jones, arranged for a Belgian family to move to the village during the war and everyone contributed furniture to make them a home in Ysgoldy. Unfortunately, the little boy died and was buried in Clocaenog Cemetery.

Clocaenog was a very busy place in those days — the forest was being felled to help provide timber for the trenches and the logs were brought down to the village sawmill by horse and cart before being loaded onto Sentinel lorries and taken to Ruthin Station.

My father never drank during opening hours but waited until after closing time to have a beer and his pipe — except on Sundays when the pub was closed and he abstained. He would never allow a woman in the pub for a chat and a drink, and even young men, 18 or so, would not be served by my father who told them, 'Wait till you are 21 and have some control'. They would then have to go to Ruthin for a drink. Although I have lived in two public houses, I have never tasted a drop of beer in my life, and my father only allowed me a lemon dash or a lemonade. When I was nursing, I had a friend whose father had been a sergeant-major during the First World War and kept a pub in Wrexham after his retirement from the army. Any woman going into his pub — even with a man — would be told to go to the next pub down the road. After we had moved to the Drovers' Arms, the minister used to come from across the road to our back door to collect his buttermilk. One day, my mother, Jane, was talking to a friend when they saw the minister approaching. 'It's

The Drovers' Arms, Rhewl.

Tŷ Coch (Cloion Inn in the past). The building beyond is the barn of Tŷ Coch Farm, now converted into a dwelling called TŷDori.

The walk from Clocaenog to Nant Clwyd Station.

cigarettes I want, Mrs. Lewis', she said jokingly. 'But I don't know what Mr. Hughes here wants in his jug!'

In addition to being a farmer and licensee, my father was also the local slaughterman and would be called to the farms to kill their animals (the killing of a pig was always a big occasion on any farm). At Christmas time he would go to Pool Park to kill 18 sheep, of which two were for the House and half a sheep each for the 32 employees on the estate.

On the first Tuesday of every month, when the auction was held at Ruthin market, Father would have a day out with his friends and there would be quite a gathering; sometimes he would take animals to sell. On dark evenings we would be waiting in the parlour for his return. We could hear him coming down Rhiwlas hill and knew he was nearly home when we heard his pony and trap crossing the bridge below Ty'n y Celyn. He would always bring us a big bag of mixed sweets from Molly Price's shop in Clwyd Street. I liked the ones called 'Fairy Whispers' best.

As children, we were often sent to check on the bullocks on Tŷ Coch 'mountain' up towards Maes Tyddyn and we walked along a green lane by the gateway to Henblas — now marked as a footpath — which my father told us had once been paved. Other long walks were to Nantclwyd Lodge, on the main Corwen Road, for my music lessons on Saturday mornings, and to school in Ruthin with Catherine Davies from Pentre Farm — we lodged in Ruthin during the week and walked home again on Fridays.

I was one of the lucky ones, winning a scholarship from Clocaenog School to Ruthin Girls' School. Eventually, I went to Manchester Royal Infirmary to train as a State Registered Nurse and worked at that hospital after completing my training. When I married, I returned to live in Rhewl with my husband and I now live, as a widow, in Ruthin.

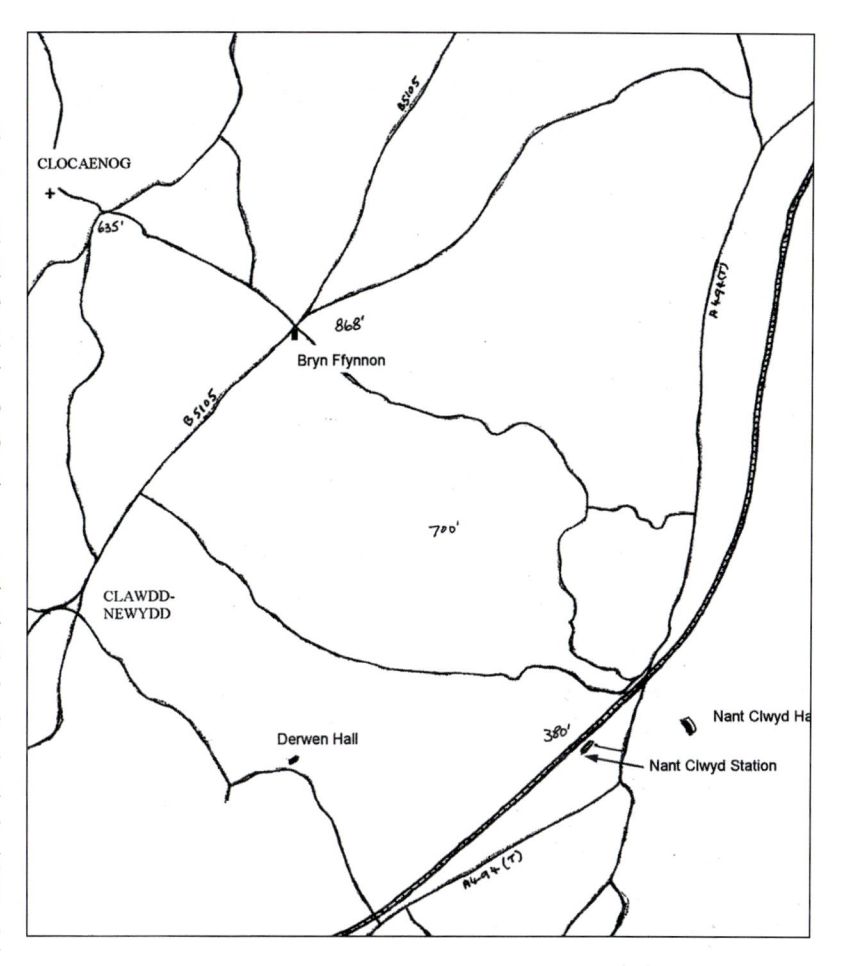

The old road 'up the mountain'.

Beryl and Dennis Bailey
5 Maes Caenog

Beryl:

My parents were Elias Davies, from Llanelidan, and Elizabeth Edwards from Llanarmon yn Iâl. My father joined the army at the age of 17 and served in Egypt during the First World War, looking after mules and horses. After the war, he took a job as a farm worker in the Pentrecelyn area where he met my mother who was looking after her uncle at Nant y Meithin, his smallholding situated high up between Pentrecelyn and the Cricor side of Llanelidan. This uncle had lost an arm in a threshing machine accident and had a hook in place of his hand. When my parents married, they lived in rooms and had their first two children there before moving to the cottage of Nant y Meithin which had been left to my mother by her uncle. It was a two-up two-down dwelling, with a shippon and barn across the yard below the house, and a *tŷ bach* at the top of the garden. That is where I spent my childhood.

Dennis and Beryl Bailey, 5 Maes Caenog.

I was born on 7 December 1946, the youngest of seven children. The oldest child, Eleanor (known to the family as Nelly), was 21 when I was born and the others, Laura (now 72), Sam, Gwen and Ellen, were so much older than me that I hardly knew them. I believe my parents lost one child, a boy, some time before the birth of Iorweth, who is five years older than me.

When I was born, only Iorweth and I were living at home with our parents, and we grew up knowing that we had a brother and four much older sisters who would visit and chat to my parents on their half-day off work. The two oldest girls worked for Dr. Hughes who lived at the Manor House, Well Street, Ruthin; one was the housekeeper and the other worked as the cook. Both were employed there until they married. The other two sisters worked in similar jobs. My brother, Sam (considered to be a bit of a naughty boy in those days), used to play truant from school for days on end and go to help my grandfather who had a threshing machine which he took round farms in the area. After leaving school, Sam worked on farms, living-in, and eventually married — several times!

My father worked full-time as a council 'lengthsman'. He walked many miles, covering all the roads between Llanelidan and the top of Graigfechan — a big area. He took great pride in his job and, each day, worked between his two red flags, culling the grass on the verges with a sickle and doing all necessary hedging and ditching — for a very low wage.

We were a poor family, but well cared for, and always had enough to eat because my father also worked hard on the smallholding, ploughing half the field for corn and, on the other half, growing vegetables for the family — always near the stream for ease of watering. In the beginning, he used to cut the corn with a scythe and, as a child, I would help with the harvest, gathering bundles together and tying each one with a twist of straw. As I grew older, it was my job to make the stooks — I think it was six bundles of corn to a stook and I remember my forearms would become very scratched and sore by the end of the day. When the stooks were dry, we would load the cart with the corn sheaves and the horse would then pull it to the barn in the yard.

The hay was cut with a scythe and turned for drying with a *picwach* (pikel) until my father bought an old green Ferguson tractor and the hay could then be cut and turned by machine, making his life easier. As my father was unable to drive, this job was taken over by my brother, Iorweth, who also had a full-time job. All the hay was loaded onto the cart and taken back to the open-sided shed in the yard where Father would build a firm, tightly-packed stack. He would first build a surrounding wall of hay which he would then infill with more hay, firming it down before building up further layers in the same manner. In later years, we became more modern and the baling machine would arrive to bale the hay which was then stacked in the same shed.

Helping Mum and Dad to bring in the hay.

All our water had to be carried in buckets from the shallow, spring-fed well in the bottom yard — the same well from which the animals used to drink and one of my mother's tasks was to feed and water the animals. One day, when I was helping her, I was knocked over by the horse; he had finished drinking at the well and decided to hurry back for his food — I just happened to be in his way! It was taken for granted that the children had to help around the place — collecting eggs, mucking out the shippon, bucket-feeding the calves and collecting the sheep from common land on the mountain where my father had grazing rights. At first, we had to gather sheep without the help of a dog, but my father did eventually get a border collie.

I remember corn and turnips being chopped and mixed together to provide feed for the animals in winter. We used to have a pig killed every year and the joints were hung from the ceiling directly above the chair where my father sat smoking his pipe — this must have helped to cure the meat! We had a blue slate floor in that room which was brushed every day and now I think of all that dust going up onto the hanging bacon. The pig-killer always came on a Saturday afternoon and, because I hated the whole process, Iorwerth and I used to go and hide up on the mountain. It was awful because we could still hear the pig screaming and, when we came back, the yard was running with blood. Gallons of water had to be carried and boiled, to use when scraping the carcass before it was cut up and salted, and I remember eating brawn for days afterwards. When I was at school, I envied the other children having lovely shop bacon when we had to eat the home-cured, fatty stuff.

Before I was born, my mother used to make bread in a big bread oven in the outhouse but eventually changed to buying shop bread. She continued to make her own butter and I would help to turn the churn but I was never good at it because I was unable to develop the sort of rhythm needed.

Sundays were different. We all walked three times to Cricor Methodist Chapel (now closed): 10 o'clock for morning service, home for lunch, back to chapel at two o'clock and again at six o'clock for Sunday School. For the rest of the day, father would sit at the side of the fireplace, reading his big Bible which was kept in a nearby wall cupboard. We were not supposed to play or do anything noisy and only did so if we could manage to be out of sight and hearing. When Iorwerth had his first sheepdog, he was told off because he went out into the field on a Sunday for a training session. My sisters later told me that we had a much easier upbringing than they had, so father must have mellowed a bit over the years!

At Christmas there would be a present each for Iorwerth and me, but never on our birthdays, and it was only after starting school, and seeing what other children had, that I realised my family was poor. We never had a family holiday, but after my sisters married, I would go on my own to stay with them for my summer holiday — one lived in Bala and the other in Glan yr Afon (on the Bala road). Fortunately, I enjoyed those times because my sisters had babies by then and it was all such a change for me because, at home, my father was often ill — I was probably sent away to give him some peace and quiet. While in Egypt, he had developed permanent health problems which were with him for the rest of his life and I was still quite small when the district nurse arrived one Sunday afternoon to give father an enema before he went to hospital for surgery. The rest of us

Plaque built into the hen house wall, now in the new extension wall. The first two lines also appear over the door of Church House, Llanfair D.C., commemorating Jonathan Beever, John Evans, John Roberts and John Wynne, church wardens in 1831. An approximate translation might be:
Don't abandon Heaven
For transient worldly things.
God is all-seeing.

Na werth y Ne,
Er benthyg byd,
Mae Duw yn gweled.
J.R. 1863.

Beryl's brother and sisters with a friend having come home from school across the fields and picked posies for Mother.

were never ill, despite the intense cold in winter, no central heating and no mains water.

At the age of four, I started at Pentrecelyn School because grandfather was poorly and my mother wanted to visit him — the school just took me in because there was nowhere else for me to go. To get there, I had to walk across five fields to the main Wrexham road, cross that road and then walk up the lane to Pentrecelyn. Before walking to school, we had to get up early to do our allotted tasks, including fetching the cows in for milking — and the same again after school. On the way to school, we called for other children who were sometimes only just getting up when we arrived — they hadn't been up for hours doing this and that and we realised that there could be an alternative way of life. Another difference was that other children were all talking about television which we did not have for a long time. I liked school, where the headmaster was a Mr. Jones, and I especially enjoyed Friday afternoons when we played rounders.

I passed my eleven plus exam and went to Brynhyfryd Secondary School, Ruthin. I would catch the bus at Llysfasi crossroads on the main road and was the only girl on the bus amongst several boys from Pentrecelyn School. I soon made some new girl friends at Brynhyfryd School, one of whom was Irene Evans from Llanelidan who later married Bryn Lewis and they have been my neighbours for many years.

By the time I started at Brynhyfryd we had a television at home but Iorweth and I were unable to go to after-school clubs, youth club or other social events in Ruthin because we lived too far away and had no transport. Another problem was the sheer isolation of the smallholding and the chores we had to do each day which left little time for anything else, so we felt quite left out of things.

When Iorweth left school, he went to work for the council and served his apprenticeship as a carpenter, continuing to work for them for many years. He married Ann Davies, a girl from Prestatyn, and they now have three children and live in Maes Hafod, Ruthin. Iorweth took early retirement in his early fifties, but did not enjoy being without work and is now employed by a firm of contract road sweepers — he likes working outside.

My parents retired when I was sixteen and we moved to live in Market Street, Ruthin, but my father found it hard to settle there after always being so busy with his job and running the smallholding — there just wasn't enough for him to do. Day after day he sat at home, bored, until Bob Lloyd from the Farmers' Auction asked him to go and help him. That completely changed everything and gave him a reason for living again.

Although my mother missed living up in the hills, she enjoyed being close to the shops and eventually accepted living in the town.

After my father died in 1980, at the age of 85, my mother went to live in one of the cottages in Church Walks (Ruthin). She was happy there but was upset when she had to move out for a while when the cottages were modernised; she went to live with my older sister in Ruthin while the work was being done, before going back to live in No. 6 again. She was 91 when she died in 1997.

When I was 18, I began my training as a State Registered Nurse at the Royal Alexandra Hospital in Rhyl at the same time as Iorweth's future wife, Ann, and my school friend Irene Evans. We lived in the nurses' home at Rhyl, only going home when we had a weekend or day off, and it was during this time

Beryl, the youngest, with her three sisters.

Nant y Meithryn today.

Below: Photograph taken on the lower yard, where the hen house was. To clean the hen house you dropped the muck down through a trap door into the pig sty and then shovelled out — keeping the upper yard clean.

Below: This photograph is taken from the upper yard where the hen house was.

that I met Dennis at the Ritz dance hall in Rhyl (later burned down). We were courting for about a year and I decided to give up my training so that we could get married in May 1966 (Irene and Ann also gave up their training to marry). Dennis and I were married in the Wesleyan Chapel in Market Street, just across the road from Maes Elwy, my parent's house, and we went to live in Llandrillo because there was a house available where Dennis was working on the Palé Estate. He was made redundant at Christmas that year and, in January 1967, we moved to live in Tŷ Capel, Clocaenog (I remember it was extremely cold that winter) and I looked after the chapel which was still in use then. Helen was born in July 1967 and Janet in 1969, so we outgrew the little two-up, two-down house and moved, in February 1971, to No. 5 Maes Caenog where Alan was born the following May. We still live in the same house, first renting it from the council, before buying it about 25 years ago; there have been fewer changes in neighbours since most of the council houses have become privately owned.

Dennis is English, but Welsh is my first language and, from the beginning, our children have been fully bilingual; when they were small there were many more youngsters living in the village — about twenty of them — and I never needed to take the children to school as there were so many of them trooping down the road together. When they became teenagers they started going into Ruthin in the evenings and at weekends, and there were always parents prepared to take them into town in cars, but they had to walk home together. We knew they were safe because there were so many of them. At that time, there was only one bus a week, at 12 noon on a Friday, going via Bontuchel and Cyffylliog before reaching Ruthin. At least they are running one bus a day now, using the same route, but few people seem to be using it so I wonder how long it will continue.

When we first moved to Clocaeneog, Mrs Jones was the postmistress at the Old Post Office (where Matt now lives) but she became ill and could no longer carry on. Mr Lake, who ran the shop and post office in Clawddnewydd, was delivering my grocery order one day and said, 'Why don't you give it a go?' I hadn't even considered being a postmistress until then but applied for the job, went to Rhyl for the interview, was given a list of figures to add up and that was it! I got the job, taking over as postmistress and running the Post Office in a small cubicle in the hall at No. 5 for over 25 years. My first customer was Mr Roberts, who lived next door until he and his wife went to live in a retirement bungalow in Rhewl. He came to draw his pension, and I find it interesting that usually the men come to draw the pensions, not the women — perhaps they are glad to get the men out of the house!

When the Post Office became computerized there was insufficient space in the hall for the necessary equipment so the downstairs cloakroom was converted into a more secure area, with a new entrance at the side of the house, and we now have our hall back. In a way, I feel as new in the job now as I was at the beginning because of changes taking place in the Post Office services. I am hoping to carry on as long as possible and perhaps, with the recent sale of Ty'n y Celyn farmland and derelict properties, there could be more families using the Post Office. I have enjoyed being a village postmistress — meeting all the people and having a two-minute transaction and a quarter of an hour's chat with each one. The sad thing is remembering all the people who have lived here, grown old and died — I saw them every week collecting their pensions, and I miss them now they're gone.

Over the past few years, I have developed hearing problems in one ear (a genetic problem) but have recently been fitted with one of the digital hearing aids which the Welsh NHS is now providing. It is wonderful when watching television but it will take me time to adjust because everything seems so much louder. I have to wear it a few hours each day and gradually accustom my brain to the increase in volume.

Dennis:
During the Second World War (before I was born) my father was a sergeant major in the army and spent the war in the desert town of Beirut. Back in Britain, my mother and two older brothers were evacuated and were billeted with a family who treated mother like a slave so, eventually, she and the boys returned to Birmingham. For the rest of the war she worked in the casting area of an iron foundry — heavy work for a woman. When my father was demobbed, he worked as a tram driver and mother started up a café near Canal Street in the city centre.

I was born on 6 June 1946 at a hospital in Birmingham (now the Princess Diana Hospital). Three early memories are of standing in a cot and hearing the radio playing, a flood which occurred at the shop, and going to nursery school where we had to lie down on camp beds for a rest after lunch. When I started primary school, I walked there each day with my cousins, through the back streets and past many bombed-out buildings.

By this time my parents were quite well off — the café was a success and my father was also earning. He always had a good car — the best — and a caravan where we spent our holidays each year, on the coast road near the Nova, in Towyn, not far from Rhyl.

I was six when, due to my mother's ill health, we moved to Holywell in north Wales in 1952. My parents bought an old foundry house between Holywell and Greenfield, with no running water or sewage, but we did have electricity, and were the first in the area to have a television set which my friends came in to watch. Many people round us were still without electricity, and their radios used batteries which had to be taken to the shop to be re-charged. We fetched all our water from a well across the road until a tap was installed, but we eventually had mains water, sewerage and gas.

Although I had two brothers — Leslie was 15 and John was seven when I was born — we never played together because of the age difference, and so we didn't know each other well and were never very close. However, I had plenty of friends because our house was near an old terrace of twelve foundry workers' houses. The area was still very rural and we went into the woods to make dens, and bows and arrows, and we played with catapults and collected birds' eggs (a popular hobby then); marbles and conkers came round in their turn, and a favourite game was 'jacks'. While working in the foundry in Birmingham, my mother had acquired some heavy cast iron stones which were used in the tumbling drums to knock rough edges off the castings. I used these as my 'jacks' and always remember them because they could be quite painful when they landed on the back of my hand.

When I first went to Greenfield Primary School I was put in the bottom class and lost over a year's education because I was always in a class below my peers. When I sat for the 11+ examination, I was still one class behind the other eleven-year olds, who had been taught to the necessary standard. So I went to Basingwork Secondary Modern School where we all sat another exam, and I was put in the top stream, eventually leaving school at 15 with nine CSEs.

My first job was with a local butcher who had two shops situated in Greenfield and Bagillt. The butcher sold good, fresh, home-killed meat which was rather over-priced for the local people, so he went to other areas selling meat from his van. I cycled for miles, taking out the orders on a delivery bike with a big frame, no gears and a large metal basket on the front. In addition, I was being taught the slaughtering skills, and it was my job to render down fat in the back shed, making dripping into one pound blocks for sale.

Although I quite liked the job, I only stayed there for about twelve months before my father, who worked on the railway, found me a job as a van boy, delivering parcels. I was earning £3 16s. 0d. weekly, paying 6s. 0d. a week for my ticket to Chester — bought at a cheap rate because I was a railway worker gave Father £2. 10s. 0d. for my keep, which left me with just £1. So I transferred to the goods department at Holywell and was then able to save up and buy myself a moped — at that time, petrol was only four shillings a gallon.

I was sent to Manchester to learn to drive heavy goods vehicles and, when I had my certificate, I delivered goods around Holywell area until Beeching's axe fell and Holywell station closed down and I was made redundant. I soon found myself back at a butcher's shop in a Holywell supermarket, working under the man who had been the manager at the Bagillt shop. He continued to train me, and I gained a slaughterer's licence. I worked there for several years, in the dark at the back of the shop, and eventually decided to return to work for the railway. For a time, I worked shifts in the goods depot at Chester but found it very boring. When I met Beryl, I found the hours did not fit in with courting, so I went to work as a tractor driver for the local council, cutting grass verges in the summer, gritting and clearing snow in the winter.

Beryl and I married when I found a forestry job with a tied house (in Llandrillo) on the Duke of Westminster's Palé Estate, but ten months later the duke died and his successor made us all redundant — at Christmas! Had I gone on the dole, we could have stayed in the house, but I eventually found a forestry job, with a house but low wages — by the time we had paid the rent there was only £6 a week left, so we found it very hard. Beryl was expecting our first child when we were lucky enough to get the tenancy of Tŷ Capel in Clocaenog where we lived for five years, cleaning the chapel and entertaining the visiting minister each Sunday. For twelve months I worked for the Forestry Commission and then returned to work for the council as a tractor driver. Sadly, during this time, my mother, who had worked hard all her life, and suffered a great deal of illness, died in her early sixties when I was 23.

My next job was with Hucon, Ruthin, making precast concrete and I did piece work there for five years — hard work, but I doubled my wage. Unfortunately I developed cement dust dermatitis that still flares up from time to time, and I had to leave. Subsequently, I worked on JCBs and bulldozers for Jones Brothers, as a machine driver with Turner & Williams, and was then asked to return to Jones Brothers, doing contract work for them all over north Wales. I eventually found the distances too great and, as my petrol allowance didn't cover my costs, I went to work for the Post Office in 1979 and am still with them. I have always liked working out of doors and am based in Ruthin sorting and delivering mail.

Sometimes I thought of getting a better job and earning more money but, once the children were settled in Clocaenog School, we didn't want to disturb their education, and Beryl was running the village Post Office from the house. More importantly, we were all happy here!

The children were our main hobby for years, teaching them all to swim, chauffeuring them when they were involved in things away from the village, and supporting them in their various interests. When the children were very young I was involved in setting up the Clocaenog football team with Glyn Jones (Beryl and David Jones' son), playing matches twice weekly in the Ruthin Junior League. Glyn was the trainer and I was the manager, and we had to drive the children everywhere. We managed to get sponsorship from Wall-Lag Double Glazing and kitted out the team with shirts; we also raised money at whist drives in the Church Hall. The football came to a natural end as the children grew up and there were no younger ones to replace them.

I was also involved with tennis from the time Alan (then about nine years old) became interested in the game and did well, playing at junior level and eventually being coached by the North Wales League. He played for Wales as a junior and then in the County League. Because I spent so much time at the clubs with the children, I started practising myself and ended up playing for Ruthin for several years — this involved two club nights, a weekly match and an occasional weekend match. It was fine while the children were little but, as they grew up, I stopped playing tennis so that Beryl and I could spend more time together.

I used to collect stamps, became secretary of the local society (these clubs always like to flog a willing horse) and have been interested in photography since I was 14, starting off with an expandable Kodak bellows camera and, at one time, doing my own black and white developing, printing and enlarging in the back kitchen. For a long time I bred and exhibited budgerigars, and now another hobby is watercolour painting — often of birds — and I have recently started going to classes at Ruthin Craft Centre because I want to widen my abilities and paint landscapes; my teacher is a local artist, Nia Northcote, who is the mother-in-law of my son, Alan.

I enjoy reading and gardening, and an on-going project has been to terrace our steeply sloping back garden which is now complete with a gazebo and a waterfall. I have also built a small conservatory where Beryl and I used to enjoy sitting — but is now full of the grandchildren's toys.

Beryl and Dennis:

We have always spent a lot of time with our children and enjoyed picnics and days out in the country or at the seaside. We never had a proper holiday until 1998 but we always managed to pay for the children to go on holidays with their schools and they each had one school trip abroad.

After leaving school, Helen trained in secretarial work and is still working part-time as a secretary with the NFU, Ruthin; Janet trained as a State Registered Nurse and Midwife at Ysbyty Glan Clwyd and now works part-time; Alan is a Senior Architectural Officer with Denbighshire County Council and in addition has acquired a BA Honours degree, as well studying for his Post Graduate Diploma to become a fully qualified architect.

Our children are all married. Helen lives in Rhewl, Janet in Clawddnewydd and Alan in Ruthin. Helen's husband, Huw, is a storeman and delivery man and they have three children: Osian, born in 1992, Llion, born in 1994 and Lowri, born in 1997. Janet and Mike (a welder) have Chloë, born in 1994 and Abbie, born in 1998. Alan's wife, Rhiannon was studying design at university but left when she married and now works part-time as a childminder in Llanfair D.C., and they have Hana, born in 2000 and Cai, born in 2002. Although all our children live locally, only Janet's and Mike's children have attended Clocaenog School.

We now have seven grandchildren — and they still keep producing them! We have daily contact with them and look after them when their mothers are out at work, so it has been like parenting all over again, but we are glad to be able to help or children in this way. All our grandchildren are bi-lingual (in Welsh and English).

In the past we have had pet dogs — first a sheep dog and then a labrador cross, but they have gone now and we still miss them, particularly when we go walking; we often go out on Sundays and one of our favourite walks is on the Great Orme in Llandudno.

We have lived in Clocaenog for 36 years and have had a busy and happy life together.

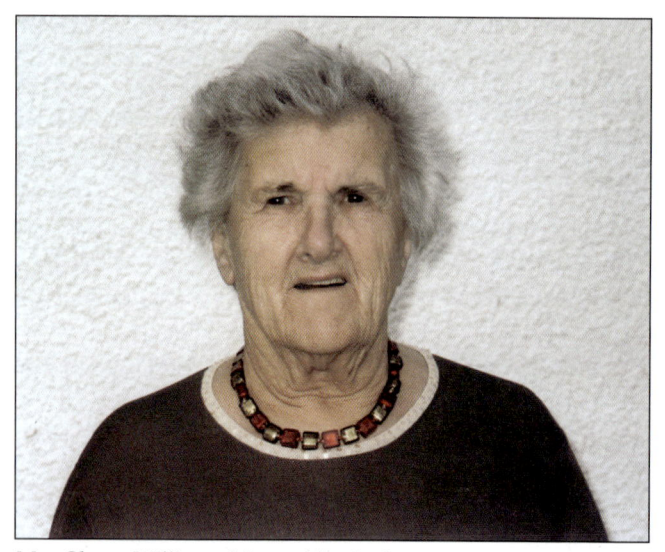

Mrs Glenys Williams, Maestyddyn Isaf.

Glenys Williams
Maestyddyn Isaf

I was born in Pwllglas, but my family moved to Allt y Celyn, Clawddnewydd, in 1927. We decided to go to Clocaenog School because that is where the neighbours' children went — although I am sure Derwen School was nearer. We didn't mind the walk as it was with other children, some of whom joined us as we went through Clawddnewydd. If it was raining, and to save us getting wet, my father would take us in the pony and trap ('Springcet' we called the pony). I imagine there were about 70 to 80 children in the school at that time, and most of the pupils stayed on until they were 14, so I remember, as a small girl, some of the boys looking more like men to me.

Mrs A. M. Jones, Maes Gwyn, was the infant teacher and I have very happy memories of that time, although what we were taught then was very elementary compared to what children are taught now. We wrote on a blue slate but later we had paper and pencil before progressing to using ink. Mr. Llew Roberts, a bachelor from Port Dinorwic, was the headmaster. He was very kind to the children, especially when we were breaking up for the holidays and there was a bag of sixpences to be handed out — and sixpence meant a lot in those days! On other occasions he would give us sixpence as a reward for good work in class or for reading well. Mr. Roberts was musical, but as there was no piano in school he used a tuning fork to start us singing on the right note. He was very religious and led our services and taught us what was right and important in life.

He lodged with Mr. Saunders Davies and family at Bryn Ffynnon, and would go there for his lunch each day. We carried our lunch to school and one of the duties of the big boys was to fill the urn with water and put it on the fire mid-morning to heat it for our lunch-time drinks. Miss Wyn from Llanarmon taught the middle class and lodged during the week in the chapel house belonging to the Methodists, coming from her home on a motor bike on Monday mornings.

During the dinner hour we were free to do as we wished and in the summer we would go up to Pincyn Llys and arrive out of breath at the top, with just enough time to tap the stones to say we had been there, before running back down to school. Another thing we did was to go to the woods in spring to collect the rhododendron flowers. An old woman called Mrs. Lewis lived in the cottage called Glan yr Afon and she was always dressed in black, and when we crept passed with our arms full of flowers she would come out and chase us with a broom and we were convinced she was a witch! Sometimes in the dinner hour some of the boys went to Bryn Fedwen where Dafydd Hughes and his son, Dafydd, lived. Dafydd was a carpenter and had a barn where the boys took great pleasure in watching him and his son making various farm implements and all sorts of carts. I remember one lunch hour walking from the bottom of Helyg Hill and going over the style and across the field to a farm sale at Ty'n-y-Celyn. The family from there was moving to live in Sarnau, Clawddnewydd, next door to my house. We couldn't stay long to watch but I remember it was the late Roger Jones who bought the land — Ty'n-y-Celyn and Cae Segwen — and moved to live there after leaving Craig Wen.

The parson at that time was Rev. Hopkins Jones and I remember him walking through the village wearing a long frock coat with a flat hat on his head. He used to keep a horse and trap in his stable or coach house, the building which was eventually adapted and converted into Clocaenog Church Hall. Their family kept a maid who would walk to the shop in her white cap and apron on errands for Mrs.Hopkins Jones. Mr. and Mrs. Francis lived next door to the Wesleyan Chapel where Mr. Francis was a lay preacher, and they ran the village shop and Post Office where, as a child, I could buy quite a few sweets for a ha'penny (halfpenny).

I spent happy years at Clocaenog School before passing a scholarship examination in 1932 to go to Ruthin County School for Girls. I travelled on the train from Derwen to Ruthin for two years but after that I went by bus from Clawddnewydd.

Glenys Williams

Maestyddyn Isaf

Rwy'n enedigol o Bwllglas, a symudodd y teulu i Allt y Celyn yn 1927. Ddaru ni benderfynnu mynd i Ysgol Clocaenog, a'r rheswm am hynny oedd gan fod ein cymdogion ni yn mynd i ysgol Clocaenog ac nid i Dderwen, er rwy'n siwr fod Derwen yn nes. Cerdded i'r ysgol gyda'r plant eraill fel nad oedd yn gymaint o boendod — plant y Clawdd i gyd. Allai feddwl bod yna tua saithdeg i wythdeg o blant yn yr ysgol. Wrth gwrs yr adeg honno roedd y plant yn aros yn yr ysgol nes oedden nhw yn bedair-ar-ddeg oed. Allai gofio fod rhai o'r bechgyn yn edrych fel dynion i mi. Os fyddai'n gwlychu fe fyddai fy nhad yn mynd a ni efo merlyn a'r trap — 'springcet' oeddem ni yn ei alw fo — a lle bod ni'n gwlychu fe fydde fo yn mynd a ni i Glocaenog. Os oedd hi wedi bod yn glawio'n arw, a ninne ar ein ffordd adre, fe fyddai'n dod i'n nol ni hefyd. Roedd hyn yn gaffaeliad mawr ar y pryd. Mae'n debyg fod yna lot o blant eraill yn cael eu cario yr un amser.

Mrs A. M. Jones, Maes Gwyn — Pentre yr adeg honno — oedd yn athrawes ar y babanod. Mae gen i atgofion pleserus iawn ond roedd y pethau roeddem ni yn ei ddysgu yn elfennol iawn iw gymharu a beth mae plant yn ei gael heddiw. Ysgrifennu ar slaten fydden ni — slaten las, a nes ymlaen yn yr ysgol wrth gwrs roeddech chi yn cael pensil a phapur, ac yn nes ymlaen wedyn byddech yn dod i ddefnyddio inc. Mr Llew Roberts oedd y prifathro, hen lanc a brodor o Port Dinorwig oedd o. Roedd o'n hael iawn efo ni'r plant — yn enwedig yn y gwylie wrth i ni dorri fynny. Fe fydde fo yno efo bag efo chwech cheiniog i ni — ac roedd chwech cheiniog yn golygu lot yr adeg honno. Hefyd roeddem yn cael chwe cheiniog ecstra ac roedd hynny am fod yn dda yn y dosbarth neu am ddarllen — roedd yne bethe y base fo'n rhoi chwe cheiniog ychwanegol i chi am wneud.

Bydde ni hefyd yn cael cerddoriaeth — roedd o'n andros o gerddorol. Doedd yne ddim piano yr adeg honno with gwrs ac i gael y nodyn fe fyddai gyno fo ryw chwisl i gael yr union nodyn gywir — ac mi fydde fo bob tro. Mi fydde ni hefyd yn cael gwasanaeth — roedd o'n grefyddol iawn ac fe ddysgodd y pethe pwysig i ni yr adeg honno. Roedd o'n lodgio efo Saunders Davies a'i deulu yn Bryn Ffynnon. Fe fydde fo yn mynd adre am ginio bob dydd. Mynd a cinio efo ni fydde ni fel plant. Gorchwyl y bechgyn mawr oedd llenwi yr yrn efo dŵr oer ac fe fydde hwn yn cael ei roi ar y tan ganol bore ac wedyn erbyn amser cinio fe fyddai na ddŵr poeth yn barod i ni blant. Miss Wyn o Lanarmon oedd efo'r dosbarth canol. Roedd hi yn lodgio yn Nhy Capel y Methodistiaid, ac yn dod ar fore Llun ar gefn moto beic o Lanarmon i Glocaenog. Yn yr awr ginio roeddem ni'r plant yn cael gwneud fel a fynnom. Yn yr haf fe fyddem ni yn picied i fyny i Bincyn Llys a colli gwynt yn lan. Dim ond digon o amser i roi tap ar garreg Pincyn Llys i ddweud em bod wedi bod yno. Peth arall fydde ni'n wneud yn y gwanwyn — pan oedd y rodedendrums allan — oedd mynd i Goed Cwper heibio i Glanrafon. Roedd yno goed o bob math yn perthyn i stad Pool Parc a fydde ni yn mynd i fano i hel rodedendrums. Ond roedd yne hen wraig yn byw yn Glan yr Afon — Mrs Lewis oedd ei henw hi, ac fe fydde hi yn rhedeg ar ein hol ni efo ffon — hi oedd yn edrych ar ôl etifeddiaeth y rodedendrums! Fe fyddai'r bechgyn yn aml iawn yn cael lot o fwyniant wrth fynd i Bryn Fedwen lle roedd Dafydd Hughes a'i fab, Dafydd, yn byw. Saer oedd Dafydd Hughes, ac roedd ganddo ysgubor lle byddai yn gwneud ei waith. Fe fyddai y bechgyn yn cael llawer o fwyniant o'i wylio fo yn gwneud offer — troliau a bob math o offer ffarm.

Dwi'n cofio mynd i Ty'n Celyn i sel ffarm — roedd y teulu yn ymddeol ac yn symud i fyw yn Sarnau yng Nghlawddnewydd, drws nesaf i ni yn Allt y Celyn. Roedd yne sêl yno a dwi'n cofio cerdded o waelod allt Helyg, dros y gamfa ac i fyny'r cae ac i Ty'n Celyn i'r sêl. Doedden ni ddim yn cael aros yno yn hir gan mae ein hawr ginio ni oedd hi. Y ddiweddar erbyn heddiw Roger Joneses ddaru brynu'r tir — Ty'n Celyn a Segwen, a nhw ddoth yno i fyw wedyn o Graig Wen.

Mae gen i gof am y person yr adeg honno — Mr Jones oedd ei enw fo. Mi fydde fo yn cadw ceffyl a thrap ac mae nhw'n dweud mai yn y stabal neu'r 'coach house' mae 'village hall' Clocaenog rwan — wedi cael ei addasu. Mr. Hopcyn Jones oedd y person, yn gwisgo ffroc cot laes — fedrai weld o rwan yn cerdded drwy'r pentref a het fflat ar ei ben. Roedden nhw yn cadw morwyn — fedrai weld honno yn cerdded yn ei ffedog wen a chap gwyn i lawr i'r siop. Yn y siop roedd Mrs Ffransis yn byw — roedd o'n Bost Office hefyd. Mae'n debyg mai fferins oedd yr unig beth y basen ni yn ei brynu fel plant — fasech chi'n cael dipyn o fferins yr adeg honno am ddime ac am geiniog. Mr Ffransis oedd y postmon oedd yn mynd a llythyrau, ac roedd o hefyd yn bregethwr cynorthwyol gyda'r Wesleaid. Hwyrach mai dyna pam oedd o'n byw drws nesaf i'r capel Wesle — bydde fo'n mynd o gwmpas i bregethu ar y Sul.

Eryl Wyn Williams
Maestyddyn Isaf

I was born on 13 Nov 1955 and have lived here all my life. My father came here from Waen, took over the running of the farm from his father in 1947, and later bought the farm from the Forestry Commission — it wasn't part of the Pool Park Estate. We had the largest piece of land isolated from the Ruthin Castle Estate to which it belonged originally, and we were on the boundary of that estate. It wasn't affected by the Enclosure, the boundaries of which go all round the edges of the farm.

When my father first came here the holding was run as a mixed farming unit with dairy, beef cattle, and sheep, having much smaller numbers of stock, with about 300 sheep, milking 20 to 30 cows and rearing beef.

In the 1950s my mother had battery hens and sold eggs to North Western Farmers from Nantwich, who came and collected from the farm.

Since my father's day, farms have gone bigger and much more intensive. A similar farm, with the same acreage as my father's, now holds 900 sheep, 200 cattle made up of 100 suckler cows and growing on 100 beef cattle. Silage in big bails has revolutionised farming and enabled the farmers to feed far more animals from the same land, given that they have the machinery to handle it. Grassland is much more productive, not because of fertilisers, but because the seed varieties grown are better and stronger and feed more animals per acre. It is because of intensification, and also there was a lack of knowledge in the old days and things were usually done in the traditional way.

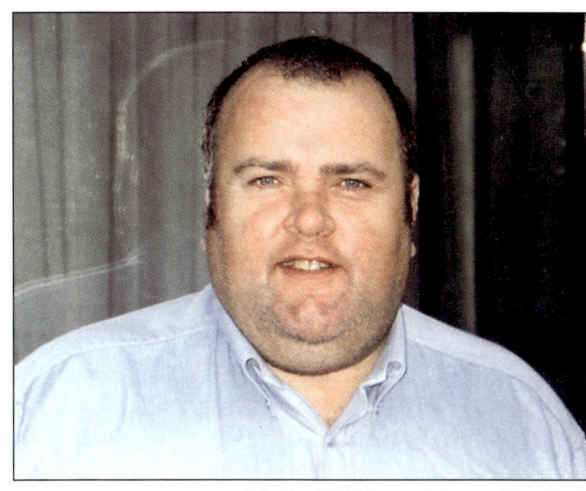

Mr Eryl Williams, Maestyddyn Isaf.

My father worked the farm himself with my mother and two or three men, depending on the season, but always two full time working here, and one part time. Now, there is myself and my nephew, with three times the amount of live stock, but we buy in contract labour to do big jobs like silage, shearing and spraying and big projects like fencing — but not just remedial work which we do ourselves. We do limited spraying on crops like swedes, or corn before harvesting. Ploughing is also carried out by contract labour.

In the future I believe the farms will be in bigger units and with more partnerships, sharing machinery and contracting in labour and machines — and farmers being more innovative in selling their produce. They might not sell to the cheapest markets but go for smaller private farmers' markets or look to premium breeding especially here on the hills. We do not use A.I. because, with sucklers when they come on heat, it is done the natural way by our own bull.

In the old days the threshing machine came round to each farm in turn and that method is coming back now. My nephew who works here makes our silage and then with two others in partnership goes round other farms with his machinery making silage for other farmers. It makes things more fair and equal, the big farmers helping the smaller ones with their machinery, which can be so expensive if only used on a small acreage.

When I joined Ruthin Young Farmers there were lots of young people from round here who joined at the same time— Sharon (Bryn Coch), Hywel, and others who were all at school together, first at Clocaenog and then at Brynhyfryd. After school I spent one year at Llysfasi Agricultural College. Everyone tried to get me to stay on to take 'A' levels, but I left Brynhyfryd School with eleven 'O' levels. That is one thing I regret — I could have gone on to university. I would do anything to have that time over again. However, I wanted to go into farming and couldn't wait to get back on the farm.

I might have done something quite different, but I went on to be Chairman of Clwyd Young Farmers and then Chairman of Wales in 1987, and became Chairman of England and Wales in 1990. In that year, 2,000 young farmers from all over England and Wales came to camp out at Maestyddyn in caravans and tents — we used the sheds and had barbecues, a kitchen fitted out with stoves and ovens, and had music and dancing on two evenings — a whole weekend of fun! They came from all over — from Northumberland in the north, to Essex in the south. It was my idea, and we all had a great time —no bad behaviour. We made £9,000 profit and started the Rural Youth Trust which I inaugurated with Princess Anne; I went to Buckingham Palace for a special party to launch it and I was made the chairman. In a short time, the fund has grown to £350,000. The fund is used to help young people travel abroad, for creating play parks in country areas, promoting youth schemes and training staff to run them; any plan to aid young people in rural communities will be considered for financial sponsoring by the board of trustees.

I joined the Community Council 27 or 28 years ago, following on from my father. In 1990 I was finishing as Chairman of the National Federation of Young Farmers' Clubs, and went into the election for Glyndŵr District Council and got in unopposed. In 1991 I stood in the Ruthin Ward elections — Rhewl, Clocaenog, Pwllglas being the outer limits — and won the seat on Clwyd County Council. Then, in the redistribution of

Clwyd, I stood for the County Council in 1995 and again 1999. I was elected Chairman in 1999, and Leader in 2002.

I stood for Plaid Cymru in 1997 General Election and came a creditable third, considering the landslide which Labour was having at the time. They wanted me to stand for the Welsh Assembly elections but I preferred to get involved with local affairs at the same time, as Leader of the Council. I get involved with national policies in that way. If I had won through to the National Assembly I don't think I would have had the time to deal with local matters back here in the same way. I have been able to delve into all the possible pockets of money which are available and which, if you think imaginatively, can be accessed and used within the community to good purpose. There is a big debate now as regards areas of Rhyl, Prestatyn, central Denbigh and parts of Ruthin, where money needs to be spent — not necessarily council money, but as with Ruthin Gaol, Welsh Assembly money — if only people would think creatively. Any idea takes time to develop and bring to fruition.

After being ill for four years, my father died 23 years ago, aged 60, very young by today's standards. I remember I used to go to the shop in Clawddnewydd' for fags for him and he would smoke like a chimney — 40 Embassy a day. He would get up in a morning and lean on the fence and cough and choke and choke — but go on smoking. He had treatment and was better for a time, but it returned. The only good which came of his illness was that all my uncles and cousins gave up smoking after seeing how he suffered.

What do I think about hunting? We have the Corwen/Bala pack of hounds which come with guns to clear out the forest. Hounds go in and flush out the foxes. The farmers who live on the edges of Clocaenog Forest pay £20 each year for the annual cull. Without that we would have a real problem.

I have seen a deer recently, maybe an escaped one. Once there were 'wild' sheep in the forest, because certain people, like those from Plas, had sheep out on the roads and some would escape into the forest and lamb there. They let them graze the woods, but then the Council would round them up and sell them so the farmers became a bit more careful and fenced their sheep in.

We hold Grass Track Racing meetings at Maestyddyn. We use seven or eight fields in succession, but ran out of flat areas this year. It is no hassle, and the money goes to help the school, Bedol or the community centre. We have re-seeded some fields and we should be able to run the events again next year.

I have had a happy and interesting life and I don't regret a single day. My mother would have liked me to have married but, if I had, I would not have had the time to spend on what I have done and achieved.

Saunders Davies
Brynffynnon

In May 1916 our family moved from Gwyddelwern to live in Brynffynnon, Clocaenog — a very friendly area. The village had one public house, a church, a Welsh Presbyterian chapel called Cades, and a Wesleyan chapel. A widow and her son lived in the house belonging to Cades, but they later moved to a new house named Derlwyn. There was also a nearly derelict house next to the other chapel, Tanllan Bach, but I do not remember anyone living there. Further on towards Bontuchel was Tanllan Farm and Glan yr Afon, where two hospitable families lived; further on again was Pentre Farm. Most of the farms belonged to Lord Bagot in those days.

Near the Wesleyan chapel was the Post Office run by Mrs. Francis. Not far away was the Rectory where the Rector and his wife lived and, next to that, John Jones and his wife lived in Paradwys. He was a hard working deacon for Capel Cades. There were also two very faithful men who attended the Wesleyan chapel — Robert Roberts (Plas Cwta) and David Hughes (Bryn Fedwyn). In Bryngwyn Farm, towards Clawddnewydd, there were two sisters and two brothers, one brother being a renowned singer. Another real asset to the chapel for years was the Davies family, Tynycelyn.

I remember the Forestry Commission planting trees round Clocaenog. The introduction of electricity instead of lamps and candles, and clean tap water, brought great improvements to the area. There were changes on the farms too, with tractors replacing horses. The Milk Marketing Board was introduced in the 1930s with milk being sold directly to them. In the 40s I remember butter being carried in baskets to be sold

The old Shop and Post Office run by Mr & Mrs Francis, adjoining the Wesleyan Methodist Chapel.

in Ruthin. Threshing day was always very busy. And lastly, I remember the great snowfall of 1947.

S. D.*

* Sadly, Saunders Davies died in 2001, aged 97. He wrote these memories the year before. His wife, Maud Winifred, died in 1978.

Saunders Davies
Brynffynnon

Yn mis Mai 1916 daethom fel teulu o ardal Gwyddelwern i fyw i Brynffynnon, Clocaenog, ac i ardal groesawus iawn. Yn y pentref yr oedd un dafarn, Eglwys y Plwyf a dau gapel; un o'r enw 'Cades' yn perthyn i'r Presbyteriaid a'r llall yn gapel y Wesleiad. Yr oedd tŷ capel gyda Cades lle yr oedd gwraig weddw ac un mab yn byw ond, ymhen amser, fe adeiladwyd tŷ o'r enw 'Derlwyn' ac aethant yno i fyw. Yn ymyl y capel yma yr oedd hen dŷ bron a syrthio i lawr o'r enw 'Tanllan Bach' ond nid ydwyf yn cofio neb yn byw ynddo. Yn is i lawr oddiwrtho yr oedd fferm o'r enw 'Tanllan'; ac yn Glan yr Afon yr oedd dau deulu croesawgar yn byw. I gyfeiriad Bontuchel yr oedd fferm o'r enw 'Pentre'; perthyn i ystad Lord Bagot yr oedd y rhan fwyaf o'r ffermydd yn yr ardal yr adeg honno.

Yn ymyl Capel y Wesleiad yr oedd y Post Office yn cael ei gadw gan Mrs Francis. Yr oedd y Rheithordy wedi cael ei leoli ar ganol y llan ac yma yr oedd y Rheithor a'i deulu yn byw. Yn Paradwys yr oedd John Jones a'i briod yn byw, blaenor gweithgar iawn yn Capel Cades. Yr oedd dau ŵr ffyddlon iawn yn Capel y Wesleiad, sef Robert Roberts, Plas Cwta, a David Hughes, Bryn Fedwen. Bron iawn yn y fan yr oedd fferm o'r enw Nantycelyn, ac i gyfeiriad Clawddnewydd yr oedd ffermdy Bryn Gwyn, lle yr oedd dwy ferch a dau fab yn cartrefu; un mab yn ganwr o fri. Teulu arall fu yn gefn mawr i'r capel am flynyddoedd oedd teulu ???

Yr wyf yn cofio y Comisiwn Coedwigaeth yn plannu coed o gwmpas ardal Clocaenog. Cafwyd llawer o wellianau wrth gael dŵr glan wedi ei beipio i'r tŷ a chael trydan i gymeryd lle y lampau olew a'r canhwyllau.

Newidiadau ar y fferm hefyd wrth gael tractor i gymeryd lle y ceffylau. Y Bwrdd Marchnata Llaeth yn cael ei sefydlu yn y tri-degau a dechrau gwerthu llaeth iddynt. Yn y pedwar-degau cario menyn cartref mewn basgedi i'w werthu yn Rhuthun. Diwrnod prysur iawn oedd diwrnod dyrnu a cofiaf yn dda iawn hefyd am yr eira mawr yn 1947.

Bu Saunders Davies farw yn 97 oed yn y flwyddyn 2001. Bu ei briod, Maud Winifred, farw yn 1978.

The great snowfall of 1947. Forestry workers and all able-bodied men turned out to clear the road from Ruthin. Here is the road where it approaches Clawddnewydd.

June Vlies
Tŷ Capel

I was born at St. Mary's Hospital in Manchester on 8 June 1929. My father was Philip Sidney McKinless and my mother was Adeline Poole before she married; they lived in High Blakeley, north Manchester and my father worked as a shipping clerk before becoming a manager there.

Thinking back, my father, who was not an ambitious man, would have made a very good househusband, whereas my mother, who was ambitious and earned more money than my father, gave up her job when she married because she intended to have a large family. Their first child died after ten days but, ignoring advice to have no more children, they subsequently had me; mine was an induction birth (achieved then by giving the patient pint pots of castor oil) which physically wrecked my mother and, afterwards, she also suffered from 'white leg' (thrombosis) causing problems for the rest of her life.

I was very happy to start school, but was soon diagnosed with a heart problem and was not allowed to walk for 18 months. After returning to school aged six and a half, I was moved up a class and life was never the same again. I didn't like the new teacher who had black stockings, and hair in a bun, and was not very child-friendly.

When I was seven we moved to Chadderton near Oldham and I had to travel quite a distance by bus to get to my new school — a little church scool which was ancient and quaint and contained a lot of children who came from a different world from me. Many of their parents worked in ill-paid jobs in the mills and the children came to school poorly dressed and wearing clogs which I had never seen before.

The school went to church every Wednesday and each morning started with the catechism being chanted — and I had been brought up as a Scottish Presbyterian! The Presbyterians were strict about Sunday activities but, on other days, held wonderful social events which were very friendly and enjoyable; no dancing was allowed because it had connotations. In contrast to that, I found the Church of England School less flexible.

At home as a child, I liked doing jigsaws, playing with dolls, playing cards, reading, and would knit, crochet and do bobbin work, using a wooden bobbin with four nails hammered into the top and multi-coloured wool; the resulting woven sausage could be made into circular mats and all manner of animals and figures. Being an only child, the family's fox terrier was often my playmate, particularly when I was ill, and I used to dress her up and even play Ludo with her! The games we played at school came in phases and included roller skating, hopscotch, ball games, marbles and whip and top (I was always good with the whip!); we used to chalk patterns on the tops and watch them alter as they were spinning. There was skipping, of course, alone or with two girls turning a long piece of washing line and several girls skipping together, often with intricate movements and songs.

Because I enjoyed learning, I wanted to take a scholarship exam. Most of the parents had no expectations other than their children following them into the mill but there was one boy, a year younger than me, who also sat the exam — he passed and I failed. The headmaster felt that this boy was not as clever as me so advised my mother to approach the education committee where a man said to her, 'I shouldn't tell you this, but it's because he's a boy'. There was no way around it at the time, but I did eventually get to Chadderton Grammar School by passing the 13+ exam and started there in 1942 at the age of 12.

When I was sixteen, I took eight subjects in the School Certificate examination. Unfortunately, the day before the exams, I had a virus infection with a high temperature and the doctor would not allow me to go to school. The headmaster sent a teacher to invigilate while I did the first three exams at home, then I was able to go back to school to finish the rest. Two years later, having passed the Higher School Certificate, I tried to get into university but was unable to get a place because preference was being given to those returning from National Service. (Education was not the only thing affected during the war and for many

Mrs June Vlies.

years afterwards when life was also constrained by the rationing of food and clothing, it was made worse by severe shortages of goods in the shops long after the cessation of hostilities in 1945.)

After killing time for a year, I re-applied and was offered an interview at Durham University where the Principal said that my chosen discipline of psychology required a special kind of mind and I would be better advised to study history for which I had gained 80%. I was too naïve to insist on psychology, started the history course, and hated it! Being at university failed to live up to my expectations as the student body consisted of two distinct layers: those of us straight from school and older students given priority places. These two strata did not make a cohesive whole.

A year later, I left university and went to live with friends in Paris for a year — an education in itself — and was able to go to the Sorbonne, becoming fluent in French before my visa expired and I had to come home.

I found work in the aerodynamics department of A. V. Rowe (the aviation company), where the Vulcan bomber was being designed and developed, and I was able to watch the first take-off and flight. My future husband, Harold Vlies, also worked for the company and we met on a social outing run by the firm. He was of Dutch extraction from a family of ribbon makers in France. Harold and I were married at Poynton Church, Cheshire, in 1953 and went to live in Brookfield Avenue, Poynton, eventually moving to a lovely house in Woodford where we lived for six years until my husband died — we were together for only 18 years.

Sadly, we were unable to have children but were eventually successful in adopting a seven week old baby girl with the help of Stockport Children's Department. We called her Hilary and she was a dainty little thing, proving to be a very easy baby and child. It was all a great experience and we became a very close knit little family.

Harold's sudden death came as a terrible shock to 14 year-old Hilary and me and it was a difficult time for both of us coming to terms with such a terrible loss. On top of this we had to leave Woodford because we could no longer afford to stay in such a big house with two stables and a tennis court. However, I was determined to keep Hilary's ponies so we moved to live in a small rented farmhouse on a friend's Llandegla estate, arriving with a Land Rover, trailer, 6 cats, 3 dogs and four horses — my brother-in-law christened me 'Mrs. Noah'. I eventually bought the house with four acres of land and Hilary and I lived there until she was 24 when I moved to Hirwaen for about five years before coming to live in Tŷ Capel in 1986. I have always had dogs but it was Hilary who introduced cats to the household. She was always very close to her father and used to sit on the bench to watch him making model railways in his workshop.

I have had a passion for horses from a very early age, although I never had one of my own as a child. Of course, most deliveries were made by horse and cart in those days and I used to wait outside just to see the horses arriving in the street — I'd wait all day for that! I was lucky to have a child who developed a passion for horses — encouraged by me, of course — and I did a lot of the work on them because she was at school but I must say she was always willing to work with them in her spare time. I loved it!

Hilary's life has always involved horses. She writes successful books about them, lectures at equestrian colleges and runs a thriving business selling riding equipment. Her main hobby now is carriage driving.

In addition to my love of horses, dogs have always been a major part of my life and I have never been without one throughout my life. When my husband was alive we had a Poodle and an Airedale, and, after moving to Wales, Hilary and I had black Gronandaals (Belgian shepherd dogs). The most special dog I have ever had was Kim, a Gronandaal, but sadly he developed epilepsy when he was only seven and had to be put down.

A couple of years later, I took on three Borzoi puppies from a rescued litter, two for me and one for Hilary — elegant, gentle dogs with lovely natures and they all lived long lives, the last dying at the age of 16. My next rescue dog was Polly who had been on the streets for months and would fight anything that moved, making my cats' lives a misery. That was when I started going to dog training classes at Llanelidan after which Polly's behaviour gradually improved — it was hard work and wore me out but was worth the effort and Polly has only recently died. I still have Cushla (another rescue dog) who has done very well at the classes and now enoys heel work and other exercises to music.

I have continued going to the classes at the Happy Days Kennels and help with the demonstrations and dealing with problem dogs. I am not at all competitive, but I do enjoy going to Crufts to see the dogs there, particularly the working dogs.

Although I have always lived in isolated houses, I am getting older and like living in the small village of Clocaenog where there are people round me who are friendly, but not intrusive. I enjoy gardening but have only a patio garden at the back because the land belonging to my property is separated from the house by the entrance gate to the field behind. I used to keep a goat and grow vegetables there.

In addition to the dog training classes and exercising my own dog, I am very interested in decorative art and go to classes in painting run by Soosie Black at Stryt Cottage. I am very happy and contented living here because I know how to keep myself occupied and, having learned to read before I was five years old, I still get a lot of enjoyment from books. I have a lovely daughter with whom I have frequent contact and one of my greatest pleasures now is to see her happy and successful.

June Vlies with some of her rescued dogs.

The Stephenson Family
Tan Llan

Mary:

Victor, Carole and I came to Tan Llan in February 1952, after our land in Prescot had been taken from us by compulsory purchase. At that time, there was no electricity in the village, but we had oil lamps, Calor gas, a septic tank and mains water which could be heated in the back boiler of the fire.

Soon after we moved here, my kind neighbour told me she would take me to the W.I. meeting and so I was introduced. There were over 60 members who met in the Village Hall, which was lit by Calor gas lamps, and the heating was a pot-bellied stove in the middle of one wall. Of course, we all wore hats for meetings.

As the years passed other Institutes opened in neighbouring villages and our numbers shrank accordingly, but when the numbers were smaller it was easier to get to know the other members. I soon found myself serving on the committee. I think we were an exceptionally talented Institute, and with a little encouragement, we found members who were willing to enter all the county competitions — with great success. I remember country dancing in Ruthin Town Hall where we had trouble with the gramophone needle. We enjoyed flower arranging, cookery, crafts, public speaking, choral speaking and a kitchen band, amongst other activities. Mostly we had members who had the skills to train us or one of us knew someone who would. In time I found myself serving as secretary or president; posts I held and enjoyed for many years as I could always rely on help and co-operation from members and so the work-load was shared between us. On request, two fellow members kept me fairly straight — one with the rules and the other with our own customs, so hopefully I did not often put my foot in it! Delegates were found to attend Group and Council Meetings and the A.G.Ms.

We played whist with patients at Pool Park Hospital, and entertained some of their residents at a Christmas party in the Village Hall each year. There was also Sports Day for the village school and tea with ice cream to follow for the children.

Our W.I. had a trip in the summer, when husbands and friends could

Mr and Mrs Stephenson.

Mary and Vic Stephenson at their first farm, in prescot, 1941.

Vic working with his horses at Tan Llan.

join us. At our own Christmas party in the Hall members would prepare the room, bring and serve the food, and clear away afterwards for games which often proved hilarious.

We had our own fund-raising efforts and occasionally one for charity; one massive one I remember was for the 'Save the Children Fund'. A sale of work was held, followed in the evening by a social for the younger ones and a big raffle; it was a financial success but physically exhausting. They were busy years, fitting in jobs on the farm, family commitments, helping with a social car service in the village and general involvement in the community.

When my husband died in 1991 I moved to Caerwys to be near Carole and for a while I still came to W.I. meetings in Clocaenog, but the travelling became too much for me. I still miss Clocaenog but get regular reports from friends in the area.

I have deliberately omitted any names because so many people were kind, helpful, and welcoming to non-Welsh speakers like myself.

Carole:
I was seven when we moved to Tan Llan and one of my earliest memories is of the primary school in the village, where every lesson was taught in Welsh — including the English lesson! However, this did not present too much of a problem because at that age it is not difficult to acquire an understanding of another language. There were only two other English children at the school then, so I suspect we probably tended to stick together. Everyone was very kind and friendly and made us welcome. I used to walk the half-mile to and from school on my own each day, quite safely. At that time, one landmark event I remember was sweets finally coming off ration and they could be bought at one or other of the two shops — Tŷ Coch or the Post Office Stores.

We had no electricity for the first eight or nine years and we used paraffin and Tilley lamps for lighting, and Calor gas and the coal oven for cooking. The fire also heated the water, although bath day in the winter was something of an ordeal; I can remember many times when the ice formed on the insides of the windows and, if at all possible, dressing took place under the bedclothes. We did have an inside flush toilet, but the old *Tŷ Bach* with the wooden seat was still in existence outside.

Pa had always had horses on the farm and he managed to avoid tractors for some considerable time, even after everyone else became mechanised.

One of those little gems of childhood, which gives me pleasure to recall, is riding home from the field on a warm

Carole Stephenson.

Vic with the old plough

Tan Llan Farm sale, 1998.

summer's day on top of a load of hay, pulled by Prince clip-clopping down the lane — time seemed to stand still.

I always had a pony from being a toddler, and during the 1950s I would often disappear for hours on end, riding alone through the maze of forestry tracks around Pincyn Llys. I doubt if any child now would have the freedom to roam in the safety that I took for granted then. There was one memorable day when the pony somehow managed to end up in the kitchen, just as a neighbour knocked at the door. As Ma was unable to actually open the door because a small, fat pony was blocking her way, she shouted, 'Come in!' The poor chap entered, only to be faced with a small, fat pony's bottom. (I do believe that it was after that we acquired a slightly eccentric reputation locally.)

Threshing day was always something of an event, with huge amounts of food being prepared for all the helpers who would be coming from neighbouring farms. Ma had to make sure everything was up to standard, in case unfavourable comparisons were made.

Before the electricity arrived, Pa had to milk by hand and I remember great bowls of milk settling in the dairy. I would sneak in to run my finger over the edge of the cream, hoping that it wouldn't show, but I could never manage not to leave a wrinkly bit.

Pa always had a variety of livestock: cattle, horses, hens, sheep, cats, dogs and pigs of many colours. In the early days the pigs were fed mainly on swill which he used to collect from the hotels in bins, that were loaded into his old Morris van. This was wonderful stuff, often containing big joints of roast meat, almost intact. The cats and dogs also thrived on this diet. Some very nice china and cutlery used to emerge from the bins as well as the meat.

In the early days after moving to Tan Llan, there used to be mobile shops delivering bread, groceries and meat round the village and the outlying farms and houses. This service declined slowly over the years as more people acquired their own transport. I looked forward to the

Clocaenog W.I., 1967, with 48 members in attendance. Mary Stephenson was the President.

weekly shopping trip to Ruthin during school holidays. There were no supermarkets then, and Ma would hand over her shopping list to the brown coated gentleman at the Star, who would bustle round packing all the groceries into boxes for us to collect after the rest of the shopping in town had been attended to. Occasionally there was a major shopping trip to Wrexham, always coinciding with Wrexham Horse Sale on the first Thursday of each month. I would sometimes wangle a day off school to go with Ma and Pa.

After Pa died, Ma sold up and moved to a more manageable bungalow in Caerwys, but I still think about life on the farm in Clocaenog and occasionally take a nostalgic drive through the village and past my old home.*

* Sadly, Mary Stephenson has died. She was always ready to take part in W.I. or village activities and had a wonderful sense of humour, which made her good company for her many friends. She lived here in Clocaenog from 1952- 1991.

Edward William Davies
Glandŵr

My full name is Edward William Davies and I was born on the 4th April 1924. My father, Edward Henry Davies, came from Denbigh and he married Mary Davies, a girl from Bodfari, after meeting her in Colwyn Bay when he was delivering coal and she was in service there. They went to live on a smallholding in Sychdyn, then moved to Llandyrnog, and from there to Bryneglwys, then Llanrhaeadr. He was without farm work for a year from 1918 to 1919, when he took the tenancy of Pentre, Clocaenog which, in 1928, he bought, when Pool Park Estate was sold. My parents had four daughters Sarah Ellen, Annie Mary, Jen, and Catherine — all much older than me. My father always said that I was an afterthought!

Edward William Davies.

I was born on the farm at Pentre, on a day when my father was out in the field sowing seeds — in those days, he used a fiddle for this task. Sadly, I never knew my mother because she died when I was only 18-months old and my oldest sister, Sarah Ellen, who had planned to get married about that time, postponed the wedding for six months, eventually getting married when I was two. Her daughter was born nine months later and was just two years and nine months younger than me. After Sarah left home, I was brought up by Annie Mary, who later married and became well known to all the locals as Mrs. A. M. Jones. She taught in Clocaenog School until she married.

When I was young, times were hard and we never had a holiday. However, there were activities in the Church Hall including whist drives, concerts and 'village hops', with music supplied by records on a big radiogram. There were also Red Cross groups, and chapel drama groups which gave performances with the children watching from the gallery at the back.

My sisters used to make bread in the old brick oven which was beehive-shaped inside, and whitewashed outside. A fire was lit inside the oven, then, when hot enough, it was raked out and the bread put in — *bara brith* and rice pudding too, sometimes. When baked, the loaves would be left to cool on the old stone table in the back kitchen. I remember one day when Goodwin, a foreman in the Forestry, came to the house and he and I made quite a hole in one of the loaves by picking at it while everybody was talking. Then one of my sisters noticed what was going on and shouted 'You're just like a mouse!' and I got the biggest clout I ever had. But it was worth it; it tasted good, you know! After my sisters all left home and there was no woman in the house, we used to be able to buy a really big loaf from the village shop — that big and that wide — for only nine pence. My father and I were on our own from 1934 to 1945 and, during that time, one or other of my sisters would come to clean and wash for us. Sadly, my sister, Jane, became a widow in 1943 and

Ted Davies, photographed in the early 1950s.

eventually she returned to Pentre with her children.

We had horses and stables up at Pentre; my father bought his first tractor in 1948, but we still had a horse for a few years to do crop work, mostly, growing nearly all the fodder for our animals: hay, corn, swedes, potatoes — we were self-sufficient, you see, although we had to buy in things like tea and sugar. My father went to Ruthin Auction on a Friday in 1943 and bought a 1933 Morris Cowley, but the damned thing kept breaking down; in the end, he shoved it in the hollow with the rest of the rubbish where it lay until 1970 when it was sold for restoration. In the summer of 1999, I went to the Malpas Vintage Rally with Matt from the Old Post Office across the road. We were looking at a tiny vintage car when I looked round and saw, to my amazement, my dad's old car DM8297!

We had a wheelwright in the village — old Dafydd Hughes — who lived at Bryn Fedwen (just over the little hump-backed bridge by Paradwys) with his son, David, who used to come to Pentre to mend the cart. Although David used to stutter really badly, he could sing marvellously in chapel. There was also a blacksmith in Clocaenog but I always used the one at Pandy in Bontuchel, which has now transferred to a big shed further up the hill. Sadly, the old smithy at Bontuchel has not been preserved.

I was educated at the village school until I was eleven. The headmaster then was Llewelyn Roberts and the teachers were Miss Wyn and Miss Telford. My sister, Annie Mary, had married in 1928 so I didn't have her teaching me. I think we also had a Mr. Savage, from Denbigh, and Raymond Edwards of Rhos (who eventually ended up as the Principal in the College of Drama in Cardiff), and there were various other teachers. Even Eryl Frances from the Old Post Office taught me for one day when the schoolmaster was missing — we are still in touch.

There was a blackboard in the school where they used to chalk up the number of pupils present in school each day, and I remember seeing 80 on the board one day. Don't forget, of course, that most of the children were there until they were 14 as there were only two or three pupils a year who managed to pass the scholarship for grammar school. The fourteen year olds looked like big, grown-up men to a child of five!

I used to play with my friends in school but, living on a remote farm, I didn't have many friends to play with at other times. At school, we played ring-a-ring-o'-roses and tag, or we made long snakes of children by hanging onto the collar of the one in front, going round the playground and through the gate in a long line. We used to go into Ty'n Celyn field to play hide and seek — it was a good place to hide when the grass grew taller than our heads — or we would play fox and hounds there; some of us were foxes, some were hounds and we would hunt for hours! Sometimes, when we were particularly energetic, we would walk up to Pincyn Llys and back during our dinner hour. A hell of a rush! We would hear the first bell and knew it was a quarter to one. Then we had to run to get back for one o'clock because, if we were late, we were frog-marched into the school and given the ruler across our hands — I had it many a time. Oh! it was painful! Sometimes, you were clouted as well. There were also bells at a quarter to nine in the morning and another at nine, and you were late if the second bell had stopped ringing. The bell was of polished brass and hung from the tower above the school — a shame it was taken down.

Childhood illnesses were often serious in those days. At the age of six, Will and his twin sister, from Fron, had diptheria — Will's hearing was badly affected and his sister died. My wife, Alwen, also had diphtheria as a child and she developed a mastoid infection. Later, at Brynhyfryd School, I remember an old woman who used to come and lecture to us on T.B. — she called it 'consumption'. Her English had a marked Welsh accent and I can see her now, holding a small, screw-capped bottle, saying, "When you spit, you spit in the bottle'; she demonstrated this and we all had a job to keep straight faces.

Ted Davies with his father.

The thing which stands out in my memory from this time is the Gresford Colliery disaster. I remember the headmaster reading the news to us from the *Daily Post* (a big broadsheet newspaper in those days) — the date was 22 September, 1934. I was ten years old then. In that year, I was one of the pupils selected to take the scholarship exam for Denbigh County School for Boys; I passed, but, sadly, some failed. Ceinwen Roberts passed the scholarship the same year, and so did Eifion Wyn from Clawddnewydd.

While I was at Denbigh County School there were two important public proclamations in the same year. The whole school went up to hear the Town Clerk, in all his livery, read out the proclamation of Edward VIII's accession to the throne from the balcony of Denbigh Town Hall; he was accompanied by the High Sheriff and other dignitaries. Then, when the king abdicated in the following December, we were all marched up there again for the proclamation of King George VI's accession.

A special occasion in Clocaenog was the celebration of the Silver Jubilee of George V in 1935. By this time, Thompson Davies had collected money from the locals to pay for the conversion of the old barn, shippon and hayloft (belonging to the Old Rectory) into a hall for the use of the village, and this was the first event I ever attended there — we had games and balloons in the grounds and tea in the hall. Then, in May 1937, we had a Coronation party in the church hall with a big tea and sports on Ty'n y Celyn field; we also played quoits using old horseshoes hammered into rings by the local blacksmith. That evening, I remember going to Ruthin Square and listening to the radio broadcast by King George VI, with his stammer, saying 'The Queen and I'. Of course, there were two jubilees in my father's lifetime — he was born in 1877, and Queen Victoria, having come to the throne in 1837, had her Golden Jubilee in 1887 and her Diamond Jubilee in 1897. I remember hearing him talk about them.

In 1938, 'dualisation' occurred — a big word in education then — and we boys were moved from Denbigh County School to Bryn Hyfryd Girls' School in Ruthin. For boys and girls to be mixed was a big change, I can tell you. I never planned to be a farmer when I was at school because my strongest point was always science and I wanted to be a doctor, but my father was ill at the time so I had to do all the milking before going to school and when I returned home. I've always been lucky, with a very good memory, and, although I had to leave school at the beginning of the war, I managed to pass my School Certificate in eight subjects, some with credit or commended. I've still got the framed certificate hanging on my sitting room wall.

When war was declared, the village had its share of evacuees, mostly from Liverpool. They had a separate school in the village hall with their own teachers who lodged with Mrs. Yates at Braeburn on the road to Clawddnewydd. The present Stryt Cottage was three dwellings at that time and I remember Peter Ball who was billetted with old Mrs. Jones in the top cottage. One Sunday, Malcolm, another evacuee, and I were on the wall by Glan yr Afon doing nothing much — it was a Sunday — when this car came along, stopped and out got a padre with his dog collar and uniform. He was a big, hefty fellow who spoke Welsh and gave us a terrific lecture, telling us we should be in Sunday School, not outside. Anyway, he wanted to know the way to Cyffylliog. For a long time after that, we kept away from the road at that time of day on a Sunday. Then we forgot, and one Sunday we were by Glan yr Afon again and along came another padre. He also wanted to know how to get to Cyffylliog but, as he was one of the Free French Forces, he didn't speak a word of Welsh or English. Eventually, we managed to explain in our schoolboy French. I don't know if he ever got there!

Of course, we had rationing during the war (and for a few years afterwards) but it didn't affect us as much on the farms as it did other people we had eggs and other produce of our own, so we never went hungry. We used to have one or two pigs killed at the farm each year for our own use, and the others were taken in to Ruthin market by horse and cart; cattle and sheep had to be walked to the market and, if they were not sold, we had to walk them all back again. We did that on more than one occasion, but this became too dangerous after 1952 when the traffic began to build up.

Before 1954, when myxomatosis was introduced to this country, rabbits were a plague to the farmer (they would eat up to 20 yards of corn from the field edges and spoil even more) but they were also a valuable source of food and were called 'the poor man's chicken' in those days. There was some shooting, but we used snares and ferrets to catch rabbits and, during the war, we earned pocket money by selling them to a bloke from Widnes for half a crown a couple. This man was originally from round here until he married and went to live in Widnes where he was employed in the copper works. He had two sons and a daughter who, with their mother, all contracted tuberculosis and died, after which he returned to work in Pentre with my father as he had worked on farms as a young man. It was this man who, finding a rabbit killed by a stoat (the stoat leaves a big hole in the neck where it sucks out the blood), just sewed up the hole saying, 'it'll do all right for them folks in Lancashire'.

There was a searchlight camp on one of Bryngwyn's fields and one in Cyffylliog; the soldiers used to race in pick-ups from one to the other and very dangerous they were, to be quite honest. One night, John William Jones and I were walking up to Clawdd past the searchlight camp when the big generator was switched on and, all of a sudden, this blooming searchlight shone across the ground into our eyes. Everything went purple, not black, and we thought we had been blinded, so we hid in the hedge until we could see again and then we saw a plane caught in the beam of the searchlight just over Bryn Coch. We used to steer clear of the searchlight after that and always walked to Clawdd the long way round, using the lane between the Old Post Office and Bryn Ffynnon and walking along the main road. There used to be a holiday camp (for children from Merseyside) where the forestry houses now stand just beyond Clawddnewydd on the road towards Cerrig y Drudion. The buildings were bombed one night and had to be evacuated. Later, the site became HMS *Indefatigable*, a naval training base, and Joe, the brother of Mrs. Jones, Brynfedwyn, was the cook there until he went into the army.

For several years, No. 49 P.O.W. Camp was sited on Pool Park land, initially for prisoners of war and, after the war, for displaced persons from Europe. The camp consisted of Nissen huts and the old foundations can still be seen from the main Ruthin to Clawddnewydd road. The German and Italian prisoners did farm work and helped us out at Pentre from time to time — but not on a regular basis as they did on some farms. We would ask for help with jobs like the harvest and lifting swedes, and we found that the Italians, who were the first to be repatriated, were a more volatile lot than the Germans. I remember one big chap, a German, helping us at Pentre just before he was repatriated. He kept asking us for coupons because he wanted to buy stockings for 'Mary' and it took us a long time to twig that he didn't know the English for 'wife', calling all women 'Mary'. Then we gave him some clothing coupons and he was able to take the precious stockings home to his wife. There were others who spoke English very well.

Later, in 1949, when the camp was filled with displaced persons, we had four Poles helping us; at another time, we had Ukrainians and Lithuanians helping to lift swedes. None of them had trimmed swedes before and one of the men cut one finger every day — he was in a state, I can tell you! He was only there four days and he cut four fingers and, if he'd been there a week, he'd have cut his hand off! So we had a lot of nationalities going through Clocaenog at that time. The camp closed down in about 1950. Some of those who remained went to an old RAF camp in Caernarfon, before eventually returning to Europe, but others stayed and settled in Caernarfonshire, many of them marrying Welsh girls. They must be getting old now, but their children have grown up here in Wales.

Eventually, I took over the farm when I grew up and married Alwen Jones, from Bontuchel, in 1952 at Pendref Chapel, Ruthin, and our three children were born at Pentre. Mary was born in 1952, married Peter Newcombe in 1973 and they have three children; at present, Mary and her

Ted's wife, Alwen, playing the harp to accompany her grandaughter.

Lee's Holiday Camp for children from Liverpool which, in 1940–2, became a naval cadet training camp known as HMS Indefatigable. When the cadets were moved to a ship on the Menai Strait, the camp reverted to being a children's camp. [DRO, Ruthin]

husband are living in Erw Goch, Ruthin, but are planning to build a house in Clocaenog in the near future. Our second daughter, Myfanwy May, was born in 1954; she married Terence Moore in 1973 and they have lived in Leeswood (Coed Llai) ever since, but now their three children have grown up they have bought a plot in Connah's Quay and plan to build there. Henry, our youngest, was born in 1959 and has lived in Buckley since marrying Avril Jones and they now have four daughters. Sadly, my wife, Alwen, has recently suffered a series of strokes and is now being cared for at Awelon in Ruthin.

It is interesting to note that Alwen's grandmother had seven children from her first marriage, then, after her husband's death, she married his brother and had another seven offspring. Of these fourteen children, thirteen lived to become adults — and that was around the end of the nineteenth century. Not all families were so fortunate — there were a lot of young members of one family from Cruglas, Cyffylliog (about half a dozen of them) who were all buried in Clocaenog Church cemetery under a blue slate gravestone near the yew tree on the Tŷ Coch side of the churchyard.

In 1952, I was Clerk of the Parish Council and was involved, with Gwyn Williams, the school headmaster, in preparations for the Coronation celebrations. I was still clerk at the time of the Investiture of the Prince of Wales in 1969, when the children of Clocaenog School were given commemorative mugs. By 1977, the time of the Silver Jubilee, I had become Chairman of the Community Council and also a District Councillor for Glyndŵr. There were celebrations in the church hall, and Clocaenog W.I. provided food for the children in the afternoon; Clawddnewydd W.I. (now defunct) provided food for the adults in the evening. There were no village celebrations for the Golden Jubilee of Queen Elizabeth II in 2002.

The first chapel to close here was the Calvinist Chapel on the first Sunday in 1974 and the Wesleyan Chapel closed in the early 1990s. I was asked to go to the chapel in Bontuchel but decided to attend the church here to help keep it going.

My father always used to say, 'There's been a hell of a lot of change in my lifetime', but I think there has been even more in mine. With change accelerating all the time, I think it is important that future generations should be aware of the past.

Glandŵr

This property, built prior to 1841, is situated by a stream in the centre of the village opposite the school. Adjacent to Glandŵr, on the road leading up to the parish church, was once a row of eight cottages (belonging to the owner of Glandŵr) but only part of the original buildings remain; these were eventually sold and now form Stryt Cottage which has been renovated and modernised over the years.

It is recorded in the 1891 Census for the Parish of Clocaenog that Robert Williams, a stockman from Cyffylliog, and his wife, Catherine, born in the county of Meirioneth, occupied Glandŵr. Also living in the house at that time were Maggie Williams, John Williams, William (infant) and William Jones who was retired. Catherine Williams farmed the meadows

Edward Henry Davies, Ted's father in the 1950s.

Glandŵr.

adjoining Glandŵr and, at one time, a field behind the former Post Office and Wesleyan Chapel formed part of the Glandŵr holding but, in later years, was in the possession of the owners of Ty'n y Celyn Farm.

In 1919, a group of Canadian workers were felling trees in the forest near Llyg y Fynydd and the timber was stacked on Glandŵr fields before being transported to Ruthin by horsepower; this was supervised by Scotsmen who stayed at Pentre Clocaenog, sleeping in the servants' bedroom which had separate access from the farmyard.

When Pool Park Estate was sold in 1928, 3.25 acres of land, described as a suitable building site and known as Erin Cochion Crofts, was bought by the owner of Glandŵr. In 1934, two council houses were built on a portion of this land and were rented out to local residents, and the bungalow known as Isfryn was also constructed nearby. In 1950, another piece of land was sold to the local authority and work commenced on building a row of Council Houses, again for letting to local people.

Further residential development of Glandŵr land has taken place in recent years, including five houses which form Erw Lâs, and, at the time of writing, three plots behind Erw Lâs have been granted planning permission and the buildings are in various stages of construction.

Gwyneth Roberts
Childhood Days

Mrs Gwyneth Roberts.

I was born in 1938 and brought up at Fferm, Llanfwrog near Ruthin, until the age of seven. Then, in 1945, following the death of my father two years previously, I went with my mother, two brothers and a sister, to live at Pentre Farm, Clocaenog, where my grandfather and Uncle Ted (Davies) farmed about 128 acres. I was already used to farm life and animals so there was little change in my pattern of living. There was no mains water or electricity on the farm and we carried water from the well at the bottom of the garden; water for washing clothes was brought from the brook to boil in the cast iron kettle that hung over the blazing fire in the black-leaded grate. On one side of the grate was an oven, on the other a boiler for heating more water, and an iron fender surrounded the hearth. Between the fire and the fender stood a polished iron stool which was used to support the big black kettle when it was taken from the fire to fill the teapot. The smoothing iron was heated in front of the fire and the ironed clothes were placed to air on a long clothes line which was hanging from the kitchen ceiling above the hearth.

It was a mixed farm: cows for milking, bullocks for fattening, sows and piglets, sheep and lambs, a dog and several cats to catch the mice. The cows were milked twice a day, and most of the milk was poured into a ten gallon container to be taken for processing at the factory. From the milk kept for use in the house we used cream to make butter and the skimmed milk was fed to the pigs and calves. On churning days, I remember turning the butter churn handle for a long time before the butter separated, ready to be shaped and weighed, and the family drank the buttermilk.

As there were not many modern conveniences, we children had to help around the house by carrying water, washing dishes, dusting the furniture, washing the floor and gathering firewood to light the fire each morning. I always liked collecting the eggs and was in my element, standing with my mother to watch chicks hatching. Sometimes, when the men were busy with the harvest, we had to fetch the cows in from the field and then take them back again from the yard after milking. We also helped in the hay fields by loading hay onto the cart and leading the horse back to the shed, loft or haystack — a slow process. We had three horses, Cymro, Capten and Prince and in hot weather, when the horses were sweating, we would use them in rotation to give each of them a rest in the stable.

Threshing day was so busy that the threshing machine had to be placed in position the previous night, ready for a punctual start in the morning when ten to twelve men from neighbouring farms would arrive to help. I remember I would see the occasional rat fleeing from the shed where it had been hiding and eating its fill for weeks. This was also a busy time for the farmer's wife as she needed to prepare food for everyone — roast beef with vegetables, rice pudding and apple tart was the usual fare for dinner and, at tea time, there would be plenty of bread and butter with jam, *bara brith* and cakes, all washed down with cups of tea.

Pentre Farm had a water mill which was used to grind corn and chop turnips and straw which was fed to the cows and bullocks. One or two pigs would be fattened each year to feed the family: after the butcher had salted it well, the meat would be put on a hook and hung from a beam in the kitchen ceiling ready to be sliced and cooked nearly every day.

I attended school in Clocaenog for about four years, walking the mile to and from home each day and it was a very happy time: I made friends, had a good education and enjoyed school dinners prepared for us in the Church Hall. I passed the scholarship examination at the age of eleven and went on to Brynhyfryd School, Ruthin, travelling by Crosville bus which picked us up by the village school at 7.50 a.m. and brought us back by 4.30 p.m. in the afternoon. Some mornings, I was too late to catch the bus in the village so would run like lightning up Allt Helyg to Brynffynon to meet the bus after it had been to the Tollbar to collect the Llanfihangel children who were brought to that point by taxi. At Brynhyfryd, I studied a broad range of subjects with increasing amounts of homework which resulted in my leather satchel becoming heavier each term.

On Sundays I attended Cades Chapel where I had good teaching in Sunday School and sometimes also went to a prayer or fellowship meeting. Everyone was very faithful to that little chapel.

Our lives were very busy, but we also had time to play, and I especially enjoyed going to the top of Pincyn Llys to look at the wonderful scenery. Rosehips were picked and sold to raise money for books for Clocaenog School, and we collected mushrooms, blackberries and nuts which we dried for Christmas. We also set snares to catch rabbits. After finishing our homework we played games like Snakes and Ladders and Ludo, doing jigsaws, or reading books and comics, and I remember learning to ride a bike, having a few falls before mastering the skill and gaining confidence. The Church Hall was the venue for many social events: the junior school Christmas Concert, a very successful eisteddfod, and a number of concerts and performances by the local drama group which played to packed audiences.

I spent eight happy years in Clocaenog and found it a very friendly place with the majority of people taking an interest in each other's activities and ready to help whenever needed.

G.R.*

* Gwyneth now lives with her husband in Galltegfa, Ruthin.

Gwyneth Roberts
Dyddiau Plentyndod

Cael fy ngeni a'm magu nes yn saith oed yn Y Fferm, Llanfwrog ger Rhuthun ac yna yn y flwyddyn 1945, ar ol marw fy nhad dwy flynedd yn gynt, symud gyda fy mam, dau frawd a fy chwaer, i fyw i Pentre Clocaenog lle yr oedd fy nhaid a'm ewythr yn ffermio rhyw

Pentre Farm, 2004.

Amser i segura ger y Tan yn yr hwyr. Mam ar y chwith, yn gweu hosanau ar bedair gweillen, Taid ar y dde. Ted Davies yn pocio'r tan.
Time to relax by the fire in the evening. Mother is on the left, knitting socks on four needles and Grandfather Davies on the right. Ted Davies pokes the fire.

128 erw o dir. Yr oeddwn eisioes wedi arfer gyda bywyd gwledig ac amaethyddol ac felly nid oedd dim newid yn y patrwm o fyw ar fferm a bod ymysg yr anifeiliaid. Nid oedd dŵr na thrydan yn y tŷ nac yn adeiladau y fferm; cario dŵr o'r ffynnon yng ngwaelod yr ardd i'w yfed a'i ferwi yn y tecell haearn bwrw oedd yn crogi uwchben tanllwyth o dân yn y grât ddu, gyda popty i goginio ar un ochor a berwedydd dŵr yr ochor arall gyda ffendar a stôl haearn o flaen y tân ar yr aelwyd. Dŵr o'r pistyll a ddefnyddiwyd i olchi dillad. Lampau olew a canhwyllau oedd yn goleuo y tŷ gyda'r nos ac yr oedd lampau pwrpasol i fynd allan ar y buarth ac i'r adeiladau. Llechi glas oedd lloriau y rhan fwyaf or ystafelloedd i lawr y grisiau, ac hefyd byddai byrddau a meinciau wedi eu gwneud o lechen yn y bwtri i gadw bwyd yn oer. Yn hongian o'r nenfwd yn y gegin, uwchben yr aelwyd, yr oedd lein ddillad reit helaeth ac ar hon y byddai y dillad yn gorffen sychu yn iawn ar ôl cael eu smwddio cyn y byddent yn barod yw gwisgo; haearn smwddio wedi ei gynhesu yn y tân agored a ddefnyddid yn y cyfnod yma.

Ffermio cymysg oedd yma, godro gwartheg, pesgi bustych i gynhyrchu cig, hychod yn magu moch; defaid ac wyn; ieir, cywion a gwyddau, ci ac amryw o gathod o gwmpas i ddal llygod. Byddai'r gwartheg yn cael eu godro ddwy waith y dydd a'r llaeth yn cael ei anfon i'r ffatri mewn cansen deg galwyn a'r lori yn galw amdano bob dydd, ond yr oedd peth o'r llaeth yn cael el gadw i'w ddefnyddio yn y tŷ, ac yr oedd angen cadw hufen i wneud ymenyn a byddai y sgim yn cael ei fwydo i'r moch a'r lloi. Cofio yn iawn gorfod troi y fuddai am amser maith cyn y byddai y menyn yn barod iw drin ar ddiwrnod y corddi, ac wedi tynnu y menyn allan beth fyddai yn weddill oedd llaeth enwyn a byddai hwn yn cael ei yfed gan y teulu. Gan nad oedd llawer o gyfleusterau a darpariaethau wrth law yr oedd yn angenrheidiol i ni blant helpu o gwmpas y tŷ gan olchi llestri, cario dŵr, hel coed tan i gynnau y tan yn y bore, tynnu llwch oddiar y dodrefn a golchi llawr. Gorchwyl arall oedd hel wyau a byddwn wrth fy modd yn mynd gyda fy mam i weld cywion bach yn deor o'r wyau. Ambell dro rhaid oedd nol y gwartheg godro o'r caeau ac yna eu danfon yn ôl wedi iddynt gael eu gollwng o'r beudy; digwyddai hyn pan fyddai y dynion yn brysur yn y caeau gyda'r cynhaeaf. Byddem yn helpu yn y caeau gwair hefyd a proses araf oedd hon cario gwair rhydd gyda trol a ceffyl a'i ddadlwytho i'r sied, y daflod neu gwneud tas wair. Os oedd y tywydd yn boeth byddai y ceffylau yn chwysu a rhaid oedd newid am yr un yn y stabal er mwyn i'r llall gael gorffwys, yr oedd tri ceffyl ar gael, Cymro, Capten a Prince. Diwrnod dyrnu yr ŷd oedd yn amser prysur iawn a'r injian yn cael ei gosod yn barod y noson cynt er mwyn cael cychwyn yn brydlon y bore canlynol ac ar y diwrnod yma byddai y ffermwyr lleol yn cyfnewid llafur er mwyn cael digon o ddynion i wneud y gwahanol ddyletswyddau, tua

Hen offer gwneud ymenyn, cynnwys noe, scimar llefrith, gwasgwgr llaethenwyn, pat siapio ymenyn, bwlen uwd, goblet llaethenwyn.
Some old farm wooden butter-making equipment, including a settling bowl, cream skimmers, whey squeezers and butter pats, a porridge bowl and a buttermilk goblet.

Mam Gwyneth, Jane, yn paratoi swper wrth olau canwyll. Sylwch ar y hamiau cig moch yn hongian uwchben ar y trawstiau.
Gwyneth's mother, Jane, prepares supper by candle-light. Notice the hams hanging above her head.

deg neu ddeuddeg o ddwylo oedd eisiau. Yn ystod y dyrnu byddai ambell i lygoden fawr yn ceisio ffoi o'r sied wedi bod yn llechu ac yn bwydo yno am rai wythnosau. Yr oedd hwn yn ddiwrnod prysur i wraig y tŷ hefyd gan fod eisiau paratoi bwyd a golchi llestri; cig eidion a llysiau a pwdin reis a cacen afalau i ddilyn fyddent yn gael fel arfer i ginio ac amser té yr oedd digon o fara ymenyn a jam, bara brith a cacen ar gael gyda paned o de. Yr oedd olwyn ddŵr yn y Pentre a defnyddwyd hon i weithio peiriannau i falu blawd, maip a gwellt a hwy oedd porthiant y gwartheg godro a'r bustych. Byddai un neu ddau mochyn yn cael ei besgi ai ladd bob blwyddyn i fwydo y teulu, ac wedi iddo gael ei halltu yn iawn gan y cigydd, byddai y cig yn cael ei roi ar fach a'i grogi oddiwrth drawst y nenfwd yn y gegin i'w ddefnyddio bron bob dydd.

Mynd i'r ysgol fel pob plentyn arall, a cherdded tua militir i fynychu ysgol gynradd Clocaenog am tua pedair blynedd. Cael amser hapus iawn yno gan wneud ffrindiau a cael addysg da iawn yno ac hefyd mwynhau cael cinio wedi el baratoi yn Neuadd yr Eglwys. Eistedd y 'Scholarship' pan yn unarddeg oed a symud ymlaen i ysgol Brynhyfryd Rhuthun. Cyfarfod bws Crosville yn y llan am ddeg munud i wyth y bore, a cael ei gollwng yn nhref Rhuthun a cerdded yn ôl ac ymlaen i'r ysgol, a cyfarfod y bws am hanner awr wedi pedwar y prynhawn in cludo yn ôl i Clocaenog. Rhy hwyr i gael y bws ambell fore a rhaid oedd rhedeg nerth fy nghoesau i fyny Allt Helyg at Brynffynnon i gyfarfod y bws wedi iddo fod yn y 'Tollbar' yn nôl plant Llanfihangel oedd yn cael eu danfon yno gyda tacsi. Cael gwersi eangach wedi symud o'r ysgol fach, a digon o waith cartref gyda'r nos a'r bag lledr oeddwn yn gario ar fy ysgwydd yn mynd yn drymach bob tymor.

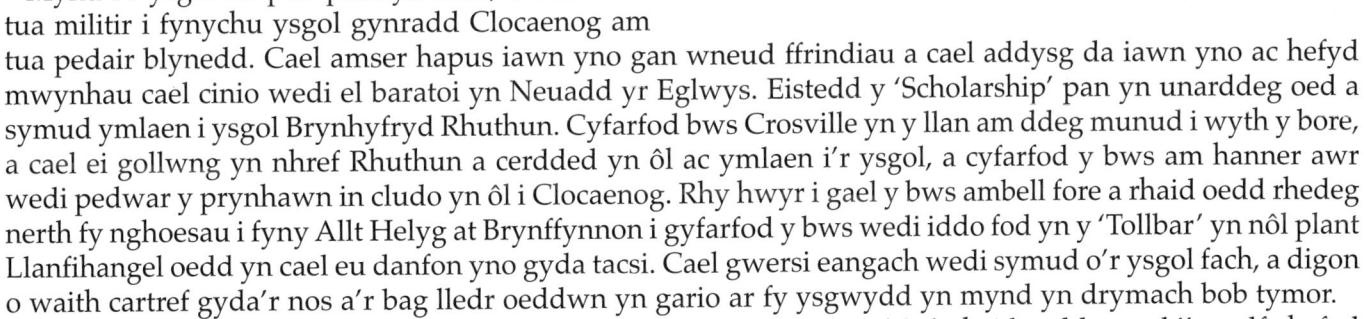

Mynd i Capel Cades ar y Sul a cael hyfforddiant da iawn yn yr Ysgol Sul, rhaid oedd mynd i'r oedfa hefyd ac ambell waith i'r cyfarfod gweddi a'r seiat. Yr oedd pawb yn ffyddlon iawn i'r capel bach yma.

Cael amser i chwarae hefyd, a pleser mawr oedd cael mynd i ben Pincyn Llys i weld yr olygfa ardderchog, byddwn yn hel cnau a'i sychu i'w cadw at y Nadolig; hel madrach a mwyar duon, gosod maglau i ddal cwningod a hel 'rosehips' i fynd i'r ysgol gynradd i'w gwerthu a'r arian yn cael el ddefnyddio i brynu llyfrau i'r ysgol. Cofio dysgu reidio beic a chael ambell godwm cyn i mi fedru meistroli y grefft yn iawn a chael digon o hyder. Ar ôl gwneud gwaith cartref yr ysgol gyda'r nos, chwarae gemau megis Snakes & Ladders, Ludo a rhai eraill, neu gwneud 'jigsaw' a darllen comics a llyfrau eraill reit ddiddorol. Cynhelid cyngerdd yr ysgol gynradd yn neuadd yr Eglwys bob blwyddyn

Amser swper yn ngolau'r lamp olew. Gwyneth yn tywallt te i John Roberts, ai brawd ieuengaf, Medwyn, ar y dde iddi.
Supper time and the paraffin lamp glows. Gwyneth pours the tea for the young John Roberts and her younger brother, Medwyn, is on her right.

ac yr wyf yn credu mai rhywbryd o gwmpas y Nadolig oedd hwn yn cymeryd lle. Byddai Eisteddfod lewyrchus iawn yn cael ei chynnal yn flynyddol ac ambell i gyngerdd ac yr oedd y cwmni drama lleol yn perfformio i gynulleidfa yn llenwi y neuadd.

Y mae yr rhaid i mi gyfaddef mai amser hapus iawn a dreuliais i am tua wyth mlynedd yn Clocaenog a'i chael yn ardal gymdeithasol iawn a'r mwyafrif yn cymeryd diddordeb yn gweithgarwch eu gilydd ac yn barod i roi cymorth pan fyddai angen ar rhywun.

G.R.

Roy Wilson and Edgar Moody
Min-y-Dŵr, Erw Las

Roy:

I was born on the 14th August 1925, at Rhos-on-Sea, but only lived there for six months before my parents moved to Littleover, near Derby, where we lived for the next seven years. My father had a gents' outfitters business there but, in 1930, the centre of the town was flooded and he lost a lot of money because most of his valuable stock was kept in the cellar. A flood was called 'an Act of God' for insurance purposes in those days, so he was unable to make a claim and never really recovered from this. He eventually had to sell up and we moved to Nottingham where Dad worked as a rep for my grandfather's millinery business. Before leaving Littleover, I attended a small private school in Derby and then transferred to a school in Nottingham. Being a sensitive only child, I always found it difficult to adjust to a place full of children and never cared much for school; I didn't experience any bullying or nasty teachers but, from beginning to end, I just didn't have a bent for it.

Edgar Moody and Roy Wilson.

Children used to pretend a great deal in those days and this came out in the games we played — dressing up, playacting, cowboys and Indians. In the school yard, there were games that children have always played: conkers, roller-skating and marbles, each in their season — I was never very good at marbles. By the time I went to the senior school, I had lost a lot of the shyness that had been a curse when I was younger and was able to quite enjoy my time there with my mates. Of course, things changed when the war came and we had to dig trenches in the school playing field. Games became more aggressive, copying the war and what was happening around us, playing at aeroplanes and avidly reading the newspapers, magazines and *Boys Own* which were all full of war stories — very different to our previous humdrum life before war was declared. It was a very exciting time for boys of that age and, as there was no television in those days, we still had to imagine the things we were listening to on the radio — inevitably, this was transferred to our games. However, living where we did, we were distant enough from the heavy bombing elsewhere to feel relatively safe.

I was 14 when the war started and continued at the Grammar School in Poulton-le-Fylde until I was 16 when I was supposed to continue my education at Rossall School. However, I found a way out of this when the Ministry of Pensions moved to Blackpool from London and my parents decided to sell their bungalow to one of the civil servants. My father was made a floor manager for the NAAFI and was sent to Saighton Camp, so we lived in nearby Chester. The war became more serious for us then, with air raids and bombing, although we didn't have any bad experiences ourselves and had quite a good sort of life. I loved dancing which I had started in Blackpool at the Tower Ballroom, the Palace and the Winter Gardens — there were always good bands playing and I had nice girl friends to take dancing which was quite the thing for teenagers then — we loved American music for dancing, with tangos and rumbas, all very different to today's raves!

I was called up into the army in October, 1943, gong first to Maryhill Barracks in Glasgow — a terrible place, now obliterated — where I did six weeks basic training which was pretty rough, gong into ex-cavalry barracks with no facilities, no heating and no hot water. I volunteered for the Royal Signals Regiment and was sent to Catterick Camp — equally chilly but I quite enjoyed life there — and was trained for signals work, teleprinting and wireless operation which was all an interesting way of getting a trade, not just playing with bayonets. Whilst training, signals developed into an obsession and, as we walked round Catterick, we would communicate with each other using semaphore signs and morse code. Tuition completed, we were sent to a camp in Epping where the sky was full of doodlebugs and, from there, back to Liverpool to embark on a boat for India and from there, eventually, to Burma, Singapore and Hong Kong.

After the war, I worked for Western Command with the Ministry of Defence doing communication work for them — most of my life has been spent in communications, except for one or two interludes when I got fed up and did something else for a change. Farming is in my blood as my great grandparents farmed in Derbyshire, at Wirksworth in the Bakewell area. For a while, I went into farm work in Willaston, Wirral, which I liked very much as I've always enjoyed country living, agricultural shows and anything to do with the countryside. Unfortunately, my old trouble returned when I developed asthma and hay fever due to handling straw, so I had to pack it in.

Whilst I was doing my signals training, I was called home urgently when my mother, who was a wonderful person and gave me a happy childhood, was seriously injured in a bus accident caused by the driver going to sleep at the wheel on Mostyn Hill and crashing into a lorry (probably due to having been up all the previous night in an air raid). Tragically, she suffered a brain injury from which she never really recovered, although she lived into her 80s. My father remained devoted to her whilst sheltering me as much as possible from the consequences of the accident, but I was always aware of what he was going through and wanted to help him — as a result, we spent a lot of time together after the war and shared many interests.

Hunting has always featured in my fife, having learned to ride a horse as a young child when visiting my grandparents who lived at Rhos-on-Sea. Grandma would give me sixpence to go for a ride and, although I had my leg pulled about it, riding always appealed to me. For presents, people used to give me jigsaws depicting hunting.

Being unmarried when I came out of the army after the war, I could follow my own interests and, after seeing an advert for a hunt in the *Chester Chronicle*, I decided to go and join it for the day. I cycled to that first meet which started early one morning at a farm in Parkgate (Wirral) and I really enjoyed it. As soon as I heard the cry of the hounds and saw the pageantry, I decided this was for me and, since then, I have ridden and followed the hunt on horse, bike, scooter and car. The hunt was an interest that my father eventually began to share with me.

Ed:
My parents were both German and I was born on the 8th March, 1943, in Hamburg, Germany, and lived there until I was eight. My only very early memories are of being in an air raid shelter and hearing bombers overhead. When I was four, a bomb fell just outside the air raid shelter, the door blew in, the shelter filled with smoke and I was badly affected by smoke inhalation. I was taken to hospital where my mother was told there was no hope and that she should leave me there to die — a traumatic experience for her. My mother immediately removed me from the hospital, hitched a lift with me down to the countryside further south and carefully nursed me back to health. I was a long time recovering (my mother, to this day, dislikes talking about that time).

My father was killed during the last month of the war, and my mother and I continued to live in Hamburg during the time Germany was occupied by Allied forces. My mother met an English soldier stationed across the road in the army fire service — the soldiers used to take the kids out for a ride on the fire engine sometimes and that is how she met him when I was four or five. They eventually married and my brother was born eighteen months later. Soon after that, we moved to Bad Oyenhausen Camp, 30 miles from Hamburg and, in 1951, my stepfather was moved back to Britain and we went to live in Chester.

I had started my schooling, at the age of seven, in the army school at Bad Oyenhausen because my mother wanted me to be taught in the medium of English, knowing that we would be going to live in Britain. I was already fluent in both English and German and would listen to the Forces Radio, but have now more or less lost the German because I haven't been back to Germany since 1956.

In my early years at school we played marbles, conkers and flicking cards — these were collected from bubble gum wrappers and cigarette packets. We didn't just exchange them — it was more like gambling with them — and if a flicked card covered somebody else's, you won that card. Roller skating was my big thing and, from the age of about 10, I played roller skating hockey with a tennis ball and cricket stumps and there would be about 30 of us with these metal-wheeled skates going up and down the street until the residents had had enough of the noise — it must have sounded like elephants going past. The street next to us was made of cobblestones so we had to go to the next one which was covered with tarmac and ideal for roller-skating.

When we first came to Cheshire, we lived at Hoole Bank (on the Helsby side of the city) which was very much part of the countryside in those days, and then to Hoole. I completed my primary education in Hoole and was then allowed to choose which secondary school I should attend and made a big mistake by picking the one nearest to home. Being rather shy and mentally a late developer (attributed to speaking German first and then having to switch to English), I always hated school and it took a long time for history, geography and maths to click. As far as I was concerned, the only good thing about it was the sports. I was in the school's athletic team, as a sprinter mainly, and I also swam for the school and played football for Chester Schoolboys Team. I won the Chester Schools' Gymnastics Championship in 1957 and, when I left school, played in the local football league, then had trials for Chester Football Club but didn't get in, which didn't really disappoint me because there was no money in football in those days. When I left school in 1958, at the age of 15, there was no provision at all for secondary modern school children to take exams to assess their level of education at the end of their schooling, so I took myself off to Chester College of Further Education and then night school where I was able to study and, with time, took five 'O' levels and, in the end, achieved two 'A' levels as well.

I remained interested in playing sport until my mid-twenties, particularly table tennis, football and tennis, but when 15-year olds start beating you, it's time to pack it in — but I still enjoy watching all sports. From the age of eight, I have always been passionate about motor-bikes, having seen the old army bikes, telegraph boys on two-stroke Bantams, and police bikes which were sold off when they'd finished with them and I had hopes of buying some day. I started off with an old Lambretta scooter when I was 19, graduating eventually, via various models, to a 500cc motor-bike. The most powerful bike I ever rode was 600cc. I would still love to own a motor-bike now, especially the new Triumph Range which has just come out — still dreaming at my age! Oddly, I love speed on a motor-bike but not in a car.

Throughout my life, one of my chief interests has been music and I once started to learn to play the mouth organ, then a guitar on which I learned to play about six chords (but could never tune it), then an autoharp — but that was even harder to tune — and now I've got a large keyboard upstairs on which I learned to play about four tunes before I got fed up with it. I'm absolutely hopeless with instruments but love music — I like almost anything except the heavy stuff and modern pop music.

Fishing was another interest of mine in my teens and twenties, mostly coarse fishing, but sometimes I went to Scotland for salmon fishing on the River Cree and the Palnure River which is one of its tributaries. I also did some trout fishing there and have also enjoyed fishing for trout at Trawsfynydd Lake which was a good fishery in years past.

Radios have always fascinated me and I used to build crystal sets and single valve radios and, being more practical than studious, would like to have taken up an apprenticeship in this field. However, instead, I've had a varied working career in offices, production companies, insurance and then, for 19 years, in the quarrying business where I eventually became Administration Manager for North Wales — an office job, really, but travelling from my base to the various quarries on certain days. Later I was less happy in my job after Redland Aggregates took over the business because I was then based in Llanarmon yn Iâl all the time.

I met Roy in Chester when he was living in a bedsit, but planning to move, and we decided to share a flat together — it was in a converted house with rising damp (we were on the ground floor) so we soon decided to buy a house at Pen-y-Ffordd and we've been together ever since — 25 years now.

I could never live in a town — even in Chester we lived on the outskirts — and I find big cities claustrophobic. I don't like flat countryside, either, and prefer mountains and hills around me. If I had my way, I'd move even further into the country than I am now. When we first came here, we had a Cavalier King

Charles spaniel, Jamie, a marvellous little dog, and everybody's friend. He was my fourth dog — and my last — because it's such a lot of upset when they go. I stick to fish now: goldfish in the garden pond and tropical fish in the aquarium.

Roy:
We've got on very well since we met because we are good friends and have many interests in common — for instance, we both like gardening and walking. At the time we met, I was working in Chester and Ed had lived there previously, so we are both Cestrians, really, and have many happy memories of it over the years. When we decided to move from our little semi-detached house in Pen-y-Ffordd, we started looking for a detached property out in the country and, after the purchase fell through of a new bungalow in Bryneglwys, we started to look in the Ruthin area and discovered there were five new houses being built in Clocaenog. We had heard of Clocaenog Forest but not the village, so when we arrived here and saw the two houses already built, and the situation, we knew we had found what we were looking for. We've always been pleased that the bungalow purchase fell through because this is a much more attractive area.

I love the country in all its seasons, but do like to see a bit of life around me. It's funny, really, because I'm the country bumpkin and Ed's the city one. But I need to have access to a small town, have a cup of coffee and watch the world go by, then retreat back into the country again. For me, that's ideal. So living in Clocaenog is a very acceptable compromise and provides us both with what we need. Although I can drive, Ed does most of the driving now and I'm just as happy as a passenger.

Ed:
I'm not a good passenger — you can see all the toothmarks on the dashboard when Roy drives and I'm in the other seat — and I can't have road rage as a passenger, either. When I get behind that wheel, everybody on the road is either a road hog or a useless driver.

Ed and Roy:
We both enjoy living here in the village; we like the people and have been very happy here for the past twelve years. The only thing that might cause problems would be if neither of us could drive for any reason, otherwise we hope to stay here until the end of our lives.

Irene and Bryn Lewis
8 Maes Caenog

Bryn:
My parents were Blodwen and Harry Lewis and I was born in Gwynfryn, Wrexham, on 20 February 1942, the last of seven boys, one of whom had already died. At that time, my parents had had seven children in ten years and my only sister, Morfydd was born three years later in 1945.

We all lived in Eisteddfod Farm, Gwynfryn, a two-bedroomed house and smallholding belonging to Minera Lime Works, where my father worked in the quarry, coming home after a full day's work to see to the animals and till the land on the smallholding. My parents' life was nothing but work, work all day long and, in the end, they had little to show for it other than successfully rearing seven children. My mother was a lovely lady but, even at the end, life was cruel to her because she developed Alzheimer's disease and died in 1993 at the age of 91. My father had died before her in 1978.

Mr & Mrs Lewis, Maes Caenog.

I was very young during the Second World War and my only memory of that time is when we were all in the wash house and a bomb landed 65 yards away from the house, making the door rattle — the hole is still in the field. On another occasion, incendiary bombs were used to set Minera Mountain on fire; this lit up the area and the locals thought the Germans were planning to drop more bombs on us, thinking there was a munitions factory in the lime works.

My parents had a massive garden — perhaps half-an-acre of land and my father used to dig it all over by hand each year, growing all the vegetables for the family with my mother's help. They had a horse to carry hay and other loads, and a few cattle and pigs which had to be let out twice a day to go to the river for water. My mother, who was never happy with animals, was always afraid of being kicked when she had to go between the cattle to release them — and she was terrified of the pigs.

One day before my sister was born, my parents went out on a Saturday afternoon and left us all at home. Father had bought a new pig that morning and the last thing he said before he went was: 'Don't let the pig out'. So what did we do? I was terrified of the pig and perched myself on top of the gate before my brothers let the pig out and it ran riot — it even went upstairs to the bedrooms! I can see that pig now, running past its hut with my brother reaching over to grab its ear to turn it into the sty. When Father came home he noticed the pig had one ear up and the other ear down. 'What's happened to the pig?' he asked. My brothers all had a good thrashing but I got away with it because I was so young.

Our parents were always very strict and, of course, the whole family attended Peniol Chapel three times every Sunday and I was supposed to learn my verses for Sunday school each week — everyone else knew them but I often failed to recite them correctly.

Quite close to the house, there were lead mine shafts which were so deep that if you dropped a stone down it took quite a while before it could be heard hitting the bottom. We used to chuck all our rubbish into one of these shafts which had only brambles and a bit of barbed wire round the top. One day, I wanted a wheel for something and, knowing there was one in the rubbish, I reached for it and slipped! I could feel myself sliding down and was hanging on for dear life, clutching at anything I could reach and screaming at the top of my voice. The lady from next door was passing on her way to the shop when she heard me and ran back to tell my mother who grabbed me by my hair and hauled me out. I was very lucky!

As we grew up, my brothers and I had to leave home and go to live and work somewhere else so, when I was 15, I went to work on a farm in Llanelidan, living in with the elderly farmer and his wife. I was taught to drive the tractor and shown how to do all the general farm work, planting potatoes and sowing the corn which was used to feed the animals. Each Saturday, after the morning milking, I cycled home with my case, full of dirty clothes, hanging from the handlebars. It was full of clean clothes when I returned to the farm later the same day and that was all the free time I was given as I had to be back in time to do the evening milking.

When the farmer and his wife retired, I moved to work for Iorwerth Jones at Pool Park Farm for seven years and that is when I met my real boss — the wife — at a folk dance in Pwllglas Village Hall. Although I couldn't dance, I went hoping to find her there and we were married on 3 July 1966, the day that the England Football team won the Cup.

Irene:

My parents were Glyn and Margaret Evans and I was born in Glasfryn, Llanelidan on 14 November 1946. Mam and Dad were then in their late thirties because, during the war, Mam was in the ATS and Dad was in the army, so I was a post-war baby, followed by my sister Gwenda, five years later. Dad worked as a foreman for the county council and Mam was a housewife but, before the war, she had been in service on the Wirral and worked in the post office at Llanelidan.

Elizabeth Edwards, my maternal grandmother (known as Nain within the family) also lived in Llanelidan and had lost her husband, William

Bryn Lewis demonstrating the seed fiddle which he used in 2004 to sow grass seed around the new approaches to Ty'n-y-Celyn — a very effective method. In the past, even large fields would be sown this way.

Edwards, in 1917 during the First World War (he was buried in France and nobody ever visited his grave until our son, Mark, went to France in 2001). She brought up their three children on her own — Margaret, Gwilym and Olwen. Olwen died in childbirth in 1945, the last year of the war, when she was only 29, and her son, Tudor, was also brought up by Nain (Olwen's older children were brought up by other relatives). Mam and Dad used to help Nain and, on the only family holiday we ever had, Tudor, then about five years old, came with us to a caravan site between Rhyl and Pensarn — I can see it now, all white caravans with a toilet block some distance away. When Tudor and I went to the lavatories together, we couldn't find our way back because all the caravans looked the same. We both ended up in tears and that is my only memory of the holiday — not the sea, not the sand, but being lost!

Nain's house was halfway between our house and Llanelidan School so I called there every morning on my way to school and she would insist on sewing a button on if one was missing, even though it meant I would be late for school. On the return journey she always gave me a 'butty' and then I went to the farm next door to collect the milk can which I had left there in the morning, carrying the fresh milk for over a mile up the steep hill to our house. I don't remember Mam ever taking me to school, even on the first day, when, if you were lucky, an older child would pick you up and off you went. We were never given any pocket money but were sometimes paid for gathering rose hips which were collected in bulk and then taken from the school to make rose hip syrup. We would also pick blackberries on the way home from school for Mam to make jam or bramble jelly.

My parents kept a pig and some hens and, because we lived right on the edge of the Naylor Leyland Estate, Sir Vivien's pheasants used to come into the garden to feed alongside our hens. When the family needed something for Sunday lunch, my father would shut our hens in their house, soak corn in rum to feed the pheasants then, when they became a bit drunk, he was able to catch a bird easily. I remember those pheasants hanging up behind the back door covered by some coats. My mother would pluck and clean the birds early in the morning and hurry to burn the evidence on the fire before the postman came by, ensuring that nobody would see any feathers come floating out of our chimney.

My primary education was completed in Llanelidan and I had already started secondary education at Brynhyfryd School when we moved to live in Dolafon, Pwllglas during my fourteenth year. After leaving school I decided to go in for nursing and worked as a cadet for nine months at the Royal Alexandra Hospital, Rhyl, before starting my State Registration training. When Bryn and I married I soon realised that, as far as my mother-in-law was concerned, there were no lads like hers, and none of her daughters-in-law were good enough for her boys! Something we all had to learn to live with. When I became pregnant with my first child, I had to give up my training and leave the Royal Alexandra Hospital so that was the end of that, but I have no regrets.

Irene and Bryn:
We married in July 1966, living in Rhuddlan for a short time before moving to Rhiwlas, Llanbedr (a tied house) where Mark was born in April 1967. We could have lived in Bryn's old home in Minera but decided against it because of the dangerous mineshafts close by (it is still standing, but has never been lived in since Bryn's family left). We put our names on the waiting list for a council house because we wanted our own home. A house in Clocaenog was the first to be offered and, as we already knew Beryl and Dennis Bailey (then living in Tŷ Capel), we accepted. We were expecting our second son, Philip, when we came to live in Clocaenog; he was born in December 1968 and our family was completed by Ian, born in June 1970 and Carol Anne in March 1973. During this period, Bryn was working for Jones Brothers, Ruthin, driving JCBs and tractors. After leaving there in 1977, he eventually got a job as a gardener at Pool Park Hospital, growing all the vegetables for the hospital, with any surplus being sold to Denbigh Hospital and some to Ysbyty Glan Clwyd. Pool Park was closed down in 1990 and since that time Bryn has done farm work, mainly for the Jones family (Ty'n y Celyn).

We had a lot of sadness towards the end of the 1970s. After losing her husband and rearing three children on her own, then bringing up her grandson, Irene's grandmother cared for her daughter, Margaret (Irene's mother) who suffered with rheumatoid arthritis. Nain was a wonderful old lady, and, unlike Bryn's mam, her mind was perfect to the end; she died in 1978 at the age of 94, when our daughter, Carol, was five years old. Irene's dad died soon afterwards in 1979 and her mam in 1981.

Our family has grown and we now have six grandchildren. Our oldest son, Mark, a joiner by trade, is building his own house on land just below Maes Caenog and will shortly return to live in Clocaenog with his wife, Alison, and their two children, Sian, 10, and Catrin, 7. Alison, who has worked for some time as an auxiliary at Ysbyty Glan Clwyd, has recently started training to qualify as a psychiatric nurse.

Philip works as a microbiologist in Ysbyty Glan Clwyd and his wife, Joanne, is a qualified nurse working in the cancer unit in the same hospital. They live in Prestatyn and have two children: Amy, 4, and Ben, 2.

Carol Anne and her husband, Arfon, have three year old twin boys, Jac and Tomos, and live in Rhewl. Carol Ann is a staff nurse in the cancer unit at Glan Clwyd, and Arfon works in Richard Williams, the builders' merchants in Ruthin.

Since Ian left school, he has been employed by E. Jones & Son, the civil engineering company based in Clawddnewydd, and now lives in Llanrhaeadr (between Ruthin and Denbigh).

Although the decision to live in Clocaenog was, in a way, made for us, we have had a good life here and we are fortunate because our children are all living in the area and we have frequent contact with our grandchildren.

David and Clair Craig
Cae Wgan

David:

I was born in Liverpool in 1946 and grew up in the sixties; two of my school mates were members of a certain well known four — and our sixth form 'lesson times' were occupied in the 'Cavern' listening to the Beatles rehearse. Most of my early and mid-teen holidays were spent in the small village of Aberdaron on the Llŷn Peninsula working in a guest house. I returned to Wales in 1976, this time to live, when I was appointed Lecturer in Educational Technology to the North-East Wales Institute (NEWI). I was based initially at the Kelsterton College site in Deeside but with some teaching at the Cartrefle site in Wrexham, on a range of full, part time and overseas teacher training courses.

The move to Cae Wgan was the result of a series of coincidences. Firstly my wife, Barbara, was born in Bersham and knew the north-east of Wales around the colleges quite well. The small villages she had known were expanding and had lost their originality. As we viewed one property after another in that hot summer of '76 we moved further and further inland. The second coincidence was that our building society surveyor (Ian Jackson), realising that we had already sold our house in Liverpool, asked if we would be interested in a smallholding just outside Ruthin. Being 'city born' I had no idea what a smallholding was, but we agreed to view the property, arranging the time of the visit so that Ian could tell his wife, Fran, of the possible sale, before we arrived. Our delight at the sight of Cae Wgan from the top of the drive instantly made the decision that here was our new home. The third coincidence was the fact that Barbara's grandparents had been born in Llanuwchllyn near Bala and therefore the move back into this part of Wales was, for Barbara, a return to her roots.

We came to Cae Wgan on December 6th 1976 with Jayne, our sixteen-month old daughter. Those first months passed in a blur as we adapted to living in the country. Heating needed to be sorted out, and we were looking after Ian's and Fran's Welsh cobs until they could take them to their new smallholding in Treuddyn, and finding the route to work, either at Kelsterton, Deeside or Cartrefle, Wrexham. With only one car it meant leaving the family without transport, but there were other priorities before a second car could be bought.

David and Clair Craig on their wedding day.

The family grapevine had been twitching and the arrival of Dic Morris from Bryn Pader heralded the family's inquisitiveness. Barbara's Uncle Dic was a friend to the Williams family of Llys and he knew many of the local farmers, as one would expect with the gatherings at the local stock auctions. His appraisal of Cae Wgan's land led to his suggesting a number of improvements. We decided to follow his ideas through and with the considerable help of Wyn Jones, Bryn Coch, we implemented these ideas over the next few years. This was my first introduction to the concept of a 'rural tomorrow', that is, that things would be completed in time, not rushed, nor put off like the Spanish mañana.

I feel some of my earlier agricultural attempts must have caused my neighbours considerable amusement: tacking the sheep netting on upside down, wearing gloves to protect my hands from the baler twine, never mind my efforts to lift a small bale and throw it up onto the trailer and the venture of planting six hundred 'christmas trees' in the long field, with the thought of selling them as they grew! This developed into giving a small number of them to friends and asking for a contribution to a named charity. The remainder have grown into a very tall, densely-packed forest — but a beautiful sanctuary for birds and other wild life.

The year of 1978 saw the birth of my son, Richard, one of the last babies in the area (another was Andrew Jones of Maes Draw) to be born in Ruthin Hospital. The early years of Jayne and Richard were spent with the added quality of growing up in the countryside, feeding pet lambs, making dens and hideaways — in the outbuildings, and hunting for Easter bunny eggs that were somehow found in the garden.

The main outbuilding to Cae Wgan was a ridged barn attached to a long shed, with various extra extensions added. After the Welsh cobs were gone, we tidied up the barn and exposed two inspection pits. Before Ian and Fran had used the barn for stables it had housed the local garage business run by Llew and Bessie Roberts. A number of humorous tales arose from this having been the local garage, firstly the inspection pits. After friends visited us one weekend, we decided to empty the central pit and, with considerable effort, we cleared it ready for use. When, in conversation with my neighbour, Wyn Jones, my comments on the nature and quantity of the infill by Ian Jackson caused him some embarrassment, which I failed to notice. It wasn't until months later that Wynne confessed to helping Llew fill in the pits to avoid competition with the new garage that Llew opened in the village. Gentlemen, both pits have since been refilled and sealed!

Two other tales linked with the now defunct garage concerned visits two years after we had moved in and were in the process of altering the house. I had taken to wearing overalls in the winter whilst working on the house. One Saturday afternoon a Land Rover came down the drive and the driver acknowledged me and asked to speak to the boss. Considering that only I allowed Barbara the title of 'boss', and then solely when a list of jobs was presented, I was somewhat concerned to hear this stranger asking for my wife. It wasn't until I curtly wanted to know his business that the realisation dawned on me that he was looking for Llew Roberts and thought I was one of the garage mechanics. He was redirected to the village, mouthing apologies for disturbing us. The second visit was a few weeks later when a lady drove down the drive followed by another car. The lady got out of the first car and, as she got into the other car, she called to me that her car was due for its MOT and she would pick it up later. Again a careful explanation that this was no longer a garage and a red faced driver quickly drove away, leaving me with the thought that, as it was six years since the garage was at Cae Wgan — do MOTs last that long?

In the early eighties I became a local councillor for Clocaenog and attended many meetings that enriched my knowledge of the community and of my fellow councillors and neighbours. I was fortunate to be elected Chairman of the council but with the appointment came

Cae Wgan as it looked c.1900.

the onerous task of leading the community to raise funds for the local hospital scanner appeal. The target at the time seemed enormous and the usual ways of raising the money seemed long drawn out. An idea emerged that was based on a rural theme and this idea proved most successful and a possible formula for future fundraising — the rural version of 'Its a Knockout` was born!

Taking what we had locally — hay bales, tarpaulins, goal-post netting, school sports equipment, lots of buckets and gallons of water, we devised team competitions against other teams from the area for a winning prize. Entries to the events were agreed and challenges sent out. The Jones family of Ty'n y Celyn generously lent their fields for the events, as well as giving a contribution to funds. The event took place and was a resounding success, not only passing the target for the scanner appeal, but leaving reserves for future fundraising and all in one evening! [David was the prime organiser of this super occasion].

The idea of a rural 'It's a Knockout' was only used twice again locally; the following year to raise funds for the Urdd Eisteddfod and secondly at Llysfasi Agricultural College to raise funds for the Young Farmers. The final performance using this idea was at a Young Farmers' competition at the Royal Welsh Show where mock cows carried milky water down a planned 'milk run', and where 'nain and taid' were pulled out of bed and everyone — bed included were moved through a three foot wide door to a new bedroom!

During all these events Jayne and Richard were growing up. Through attending the local village school in Clocaenog they both became bilingual and became involved in many local and regional projects as members of the Urdd. Richard was part of a successful team that won at the Merthyr Tydfil Eisteddfod and whose performance recorded by HTV is surely going to embarrass him when shown to future girl friends. The bilingual approach within Clocaenog school had an even greater effect as we ventured on holidays abroad. As any concerned parents, with children away from home, you keep a watch on what your children are doing and on numerous occasions I observed both Richard and Jayne attempting to speak in the language of the country where we were staying, by adapting their listening to the new language as they had done back in Clocaenog.

Time was passing and Barbara, now with her own car, returned to part time teaching of maths education at Cartrefle in Wrexham. My job in NEWI changed and the British Council sent me abroad as an educational consultant, firstly on two visits to Sudan and secondly on two trips to Zambia. Seeing the poverty in the Sudanese camps and the first hand experience of the impact of Aids brought home to me how privileged we really are, in our own small community in Wales, and the quality of our lives. The realisation of the beauty of our environment has been reinforced many times and Africa only served to increase my appreciation of the lush greenery of Wales.

In 1991 following a suggestion by Richard, who was now fourteen years old and a keen fisherman, we decided to do something about the natural streams which flowed through our land. The idea appealed to me because it was giving something back into the area which I hoped would add to its beauty. A proposal for a small lake was put forward to local planning and the Natural Rivers Authority. On agreement with them and the help of Alan Jones's machines we created a lake, one hundred metres by fifty metres and a depth of about $2^1/_2$ metres. Here, the realisation and concept of a 'rural tomorrow' spoken of earlier comes in again. As a city dweller of fifteen years ago, I would have expected grass, trees and other vegetation surrounding the lake — the instant rural picture. Now I accepted the slow development as plants and trees took hold and grew, and have experienced much pleasure in watching the progress. A tale that accompanies this changing scene is how, one morning, I noticed the water coming down from Bryn Gwyn's fields was a milky colour. Being a lovely day I decided to follow the stream up and came across my neighbour, Gwyn, digging out the stream bed. On enquiring what his idea was, he replied that he was making a small pond, following my example, and he would put twelve trout in it when the pool was finished and the water had cleared. I returned to Cae Wgan and thought no more about it until I heard, weeks later, that after heavy rain the pond had washed away. This was too good a joke to miss and I still remind Gwyn how tasty his trout were!

Links with Clocaenog school remained even after both Richard and Jayne had left for Brynhyfryd Secondary School in Ruthin. This was because the idea of friends of the school forming the Fifty Club developed; the initial group was to be fifty people who would pay a donation fee to join, which would be added to other fund-raising activities such as barn dances, BBQs and treasure hunts. The treasure hunts were fun, following the clues given on sheets of paper and, hopefully, ending at a local pub for food and a drink, although sometimes search parties had to be sent out to bring in those souls who claimed to have followed the clues correctly but still got lost. On one occasion the route was over the Clwydian range. It was well planned and agreed with local farmers and the dues written. Unfortunately, when half the party had (correctly) passed the Moel y Parc transmitter station, one farmer decided to close a gate being used on the route. This meant that the second half of the treasure hunters had to go all round the mountain to reach their destination. A few choice words were exchanged on that occasion with the organisers.

In 1992 two strong community events took place with which I was involved. Firstly, there was the forming of an Action Committee on behalf of the school to request that something be done about the size and facilities of the school. There had been outline planning detail and a compulsory purchase order on Ty'n y Celyn fields opposite Stryt Cottage since the early eighties. Although protests and petitions had been signed, the only real development gained was the positioning of a large mobile classroom in the top part of the school grounds.

My second involvement was with the three communities of Clawddnewydd, Derwen, and Clocaenog concerning the proposal for a new community centre, with a hall large enough to meet the combined demands of the three communities. Meetings and planning looked at ideas and a rough costing was reached. My role was to look for Lottery funding which I did. Others within the group looked towards other methods of fund-raising, together with putting more detail on the initial idea. Praise must be given to the community as a whole when an Auction of Promises was held in May 1993 at Bryn Coch farm and promises were collected and put into a bilingual booklet. Ivor Lloyd, a local auctioneer, took the bidding and to record that we raised just under £7,000 in one night shows the support and commitment of our community.

Over the years I had become accustomed to distances that had to be travelled between places. Five miles into Ruthin for DIY parts was normal and yet I had a slightly guilty feeling when I thought back to how I would complain about my late mother's requests to be taken by car into the city centre of Liverpool from her home, and yet it was less than from Cae Wgan to Ruthin. Distance became another factor in my life when Barbara was interviewed and accepted a Regional Co-ordinators job for a National Maths Education Project based in Manchester Polytechnic. Therefore, with a new car, she travelled to Manchester and back every couple of days during the week. Because of my concern over the distance, the motorway traffic, and especially during poor weather conditions, I pressed her to stay with some of her new colleagues and we would see her at weekends. In this situation we grew more and more apart until Barbara had developed a second life in Manchester. The result was an agreed divorce that took place in September 1995, five weeks after our silver wedding anniversary.

To say that life carried on is true. Both Jayne and Richard stayed to live at Cae Wgan and they were the strength that kept the process going. Jayne had been Head Girl of Brynhyfryd School and in 1994 she left to study maths at Bristol University, but she withdrew, and after a number of temporary jobs found her vocation in nursing and followed a degree course at NEWI in Wrexham. Jayne graduated in July 1999 and went to work at Wrexham Maelor Hospital where she met her future husband, Graham. Richard meanwhile, ever practical, left school and worked with a local landscape company, who were setting up play areas for children. He decided to move to Bristol, where he has since qualified as a maintenance engineer at a Bristol leisure and conference facility.

Whilst they were finding their futures, I was still involved in community happenings and the necessity of raising money towards the new community centre. Lottery funding had come up trumps with a donation for just over £180,000. Donations from Denbighshire County Council added to this, but the real hard fund raising came from the villages. Again and again coffee mornings and race nights, barn dances, whist drives and many a *Noson Lawen* fed in money until we were within sight of our target. Architectural drawings were finally agreed, tenders requested and the building started.

Autumn, winter and spring went by and in the summer of 1996 a new page opened in my life when I met Clair. During the past years the community had held the annual sports/gymkhana events in Clawddnewydd and Derwen and then rounded off a pleasant day with a BBQ based at the village pub, the Glan Llyn. After one such day and having finished and left the field tidy, we retreated to the Glan Llyn for a well-earned drink and a snack. I have been told since that I 'worked the room' chatting up every lady there — but then I did know a lot of the people who were present. One exception was a dark haired beauty who stood out. I asked her name and told her mine was David, and to my consternation Clair replied that she already knew. How? I asked. It seems that, as happens in any area, Richard was in school with Clair's eldest, Sophie and I had dropped Sophie home on a number of occasions when I was bringing Richard and his

Cae Wgan as it looks today.

friends back from town. Eventually Clair and I met on our own and over a coffee we talked about our years of living in this community, past history and jobs we had done. From this very chance meeting our relationship grew until in January 2004 Clair and I married and a new chapter started for us both in Cae Wgan.

Later in the same year Jayne married Graham and the following November presented us with our first grandchild, a boy, Thomas Jack.

Clair has three daughters, Sophie, an arts graduate; Laura who is a beautician; and Rachel, the youngest, who has qualified and worked in catering, but is now looking for a career in other directions. Sophie is the only daughter now living in Cae Wgan, but Laura and Rachel live not too far away, in Trefnant and Llanelidan respectively. Laura is, at the time of writing this, expecting her first child.

The house has changed a lot from when we first bought it. All the windows have been replaced with double glazed units and the wall rendering has been reapplied. In place of the old pigsty, a conservatory has been built, which has created a place of quiet retreat to read a book or to gently snooze. In the latter years we have tried to make the house maintenance free, as well as a sanctuary to which the grown up children can return, especially with the new generation of grandchildren.

Clair:
As David is unable to finish this chapter, I know he would like me, Clair, to take you up to the present day.

Emily Anne was born to Laura and Shôn in December 2005, and Cae Wgan enjoyed a wonderful family Christmas, introducing the new generation into the spirit of the house.

As we entered a new year with the additions to the family, life at Cae Wgan settled into a normal routine. David returned to work and the calendar on the wall showed the usual Community Council meetings and events. Sadly, this was not to continue. On January 12, 2006 David suddenly, but very peacefully, passed away at Cae Wgan.

To celebrate David's life, we held a funeral service at Wrexham Crematorium, where family, colleagues and friends from all walks of life came together. Then to complete the celebration of the man whom we knew as David Craig, we returned to the village where a funeral tea was held at the Canolfan Cae Cymro, bringing together the community that David thought so highly of, and which accepted him so easily.

The Griffiths Family
Bryngwyn

Ifor Wynne Griffiths:
My father moved from Caernarfonshire about 1890 and took over the tenancy of Bryngwyn until 1928 when he bought the farm from the Pool Park Estate. I was born on 10 September 1915, the only child of my father's second marriage to Margaret Davies from Cae Segwen, here in Clocaenog. His first wife had died some time earlier, leaving him with their four children — Rowland and Richard and two girls, Sydney and Laura.

My father was a farmer dealer. At certain times of the year — mostly during the winter months — farmers would take pigs to Ruthin, where Dad weighed and bought them, then, on foot, drove them to the railway station where they were loaded onto trucks and transported to customers such as George Samworth in Birmingham and J. A. Price (pork butcher) of Wolverhampton. On Fridays, Father went to the Hawk and

Buckle, Denbigh, and a similar procedure took place. At Bryngwyn, he kept a few sheep and cattle; he had farm horses which made the work a little easier and, when I left school, I used to love working with them. When there was an 'R' in the month, a pig would be killed for us by either John Lewis (Tŷ Coch), Ifan (Foel Bach), or Jack y 'Llys' who slaughtered pigs on many farms in the area.

The women had to work hard too; I remember my mother had a task each day. Monday was wash day, Tuesday she had to bake for the family, Wednesday there was butter to be made, and so on through the week, as well as all the cooking for her large family-- she used to make 40lbs. of butter a week which would be taken to Dowell's shop in town and bartered for other goods.

Ifor Griffiths, surrounded by members of his family, 2005.

One of my earliest memories is of Mam's cousin, whose family had previously emigrated to Australia and he returned as an Anzac soldier and, when on leave in 1918, he came to visit us. As a three-year old he held me up in the air above his head and I vividly remember the unusual style of his Australian hat. Sadly he was killed in France shortly afterwards.

I remember a cart used to come to the village carrying ale from the Hand public house in Ruthin to supply Tŷ Coch inn (the licensee was not brewing his own ale in the house by that time) and another cart would bring a barrel of fresh herrings for sale — I recall how the man would shout, '*Penwig* fresh!' In those days the mail was always delivered to Pool Park and Mr. Francis from the Post Office would cycle there daily to collect the village post. Pool Park employed many local people and the keepers, some of whom lived in the village, were breeding pheasants at Bron-y-gôf and other places on the estate. A lot of poaching was done of course — of pheasants and rabbits.

My brother Rowland had a good tenor voice and competed successfully in eisteddfodau, and in 1915, when the event was held in Nantglyn, he was awarded the Chair; the carving of the date on the chair back had been altered from 1914 to 1915 because nobody had been judged worthy of the honour in 1914. My other brother, Richard, worked in a bank, progressing to become a manager, and when I was still quite young my sisters married and moved to their own homes.

In 1928, a bailiff from Pool Park built a bungalow, Braeburn, above the old

Ifor's father (tall man with stick) with local farmers who have brought in pigs for sale. They are standing in front of the old cock-pit, Denbigh (which is now in St. Fagan's Museum).

A bailing machine worked from a tractor. On the left is one of the Italian farm workers. Ifor's future wife, a Land Army girl, in the centre, and Ifor, with another farm worker, on the right.

cottage of Cefn Isa, with the intention of retiring there but, instead, he sold it to Mr. and Mrs. Yates, a cotton broker and his wife, who were very generous to all the children of the village.

I attended Clocaenog village school when Llywelyn Roberts was headmaster. He used to lodge at Brynfynnon with R. E. Davies (the father of Saunders Davies) and always went back there for his meal during the mid-day break while many of the children ate packed lunches and heated a drink on the school stove. Sometimes, on my way to school, I used to spend a penny on sweets at Mrs. Jones's shop, Paradwys.

When I was eleven I won a scholarship to Denbigh County School and Hywel Clwyd Evans and I were the first two scholarship winners mentioned in the school records. I went by train from Ruthin and lodged in Denbigh during the week at 34, Post Office Lane, with a lady we called 'Nain'; her daughter kept a café where Woolworths now stands and her son played a ukelele and sang comic songs. I was good at most subjects — except mathematics — and when I took the School Certificate exams, maths was the only subject I failed, so the Headmaster called me into his room and suggested I re-took maths because it was essential. But I preferred to leave school and went home to farm.

We kept about a dozen milking cows, along with sucklers out in the fields rearing calves, and some sheep and hens; we grew swedes and hay for the animals and were largely self-sufficient. Fairs were important, not only for selling but as social occasions, and were held on Tuesdays each month, the first in Ruthin, the second in Denbigh and the third in Corwen.

During the Second World War, a search-light was positioned near the gateway to Bryngwyn, and the soldiers manning it were living in Nissen huts nearby — there were a lot of soldiers and always a guard on duty. We also had German and Italian prisoners-of-war working on the farm — Rocco Blago was one, and after the war he brought his wife over here and they lived in Tŷ Cerrig which belonged to Bryngwyn. My father also bought the small-holdings of Hafotty and Plas Newydd.

During this time I first met the lady who was to become my wife. Her name was Blodwen Mary Watkin and she came to this area as a land-girl from Llanfihangel yng Ngwynfa. We were married in the early 40s and had seven children together. Sadly she passed away in March 1983 aged 60.

I lived and worked at the farm all my life until this year (2004) when I moved to Llanrhaeadr Hall. It is a nuisance not being able to walk now but I am still very interested in the farm and all that goes on there. John keeps me well informed and sometimes takes me for a drive round to see the land and stock for myself.

The old clapper bridge which was once the main way up to Bryngwyn.

John:
My name is John Griffiths and I was born on 5 January 1953, the youngest of seven children, and have three sisters and three brothers — Elsie first, then Llinos, Valmai, Thomas, Jesse, Oswyn and myself.

When I went to school, Mr. Gwyn Williams was the headmaster, and we all respected him for being strict but fair. When we were playing in the yard after dinner, someone would spot Mr. Williams, with his briefcase, coming back from lunch at his home in Maes Caenog, and a hush fell over the whole playground as he approached the school. Mrs. Ceinwen Roberts was the second teacher throughout my time at the school. She too was greatly respected, and is still living locally in Clawddnewydd. It is strange what you remember, but on one occasion, because there was a bull in Ty'n y Celyn field (now the school football pitch) we all had to walk quietly through the Rectory garden on our way to the Church Hall for lunch, but we were allowed to walk back along the lane past the field afterwards as the bull had gone out of sight. One particular day in school stands out in my memory because Mr. Williams asked us all what we knew about John F. Kennedy; I for one had never even heard of him, so we spent the whole morning learning about him and how, the day before, he had been assassinated.

Every Sunday, the whole family walked to Cades Chapel, up the fields to Tŷ Cerrig, through Nant-y-Celyn yard, over the bridge and across what is now the car park for Maes Caenog. Our chapel was unusual because as you walked into it everyone was facing you, unlike most other chapels, and there was a big

Liz and John Griffiths, Bryngwyn.

stove on the left hand side which was always well stoked up in the winter to keep us warm during the sermon. After the service we were sometimes invited to tea by Auntie Gwen (Evans) at No. 4 Maes Caenog, or by Mrs. Chapman at Isfryn — all seven of us — and the visiting preacher would come back to Bryngwyn for tea on Sundays for one month of the year — our month was July. Mam would remind us to be on our best behaviour and we would all sit at the table; nobody was allowed to begin eating until the minister had said a prayer and had picked up his knife and fork. After tea, he and my parents went into the parlour for a chat and then we would all set out again to go to the evening service.

What did we play? I don't really remember any particular game — just helping and messing about on the farm. However, as children, we tried to help as best we could for most of the time.

I remember the milk churns being taken down to the stand at the end of our lane, then, as we modernised the shippon, the milk would be piped and cooled until the bulk tanker came up to the farm to collect it. We employed men to help with ploughing and sowing — Dad ploughed a lot in those days and, like most farmers, we were fairly self-sufficient.

The night before the annual ewe sale in September, we would help Dad walk the sheep down and pen them in a field near Ruthin and then take them into the market very early the following morning. We boys would be on bikes, riding ahead to block the side roads — most of our bikes were old and battered!

The search-lights were before my time but, when I was a boy, the three Nissen huts where the soldiers had lived were used to house chickens. Otto Führer was a German who had settled in Wales and was a good fencer; I enjoyed helping him. Another ex-prisoner-of-war was Jo Priamo who, with his Italian wife, lived at Plas Newydd and their children went to school with us in Clocaenog. We were quite scared of Mrs. Priamo, who had black hair scraped back off her face and a big mole on her cheek. One day my brother, Jesse, wanted a drink of water so we called at the Priamo's house where Mrs. Priamo had just mopped the kitchen floor and spread newspapers over it — to soak up the water, we thought. She told us to wait at the door, but Jesse stepped inside, carefully avoided standing on the papers, went over to the tap and then was terrified when Mrs. Priamo screamed, '*Mama mia!*' and a lot more Italian at him.

I went to Coleg Llysfasi on day-release after I finished at school and found it very useful, particularly for making friends, widening my contacts, and meeting other farmers' sons of my own age, some of whom I still meet at the markets today. Richard, our son, went two days a week to the college for two years after leaving

Brynhyfryd School. He is very keen on farming and is working with us here at Bryngwyn.

We do not milk any more, but keep a fair number of sucklers that run with a Charolais bull. We run blue-faced Leicester rams on Welsh ewes to produce mule ewe lambs, and a Texel ram is put to the mules to produce fat lambs that are sold in local markets. Grants through the FHDS (Farm and Horticultural Development Scheme) helped us to improve housing for the animals and our livestock is now kept in more comfortable conditions with housing wide enough to take a tractor in to muck out — a very labour-intensive job in the old days.

We lamb some of the ewes in sheds, a great help in bad weather, but it is not always ideal and someone has to be with them to prevent terrible mix-ups with ewes and lambs. We have a rota, but Liz is the expert at pulling lambs, with her smaller hands and her patience, and I honestly cannot remember when we last had to call the vet out to help with a lambing. We scan the ewes about mid-way through pregnancy to discover how many lambs they are carrying, in order to feed and manage them appropriately, if left until later, one lamb can become hidden behind the other on the scan. Before and after lambing, those with twins are fed extra to help them produce strong lambs and sufficient milk. The barren ewes are sold on. We have been scanning for 12 years now and during that time the equipment has changed and is more efficient and accurate. One of the early methods was a lengthy and strenuous procedure but now, with the present system, we can scan 200 to 300 sheep in an hour.

It is difficult to say what the future might be, but there have always been ups and downs in farming. We don't yet know how C.A.P. (Common Agricultural Policy) reforms will affect us and only time will tell if it is the right way forward; next year (2005) will be its first functioning year. If nothing else, hopefully it will reduce the number of forms to be filled — each with their submission date, deadlines and retention periods.

The amount of paper work and record keeping is now unbelievable. Every animal on the farm is ear-tagged and subject to 'traceability' and all the ear tag numbers logged; accounts, medical records and the herd and flock books must all be kept up to date. We have always kept a record book but, since the foot and mouth crisis of 2001, the changes have been immense — for example, the six day standstill rule (that was originally twenty days!) when moving animals or introducing new stock. I am fortunate to have a good wife to do this essential paper work.

Liz:

I was born on the Wirral on 3 March 1962 and lived there until I was ten. My surname was Ashworth, but became Taylor when my mother re-married, after which the family lived on a smallholding at Hendre, Mold where I went to Mold Alun School up to taking my 'O' levels. Most weekends during the summer months I would ride miles to local shows over quite a wide area and would thoroughly enjoy taking part in the jumping and gymkhana classes. Punch was my first ever pony and then I graduated to Tony, who was much bigger and great at jumping.

We then moved to Tŷ Cerrig, Melin-y-Wig in 1978. There was some hay left behind on the small holding and we asked if anybody knew someone local who could fetch it for us. John was suggested as he had a suitable lorry — and that is how John and I first met.

My Dad also re-married — to Anne — and continued to live on the Wirral. Unfortunately, he died very suddenly and unexpectedly on 15th April 1990, aged 58. Anne still lives in the bungalow they shared in Heswall.

I have an older brother who lives in Devon and a younger half-brother and sister, one of whom lives in Ruthin and one in Cyffylliog, and a step-brother who lives in Cheltenham.

The 'old' and 'new' Bryngwyn.

Although I was not born on a farm, I was used to animals as we had a few sheep, cows and a horse when I was growing up. During the spring of 1979 I helped with the lambing for Eryl, Maestyddyn, and then I went to work with race horses in Llandyrnog for Hollister Owen.

John and I married in October 1983 and have had four children, Richard born in December 1984, Bethan July 1986, Ellen February 1988 and Gareth August 1990. The children were all born at H. M. Stanley Hospital, St. Asaph. They attended Ysgol Feithrin in the Church Hall before going to Clocaenog School, then on to Brynhyfryd where they have all been taught through the medium of Welsh.

I suppose on the farming side of life, lambing and book-keeping are two of my more useful roles. We both like farming and living in this beautiful part of the country. It's a good way of life that we enjoy as a family.

Catherine Susan Black
Stryt Cottage

I was born 19 January 1944 in a nursing home at Upton, Wirral. Father wanted the name Catherine but my mother preferred Susan and always called me by that name, although I have always been known to my friends as 'Soosie'. My first name has caused me problems throughout my life, as when I was waiting for a medical to go to live in Australia, I failed to respond to the name Catherine Black when it was called. I always have to remind myself to sign officicial documents with Catherine first — and often make mistakes!

Mrs Soosie Black, Stryt Cottage.

Mother was born in Liverpool, father in Birkenhead, and they met at a New Year's party. My father had been a marine engineer in the Merchant Navy before the war, but then set up his own successful electrical engineering business and fitted Asdic detection equipment to the ships coming into port throughout the war. My paternal grandfather was a civil engineer, working on the layout of tracks for trams, both here and abroad. Sadly, he died in the terrible influenza epidemic of 1918, leaving my grandmother with four children to bring up on her own. Fortunately, she already had her own small millinery business which she developed further with the help of her two daughters, eventually becoming quite wealthy, and I feel that my passion for hats stems from seeing all the hat blocks in the large milliner's shop in Birkenhead. My aunts continued to run the business until they retired in their sixties. Incidentally, I have some Welsh roots which I inherited from this grandmother whose Welsh parents were called Roberts.

I have many memories of early childhood and these include: my father coming home from work and waltzing me around the room; my mother taking me to the launch of the *Ark Royal* at Camel Laird's shipyard in Birkenhead; visiting my grandmother who made sweets from the fairies appear on the table when I closed my eyes; finding out that nobody else could see the small, brownish man who often stood in a corner of my room.

I always looked up to my two brothers, Paul and Michael, as they were several years older and usually very good to me, but, on one occasion when we were playing hospitals, they actually amputated my teddy bear's leg and I retaliated by chopping off the heads of their 'Jack Sharps' (sticklebacks) — still feel ashamed of that episode.

Soon after the war, my two milliner aunts, Grace (always called Googs) and Doris, returned from a holiday in Switzerland bringing me a little Swiss sundress. I loved the dress but my mother decided to shorten it and I was very angry. So, when she was engrossed in conversation with the next-door neighbour, I went indoors for the scissors and came out to start cutting round the edge of the dress my mother was wearing; I was half-way round before she became aware of what I was doing. I can see my mother in that dress now — it was pretty with pale green stripes and lilac flowers and, to repair it, she had to insert a band of plain green fabric. My mother must have despaired of me at times!

Clothing was still rationed in those days and, when my mother went to a Masonic Ladies' Night, she would make a long dress from a *Vogue* pattern. I used to think she was the most beautiful person in the world and I loved the smell of her perfume. Smells are very evocative for me and will sometimes take me straight back to my childhood, like the smells of blancmange powder and the back of the garage in the hot sun where I used to play shop with the nearly empty packets my mother had cleared out of the sideboard. I would eat what was left in the packets and then be sick afterwards! I also had a habit of giving things away as a child — doll's clothes and toys, and, if my mother was talking to someone, I'd run to get a few currants and wrap them in paper as a gift for the visitor.

Sometimes, my brothers would build magnificent dens in the garden — almost fit to live in — with books, chairs and a small table with a vase of flowers, but would eventually go off to play their own games in the air raid shelters nearby. I spent a lot of time playing on my own but, although occasionally lonely, it was a happy childhood and, as I learned to read very early, I could always lose myself in books.

I remember starting at Barnston Lane School and finding it horrendous — even worrying my mother by returning home one day when I should have been eating my school dinner. When I was seven, I developed Bell's palsy and was away from school for two months, returning to find that I had been put down to the 'B' grade. Whilst ill, my long plaits had been cut off and, on the day I got all my arithmetic wrong, the teacher stood me in front of the class and commented,' When they cut your hair, they must have cut out your brains!' All this increased my hatred of school and undermined my self-confidence. Another incident which had a long-term effect happened on a thundery, overcast day when we were sent home early — my mother was not at the gate to meet me and some of the children told me she must have been killed by the thunder. I was terrified of thunderstorms for years afterwards.

At the end of junior school, I failed my 11+ and, for a short time, attended the local secondary school but my parents then sent me to a private school which I liked a bit better — my brothers were already at Skerries College in Liverpool. I left school at 17 and went to secretarial college because I was told it would be useful to have secretarial skills. I then spent five years working as the manager's secretary in the wholesale department of W. H. Smith & Son in Birkenhead but didn't really enjoy it. In 1967, my brother's girl friend, who worked for the airline, BOAC, suggested I apply for a job as an air stewardess. Having tempted me with real Russian beluga caviar and vodka brought back from Moscow, she picked up the phone, passed it to me and, primed by the vodka, I asked for an application form. Much to my surprise I was offered the job and then spent ten years flying and another eleven years working on the ground for several different airlines while the industry was expanding rapidly.

My working life was full of interest and I would never have swopped it for anything else although it entailed long hours, hard work and we were often utterly exhausted. In the late 60s we flew many hippies out to Canada and Los Angeles and I remember, in Canada, a whole orchestra boarding our plane at the beginning of their world tour. On a few flights out of Geneva for the Red Cross we had the sad task of carrying wounded children from the Vietnam War and, one weekend, expecting to fly from Manchester to Toronto, with my suitcase full of winter clothes, I learned we were being sent to Entebbe to help with the evacuation of the Asians being expelled from Uganda by Idi Amin. We did several of these trips bringing those desperate people back to Britain — a very frightening and scary task in a strange and unpredictable situation. In the end, we were so frightened that the aircrew all stayed together in one room at the Lake Victoria Hotel until it was time to fly out. This was one of the last flights out of Entebbe and most of the refugees had had to walk many miles to reach the airport where they had been held at gunpoint. I was also involved in the Haj flights, taking Muslims from Bahrain into Mecca, including village people who had never even seen an aircraft and, because some of them were old, we did have two deaths in the air, which was very sad. I also lived in Bahrain for two years, working for Gulf Air, flying to places like London and Bombay in sumptuous VC10s.

When I left Bahrain, I returned to London and started to work on the ground with TWA becoming involved in many different aspects of the job i.e. check-in, gates, documentation, lost luggage (we called it the 'gaol job'), ordering food for the flights, PR and over-bookings. The arrival of computers made life easier but we still had to collect the tear-off strips from the boarding passes (as many as 400 on the 'Jumbos') — these were, and still are, the means by which the individual airlines are paid. I was in a team with a super bunch of people, working hard but also having a lot of fun; they are still my friends and we all meet regularly, even Annie who now lives in America.

Soosie Black (centre in uniform) in her days as an air hostess.

I met my future husband, Peter, at the Farnborough Air Show where I was working as a hostess in the TWA hospitality lounge. He was an Australian airline pilot and I knew him for four and a half years before we married in 1988 and set up home 40 minutes drive from the centre of Sydney, Australia. Our house was high up and stood on a large plot in beautiful bush land with extensive views towards the beaches at Gosford. I loved the wonderful lifestyle we had there and, being married to a pilot, was able to come back to England frequently to visit family and friends. Sadly, Father had had a fatal stroke in 1983 and never saw my Australian home, but my mother spent time with us there. During her last visit, she was not well and, after returning home, her illness was diagnosed as terminal, so I returned to England and was glad to be able to nurse her for the last six months of her life.

My husband and I lived in Australia for six and a half years before, sadly, our marriage eventually broke down. I remained there for another 18 months because, during the divorce proceedings, I was in no fit state to make decisions about my future. Finally I returned to Britain to start a completely new life on my own and, two years later, when I went back to visit friends in Oz, I knew I had made the right decision.

On my return from Australia, I bought a little house in Cheshire before deciding to move to Wales when I bought Stryt Cottage in Clocaenog. I already knew Ruthin and north Wales well from my childhood because the family used to spend holidays in the area or drive out from the Wirral for a picnic on Sundays and, later, I would visit my brother and his wife at their cottage in north Wales. Clocaenog is one of the most friendly places in which I have ever lived, with good neighbours and everybody stopping to pass the time of day. Enjoyable community events are held in the church hall from time to time, usually with good home-made food (I always have seconds) and music and entertainment by local people.

I am passionately fond of animals and was determined to bring my cat, Misty, and golden retriever, Sam, back from Australia, even though it meant they would have to spend six months in quarantine. I went to visit them regularly during that time but, unfortunately, Misty died the week before she could be released with Sam — a devastating experience I cannot forget. I still have Sam who is now 13-years old; Helston, the cat who came from my holiday in Cornwall; a cat, Gwydd, rescued from Gwyddelwern, who promptly produced a litter of kittens — of which I still have three — and, latterly, a stray tom who needed immediate surgery to remove a damaged eye and is now (predictably) called Nelson.

Whilst living in Australia, I developed my skills as a folk artist and this became a way of earning a living on my return to the UK — I now teach folk art in classes and workshops and undertake commissions. After various improvements to the house and garden, I had a large conservatory built to enable me to take my art classes out of the kitchen and this meant I could also develop another sideline with a self-contained bed and breakfast area for two people — I enjoy this as I meet some interesting and pleasant people. This has

Soosie Black in front of Stryt Cottage.

become a very successful and satisfying way of life and my six and a half years in this village have been very pleasant. I plan to stay here for the foreseeable future.

William George Roberts
Y Fron

William George Roberts.

In 1869, my grandfather moved from Bala to Fron, a farm on the Pool Park Estate, but I don't know why he came here. Initially, the family lived in the old farmhouse (later demolished) and the present house was newly built for them shortly after they arrived, so that is how my family history in Fron began. There were three children — my father and his two sisters — and eventually my father, Robert William Roberts, married, took over the running of the farm, and his two sisters then returned to live in Bala. Sadly, my father's first wife died, leaving him with two young sons, Arthur and Hugh, so the following few years must have been very difficult for him. However, he later married my mother, Ann Ellen Edwards, and I was born three years later, one of twins, in 1923.

My name is William George Roberts and my twin sister was called Margaret Louise. When my sister and I were five and a half years old, my mother, my twin sister and I, and a brother, all had scarlet fever which was a dreaded illness in those days. Nobody would come near us to help so we were taken by ambulance to a hospital in Wrexham where my sister died three hours later — it still upsets me now to tell you about it because it is very sad when you lose one of the family, so young and my twin. I was left rather deaf after the illness. I don't remember about paying for the doctor — it's hard to remember the details — but I know he didn't charge us much for coming to the house. My mother and father felt very low after losing their daughter and almost lost the will to go on but, as time passed, they were able to carry on and keep the family going. At the age of seven, I went to Wrexham hospital again to have my tonsils and adenoids removed. My mother took me by train from Ruthin to Chester, changing trains and going a long way round to reach Wrexham where we had to stay in lodgings because there were other young boys waiting for an operation. At nine, I had yet another operation, for a mastoid, but this time I was too ill to be taken to the hospital in Liverpool. There was danger of the infection spreading into the brain, so a doctor from Ruthin Castle (then a hospital) and the old doctor, Trefor Hughes, did an emergency operation. I was in hospital for seven weeks but they saved my life and, although I recovered in time, it left me stone deaf in one ear, affecting much of my schooling.

I hated Clocaenog School because the schoolmaster couldn't (and wouldn't) understand why I was unable to do the lessons. How could I? I couldn't hear what the lessons were! The teacher would bring me out to the front of the class and ridicule me, so I didn't get a good education and I've had to do the best I can. It shouldn't be like that, and I think things have improved now as the teachers are better trained and are more understanding. I left school just before I was fourteen and was glad to go from such a hateful place. Even so, I have done better than many who have had a good education, and my brothers and I made a success at Fron despite some setbacks.

In my childhood, farming was very different and we didn't keep much stock, just enough to feed ourselves, buy clothes and to give us some kind of a living. We didn't go to town very often but depended on the village shop for some essentials. We would only go to town on fair days which were the first Tuesday of every month (it is still the same day for market days in Ruthin) and that was a big day. Often a dealer would come round to the farm to buy whatever cattle we had to sell, but we would go to town with sheep or pigs, putting them in a cart or, sometimes, walking the sheep to market — it was easier to do that in those days because there was little traffic. If nobody bought the animals, or the price was not good enough, they had to be brought back the same way. We would try again another time and perhaps have to sell them for less anyway.

We sowed seed, either by hand or using a fiddle, and grew enough wheat, oats, barley, potatoes, swedes and turnips to feed ourselves and the farm animals. We grew hay, of course, which was cut by the old type of mowing machine, and the corn was cut with a side delivery mower with paddles on it. Every time the sheaf was big enough, out it came to be tied by hand and I was very good at that. I also used to go to other farms, tying the sheaves by taking a few strands of corn, twisting them, wrapping them round a sheaf and tucking it in, before stooking it to dry — work which took time and skill to keep up with the cutter. The big farms, of course, had binding machines.

In our farmhouse, there was a step going down from the kitchen into the dairy, which was like a half-cellar, built into the earth bank with only a few stones to keep the soil back. It was very cool down there, with slate slabs on which we kept all the food and butter. To make butter, I had to harness the horse to a beam in the yard and lead it round and round; at every turn, the horse and I had to step over another beam which connected with cogs to a square churn in the dairy. Later, we had an end-over-end churn which was turned by hand and did the job well — another task for my mother, but we helped her when we could.

It was a hard life for Mother. To make enough bread for the family, she would buy a big sack of white flour and would make the family's bread once a week, cooking it in the big oven in the outbuilding in the yard (*pobty mawr*, we called it). We would stoke the oven until it was very, very, hot and, once the firewood had all burned to ashes, the dough would be put in tins which were placed in the ashes to cook. They were big loaves for a big family and it was wonderful bread — much better than today's.

Then there was the washing which took one whole day a week, using a big old-fashioned washing tub and dolly pegs, with the water heated over the fire and in a boiler to one side of the grate. The boiler had a lid on top and the water had to be ladled in and out with a can. As the water level dropped, it would be topped up with hot water from the kettle which stood on a trivet attached to the side of the grate and could be swivelled back over the flames when needed. This method of water heating was also used when we had a bath and, as there was no bathroom, we used an old tin bath which we brought out into the kitchen before filling it with water. Electricity only came to Fron in 1959 and, until then, it was oil and paraffin lamps.

As my brothers grew up, they went out to work when they finished school. In the early thirties, my older brothers started off as farm labourers for two shillings a day, and brought home all the money to help the family. I was still at school and living at home but went out to work on some days, earning the same rate of pay as my brothers. To start the day, I did a lot of jobs at home and then walked two miles or more to get to work by eight o'clock. Walking was no problem in those days and we didn't even think about it because it was easy and the only way of going places. You couldn't afford a bike in the early thirties but, eventually, my older brother bought a second-hand bike for thirty bob for us two younger boys — we were delighted with it. The work was really too hard for lads of 14 or 15 but that's how it was. At some farms, they only gave us very poor food, because those farmers were hard up too, but some were very good to us and that helped a lot. At the end of the day, we would go home to do some more work in the house and on the farm to help keep things going.

With three boys at home throughout the Second World War, our parents didn't need to use the Italian prisoners from the camp at Plas Efenechtyd. On some of the larger farms, like Maes Tyddyn and Bryngwyn, there were gangs of prisoners, with a supervisor, doing drainage and other work. Some of the prisoners stayed in this country after the war. In the earlier 1914–18 war, my father had had a prisoner-of-war, Robert Lomax, working on the farm — probably a conscientious objector.

At home, we were farming with a pair of horses and we didn't get a tractor until the early fifties — it was a matter of affording one, you see. There was a tractor in Plas Clocaenog in the forties — they were more fortunate, but the land on our farm was so steep it was not very good for

Washing the hard way!

A tractor with cleats (or lugs) on the wheels was particularly useful when working on steep hillsides. This tractor was photographed with the permission of Mr Edwards, Mynydd-bychan, Betws-y-Coed.

a tractor anyway. Our farm income was so low that the bank wouldn't lend us any money and, if you had an overdraft of around £10, you would have a hard word from the banker and then you had to sell something to pay the money back. That's how it was! You couldn't move away, so you just did your best with what you'd got. Things began to improve when the war started because all the talk then was about home produced food. Before the war, a lot of cheap food was imported, which made things very difficult for the Welsh farmer. So, slowly, things did come better but then we didn't have the capital to invest in farm machinery and we couldn't borrow money because the bank didn't think we were viable.

In the fifties, there were some interesting ideas coming up in farming and, with that and a bit more for our produce, it gave us more incentive to try to do something better. From keeping a few poultry, we gradually increased the numbers until, by 1959, we built a big shed and we then had over 3,000 laying hens. From that time on, we had a better living from the farm, as did most farmers, and eventually had a Ford van and a Fordson tractor on cleats. I remember once when my brother was on the Fordson, spreading manure on steep land and, due to its lack of power, it slid backwards, turning over many times before finishing in the stream at the bottom of the hill. Fortunately, my brother managed to jump off, so he was very lucky.

My two brothers and I continued to live here after our parents died and we worked the farm together until Arthur died in 1986 and Hugh in 1991; we were a close-knit family. I am still in touch with two cousins (my only living relatives) who live in St. Asaph.

All the families from the farms around us used to come over for a chat, telling the local news, and were always helpful if anybody had a problem, so we had some happy times together. Nowadays, nobody wants to know you but, at that time, there was a lot going on in the village. In the evenings, we would go and play football in the field (which the village children still use today) and the lads would arrive, one after the other, going into alternate sides as they came — sometimes we had as many as 30 players and we would all chase the football like hell, passing the ball until near the goal, then we couldn't get it between the posts because of the crowd! It was a lot of fun.

We also played games in the Church Hall at the youth club run by Emlyn Jones, Tŷ Capel; sometimes 50 or more attended, some coming from Clawddnewydd because they had no hall there in those days. The church hall was also used for village social evenings, starting with a big meal which was all laid out in advance, followed by entertainment with local people reciting, singing and acting little dramas. We thoroughly enjoyed those evenings. We had to entertain ourselves because we didn't have cars to go into Ruthin although, on some Saturday nights, we would go to the cinema there. I remember going to see *How Green Was My Valley* when, after working all day, my brother and I ran all the way there only to find the cinema was full and we had to stand by the wall. I remember sliding down the wall slowly in a faint because I had run too much! Somebody brought me some water — then we had to walk all the way home again! That was a sad film wasn't it? Sometimes we would get very hungry on the way home from Ruthin and would call in for a snack at a pub called 'Labour In Vain' (a house by the steps leading

The old double furrow plough is still in use for competition ploughing, but pulled by a tractor now instead of horses. [Mr Edwards, Mynydd-bychan]

Right: An early photograph of the Labour in Vain Inn, Llanfwrog, which was alongside the steps leading up to the church. [Roger Edwards]

Below: The same scene in 2004.

up to Llanfwrog Church). Later on, we used the bike and, in the early fifties, we bought a car — a green Austin 8 — and we were very proud of that.

We three brothers were always very close and, after our parents died, we worked the farm together for many years, caring for our stock and always keeping the land in good heart. After the deaths of my brothers, I managed to continue on the farm until my sight deteriorated to a point when I could no longer carry on. For the past few years, I have been very well looked after in Awelon, Ruthin but, sadly, Fron had to be sold.

Morfydd Edwards and Lilian Jones

Our names are Lilian Sarah Jones (born 15 April 1934) and Morfydd Mehefyn Edwards (born 22 June 1928); we are sisters and were brought up in Clocaenog by our grandparents Ellen and Gabriel Tomos Edwards.

Gabriel Edwards was born in Stryt Ucha Cottage, and was still living there with his parents when he married Ellen Rowlands of Pen y Baric, Betws Gwerfil Goch, but, soon after, they moved to live in one end of Old School House. During their married life, they moved house many times but always within Clocaenog parish and into rented properties owned by Lord Bagot: Glan yr Afon, Pennant, Tŷ Isa (Morfydd born), Graig Wen, Paradwys (Lillian born) and, in 1934, they became the first tenants of a new three-bedroomed house, Haelfryn (2 Maes Caenog), where Morfydd still lives.

At the time of his marriage, Gabriel Edwards was a tailor, trained in tailoring by Mr. John Hughes of the Post Office. Later, he worked for Lord Bagot and, for many years, as a lengthsman for Denbighshire County Council; his length was from Bryn Ffynnon down to Nant Clwyd. Eventually, Gabriel became school caretaker as his father, David Edwards, had been years before. One of the caretaker's duties was to climb a ladder and light the paraffin lamp hanging from a bracket on the school wall — this lamp was bought in April 1903, at a cost of 10s. 9d. to celebrate the coronation of King Edward VII. At first, John A. Jones, Paradwys, lit this lamp, and Gabriel Edwards took over the job in 1905. Sometimes, on windy nights, the lamp would have blown out by the time he reached home and he would have to return to re-light it. Years later, our mother became the school caretaker and, in addition, she also looked after the Church Hall.

Our grandfather, a deacon at Bethesda Wesleyan Chapel, was very strict about carrying on the family tradition of attending chapel three times every Sunday. One Sunday, when we were getting ready to go to

Morfydd Edwards and Lilian Jones.

chapel, Aunty Ellen and Uncle John turned up to see us on their only free day from running their shop in Llandderfel — but we still went to chapel, leaving them in the house to await our return.

At the time of Lillian's birth in 1934, Paradwys was divided into two dwellings — Ucha and Isa — and we had only one bedroom and a living room to accommodate our family of six: Gabriel and Ellen, their son, Will and our mother, Mary Ellen, with her two children. Big families in small properties were not unusual and, in the 1940s, a married couple brought up five girls in one half of Old School House. People who were brought up in such crowded conditions and economic hardship appreciate what they have far more than today's young generation.

As small children, we spoke only Welsh at home but, at school, we were taught in the medium of English and became bilingual. The Welsh language was introduced into the school curriculum after the war and Lilian's son, Arwel, was educated throughout in the medium of Welsh, read for his mathematics degree in Welsh and is now a maths teacher at Ysgol Berwyn, Bala.

Miss Telford, the infant teacher, used to cycle to shool from Bod Petrual, in Clocaenog Forest, where she lived in the Old Lodge which is now a visitor centre with a picnic area. Later, she came to school in a Morris Minor.

The middle class was taught by another teacher, Miss Blodwen Evans, an ex-pupil of the school, who became Mrs. Davies when she married; she lived in Ruthin until she died. The headmaster, H. F. Jones, lived at Henblas and regularly attended our Wesleyan chapel until he left the village in 1946 to become headmaster of Penmaenrhos School, Old Colwyn. Lilian was in his class when she gained her scholarship to go to Ruthin Grammar School.

There were two yards in the school — one for the boys, one for the girls — and the field was also divided between the two sexes. We used to play rounders and singing circle games:'Here we come gathering nuts in May', 'Nebuchadnezzar, King of the Jews', and 'I wrote a letter to my love' in which one child would go round the circle carrying a handkerchief and drop it behind another; both children would then race each other round the circle in an attempt to get to the space first. The loser picked up the handkerchief and the game began again. Although 'Welsh Not' was no longer obligatory, the lesson remained and the singing games in the playground were all in English, We used to play hopscotch, drawing the squares in the schoolyard or on the lane, or skipping, ball games, quoits and making our own *tŷ bach* in the fields. We used to play ball a lot, particularly with two tennis balls against the house wall — you could hear the vibrations throughout the house. We had a little doll and rag dolls but no doll's house. Teddy was Lillian's favourite and, when she moved house recently, she found him in the attic and was really upset to discover that he looked terrible — all raggedy with no eyes except the ones stitched in long ago — not a bit as she remembered him. She had cut his hair at one time and he's now quite bare, poor thing, so she would like to send him to a Teddy hospital for repair. We also had old games of Ludo, Snakes and Ladders and a jigsaw called 'Pinnocchio and Jimmy Under the Sea'. But on Sundays, games were not allowed — no ball, no scissors, nothing.

In 1939, daily drinks of Horlicks commenced at the school — we all enjoyed this, particularly when Miss Evans, the teacher, prepared the drinks and made them stronger and sweeter than anyone else. Another memory is having our gas masks examined in the afternoon — the children were then taken out in the playground and we had to walk about for fifteen minutes with the masks on — we can still remember the smell of the rubber.

At the beginning of the Second World War, evacuees from Liverpool arrived at the village in a bus, with two teachers, Miss Maxwell and Miss Woodward. Some of the children were billeted in Clocaenog, others in Clawddnewydd, and we remember Doris and Megan Hughes who stayed with Miss Evans in Ty'n y Mynydd, and Shirley Brown and Ann Gristenthwaite who were billeted in Glandŵr. Ann trained to be a teacher; Megan married and lived in Llanbedr, but the two of them kept in touch over the years. When visiting Megan, Ann met her future husband, Reg Jones and they eventually settled in Ruthin where she still lives. Marjorie and Peter Ball lived with Mrs. Jones in Stryt Ucha (one of the three Stryt Cottages); the middle cottage was occupied during the war by Mrs. Slight from Liverpool and her two children; in the third cottage, Stryt Isa, lived a couple who ran a small shop in an adjoining shed. Although not official evacuees, Ian and Diane Walker and their mother lived throughout the war years at Derlwyn. Two children, Ursula and Malcolm, stayed at Glan yr Afon and we met Ursula again when she attended the school reunion in 1998. Being evacuated did have a big influence on many lives.

During the war, we all had identification cards and collected them from the Post Office, while many of us also wore a bracelet engraved with name and identity number. Everybody had ration books and, as we were not living on a farm, we had to manage on our rations alone — we especially disliked the taste of the 'Special Margarine' and preferred dripping on our bread. Another thing we remember is dried egg — a bright yellow powder, which didn't really taste like egg, but was good scrambled, and worked very well in baking. Food has changed enormously since we were children, although it was plain food then, and mainly organic. About once a week, we had meat which we bought from the travelling butcher who came round every Friday evening. The fish man delivered once weekly and fresh bread was available from the village shop; this was run by Mrs. Frances who took over the shop and Post Office (in the Weslyan Chapel House) from her father, John Hughes.

Throughout this period, the whole civilian population (including children) was involved in the 'War Effort'. Because of food shortages, all children and pregnant women were given bottles of orange juice or rose hip syrup to supply essential vitamin C, and the teachers took us on nature walks to gather rose hips. We would also gather hips out of school hours and were paid sixpence a pound if we were lucky enough to find so many — a fortune to a child in those days. Another school activity, in the needlework class, was knitting garments for the forces: mittens, gloves, scarves and balaclavas. Mrs. Yates, Braeburn, used to go round the village selling National Savings Stamps which would eventually lead to a National Savings Certificate — a vital part of the war effort. At the end of the war, in celebration of VE day, Mrs. Yates and her friends entertained all the children to a splendid tea party on 14 June 1945.

We collected for the 'missionaries' and would practise saying the word before going to Mrs. Yates'

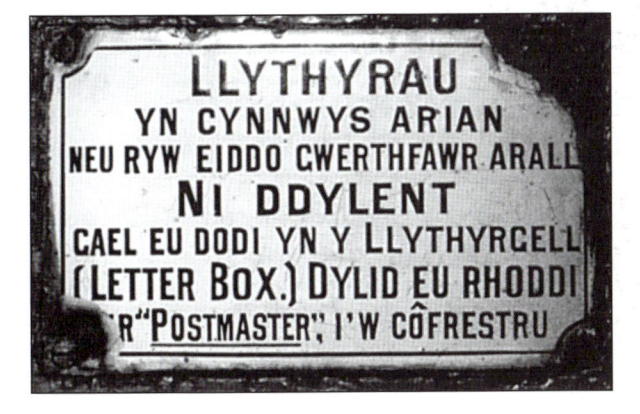

Top left: The 'New' School, clearly showing the bell and the lamp. Lilian believes the figure holding the baby is her grandfather. Above: The same view in 2004.

Left: The post box sign on the old Post Office (which was the building on the left in the two photographs above). It is one of only a few Welsh language signs from that time.

The children of Bethesda Wesleyan Chapel at a party at Llidiardau. Back row (L–R): Tecwyn Jones, Morfydd Edwards, Alec Jones, Ifor Jones, Herbert Jones. Front row: Mrs Williams (Llidiardau), Lilian Edwards, Mr Caradog Williams, Cynwyl (Rhos).

house, because she always used to give us a sixpence. She was the lady who gave all the children, from the two chapels and the church, a party at Christmas time with a big Christmas tree in the corner from which each child was given a present — Lillian remembers receiving a little elephant brooch set with blue and red stones.

We have a vivid memory of lying in bed, listening to German planes flying overhead towards Liverpool which seemed a long way from us, although we could see the sky all lit up during the bombing raids there. We only remember one occasion when bombs were dropped near here. We were eating supper, around 8 o'clock, and the explosions sounded very near but next morning we learned there were two craters in Llanelidan; when we went to see them we saw one large and one small crater. Going for walks through the fields during the war, we sometimes came across strips of silvery paper which were dropped, presumably, from the German planes to fool the radar. We also remember going to school and seeing many army lorries parked in the village — the soldiers were taking part in a mock invasion that day and some of them were having a wash in the river by the Old Post Office. If we met somebody in the dark during the blackout we'd say '*Nos da*' in a particular way and, by the reply, we would know if they were friend or foe (remember we were expecting to be invaded). Listening to the 9 o'clock news was a must and we remember the names of the newscasters — Alvar Lidell, Frank Phillips and Joseph Macloud.

For a time, there were some sailors at a camp in Clawddnewydd and they used to march down to Clocaenog on Sunday mornings to attend the 11 o'clock service at the church. We don't remember any other details because we attended chapel but we can recall hearing the bugle from the distant camp, playing Reveille and the Last Post.

Coming home from town on the bus one Saturday evening during the war, we saw a glider which had landed on the side of the road between Bryn Ffynnon and Bryn Golau (now demolished). However, when Mair and I walked up to take a look, we were told we would have to pay two pence to have a peep inside — as we did not have a single penny between us, we weren't allowed to look and went home disappointed.

The Crosville bus service in this area was very good and some buses came to the village; at other times we would have to use the bus stop at Brynffynnon on the main road. Although there were no buses during the day on Saturdays, a special bus left Clocaenog at 5 o'clock in the evening to take people to the Ruthin cinema (this was in Well Street opposite Bethania Chapel), returning at 9 p.m.

During our childhood, we never went away on holiday as people do today but, sometimes, we went to stay with family; once, Lillian stayed with mother's brother in Stoke-on-Trent, but that was unusual. Most of our relatives lived locally and we thought nothing of walking to visit our mother in Llanelidan when she worked and lived there, and where her other brother also lived. Another regular walk was to visit our grandfather's brother in Eyarth, and Morfydd used to accompany our neighbour, Dilys Jones, when she took flowers to her husband's grave in Derwen. Aunty Dil (as she was known to everybody in the village) was well used to walking to and from Ruthin where she worked.

On fine days during our childhood we often saw the patients (all men) from Pool Park Hospital going for a walk through the village; there would be about 50 patients, with one or two male nurses, going on their round trip down Rhiwlas Hill, through the village to Glan yr Afon, then up the hill that leads to Pen y Maes. Some of these men continued to do their walks alone until Pool Park closed as a hospital in 1991.

The big treat for everybody was the yearly summer day trip by charabanc to Rhyl, organised by the church and chapels; we all grew very excited when we saw the water tower on the left, about a mile before reaching the town itself, because we knew we were nearly there (the tower has gone now). We would go onto the sands but were not allowed to paddle; most of the time was spent at the Marine Lake, where we had donkey rides and a trip on the miniature train round the lake. There were also tricycle rides in a sunken area on the prom, and we would try to find amusements for a pennya-go while we ate candyfloss and got it up our noses. We all took our own picnics and, in later years, we were given £1 spending money as part of the trip.

We were happy as children and felt no need to look outside the village for our entertainment. As we grew up, there weren't many opportunities to spread our wings although there were dances in the church hall and, if you were new to dancing, Caenwen's boyfriend, Will, who was a good dancer, would take you round the floor to get you started. 'Y Gymdeithas' was held regularly during the winter months when members of Capel Bethesda, Capel Cades and St. Foddhyd's Church would meet in the Church Hall. There was a joint committee which planned a varied programme for the winter when we met each month to hear speakers from outside the village, held debates or quizzes, or be entertained by visiting singers and musicians. These social activities brought us all together

Morfydd and I grew up in a close-knit community. We consider we were privileged to live in Clocaenog village at that time where we all knew each other and everybody cared..

Morfydd:
Our mother eventually became the school caretaker and, in addition, she looked after the Church Hall. Later still, I helped to cook meals for the school for many years with Mrs Gwladys Edwards from one of the Stryt cottages. I have two children; Michael who now lives in Ruthin and works for British Telecom, and Nan, who is married to Arwel Wyn Roberts, and lives at Pant Galltegfa with their two children.

Lillian:
When I left Brynhyfryd School I worked as a receptionist for Vernon Jones, the dentist in Ruthin, for a few months. Then I went to work for some years as a clerk at the North west grocers, E. B. Jones & Company, in Ruthin (head office in Rhyl). I subsequently worked as a clerk with R. Ellis & Son, the mineral water manufacturer, in Mwrog Street, Ruthin, until I married George Emlyn Jones, a Presbyterian minister, in 1960. We moved round a lot during our married life, living in Llangernyw, Ffestiniog, Abersoch and Glan Conwy, before my husband retired and we settled in Denbigh.

Beryl and David Jones
7 Maes Caenog

Beryl:
My father worked at Llysfasi with the horses, and I was born in Llysfasi Cottages, Llanelidan, in 1929. When I was three months old, we moved to Craigadwywynt to live in a cottage and smallholding belonging to Eyarth Hall where my father worked; we stayed there until I was fourteen. In April 1943, my parents, two sisters, Dorothy and Rita, and brother Kenneth and I, moved to a cottage and smallholding on the mountain at Llanbedr where I lived until I married. My sister, Dorothy, married in June 1943 and my mother broke her leg in the July, so I had to leave school to look after her until she was mobile again.

Mr & Mrs Jones, Maes Caenog.

When I was a child, we often played hopscotch in the yard at school. At home, we played 'little house' in the field where we kept hens. Using small stones, we would lay out the plan of a house on the ground, leaving gaps for doors and windows, with little passages and various rooms; our pots and pans were made up from all sorts of rubbish. Then my father would be invited to tea but, if he walked over the wall, he was sent out again to come in through the doorway. We would offer him imaginary

Llysfasi Cottages.

Right: Students at work in the dairy at Llysfasi. It was white coats such as these that Beryl's mother used to wash.

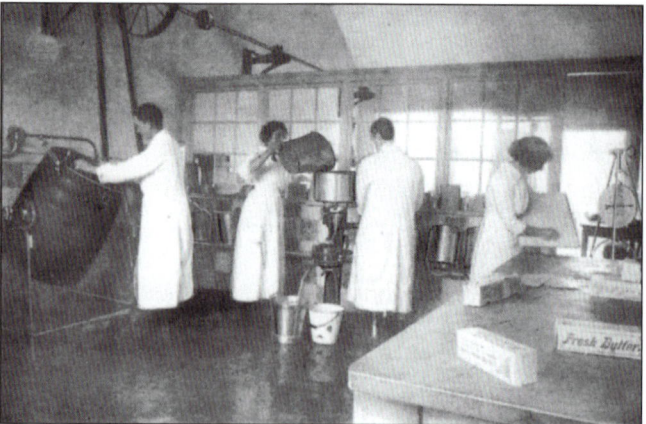

tea and cakes which he would pretend to drink and eat, fully entering into our game.

My father thought of himself as a bit of a barber and he used to cut men's hair. When we lived on the side of the road at Graigadwywynt, men would call at our house to have a haircut but it always turned into a social occasion with a chat and a bit of supper afterwards — it was all part of the ritual.

My mother went out to work and my older sister was supposed to look after us. One of our tasks was to gather sticks from the woods behind the house, ready to light the fire in the morning. One day, when we were playing in the woods, we made a wigwam with dead branches and lit a fire inside it and the whole thing caught fire, so we all had to dash out — it's a wonder we weren't all burned. The fire spread and we had to carry buckets of water to put out the flames before anybody found out — but they did! And we were never allowed to play in those woods again.

At Christmas time, my father's employers were very good to us and always sent us a hamper of fruit and we often had enough oranges to last us until March. My brother always had a torch in his Christmas stocking and would look for this first so that we could all see to open our stockings and parcels. We weren't given expensive presents but it was always a great thrill unwrapping each small gift and finding an orange in the toe. Once, I remember my mother coming into the bedroom at three or four in the morning and catching us all sitting up, so she bundled all the presents into a pillow case to take them away and we had to go back to sleep. The next day, it was a struggle to find what belonged to whom! We always had Christmas decorations but I was eight or nine before we had a Christmas tree; we used the same tree decorations year after year — including tin soldiers and little tin whistles which my own children, in their turn, have enjoyed using through the years. Sadly, some of them are now showing their age.

My oldest sister, Dorothy, married a railway signalman and lived in Warrington, visiting us once a year when she would bring us presents. I remember a doll's settee and two chairs and, once, she brought us a lovely doll's tea set which my sister and I played with until one plate was broken and my mother locked it all away in the glass cupboard — I still have it in my display cabinet.

When I left school, I went to work in Ruthin at Irwin's, the grocer, where the bakery now stands opposite the Wynnstay Arms. I only received 15 shillings a week in wages and was treated like a dogsbody because I was the youngest, and I wasn't allowed to serve at the counter. I eventually left and went to work at E. B. Jones (another grocer) for £1 a week — a big rise -and I was allowed to serve at the counter, but paying for my own bus fare and lunch each day made quite a hole in my wages (the shop was at the bottom of Clwyd Street where ' Swings and Roundabouts' is at present). I stayed there until I went to work at Plas Efenechtyd for £1. 17. 6d. (later £2) a week plus my keep.

In the winter of 1947, while I was still working at E. B. Jones, we had a lot of snow and the buses were not able to get through so, for about six weeks, I had to walk the two miles to work in Ruthin each day. My father would accompany me for part of the way, for which I was grateful. I survived!

David:
My name is David Gruffydd Jones and I was born on 22 December, 1921 at Croes Foel Farm in Dinmael (between Maerdy and Cerrig y Drudion). I had one brother, who later went into the RAF, and two sisters, one of whom married, and the other became a nurse. My early childhood was spent at Croes Foel and, as all my relatives were farming, I always wanted to be a farmer but, when I was twelve years old, my father died and we had to give up the farm.

Times were very hard in the 1930s and people nowadays just don't realise how we had to make do. We always had plenty of food — not the variety available today — but good, wholesome fare. Everybody around us was in the same boat and we didn't have many toys, but we made up for this by doing other things — like making dens in the woods. We never played in the farmyard, always the woods, and there were different crazes at various times of the year such as conkers and marbles. I do remember getting my first bike — a second-hand one of course — and this later enabled me to go to work on various farms until I found permanent work with the Forestry Commission with whom I stayed for the next 31 years, working my way up the ladder until I retired in 1978.

Working on farms entailed very long hours and, with double summertime, we thought nothing of working on the harvest until twelve o'clock at night, leaving no time for leisure at that time of year. In addition to cycling to work, we also travelled on buses — there were plenty of them in those days — but, of course, things improved as the years went on and I eventually had a motorbike and, just before we married, I bought a little car — quite an event! They were hard times but we were very happy.

While working on the farms, I never had a holiday, just the odd day off. When I went to work in the forest, we were given an annual holiday which I always used for working on the holding, perhaps taking a day off to go to one of the agricultural shows which were important social events where we met a lot of people — and I still like going. For example, when I was working at Ty'n y Maen, I used to take animals, mainly cattle, from the farm to some of the shows i.e Cerrig y Drudion, Abergele and the Royal Welsh and we won a cup for a prize bull one year.

As far back as I remember, people used to visit each other regularly for supper and to play cards (stack or whist). There would be a lot of conversation and socialising — unlike people nowadays who watch their television sets and forget how to talk to each other. I suppose we must accept that things have changed, but one can't talk to a computer! On the other hand, we do need people working with their computers — we couldn't do without them now.

I believe everybody should be interested and happy in his job. I was, and am still, interested in farming matters — I think it must be in my blood — but I retired for health reasons in 1978 and, when we turned the key in the lock of No. 7, we knew we were coming home and we've been very happy here ever since.

Beryl:
I met David in his sister's house when I was working at Plas Efenechtyd. We married on 10 September 1949 and, for two years, we lived in part of Glan yr Afon, Clocaenog, where our son, Geraint, was born. When he was three-months old, we moved to a brand new council house — 9, Maes Caenog, where Glyn and Llinos were born. David still wanted to be a farmer so, when we heard about Rhos, a smallholding for rent just below Fridd Agored near Pwllglas, we moved there and kept sheep, two milking cows, calves, pigs, pheasants and ducks — a busy life leaving little time for leisure.

Our breeding sow was a good one and, when she was making her bed, she would carry all sorts of rubbish — even wire netting — to make her nest and we knew then that she was ready to farrow.

We were living in Rhos when we rented our first television set. We collected it from the shop on the day President Kennedy was assassinated in 1963 and that was the first thing we saw when we switched the set on. You remember these things and the little cottage has now been altered out of all recognition by its present owners. Our next move was to Lodge Isa in Clocaenog Forest at Melin y Wig, when David was working with the Forestry Commission. Finally, when David retired, we came to live in No. 7 Maes Caenog — only two doors away from our previous home at No. 9.

Throughout the years, we always attended the chapel in Clocaenog and our children went to Clocaenog School, so we felt we had never really left the village. I went to the W.I. in Clawddnewydd until we moved back to live in Clocaenog when I transferred to the Clocaenog branch.

Beryl and David with their children when they were living at Lodge Isa.

When the Calvinist Chapel in Clocaenog closed down in 1974, we didn't want to go all the way to chapel in Melin y Wig or Clawddnewydd, so we decided to try the Anglican church in the village here, as my grandmother had been a churchgoer. In fact, 14 of us from the chapel transferred to the church and were confirmed at the same time — all except our son, Geraint, who was already married. I am now the caretaker for St. Foddyd's church and the Church Hall, and have been since the death of Mrs. Jones of Bryn Fedwyn. David has been the bellringer there for many years.

Beryl and David:
Clocaenog has always been central to our lives and we are delighted to be able to spend time with our grandchildren and to see them growing up and attending the village school.

Mair and John Roberts
Glan Aber

Mair:
My maiden name was Mair Williams and I was born in this parish — in this house, and have lived here ever since. This property used to be the village smithy and my grandfather was the blacksmith and farrier, so three generations of my family have lived here. My grandfather employed two workmen, one of whom, Dafydd Hughes, used to live in Bryn Fedwen — he was a joiner and made the wooden wheels on which my grandfather would put iron bands. Outside the house, near the stream, there's a stone with a hollow in it. They used to place the wheel on the stone, with a pole down the middle to hold it firmly while two men fitted the heated metal band round it. Then, by pouring cold stream water over it, they would shrink the metal to give a tight fit.

I was brought up by my mother and grandmother and never knew my grandfather who died when he was only 35. My grandmother was left with three daughters. The eldest was Mary Catherine, who later married Thomas Chapman, a barber with a shop in Llanidloes. Later, when they retired, they came to live in Isfryn in Clocaenog. My mother, Nellie, was the middle child and the youngest, Margaret Ann, was only a baby of three months old when my grandfather died.

My grandmother had to bring up her three young children by herself and, as there was no widow's pension in those days, she had to go out to work to keep herself and her family. She had a job at Poole Park and had to pay Mrs. Roberts, of Cefn Isa, to look after the baby but, later, the widow's pension was introduced.

I attended Clocaenog School when Mr. H. F. Jones was the headmaster — there were about 70 pupils at that time and two other teachers, Miss Telford, and Miss Wynne who lived in Llanarmon yn Iâl but lodged during the week in Derlwyn at the top of the village. School was alright and I liked playing rounders in the field with the others. After school, I

Mr & Mrs Roberts, Glan Aber.

used to play with my friend, Iris, who lived in Old School House where Mr. and Mrs. Mitchell now live. We used to play with dolls and make little pretend houses in the field by my house — that field has been very important to this village and all the children played there.

When I was a child, we didn't celebrate birthdays the way they do now — we just had a card and one small gift, and there was never a party. It was a special treat to go on a train — once we went on a day trip from Ruthin to Rhyl with the Chapel Sunday School but, usually, we would go by coach. The two chapels had one coach and the church another and we all went out on the same day — a Friday because that was not a market day. Both coaches would be full with mothers and children and some of the fathers used to go too, always to Rhyl. Now, I think they get too many treats. For instance, holidays were unknown when I was a child but now we go to a caravan with Glenys, our daughter, and her family. At Christmas we used to hang a stocking up on the side of the bed and in the morning there would be a doll, fruit, sweets and a few small toys. We did not have a Christmas tree in the house but there was a tree for the village children in the church hall each year, and a present for every child — all provided by Mr. and Mrs. Yates of Cefn Isa.

There used to be a bus from Clocaenog to Ruthin on market and fair days; there was also a school bus each weekday, taking some of the older children to Brynhyfryd School in Ruthin, and we could use that as well. There was a village shop then and a grocer used to come round with his van once weekly. We bought our bread from him — I don't remember my grandmother baking — and there were also a greengrocer and a fishmonger, and a butcher who used to come every Saturday, so we didn't need to go to Ruthin much. We bought our milk from Bryn Fedwen and used to carry it home in a milk can with a lid on it and we would also buy buttermilk there. Cheese was bought from the shop and we always kept our own hens, ducks and a pig. Although we were rationed during the war, we managed to get enough food because everybody grew their own vegetables — Morfydd's grandfather from No. 2 Maes Caenog, used to come down and do the digging for us and keep the garden tidy. We rarely used tinned food.

All our water came from a well in the garden — lovely spring water that we used even after mains water came to the village but it was filled in eventually because they said it was dangerous for the children. Mr. Purcell from Tank House, Clawddnewydd, laid the water pipes in the village to bring the water from Llyn Alwen reservoir and our supply was from a cold water tap inside the house from the mains supply.

We had a radio with a big battery that we had to take to Butland's shop in Castle Street, Ruthin, for changing and re-charging. Lighting in the house was by Aladdin paraffin lamp but, in the old kitchen here, we had a little oil lamp with a wick; going to bed with candles made an awful mess, especially in a draught, because the candle grease used to drip. My grandmother cooked on the fire and in the oven by the grate, and we used to have a little oil stove to boil the kettle — it was quicker and handier in the mornings. With the fire, you had to wait for it to burn up, of course. In 1993, we had a lot of work done on Glan Aber, modernising and improving it.

When I left school, I worked as a clerk in the Cambrian drinks factory and, later, I went to work for Clifford Hughes as a wages clerk. John and I first met shortly after he arrived to work at Pentre but we didn't go out together until about five years later, and I was 27 when we married at Bethania Chapel, Ruthin. There was just the wedding and then we went straight off in a hired car to our honeymoon in Southport where we had a wonderful time, with lovely weather, a bit cold, but fine and dry even though it was November. There was plenty to do, walking on the beach, going to the pictures and things like that, then we came back to Ruthin by bus at the end of the honeymoon and caught a taxi home. We have two children. Glenys, who has a degree in Welsh from the University of Wales, married to an engineer who works

Glan Aber.

for the Snowdon Mountain Railway, and they live near Llanberis. They have one child, now eleven-years old, named Alwyn. Our second child, Bryn, is also married and lives in Isfryn — the bungalow below the council houses — which used to belong to my mother's sister, Mrs. Chapman. He and Gwenan, his wife, have two children, Ffion (6) and Dewi (4). After I married, I worked in Ysgol Clocaenog canteen in the Church Hall and occasionally stood in for the cook. I enjoyed the job and worked there for 20 years.

I used to to attend Capel Cades, the chapel at the top of the village but when it closed, I started going to the church. Far more people attended services in those days and, up to a few years ago, Harvest Festival services used to be packed out and you had to go early to get a seat.

John:
My name is John Roberts and I was born at the family farm of Tŷ Newydd in Bodfari, just above Bwlch Isaf where my younger brother, Will, still lives. I attended Llandyrnog School and liked it there because I used to help the headmaster with the school garden and, as a young lad, I kept canaries, fantail pigeons and mountain ponies. My brother, Tom, and I did a lot of work with ponies and horses which we really enjoyed. When I left school at fourteen, I went into farming as a cowman and had to milk twenty-two cows by hand twice a day for Mrs. Hughes at Tre Goch Uchaf. My older brother, Tom, and I did a lot of work with horses and ponies working together with two teams of horses, Tom ploughing and I followed with the harrow. All sowing was done by hand, using a fiddle- there were no drills then — and it was all very hard work. Then Will bought an old industrial Fordson tractor — what I'd always wanted — and we did winter contract work for a long time. Later, Mrs. Hughes bought a Fordson Major and I used it to do contract work for Tre Goch.

I came to Clocaenog in 1950 when I was 20 to work for my uncle, Ted Davies' father, in Pentre. Ted and I are cousins and we laid all the hedges right round there and the one going up to Llyg Fynydd was massive, I remember. I did all types of farmwork at Pentre — milking, ploughing, haymaking, shearing and general stock work. I first met Mair at the Derwen Eisteddfod and, when I was 28 and she was 27, we married, and I have been involved in farmwork ever since then. I also worked for the Forestry Commission for 16 years with the Jones brothers, Glyn and Elwyn, who now have the depot on Denbigh Road in Ruthin. I eventually bought the two fields between Paradwys and Bryngwyn, and another by Cefn Isa, and still have a few sheep of my own on these fields and other land which I rent.

Since I was a boy, I have always trained sheepdogs for work on the farm, taking pups in, training them and then selling them on. I've sold trained dogs at the Bala sheepdog sales and have worked a lot with Don, Llanerch Las, Bala, over the years. I never went to trials because I worked all the time and couldn't get to them although I did have a try but never really got going with it. Will did better at it than I did.

My lifetime's hobby has been making shepherd's crooks — I have one that I made when I was only 16 and I still make them when I have the time. The heads are made of ram's horn and the shanks are of hazel sticks — silver hazel is the best because the shaft will never snap, but only splinter a little, when catching a ewe. Shanks will break after a while but crooks can be repaired if they are brought back to me with the horn intact. Nowadays, ram's horns are quite difficult to get unless you have the right contacts. Not all horns are suitable — they need to be of a good length and solid throughout. For instance, some horns are soft and/or have a hole in the middle so they are of no use and, of course, there are various horned sheep such as Dorsets, Welsh or Scottish Blackface, all of which are suitable.

When I'm making crooks, the horns are kept for about two years to dry out well before I change the shape by boiling and bending it — the smell while I am doing this is awful! I have one that I use for lambing and another that I use for catching sheep and as a walking stick when going round the fields and up and down hills. I have one with a bone handle I have carved into a whistle that makes a loud, sharp sound.

Sheep have been at the core of my work, hobbies and life for as far back as I can remember.

Audrey and Eddie Naisby
Paradwys

Audrey:
I was born in Burnage, Manchester, on 7 August 1929, at home; I was an only child. My father was an apprentice buyer in the cotton trade with Courtaulds, before the First World War interrupted his training and he went into the Royal Naval Air Service, based at Felixstowe where the flying boats were stationed. Soon after my parents married, the great recession of the 1920s took hold and my father was out of work, his promising career in ruins, and there was little hope of finding employment. Eventually, his father came to the rescue and loaned him the money to buy an insurance book with the Royal Liver Insurance Company; every agent was self-employed and worked on commission. My parents had married almost immediately after the death of my mother's father and they took my grandmother and my great aunt Grace to live with them. We were comfortable and well fed but there were few luxuries. Our house was on a new corporation estate, one of only four which was bigger than usual. The rent was high, but to have bought the equivalent would have been beyond my parents' income and consequently they never moved. I was seven before Grandma and my great aunt Grace left us to live on their own.

Mr & Mrs Naisby, Paradwys.

My junior school, was an ordinary council school, but based around an old house called the Acacias. The headmistress, Miss Shepherd, was very strict and very religious. Her pupils were expected to go on to grammar school and children came from near and far to be 'educated'. I remember when I was eight she came into our classroom, after a table test, and enquired about how well we had done and because nobody had full marks we all had to stand and be 'rulered' on both hands.

My father's parents retired from a terrace house to a bungalow in the country at Heald Green, outside Manchester. As a child I often went to stay with them for holidays. One of the rooms was called the Library because one wall was covered in bookshelves. I was allowed to read everything, and liked nothing better than to curl up with a book surrounded by the smell of the apples stored on the top shelf. Another favourite occupation was going to the farm down the road and bringing in the jersey cows to be milked; the reward was often a glass of milk, warm from the cow. It was there I was taught to milk, by hand of course. I had friends in the neighbourhood and we used to wander across the fields for miles, collecting berries or fishing (the catch was brought back to the farm pond) or climbing trees. I was a real tomboy and loved the country.

Every Sunday in the winter I would go by train with my parents to visit my grandparents, and every weekend in the summer we would meet them at 'the Hut'. As boys, my father and his brothers had camped on a farm near Styal, in Cheshire with Grandma and Grandpa, but when girls appeared on the scene my grandfather had a large

My mother, dressed for the Manchester Whit Walks.

Far right: My father in Royal Naval Air Service Uniform in 1917.

Mt father, back right, has just pulled the thread to click the shutter to take this photograph.

hut built so that the girls could sleep inside, while the boys continued to camp in tents. His intention was to keep the family together and it worked. The Hut, made in 1919, now stands in our garden.

At the beginning of the war in 1939, the Acacias school was evacuated to Wilmslow, Cheshire, near Ringway Airport (now Manchester International Airport) where the paratroopers were training — a safe place one wonders?

We went to sleep at my grandparents' bungalow. I had to walk over two miles to catch a school bus which took me a further two miles out to Wilmslow, where we shared the local school building, each school attending for only half a day. This was my scholarship year, and we sat the examinations in the church vestry; my parents had to buy me a fountain pen because we were not allowed to have inkwells on the rickety green baize card tables.

My favourite lesson was writing stories, but nobody was more surprised than I when an invitation arrived to have tea with the Lord Mayor of Manchester to receive a prize for the best essay written in the examinations (one boy and one girl had been chosen). In a separate examination I had won a free place at Withington Girls' School; there were nine places that year and the Acacias had won all nine! My parents were still responsible for my uniform, books and equipment.

I enjoyed my time at W.G.S. even though my Lancashire accent was a problem — I was not alone. It was a purely academic education, with stress on languages and science, but also plenty of P.E. and games. Because we were sleeping at my grandparents at that time I had to cycle eight miles to school and back every day.

There had been some air-raids and even more false alarms, but it was over a year after the war began that the Blitz hit Manchester on three successive night just before Christmas 1940. In the darkness we used to watch the fires started by the bombing, and the search-lights sweeping across the darkness hoping to pick up a German plane in their beam. Soon the whole sky was glowing red in the direction of Manchester and still we could hear the heavy throb of the German bombers going over. Each morning we cycled back to see if we still had a home.

After a while we returned to Burnage because, like everyone else, we became accustomed to the danger and tried to carry on with our lives. It meant my father reached home after work sooner, even though he often had to go out again on A.R.P. (Air-Raid Precautions) duty locally, and once a week he went back to his office building in Piccadilly, in the centre of Manchester on fire-watch.

Everywhere you went you had to carry your gas mask and when the sirens sounded we used to sit in the long corridor at school, which had been strengthened and sand-bagged, huddled on the benches. Can you imagine the cacophony with groups of girls reciting Latin declensions or saying tables through our gas masks-just to keep us occupied? We could make the most awful noises by blowing and lifting the side of the rubber round our cheeks. I shall never forget the rubbery smell.

We had an Anderson shelter dug into the clay in our garden. Of all the shelters around us, ours was the only dry one because it had been built, not deep enough, but over some land drains. At first several families crammed into our shelter, but in time they became the owners of Morrison table shelters, so instead of sitting cramped, with condensation running down the curved roof, we were able to put in a double mattress to sleep and I could do my homework. One night a stick of bombs fell very close and the wooden door on the shelter was sucked out and in but, apart from being temporarily deaf, we had survived. My father went out to see if anyone needed help and when he returned found our locked front door had blown in, without the glass breaking — blast could do strange things — several of the house windows were shattered.

We lived close to Fairey Aviation works where the fighter bombers were being made, but the Germans never managed to hit it. The McVite biscuit factory next to it was hit more than once and we knew, because next morning the air would be full of floating, charred paper from the packaging — no plastic then. Western Circle, where I lived, proved useful for an anti-aircraft gun, mounted on a lorry, to drive round and round

Audrey, with her mother and father.

firing at the German planes and making a terrible noise. Every park had its flotilla of barrage balloons and the games and football pitches were trenched to prevent enemy planes from landing. One of my jobs was to go and look at the notices fixed to the church gates reporting the names of people killed, in case we knew them. Few people had telephones and travelling around the bomb damaged city was difficult. My mother's brother was killed in Coventry, right at the beginning of the war, by a land mine that had floated down. Its parachute had caught in a tree and all the men in the road went out to move it away from their homes, not realising it would explode as soon as handled. Not one of them survived.

The war had a big impact on us all. For me, it lasted from when I was ten until I was nearly sixteen, and beyond that, the rationing continued until 1954.

My first trip abroad was with the French teacher and her husband. We went to stay with families in Bruges, Belgium. Another girl and I stayed with a professor who expected us to speak French at every meal and during evening walks along the canals with him and his daughter, Rika. I made friends with her and she came to stay at my home and we were pen-friends for many years before losing touch.

I belonged to the church youth club which met after Sunday evening service when the minister led discussions which ranged far and wide. We also had a mixed hockey team which played in the Manchester Youth League, played tennis, went to dances and the 'pictures' on Saturday nights and went for 20-mile hikes in Derbyshire before returning for church on Sunday evenings. Oh! the energy we had then. Eddie was invited for the weekend by one of his friends at Chester College to go on one of these hikes and that is how we met. We were soon commuting between Liverpool and Manchester every weekend to stay at each others' homes. Soon I went away to college in Cambridge, and Eddie, after only six weeks teaching, went into the army to do his two years National Service.

Eddie:
I was born in April 1928 in Liverpool. My paternal ancestors (weavers) were from north Yorkshire in the eighteenth century, and my maternal ancestors were from Benllech Bay in Anglesey, where the men-folk owned a schooner carrying slate from Port Dinorwic to Liverpool. My father was a blacksmith, having learned his trade during the 1914–18 war. He joined up on the first day of the war and spent the next four years with the artillery in France. Rarely would he speak of his experiences, except to say that on one occasion, the horse he was riding was killed under him and he was wounded. While in hospital recovering, he taught himself to play a flute, in order to regain the use of his hands. I owe my love of music to my father, who taught me to play from the age of eight, giving me a life-long hobby, which eventually became a source of income; so I am grateful to the Kaiser for landing a shell at the feet of the horse without actually killing my father!

In September 1939 I was due to start at a grammar school but, instead, had to report to the nearest school, to be evacuated to Farndon, and, after a while, to join my grammar school in Cardigan, where the education was fitful, but the liberty to roam was unlimited.

I returned to Liverpool when the Blitz was becoming intense, so once more schooling was disturbed, as was a rare good night's sleep, and homework was difficult to write on your knees, in the home made air-raid shelter, built like a First World War trench! My road was hit by six high-explosive bombs, as well as incendiaries, and on several occasions we were temporarily evacuated to a nearby church, while unexploded bombs were made safe. One night I had foolishly remained in bed after the siren had sounded, when I heard a bomb screaming down. I dived under the bed, but not before being covered with glass, plaster and soot. The house next door had taken a direct hit, and all our neighbour's family were killed. It was always the air-raid shelter after that!

Having taken my Higher School Certificate (the equivalent of 'A' Levels) I trained as a teacher at Chester

Elsie and Fred Naisby with Peggy the 'kid, when they were living in Betws-Gwerfil-Goch.

College before doing my army service, which proved to be interesting and varied. There were the usual punishing few weeks of initiation, followed by six months teaching English to Polish officers, at a resettlement camp at Haverigg in the Lake District. Then I was posted to Gottingen in the Hartz Mountains in northern Germany to join the 'Ox and Bucks' Light Infantry, whose job it was to keep an eye on the Russians just over the border, only a mile away — this was during the Cold War.

In Gottingen I became friendly with a German family whose daughter was the camp interpreter, and these people became the recipients of welcome gifts of N.A.A.F.I. soap, chocolate and ex-army blankets; the latter could be made into winter coats, even though they still had W.D. stamped on them. In return I was able to relax, in a family atmosphere, out of the army camp. The German civilians were still suffering great shortages and hardships long after the war was over, far more than in this country. The rest of my leisure time was spent in Brigade Cross-Country running events — in army boots; in rowing for B.A.O.R. (I had rowed at Chester); and teaching myself to play a borrowed clarinet. Life in an occupation army proved to be varied and interesting, but the downside was seeing the terrible destruction of the German cities, and in watching the long lines of refugees streaming across the border from the East.

Audrey and Eddie:
We both taught for a further two years, travelling between Manchester and Liverpool to see each other, and trying to save up enough to get married. When Eddie's parents came to live in Betws Gwerfil Goch at the end of 1950 we decided to bring our marriage forward and started looking for a house in Liverpool. We bought one in Mossley Hill and married at Easter, 1951.

Eddie had a teaching post, but as a married woman Audrey could not find work, as all posts were offered to the men returning from the forces. Eventually Audrey taught English and music part time, at Aigburth Vale Girls' Grammar School. We scraped by, and having decided that we had to eat anyway, we spent each summer holiday travelling all over Europe on a tandem, camping and cooking on a fire. We visited Scandinavia one year, journeyed across Belgium to Germany and Austria another, and cycled through France to Switzerland and Italy, usually travelling about 1,000 miles in the six weeks of the summer holidays. Our school linguistic skills were often severely tested!

It was $3^{1}/_{4}$ years before we had our first child, Paul, and, two years later, Andrew was born. During their childhood Eddie studied for a London University External Honours degree in Geography with Geology — no Open University to help in those days. In 1963 we left Liverpool to live in Berlin where Eddie taught at an RAF secondary school at Gatow. We were fortunate not to have chosen to go to Addis Ababa where Eddie was also offered a post, because Audrey was hospitalised for seven weeks soon after we arrived in Germany, and following an emergency operation our daughter Linda was born, still seven weeks premature, but very healthy. They both owe their lives to a young army doctor, Captain Lynd, and the nursing care at Spandau Military Hospital.

It was during the time of the Berlin Wall, but despite the difficulties of the situation — we always had to keep a case ready-packed to evacuate at a moments notice — we had a wonderful three years there. It opened our eyes to a much wider life style, we had a higher standard of living and could save, and still have a large house, a maid, a boiler-man, and subsidised tickets to the Berlin Philharmonic Orchestra, two opera houses and a third one in East Berlin, when we could persuade an officer to take a party through Check Point Charlie (we were civilians attached). We were living on the edge of the Grünewald Forest and within easy reach of the Havel river and our two boys had a great time cycling with their friends, sledging in the snow in the winter or tobogganing down the Rödelbahn (a hill made out of the Berlin bomb rubble) or enjoying family picnics by the open-air swimming pool after school in the summer. Eddie joined the officers' sailing club on

Eddie and Audrey Naisby when they first moved to Paradwys.

the Havel, and we opted out of all mess cocktail parties!

Every school holiday we were motoring and camping all over Europe, plus one trip back to Britain each year. Weekends were often spent in the Hartz Mountains camping with other teachers and their families, having travelled the somewhat fraught journey across East Germany; the problems, apart from when the Russians closed the borders, were not with the Russian soldiers but with the aggressive East German *Polizei*.

Having lived with the Berlin Wall for three years, Paul, our eldest son, arranged for us all to fly out and help to pull it down in 1989; Eddie's souvenir is a piece of concrete with graffiti which he himself broke off. We have vivid memories of Potzdamer Platz with jazz bands playing, people dancing and cheering — and emotional scenes, when people just stood with tears rolling down their cheeks, as they looked at the unbelievable gaping holes in the Wall. East Berliners were pouring through, to gaze at the wonders in the shop windows, to receive their 'Welcome Marks' and later in the day returning with bags of oranges and bananas.

During the last year of our stay in Berlin, our eldest son had chosen to return to England to live with Audrey's parents in Manchester, rather than to go to boarding school, but he flew out to join us each holiday. So, instead of extending Eddie's contract, we came back to Manchester where Paul was attending Chetham's School. We only lived in Cheadle Hulme for eight years, until it was nearly time for Linda to transfer to secondary school, and we came to live in Clocaenog in 1974.

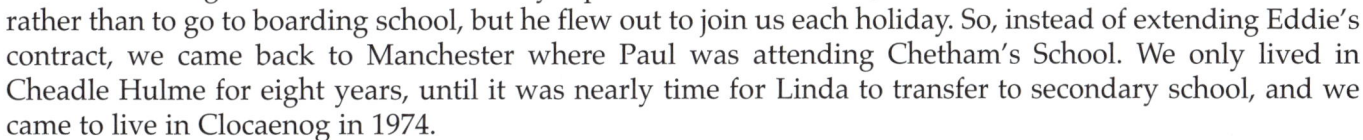

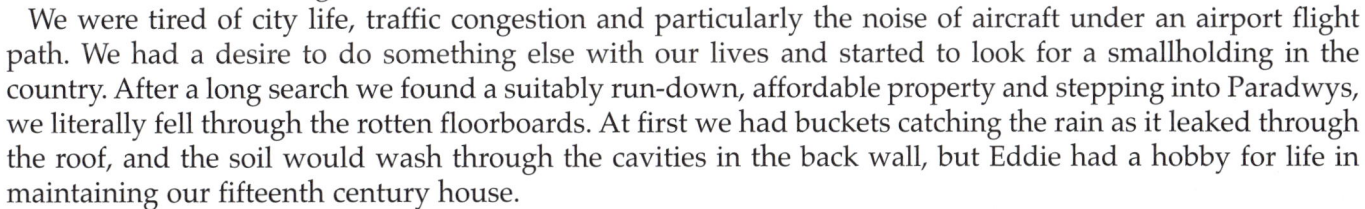

We were tired of city life, traffic congestion and particularly the noise of aircraft under an airport flight path. We had a desire to do something else with our lives and started to look for a smallholding in the country. After a long search we found a suitably run-down, affordable property and stepping into Paradwys, we literally fell through the rotten floorboards. At first we had buckets catching the rain as it leaked through the roof, and the soil would wash through the cavities in the back wall, but Eddie had a hobby for life in maintaining our fifteenth century house.

We aimed to be self-sufficient (and almost were, but for the bills!) and kept sheep, goats, pigs, hens, ducks and geese, as well as bees, growing all our own fruit and vegetables, salting bacon and making cheese. But to live here, a car was essential, and a telephone was handy to keep in touch, and we did need electricity, so somebody had to 'work'. Audrey was a home help for nearly three years and that was an asset in enabling us to make many friends in the surrounding villages. She also made lasting friends with one family when she helped to nurse the mother at home, until her death. Gradually Eddie was drawn back into teaching — not geology, but wood wind instruments at Howell's School, Denbigh; Audrey also went back to teaching, but this time with piano pupils. We both taught pupils at home and had enjoyable Christmas parties with pupils and their parents.

We arrived with only a limited knowledge of animal husbandry based on the childrens' rabbits, hamsters, gold fish and stick insects; it was a steep learning curve coping with all our animals and cultivating our $2^1/_2$ (later 6) acres. We have never regretted coming to live in Clocaenog and have enjoyed our life here.

As a child, Eddie's father inspired him with a love of sailings ships. This led Eddie to apply for a sail-training voyage on the three-masted *Winston Churchill*. The trip was only in the English Channel and the North Sea in December but it felt like rounding Cape Horn!

After travelling far and wide, working in Africa, South and North America, and having had many adventures on the way, our children are now settled with their families. Paul and Margaret, with Owen, live in London; Paul, having gained a 1st Class honours degree as a mature student at London University, works with asylum seekers, and Margaret, who has just given up full-time managerial work in the Health Service, is doing consultancy work from home. Andrew and Annie and their three children, Bethan, Sally and Hugh,

Left: About to set off from Betws Gwerfil Goch to Liverpool. Above: Audrey with the three children in the Hartz Mountains, Germany. Right: Paul and Andrew at Melin-y-Wig, 1959.

live in Sheffield, where they both trained as nurses, having previously gained degrees in English and TEFL qualifications; Andrew is in charge of trying to control T.B. in Sheffield and Annie has just re-trained and gone back to work in a cancer unit. Linda and Laurence with their three boys, Sam, Gareth and Callum are only twelve miles away towards Bala; Laurence works in the family business based in Corwen, and Linda, a qualified teacher, has only just started her third child in school and manages their two holiday lets which they have developed in the old out-buildings of the farm where they live. They have spent years restoring the derelict farmhouse and its surroundings.

We have both been reasonably healthy throughout our lives, and this has enabled us to follow an active life. Eddie discovered he could run without too much pain and has completed 20 marathons in Europe and North America, which have also been a good excuse for holidays abroad. As a 70th birthday present, the family financed a special effort which was an expedition to climb Kilimanjaro, Africa's highest mountain at over 19,000 feet — an unforgettable experience.

We are delighted to watch our family growing and developing into happy and independent people whom it is a pleasure to know as our friends, and to pass on the security of our own happy childhoods to the next generations. That is a worthwhile heritage.

Eddie at the end of one of his London Marathons. He has also sailed on the Winston Churchill *sail-training ship in the English Channel, on the last trip of the season, when a gale nearly blew the sail away! He climbed Kilimanjaro when he was 71.*

History of a House — Paradwys

Paradwys was probably built about the year 1450, according to the historian Peter Smith, who bases this hypothesis on the evidence of the structure of the building, which is relatively crude and so of an early date. Even then some of the internal timbers were recycled from other structures even older; for example, part of the frame between our kitchen and dining room contains an old newel post and a piece which looks as if it is grooved and worn by ropes, and there are sections of oak panelling — out of context — which had been pegged with wood. These pieces are structural in that wall but were covered at a later date with short, red-stained curves of barrel wood, nailed horizontally with hand-made nails, to fill in the frame and act as a base for the plaster.

Though of an early provenance, Paradwys was a much more finished dwelling than many houses known as '*tai unnos*' (one night houses) so called because they had a habit of appearing over-night like mushrooms. An example, though probably built much later at the time of the enclosure movement in the early 1800s, is one beyond Braich farm called Twll y Mŵg (Smoke Hole) which must have fulfilled the criteria required — to be built over-night and to have the smoke coming out of the chimney by morning; then you could claim the site and the surrounding land 'as far in each direction as you could throw an axe'. Few of these houses are still in existence because of the poor materials from which they were hastily made.

Essentially Paradwys is a Welsh 'long house' that began with a cruck construction. This was quite a rough method and these houses, although now rare, were once fairly common in north-east Wales. Suitably large oak trees would be felled and then, using a saw-pit, split down the length, (a method long used in ship building — perhaps a reason for people mistakenly saying they were built from ships' timbers). Every piece of wood was adzed and jointed by simple over-laps and then held together with wooden pegs. The pegs were square in section and driven into round holes until they were tightly wedged — no nails were used. All the timber was green oak newly felled, so that as the wood dried it would shrink and knit together.

The split trunks were laid out on the ground and the tie beam positioned before the structure was raised to the vertical. Each split pair of timbers was used to create the height and width of the house, meeting at the top at a ridge pole and held apart by a tie beam. It was usual for even quite complex timber frame houses to be built in this way, firstly on the ground where all the separate pieces would be numbered and the main ones pegged together, and then the frame raised upright. Take a look at

Top right: Twll y Mŵg.

Lower right: Elizabeth Jones standing in front of Paradwys Isaf, a photograph taken to show alterations that had been carried out to the house in 1912.

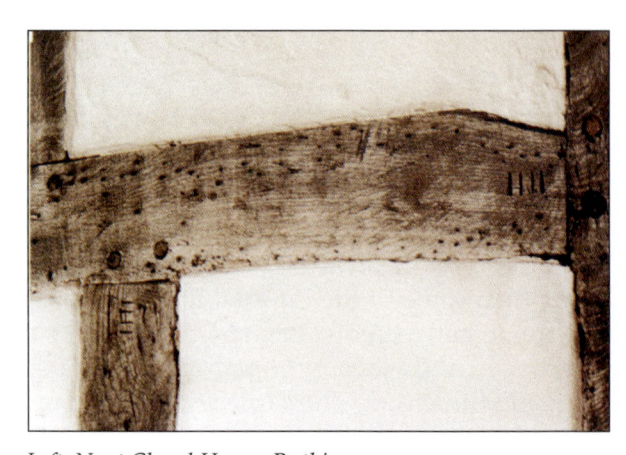

Left: Nant Clwyd House, Ruthin.

Above: Oak timbers on the outside of Nant Clwyd House showing the joiner's numbered marks.

the side of Nant Clwyd House in Castle Street, Ruthin, and you can still see the joiners' marks numbering the timbers. I recently read of a builder in the seventeenth century, who was given permission to 'lay and frame his timber in the churchyard' next to where he was building.

The 'A-frames' were placed on stone plinths with a slab of slate on top to act as a barrier between the wood and any rising damp which might rot the wood as this was a critical point in the structure. Next the whole frame would be stiffened by means of purlins and tapered secondary rafters were pegged to the back of the crucks to even out the slope from ridge to wall plate. The house would be built as a series of bays between the pairs of crucks; in the case of Paradwys there are three pairs of crucks and so it would have started out as a two bay cottage.

The site had to be near a water supply, in this instance the stream, but in order to avoid the hazard of flooding the site was prepared by using a common practice called step and fill; the cruck cottage was raised on the platform created. There were — and are — no foundations as such, though advantage would be taken of the slope behind to roll down huge erratic boulders to form the bottom of the walls. These stones were mainly granite and would give a dry base to the wall; often they were so large that they formed the whole width of the wall, over two feet thick. An oak wooden sill (wall plate) was placed on these and the rest of the wooden frame built on it. All this forms a framework for the wattle and daub, some of which is still visible in parts of the house. Vertical oak staves were fixed in the main framework and ash withies were woven horizontally to form a matting which could then be daubed with mud. This was next covered with a mixture of lime plaster and horse hair (tail hair preferably) as binding.

The floor was merely beaten earth with a central slab fireplace. We have found a burnt area beneath the central chimney that was probably the site of this original fireplace. Later a slate flag floor was instated in the family's section and there would have been cobbles in the cattle end of the homestead. Certainly it was common practice for people and animals to be under the one roof. This roof was still thatched in 1853 when an insurance was taken out for Paradwys by James Maurice of Wells Street, Ruthin on three properties in Clocaenog.

At first the windows would have been barred openings that could be shuttered when necessary and not

Paradwys Uchaf and Isaf in 1976.

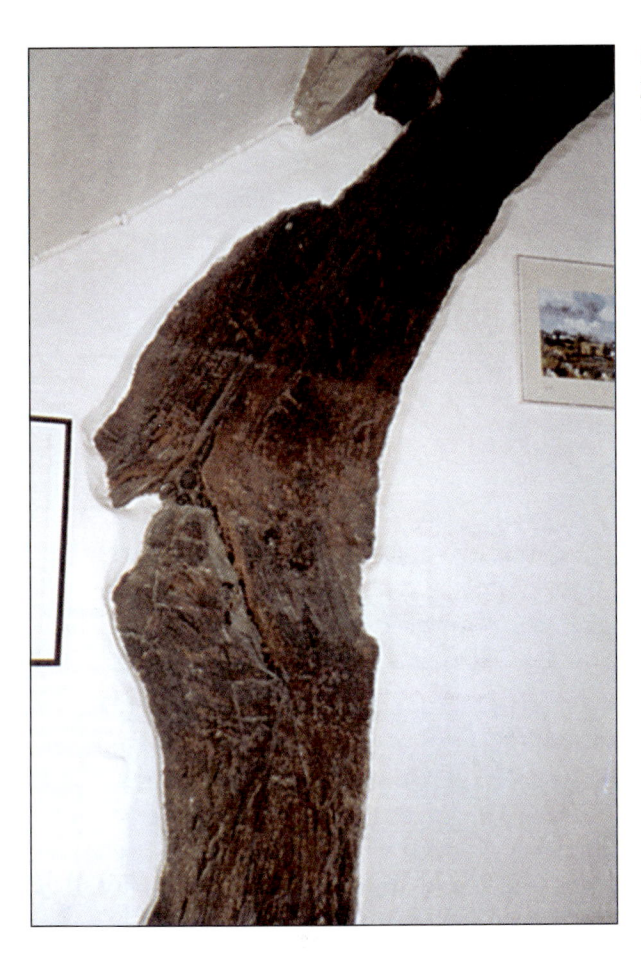

Left: A cruck, showing the purlin raised when the roof was slated.

Right: Hand-made bricks from the sixteenth century.

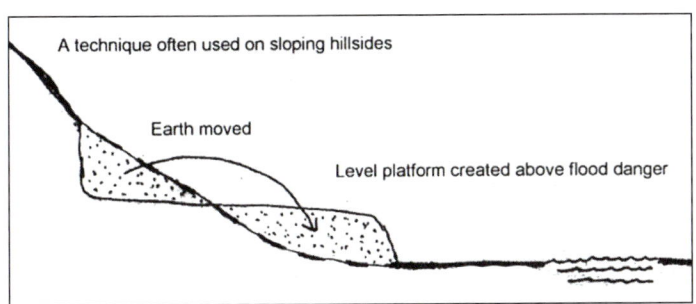

'Step and Fill'.

Below: Because Paradwys is so old, a variety of methods and building materials have been used. In part of the house the walls are made of 'wattle and daub'. The main frame was built of oak, slotted with spaced uprights of small oak staves, interwoven with ash withies — supple when newly cut. Some of the original plaster still adhers in this picture.

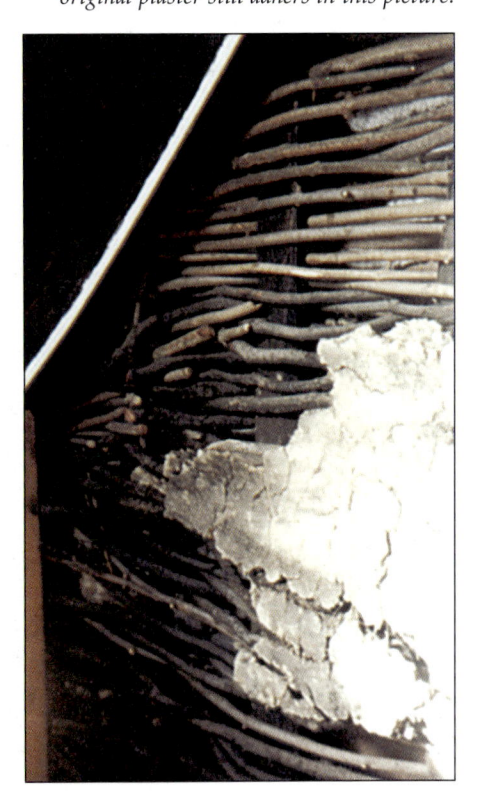

Left: Huge granite boulders in the walls.

> **Insurance in 1853**
> Insurance taken out by James Maurice Esq., of Well Street, Ruthin
> on three buildings in Clocaenog
>
> 1. £60   On the building of 2 dwelling houses and shop communicating, stone built and thatched in the occupation of R. Roberts, grocer.
>
> 2. £60   Stryt (3 dwellings) thatched. 1854 tenanted by Robert Lewis, Edward Hughes, and John Roberts and their families.
>
> 3. £80   4 adjoining dwellings, stone built and slated. 1854 tenanted by William Hughes, John Lewis, Robert Davies and Margaret Evans and families.
>
> This insurance was taken out on behalf of the Bagot Estate which owned the houses, but would not cover the contents of course. The last four dwellings have now completely disappeared.
> [Denbighshire Record Office, Ruthin]

only allowed some light to enter but some smoke to exit; there would be no glass in such a poor dwelling. At some stage it was decided to extend and 'modernise' Paradwys. Some alterations were carried out in the Tudor period and during Elizabethan times the central chimney was built; prior to that much of the smoke would have found its way out through a hole in the thatch or under the eaves. The central chimney can be roughly dated because it is constructed with hand-made bricks and these were only introduced into the Vale of Clwyd in the sixteenth century, by Flemish craftsmen who were brought here by Sir Richard Clough to build his house Bach-y-Graig, erected in 1567. The influence of these builders can also be seen in Denbigh Green, at Plas Clough, with its Dutch stepped gables, also built for Sir Richard, at the same time. Once the chimney was built, an upper floor could be added as it gave support for more timbering. At first it was only a garret (*croglofft*) reached by a ladder fixed to the wall. A cellar was dug and the dwelling was extended at both ends, though not necessarily all at the same time. Perhaps it was then that it became a tavern at the lower end of the house over the cellar (there are stone steps from inside the house leading down). When we put a window in the back wall of what we believe had been the inn parlour we found the bevelled edges of an old opening — perhaps a doorway into the inn — we also found beneath the more recent plaster a hand-blocked pattern; this we have left until we can get help to preserve it.

The extension walls were built with some granite boulders but mainly of local stone which is shale and subject to frost-fracturing, so there was need to cover them with a thick lime coating. Two more chimneys were built into the end walls but the back wall continued to be dug into the slope and there were no windows at the rear of the house, because the roof came almost to ground level.

One of our first tasks was to remove the earth at the back of the house because the walls were so damp and we were told that, in wet weather, the ground water ran down the back wall, across the floor and was brushed out of the front door — we did not fancy that! However, when a JCB removed the earth we found to our dismay that the wall was less than adequate in places! My husband, Eddie, had to support the roof with timbers and then rapidly build stone pillars, with the gaps.

When the house was divided into two dwellings, the

The roof supported by timbers after a JCB had dug out the earth bank.

Cruck Buildings: A building is primitive and therefore of early provenance when, as in Paradwys, the crucks overlap at the apex and there is a ridge-pole resting on the cross pieces. This was a particularly common method used in north-east Wales where 88 examples are known. The length of the structure was stiffened by purlins and wall plates which were placed on the ends of the cross-beams, so that the wall itself need not be load bearing.

The crucks were raised upright with the cross-beams in place, fixed with half-lap joints. Tapered secondary rafters were pegged to the back of the crucks to even out the roof slope from ridge to wall plate before thatching was put on.

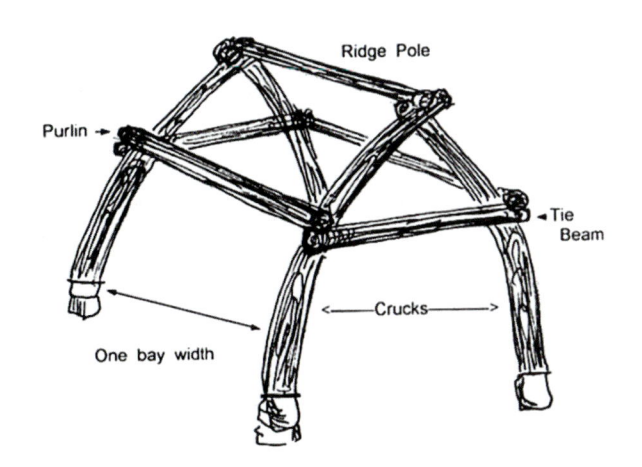

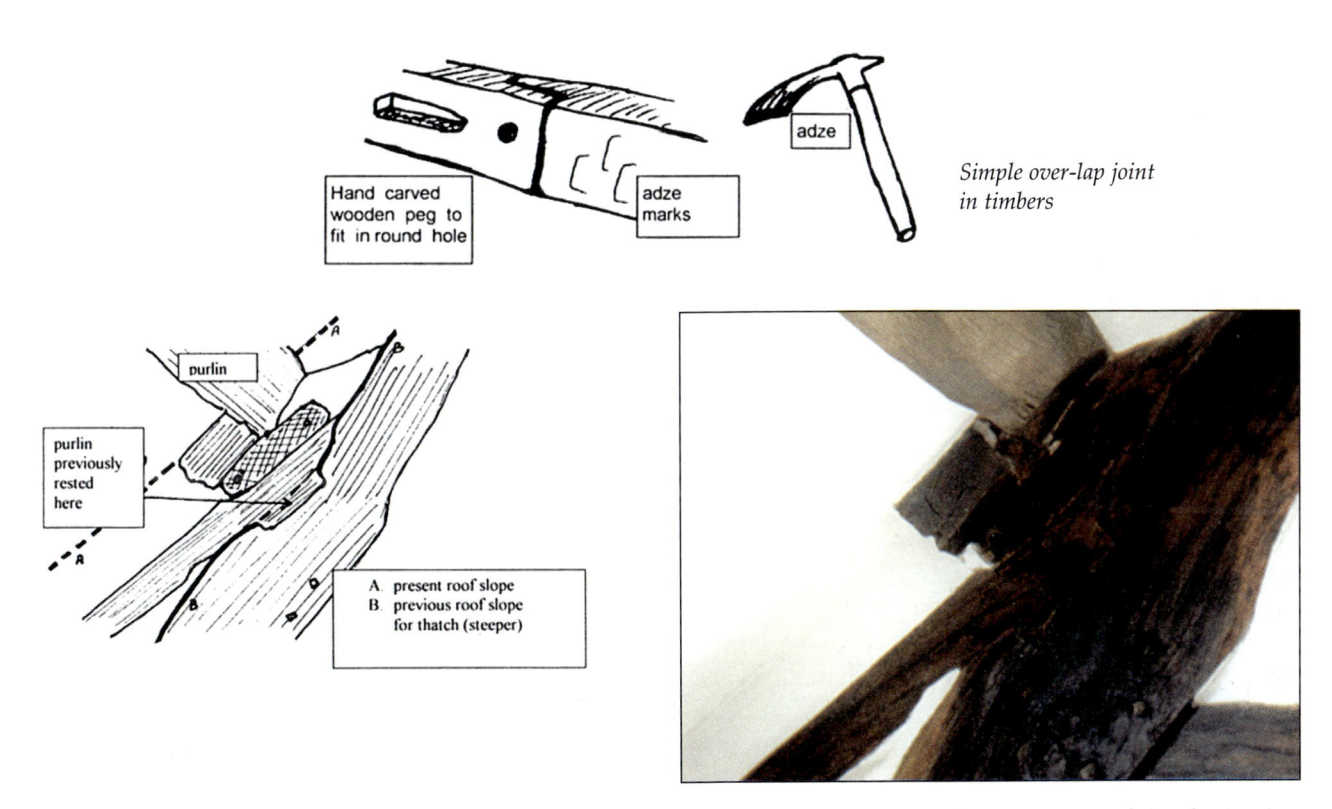

Simple over-lap joint in timbers

two separate lean-to rooms which had been added at the back were less than shoulder high on the outside and probably continued the line of the original thatched roof. Later when the main roof was slated (sometime in the nineteenth century — after 1853) these stone walls were built higher with bricks, giving a thinner upper wall and better head height inside.

When the main roof was slated in the late nineteenth century, the pitch was altered because it no longer needed to be as steep as for thatch and the changes are visible in the bedrooms. The higher eaves would then allow for windows to light the upper rooms. The bedroom above Paradwys Uchaf was reached by a ladder straight up the wall (the notches are still there) but in the nineteenth century a staircase was added and a second staircase lead up to the two bedrooms in Paradwys Isaf. We have made another bedroom above the kitchen, which incidentally only had a lath ceiling, so we had to install joists and floorboards.

We have tried to uncover and restore, at the same time as making the house acceptable as a twentieth century home. Paradwys has been altered many times over the centuries and yet still stands as an example of Welsh house design, and a true Welsh Long House.

The three-stall shippon with its cobbled floor on two levels and iron bar divisions has now gone and is the position of the holiday let's sitting room, whilst there is a bedroom built above, but without altering the

Paradwys as one house (with the holiday let on the left).

façade. The old site of the dairy has become the new kitchen/dining area for the holiday-let.

In Roman times, a tavern would hang out a bunch of ivy leaves to attract customers, probably because of the association with Bacchus. In this country it was common practice to advertise the fact that a house was a tavern and the ale was brewed, by hanging out a bush on a pole, or by standing the 'ale-stake' in front to announce that the brew was ready to be sampled, and this was required by law from about the fourteenth century. This lead to competition and various fancy signs were invented as we have today; the Bull & Bush was an early one.

Once more Paradwys is providing accommodation for people to stay and, although it is no longer a hostelry 'at the sign of the Paradise', and I have no idea what sign it ever had, if any, I think I would choose Adam and Eve in the Garden!

People who have lived in Paradwys and related topics

Although Paradwys has been said to date from about 1450 there are very few extant records that mention ordinary people from those earlier times. Few names are to be found before parish records began in the seventeenth century and, although Clocaenog has some of the oldest records in Denbighshire, dating from 1677, it is necessary to look first at legal transactions and deeds.

There were very few freehold properties in the parish of Clocaenog and most families were tenant farmers or small holders. A family called Wynne lived in the farm called Bryngwyn (off the road going from Clocaenog to Clawddnewydd). In the seventeenth century they seem to have been involved in leases and bonds with the owner, Sir Thomas Middleton, of Pwll Parc, concerning a 'messuage and tenement' called Paradwys. In effect, although owned by Sir Thomas' estate, as was nearly every house and holding in the parish, many dwellings were sub-let on quite a regular basis.

The first name in the records to connect Paradwys to a specific person was a Johannes Evans who paid his hearth tax in 1671 (the tax was abolished in 1688) and died at Paradwys in 1718. Then in 1722 Paradwys was leased to David Williams, junior, of Lodge.

In 1699 Rowland Wynne, of Bryngwyn, married Margaret Powell and in 1701 their son David Wynne was born. When he grew up he married Margaret Jones in 1730 and they moved to a house 'nearby', because they are next found in the records, living in Paradwys (just down the road from Bryngwyn) and in 1733 David is named as an innkeeper. His family was born here between 1730 and 1744, Margaret, Elizabeth, Rowland, Jane, Katherine, Hanna and David — this David died, aged 15, in 1760.

Over a long period David Wynne, senior, is named as licensee or is standing surety for other publicans. Margaret, his wife, died in Paradwys in 1769; David lived here until he died, aged 87 years old, in 1788, remaining the publican of Paradwys to the last. David Powell 'of Paradwys' died in 1797 he was probably David's maternal grandfather).

The next licence found, for 1793 (the records are not complete) was issued to Robert Jones, publican, who had married Jane, daughter of David and Margaret Wynne. Jane died at Bryngwyn in 1804, aged 72. In 1799 another Jane, wife of John Jones of Paradwys, died — they were obviously sharing the accommodation in the tavern within the family.

In the 1811 census we also find two families living in Paradwys; John Jones and Robert Jones were still there, but also Robert Roberts, who had married Anne Jones, the daughter of John, the previous year, when Anne signed her name but Robert could only put his mark. In the year 1813 David, son of Robert Roberts, publican, and his wife Anne, was born at Paradwys, whilst Mary was born at Tŷ Coch to William Roberts, publican, and his wife Elizabeth — Tŷ Coch, as well as being a farm, was also the Cloion, serving ale.

In 1823 Robert Roberts gave 2/6 (2 shillings and sixpence) towards the building of the new school, as did the other publican in the village, now Edward Lewis. Robert Jones 'of Paradwys' had died in 1821, John Jones lived on to be 84 in 1885, when he died and was buried 'from Paradwys'.

There are several extant licences issued to Robert Roberts 'at the sign of the Paradise' and we have a copy of one for 1827 when Edward Lewis is named as publican of the Plough, Clocaenog, (but this is the only time I have found the name 'the Plough' used) and 'stood surety to our Sovereign Lord the King in the sum of twenty pounds', while Robert paid thirty pounds in order to run a public house at the Paradise.

Edward Lewis lived with his wife, Ellen, at Tŷ Coch and in 1824 when his son, Edward, was born, Edward senior, was called a wheelwright in the church records and again in 1825. This may be because his father still held the licence. It was only in 1828, when John was born, that Edward was named as a publican at Tŷ Coch. Although in 1827 we see Robert Roberts as licensee and victualler, during that year Paradwys must have ceased to be a tavern. When Paradwys stopped selling ale, Tŷ Coch became the only village pub; it was never an inn.

In 1853, when an insurance for £60 was taken out by James Maurice of Well Street, Ruthin, 'for a house communicating, stone built and thatched, in the occupation of R. Roberts, grocer — Paradwys had long ceased to be run as a tavern. Robert and his wife Anne continued to live here and bring up their family, John, David, William, Anne and Gabriel — son Robert died, aged 3 — but then they disappear from the records and the parish. I should be delighted if anyone could tell me where they went; I have searched and failed.

(Incidentally, there was a Robert Roberts, publican and victualler, being issued licences to run a tavern in 1817 and 1824 at the Admiral Lord Nelson in Llanfwrog, and yet another Robert Roberts in 1822 and 1823 at the Antilope, Llanrhydd — but Robert Roberts was a popular name!)

Another £60 insurance taken out by James Maurice in 1853 was for Stryt (three dwellings) thatched, tenanted by Robert Lewis, Edward Hughes, and John Roberts, and their families. The third insurance of £80 was for 4 adjoining dwellings, (now gone) stone built and slated, tenanted in 1854 by William Hughes, John Lewis, Robert Davies and Margaret Evans and their families.

Who else has lived in Paradwys? In 1820 John Price, the schoolmaster could not afford his lodging and so part of the school was sectioned off for his accommodation, but it was very damp as the school was built against the graveyard. Money was raised to build a new school on land donated by Lord Bagot, and this was completed in 1823.

By the tithe returns of 1839 this John Price was lodging in Paradwys, the 'owner being John Jones, Maestyddyn, but in the census returns of 1851 there is also Thomas Hughes, 30, his wife, Elizabeth, 26, daughters Elizabeth, 4, and Margaret, 2. This is confirmed in the 1871 census where we read of Thomas Hughes, 49, Elizabeth, 46, and their lodger, Henry, 25, a carpenter; and Thomas Evans, 59, an agricultural labourer, with his wife Mary, 62, and their lodger John E. Roberts, schoolmaster, aged 17; also Elizabeth Price, 70, annuitant, (wife of John Price the schoolmaster, deceased) and her unmarried daughter, Mary, aged 40 — the three families with two lodgers, living under one roof with only, at the most, three bedrooms!

In 1874 two babies were born to parents living in Paradwys and were christened on the same day, April 5th: Margaret Roberts was the mother of baby Elizabeth, and Mary Hughes was the mother of Jonathon.

John Jones was on the electoral roll for 1900 and he and his wife 'kept shop'. Grandfather Jones, aged 84, died in the bedroom above the shop in 1916 and because there was only a ladder up the wall to reach the *croglofft*, I have been told that they had to wait until rigor mortis had taken hold before he could be lowered down through the hole in the ceiling — the notches where the narrow ladder went up can still be seen in the timbers.

As often seems to have happened, the schoolmaster lodged here in Paradwys and he married Elizabeth Jones, the daughter of his landlord; his name was Mr. J. H. Richards; their daughter, Nesta Elizabeth, was born in 1918 but died, unfortunately, seven months later. Her grandmother, Elizabeth Jones, the shopkeeper, died in 1925, aged 67 and John, her husband, died in 1927 aged 74.

1928 was the great divide, when the Bagot estate was broken up and sold which concerned almost every dwelling in the village of Clocaenog. Paradwys was sold in 1929, to be bought by Thomas Jones, a railway traffic inspector of Rhuallt, near Ruthin; the property was sold as one cottage and garden with two fields — almost three acres of land. One field known as Cae'r Aber was sold on to John Roberts, of Glan Aber,

> A Very Desirable Country Cottage and Garden
> **PARADWYS**
> together with
> over 2 Acres of Land
> situate in the village of Clocaenog, now or late in the occupation of Mr John Jones.
> The Roomy House, which is probably of seventeenth century origin, has a pleasant position and contains: Parlour, Kitchen, Back Kitchen, Living Room, Pantry and 3 Bedrooms, separate Wash-house and Bakehouse.
> An Excellent Garden
> Studded with Fruit trees, adjoins the House.
> The Outbuildings include: 2-divisioned Hayshed, Piggery, Shippon for 2 cows and Calfcote.
> Altogether a very Attractive Small Property, such as appeals to the Retired Countryman or as a Country residence for the Urban Dweller.
>
> Schedule
>
> | Description | Area |
> | --- | --- |
> | House, Land and Buildings | 1.122 |
> | Field | .793 |
> | Garden | .140 |
> | | 2.055 |

Extract from the 1928 Pool Park sale catalogue.

Paradwys keeping the field behind and the one opposite the house.

When a young couple Evan Evans, 21, and Ellen Roberts, 19, were married they came to live in the cottage in 1930; they had two children, Norah in 1931 and Glenys in 1933, then Elined in 1937 and Norman, born in 1943. A timber feller, Ernest Sydney Bignell and his wife, Mabel Evelyn, had a son, Robert Albert in 1933 whilst living in Paradwys Uchaf.

Other tenants were the Edwards family and Lilian Sarah was born here in 1934 but they left to go and live in No. 2 Maes Caenog when Lilian was only six weeks old. For a short time an auctioneer, Mr. H. Roberts and his wife stayed in the house. Then Mrs. Catherine Richard Jones of Nant y Celyn bought the property in 1945 and moved from the farm with her son, Meirion into Paradwys Isaf, whilst in Paradwys Uchaf lived her niece, Miss Gwen Evans, who loved to talk about times gone by and I regret not having taken the opportunity to record some of her reminiscences. She eventually moved to No. 4 Maes Caenog when it was newly built, where she lived until her death in 1981. When her aunt, Mrs. Catherine Jones, died, Meirion sold the whole property to Mr. and Mrs. Frost from Birkenhead. They used Paradwys Uchaf as a week-end home until the death of Mr. Frost, after which Mrs. Frost never visited the cottage again and the property was sold to the present owners, Audrey and Eddie Naisby in 1974.

Paradwys may have been a pilgrims' inn

It is hard for us to realize how overwhelmingly important religion was to all the people in this country before modern times. In the Middle Ages everyone in Europe supposedly belonged to the Catholic church which taught that it was necessary for each person to aim for a state of absolution in order to attain forgiveness and not be condemned to purgatory for one's sins. In real life, knowing everyone to be 'sinful', one solution was to seek forgiveness by going on a pilgrimage before it was too late. This was not an easy thing to accomplish because of personal commitments, apart from the difficulties of the journey. Gerald (*Geraldus Cambriensis*), when he travelled around Wales in the twelfth century, was gathering support for a major pilgrimage, a

St. David's Cathedral, Pembrokeshire.

crusade to the Holy Land. Towards the end of the Middle Ages pilgrimage was sometimes meted out as a punishment for a civil crime, so it was not considered an easy option e.g. Henry II went to Canterbury after the killing of Thomas à Becket. Despite the problems, thousands of people went on a pilgrimage during their lifetime, in order to avoid hell-fire in the after life. Chaucer's *Canterbury Tales* tells us about people of many walks of life seeking forgiveness through travelling on pilgrimage.

To go to Jerusalem was the ultimate aim but not always possible, so there were alternatives. One could visit and pray at various holy places recognized by the Church, such as a local shrine to a saint, and it was considered acceptable if you made the journey twice between St. David's in south Wales and Holywell in the north — it was the equivalent of going to Rome once! An old saying said, 'Seek St. Davids twice if you wish to visit Rome.' The Welsh poet, Iolo Goch, wrote that he was getting old and his feet would not take him to Jerusalem:

> *Cystal ymofal im yw*
> It is just as beneficial to me
> *Fyned deirgwaith i Fynyw*
> To go three times to Menevia
> *a myned, cymyrred cain,*
> as to go, fine dignity
> *Yr hafoedd hyd yn Rhufain.*
> in the summers as far as Rome.

You did not have to be rich to make these pilgrimages as the normal form of transport was on horseback and if you did not possess a horse then you did like most people and walked. Men and women were used to walking great distances in their daily lives — to church, to school, to market, or to visit relatives. On a long journey you would always try to join other people going the same way as yourself, for the company and for the safety of numbers, so there was no problem finding your way; there were well defined routes between one overnight stop and another, and as a pilgrim you could claim food and lodging. You had to apply to your local bishop for your '*testimoniales*' proving you were genuine; in fact in 1388 Richard II passed a law whereby any pilgrim could be arrested if he could not produce his papers.

Holywell to St.Davids

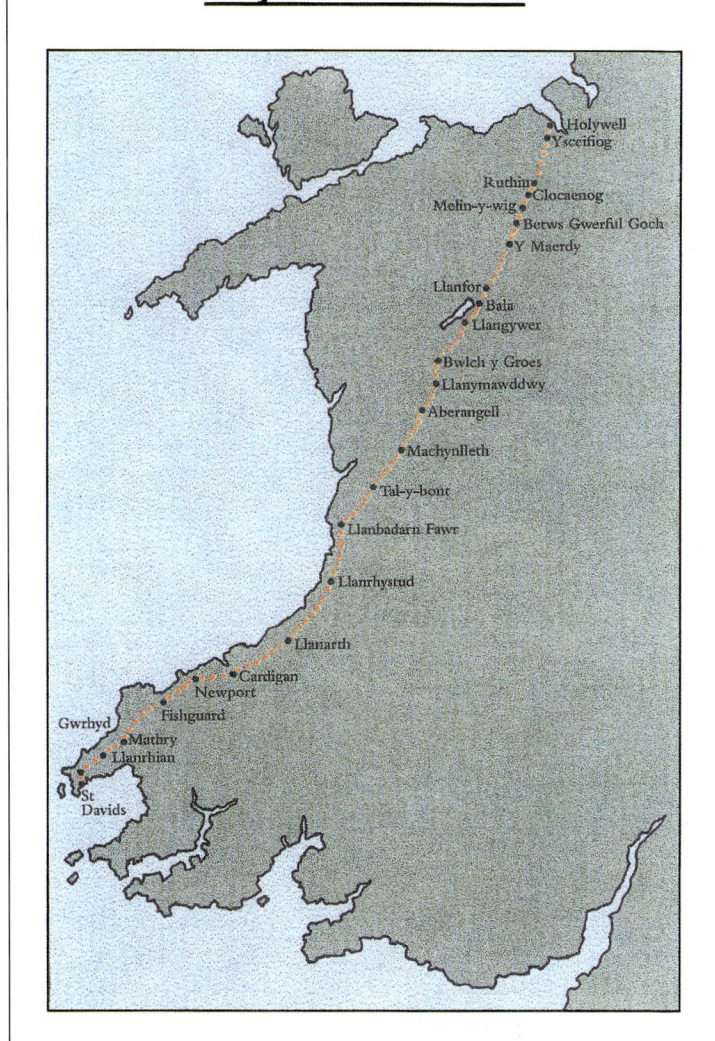

John Ogilby's Route of 1675, Holywell to St. Davids

From a map shown in **PILGRIMAGE A Welsh Perspective** by Terry John & Nona Rees With the permission of Nona Rees & the Gomer Press

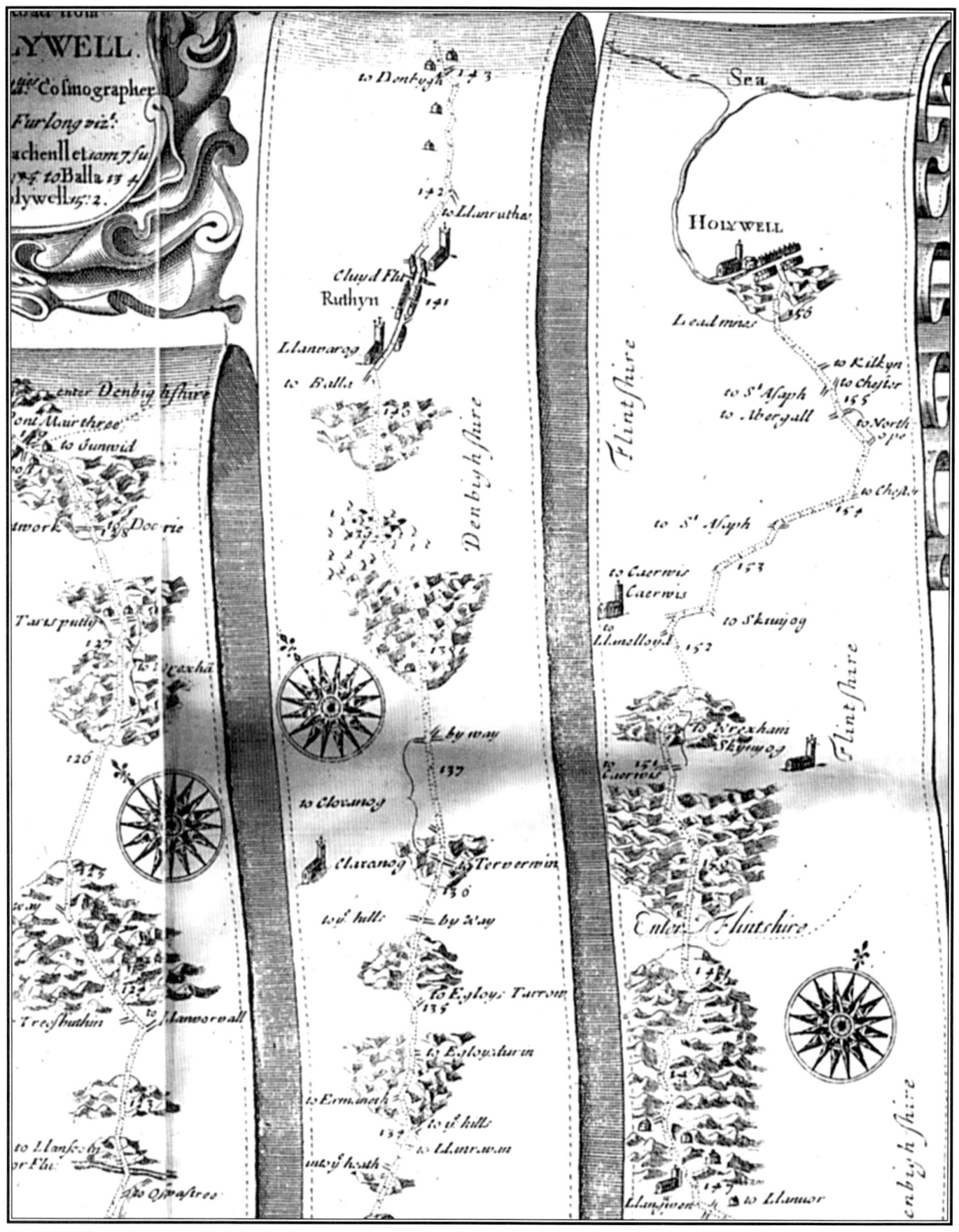

Part of Ogilby's ribbon map of 1675.

Old sunken way across the fields. Llewyn Bresych can be seen in the background.

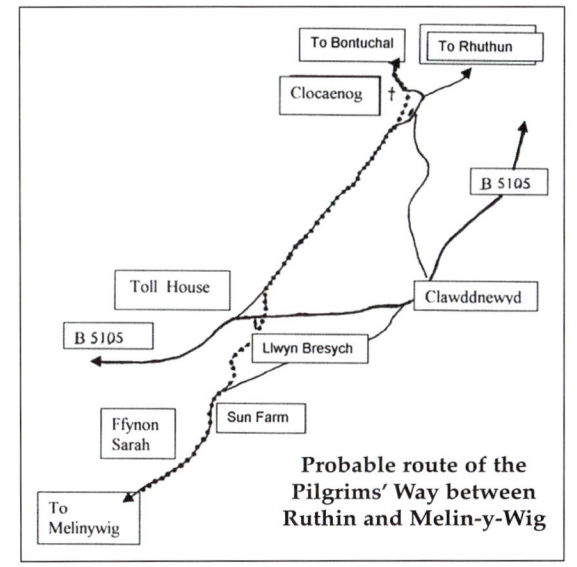

The lane down to Clocaenog from Toll Borth.

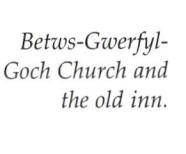

Probable route of the Pilgrims' Way between Ruthin and Melin-y-Wig

Betws-Gwerfyl-Goch Church and the old inn.

The 'holy well' of Ffynnon Sara.

Before setting out you would arrange your affairs, ask others to look after your family, property, animals, etc. and pay your 'Great Tithe', one tenth of all you possessed to the Church. You would then attend a service with other pilgrims to confess your sins and be blessed, put on your pilgrim's loose, grey, woollen robe with a monk's cowl, and take up your wooden staff and your satchel in preparation for your journey. Friends and neighbours would ask you to pray for them at the various holy places on the way. You were then ready to set out on a hazardous trip not knowing when, or if, you would return, but which you must have considered totally essential for your well-being in the next world, if not in this one.

In the late sixteenth century Saxton's map was the first to show Wales in any detail and even then it did not show routes. It was 1675 before John Ogilby published a 'ribbon' map depicting towns and villages with roads linking them and even some outstanding features of the landscape. These maps were a travellers impression, rather than an accurate depiction and although they gave mileage (St. David's to Holywell was given as 156.5 miles) they naturally followed the main routes in general usage which went north–south, as did the pilgrims, but they had less than adequate instruments to help them produce their drawn maps with accuracy. The fact that such a small hamlet as Clocaenog is given a mention indicates its importance in those days to the travelling pilgrim.

The stretch which concerns us went from Holywell through Ysceifiog to Ruthin, on to Clocaenog, Melin-y-wig, Betws Gwerfil Goch, Maerdy, and up over the moor below Caer Euni to Bethel and Bala, down the east side of the lake to Llanwchlyn and on over Bwlch y Groes (the Pass of the Cross).

A later version of a 'ribbon map' showing more of the route

Clockwise from top left:

An old postcard of Betws-Gwerfyl-Goch.

The old Pilgrims' Route over the moor below Caer Euni.

Old bridge at Maesmor.

The massive arches below the bridge at Betws-Gwerfil-Goch.

The width of the bridge at Betws-Gwerfyl-Goch.

At Clocaenog, Paradwys, by virtue of its name and age, was a likely hostelry along the way, particularly as St. Foddhyd's Church is of such antiquity and would be a useful prayer-house on the journey. From Clocaenog the route went up the much older road, not the one to Clawddnewydd, but the road connecting Cerrigydrudion to Ruthin, down the track to Llwyn Bresych, along the sunken way across the fields towards Ffynnon Sarah, (dedicated to St. Saeran, an Irish saint), which was restored in 1972 by the Rector of Derwen. This well was believed to cure cancer and rheumatism, and pilgrims would go down the steps to bathe or drop pins in the water with a wish and a prayer. Below the bridge to Braich farm is an old clapper bridge and just nearby, at the road-side stood a cottage where the keeper of the well lived; there is a narrow strip of land, still hedged, that belonged to the cottage, which only burned down in the 1860s. St. Saeran was buried at Llanynys, 'to which place a branch of an ancient road led direct from this spot through Clocaenog and Cyffylliog'.

Not far away, near Cefn Bannog, a stone was found with two crosses and 'HR 1630' carved on it. The initials link this with Hugh Reinallt of Hendre farm, who held his tenancy from the Salesbury estate on condition that he gave free lodging to travellers and pilgrims.

The small gate leading to Ffynnon Sara, by the gateway to Braich Alarch.

From Ffynnon Sarah the route joins the road to Melin-y-wig and down the valley to Betws Gwerfil Goch (the prayer-house of red haired Gwerfil, grand daughter of the twelfth century king, Owen Gwynedd); here the Church of St. Mary, founded by Gwerfil, is built alongside the pilgrims' way and from the raised sanctuary graveyard opened directly into the hostelry (which some of you may remember as the Post Office and the Hand shop — open until the 1960s — and now a private dwelling). St. Mary's Church contains some carved panels which are unique in Britain because they were once part of a rood screen depicting a crucifixion scene and are the only ones to have survived the Reformation when thousands of similar carvings were destroyed as idolatrous; this carving is so lucky to have survived as it was rescued a second time from a rubbish heap in 1840. As in Clocaenog church there is also an unusual chandelier. Next we can see the beautiful arched bridge over the Alwen, built in 1785 when the road must have been far more important as a route than today, to have been made so wide. A drovers' road crosses at right angles below the chapel, coming from the Denbigh moors, with an over-night stay at Y Gro, with its holding pens and where there was once a cockpit (now in St. Fagan's), then through the ford and on to Shrewsbury and the English markets.

At the bottom of the valley our pilgrim way crosses the A5 by the Goat Inn, over the Afon Ceirw on a mediaeval pack-horse bridge, follows a short section of the pre-Telford road, and climbs up to pass between Hafod Tudur (where our daughter and family live) and the Iron Age hill fort of Caer Euni, then on over the moor to Sarnau, Llanfor and Bala, going between two ring cairns on the way — it is strange how often these old Christian routes utilise even older pagan pathways and holy places. Many holy wells are thought to be of early Celtic origin.

Paradwys was well placed to accommodate people who were travelling on this busy route, either to market or on pilgrimage.

St. Winefride was the patron saint of virgins, based on the legend that she was beheaded by Prince Caradoc for refusing to marry him. She was Welsh by birth, and the story goes that where her head fell on the ground a healing spring began to flow — this is the well of St. Winefride in Holywell, Flintshire. She is usually depicted, like St. Denis, carrying her head in her hand. St. Winefride's Well has always been celebrated for the miraculous healing properties of its waters.

St. David/Dafydd/Dewi was the son of Xantus, Prince of Cereticu, now called Cardiganshire. As he grew up he was trained to be a priest, became an ascetic living in the Isle of Wight, preached to the Britons, argued successfully with Pelagius, and was then sent to the See of Caerleon. There at Menevia (*main aw* — meaning narrow water or *frith*) he continued his education, and when Dyvrig, Archbishop of Caerleon retired and appointed David to succeed him as archbishop, he built his episcopal residence at Menevia which ever since has been called by his name, St. David's. He died in 544A.D.

Early Worship and Holy Wells

Water, springs and wells have been venerated since pre-Christian times and there is archaeological evidence of a Celtic water-cult in Anglesey. By tradition there are two wells called Dwyfan and Dwyfach from which flowed two streams that flowed through Bala Lake 'without mingling with its waters'. Dwyfan and Dwyfach were believed to be the names of two men 'who escaped from the Deluge'. Another legend, again probably pre-Christian, but common to many other places, was about a guardian of the well — often a woman — who faded to cover the well at night with a sealing stone and so the well overflowed and a lake was formed — an alternative explanation for Llyn Tegid.

The cult of St. Patrick is shown in Cerrigydrudion's Fynnon Gwaspatrick nearby the church which is dedicated to Ienan Gwas Badrig with Mary Magdalene. The round churchyard at Efenechtyd is a sign of Celtic origins and, like Clocaenog, was probably founded by the monks from St Saeran's community at Llanynys.

St. Winefride's well-shrine, at Holywell, was perhaps one of the most famous in Britain. The well and chapel were given to the monastery of St. Werburg in 1093 by the Countess of Chester and in 1115 her son, Earl Richard, made a pilgrimage to the well. In 1240 the well reverted to the Welsh lords and Dafydd ap Llewelyn gave it into the care of Basingwerk Abbey. King Richard I sheltered at Basingwerk when he was attacked by the Welsh when on a pilgrimage to St. Winefride's Well. Edward IV (1461–83) is said to have made a journey there on foot from Shrewsbury and Richard III gave the Abbot of Basingwerk an annuity in order to maintain a priest at St. Winefride's. Many miraculous cures were recorded in the 'Lives' and in bardic songs of the tenth and fifteenth centuries. Offerings at the well were worth £10 for the year 1535.

Another church which benefited from its well was Llanrhaeadr-yn-Nghinmeirch where visitors to the local well called Ffynnon Ddyfnog left offerings which, it is said, paid for the fine Jesse window erected in 1535 in the church close by; here the well water was believed to cure skin diseases. On our local pilgrims' route Ffynnon Sara, also known as Pyllau Perl, was 'of great local repute for the cure of rheumatism'. By the well is the site of a cottage, burnt down about half a century ago, where crutches of those cured were preserved'. (1911) *Ancient Monuments*, page 48.

> Holy wells, which generally, though not always, are near a public road or pathway, and it has been thought that the pilgrimages --- account for the existence of these holy wells; but it is a question whether the wells were not venerated before these pilgrimages took place. [*Archaeologia Cambrensis* LI, 5th Series, XIII, page 167.]

This is much more likely.

The Licensing of Alehouses

Even in early times the Crown tried to keep control over public houses and attempted to restrain drunkenness. Anyone could, if they wished, brew ale, but when they wanted to sell it, the state stepped in and laid down the law. As early as the fourteenth century, anyone who brewed ale was required to place in front of the house an ale-stake, which was a long pole, with a broom or gorse attached, to announce that the ale was ready to be sampled. This led to catching passing trade by advertising the tavern with a sign hung out. Once the publicity campaign got under way in the towns, the sign boards became more and more elaborate, even being suspended right across the road in some cases where they became a hazard. In the reign of Charles II, legislation was introduced restricting their size, and the inn signs of today, with their diverse names and topics-many historic-evolved.

At first the ale would be taken away to drink, but what could be more natural than a chat with the maker of the beverage and anyone else coming in to buy, and before long a bench would be provided in the parlour, to encourage the drinkers to stay and perhaps buy a second drink. The description given by Begw Lewis is still true to this image of the inn in the front parlour.

> 1552 — Under the Acts of 5 and 6 in the reign of Edward VI were inserted recognizances by which keepers of 'common Alehouses and Tiplinghouses' were to be taken for good behaviour before two justices of the peace who were to 'certify the same recognizances at the next quarter sessions there to remain on record'. A recognizance was a bond served by the court on persons held responsible to keep the peace in their house, where ale was being served.

> 1729 — George II established the yearly petty sessions to be held within the first twenty days of

September and the Act of 1753 ordered 'that the Clerks of the Peace shall keep a register or Calendar of all the recognizances, sent or returned'. An Act in 1772 abolished the need for the keeping of a register---it must have been proving difficult to carry out.

Ruthin had over 50 'beerhouses' at this period and even in a small place like Clocaenog there were three licences issued for the year 1753.

Women could be licensees, and in 1753 the publican at Tŷ Coch was Margaret Edwards, a widow, while at Paradwys it was David Wynne, and the third tavern was run by John Williams in an unknown house. This third inn disappeared from the records after 1760, leaving David Wynne still in charge at Paradwys and William Roberts, the new innkeeper at Tŷ Coch. By 1782 William had died and Jane, his wife, is named as the publican, which she continued to be until her death in 1809; I think it is possible that their son, William took over for a short time.

In 1811 Robert Lewis is known as a carpenter and Edward, his brother is a wheelwright, but Edward moved to Tŷ Coch as a farmer and his wife seems to have kept a shop and run the public house there. After that the Cloion inn at Tŷ Coch was run by the Lewis Family until 1927.

1828 The powers of justices of the peace were severely limited by Act 9 under George IV and again in 1830 under William IV and led to the opening of a large number of beerhouses.

The chapels tried to curb drinking, with some success, particularly as regards controlling the opening hours of the ale houses. Wales was the area most resistant to Sunday opening, right up to the late twentieth century, the Llŷn peninsula being the last area to sanction it and then, only for the sake of tourism.

A.N.

Two examples of licenses

Be it remembered, that on the 16th day of September in the Sixteenth year of the reign of George the Third [1776] Rowland Wynne of Ruthin in the county foresaid, Carrier and John Jones of Ruthin aforesaid, Shoemaker personally came before us two of his Majesty's justices of the peace of ther said county, and acknowledged themselves to owe to our sovereign Lord the King that is to say, the said Rowland Wynne the Sum of Ten Pounds and the said John Jones the sum of 10 of good and lawful money of Great britain, to be made and levied of their Goods and Chattels, Lands and Tenements, respectively, to the use of our said sovereign Lord the King, his heirs and successors, if David Wynne shall make default in the condition underwritten.

THE condition of this Recognizance is such; that whereas the above-bounden David Wynne is licenced to keep a common Inn and Alehouse, for one year from the 29th day of this present Month of September in the house where he now dwelleth at Clocaenog, if the said David Wynne shall keep and maintain good order and rule, and shall suffer no disorders nor unlawful games to be used in his said house, nor in any outhouse, Yard, Garden, or backhouse, thereunto belonging, during the same term, then this Recognizance shall be void.

Taken and acknowledged the day and year above written, before us

R. Parry
Jn. Mostyn junr

At a General meeting of his Majesty's Justices of the Peace, acting in and for the Hundred of Ruthin, in the County of Denbigh, held at Ruthin aforesaid, on Saturday the 29th Day of September, one thousand eight hundred and twenty seven.

Robert Roberts at the sign of the Paradise in the Parish of Clocaenog in the said Hundred and County, Victualler, acknowledges himself to be indebted to our Sovereign Lord the King in the Sum of thirty Pounds and Edward Lewis of the Plough Clocaenog, Victualler, acknowledges himself to be indebted to our Sovereign Lord the King in the sum of twenty pounds to be levied upon their several Goods and Chattels, Lands and Tenements, by way of Recognizance to his Majesty's use, his Heirs and Successors, upon Condition, that the said Robert Roberts do and shall keep the true Assize in uttering and selling Bread and other Victuals, Beer, Ale, and other Liquors, in his House, and shall not fraudulently dilute or adulterate the same, and shall not use in uttering and selling thereof any Pots or other Measures that are not of full size, and shall not wilfully or knowingly permit Drunkeness or Tippling, nor get drunk in his House or other Premises, nor knowing suffer any Gaming, with Cards, draughts, Dice, Bagatelle or any other sedentary Game in his House or any of the Out-houses, Appurtenances, or Easements thereto belonging to Journeymen, Labourers, Servants, or Apprentices, not knowingly introduce, permit or suffer any Bull, Bear, or Badger baiting, Cock fighting, or other such Sport or Amusement in any part of his Premises, nor shall knowingly or designedly and with a View to harbour or entertain such, permit, or suffer Men or Women of notoriously bad Fame, or dissolute Boys or Girls to assemble and meet together in his House, or any of the Premises thereto belonging, nor shall keep open his House, nor permit or suffer any Drinking or Tippling in any part of his, her, or their Premises during the usual Hours of Divine Service on Sundays, nor shall keep open his House or other Premises during late Hours of the Night or early in the Morning for any other Purpose than the Reception of Travellers; but do keep a good Rule and Order therein, according to the Purport of a Licence granted for selling Ale, Beer, or other Liquors by Retail in the said House and Premises, for one whole Year commencing on the Tenth Day of October next, then this Recognizance to be void or else to remain in full force.

Acknowledged before us

Joseph Peers
Ellis Roberts

---

* This is what happened when you did not keep good order. The magazine *History Today* reported, in May 2006, that in 1664 a murder was committed on the premises of the Swan Inn, Ipswich, Suffolk and in consequence the landlord was fined 40 shillings for not keeping good order; the money to be used to buy coals for the poor and to be distributed on St. Thomas's Day.

Coleg Llysfasi

History of Llysfasi

The name Llysfasi may mean Massey's Court as there are references in the mediaeval documents to a Massi or Massey, one of the followers of de Grey of Ruthin, whose descendant built the Elizabethan mansion at Llysfasi.

Generally the incomers after a conquest do not break with tradition, but, for ease and smooth running of the land and its people, allow towns and governed areas to continue to function but with a new overseer. After the conquest of Wales in 1282, Edward I granted the lordship of Dyffryn Clwyd to Reynold de Grey of Wilton; Dyffryn Clwyd was obviously a governable unit. This was very soon after fighting ceased. Included in his new demesne were the native Welsh centres of Ruthin and Llys Llanerch. The first Court to be held at Llanerch was in 1295 and 'Massey' was one of four, listed as giving a verdict. A Richard Maysey 'found one pole axe in the hands of Pistele Ddu which was stolen at the commencement of the war; this was the Revolt of Madog ap Llewelyn in December 1294. Later, in 1324, a register was made of tenants of Roger de Grey and there were only nine tenants in the commote of Llysllanerch, and in the rental of 1465 there were eleven. No one named 'Massey' or anything similar appears as a tenant. The form 'Masci' is seen as 'Lannayr with Masci' in 1346 and the pasture land of the lord of Dyffryn Clwyd was at 'Mascoys' in 1349. In the l465 register Howel ap Gr ap Thomas held land in 'Ewarth', 'Nantcloyd', 'Kelan' (Euarth, Nantclwyd, Cilan) and 'Llesllanergh'.

In the Peniarth MS the name Massi occurs a few times, both Sir John Massi of Flintshire and Robert Massi of Denbighshire, who each occupied the post of sheriff on more than one occasion in the sixteenth century. By 1649 there is a clear reference to the manor of Mayses and to the messuage (dwelling house with outbuildings and land — perhaps from French mesnage) called the hall of Llysfasie, a water-driven corn mill in 'derwen llanerch called llysfasi mill'. After this the name Llysllannerch gradually ceases to be used.

The land would be ploughed and cropped for several years until it failed to be productive when it was allowed to lie fallow and revert to grass. There was no crop rotation practised until much later, following the agricultural revolution in the eighteenth century.

A tenant paid a rent to the lord (generally in kind) or did military service and held his land free of rent, or only paid rent in part. Sometimes tied tenants (or *taeogion*) held land in return for working on the lord's demesne whenever called upon to do so — even if his own hay rotted meanwhile. Bondsmen held neither *tyddyn* nor land and were mostly treated as household slaves. When Ruthin was attacked in 1400 many bondsmen escaped and more use was made of hire labour in this area.

The lords Grey held Dyffryn Clwyd until 1504 when it was given to the Crown. Henry VIII gave it to his illegitimate son, Henry, Duke of Richmond, who died in 1536, when it returned to being Crown property. Queen Elizabeth gave it to the Earl of Warwick. It again became Crown property during the reign of James I.

In the reign of Edward VI (1547–53) it was granted to Lord Robert Dudley, during whose ownership the Manor of Mascis was sold to John ap Edward Lloyde, gent. of Llanvayre, Co. of Denbigh, who was probably already a tenant there. John Lloyd bought the manor in 1556.

When, in 1586, the second Sir Thomas Myddleton became lord of Chirk Castle after his father, he set about adding to his land, including the purchase of Ruthin Castle, as he already owned much land in Dyffryn Clwyd. The whole lordship eventually came into his possession in 1677. In 1633 he had already bought the 'manor of Masseys, together with the hall of Llysvassie and the lands thereto, belonging to the second Sir Thomas for £560'. This final concord or settlement was between Edward Lloyd Esq. and Mary his wife and Sir Thomas Myddleton, Kt. and Watkyn Kyffin, gent. (steward to Sir Thomas). It was to remain in the Myddleton family for 277 years until, in 1796, the estate was divided, because there was no male heir, between his sisters Charlotte and Maria, and Harriet, a half-sister. Ruthin Castle went to Maria, Harriet inherited her one-third share of the Ruthin estate, but their brother Richard left his personal property to be divided between his two sisters, Charlotte and Maria.

Llysfai manor house before the First World War

Maria married Frederick West, and their children, Frederick Myddleton West and William Cornwallis West, inherited from both their parents, and also from Harriet who never married. Under Colonel Cornwallis West a Mr. Davies came from Penlan, Carrog, near Corwen, to farm at Llysfasi. He left in 1897 and the farm was taken over by Mr. Hugh Jones of Tancaeau, Rhewl for a rent of £310. He died in 1909 and his executors received twelve months notice to leave.

The estate was sold in the early twentieth century to ease financial problems and Llysfasi was auctioned on 7th September 1909 at the Castle Hotel, Ruthin for £13,680, when it was bought by Mr. Charles William Sandles of Sutton, Great Sutton, Cheshire. He bought 'the Old Manor House', outbuildings and land in one part of 164 acres, other farm lands or 'accommodation fields' and a grouse moor of 297 acres and the mill with nearly 19 acres; a total area of some 480 acres.

Now the mill, apart from doing all the milling for the farm, also provided a service for the neighbourhood. The miller lived in a substantial house and a man lived in to help in the mill and on the miller's smallholding. He would collect the grain and deliver the milled corn back to the various farms. In 1633 a Thomas Wytcherley, tenant, paid £90 to farm Llysfasi and run the mill. Often in the past the mill had been let separately, so that the lord collected an additional rent, and according to mediaeval law the lord could compel all his tenants to use 'his' mill and he would extract a toll. The mill was water-driven with two pairs of stones and a dressing machine.

Mr. Sutton owned Llysfasi for only two years during which time he had to mortgage it to the tune of £7,000. He could not live in the house until the expiry of the notice to quit, so, until then, he lived at nearby Sinet farm, which he sold before moving into Llysfasi.

Soon he was calling it 'Valley Ranch' a 'Colonial and Agricultural College', and running courses for young men who intended going out to work in the colonies. The students needed to have: '1 pair spurs — hunting pattern, 1 Stetson Hat, 1 pair of Field Glasses' and could bring their own horse and saddle and gun, because shooting would be part of the course. Term would begin on 1st January 1911.

In the following March, Llysfasi and its 'college' was sold to a Mr. Brown who employed a farm manager — a rather strange choice as he claimed to have been a Wild West cowboy in a circus called 'Bronco Jack'; his real name was J. H. Lowrie. He was not a good farm manager and was replaced by Mr. Ronald Haydon who was an experienced farmer. It then became 'Llysfasi Manor Farm School' which seemed to be better organised.

Eventually, in 1919, negotiations began with Denbighshire County Council and they bought and took over the running of the college and the estate for £19,500. The first term under the new principal, Mr. Isaac Jones, commenced in October 1920 with 24 men. Now known as Coleg Llysfasi, it is run primarily as an agricultural college.

Llysfasi Estate sale catalogue, 1909.

Mr D. F. Cunningham.

Interview with Mr. D. F. Cunningham, Principal,

Seminal periods for Llysfasi were the two World Wars; in particular the First World War, which directly preceded the opening of the college in 1920. This had shown the government that home produced food was essential for the survival of the population in times of crisis. Local authorities played a pivotal role in supplying and distributing food, working in conjunction with the farmers who produced it and the need to further develop farming methods was realised.

Many local authorities already owned smallholdings which were rented to people in the countryside who had not inherited land but who wished to work in agriculture — even if only part time — because the holdings were never big enough to support a family. Denbighshire County Council decided to buy Llysfasi and run courses which would increase the knowledge and skills of young people from the surrounding area about crops and animal husbandry. A dairy school for girls was opened in May, 1920 at Llysfasi Manor Farm House, followed in October by a course for boys in agriculture.

Farms were then more self-sufficient (not necessarily more productive) and there were greater numbers of people employed on the land; in this area there were also the big estates to be considered, of which Ruthin Castle and Nant Clwyd are but two examples. These estates owned vast acreages of land and managed large numbers of tenanted farms. In order to improve the quality of production and the breeding on all these farms there was a need to disperse knowledge from the applied sciences already taught in the universities, and spread the new techniques in husbandry to the wider community. Llysfasi was well placed to disseminate this know-how to young people training at the 'Farm Institute', as it was then called. Contemporary with this was the setting up of a Welsh plant breeding station by George Stapleton at Aberystwyth.

Llysfasi offered practical vocational training in what, in each era, were considered ideal conditions, showing how to improve skills such as butter making for the girls or ploughing for the boys. At first there was a strict division of teaching — girls were taught home-making in the summer term and boys field work in the winter term. Apart from land management and husbandry, the college was also involved in teaching forestry, and has the largest forestry department in Wales, still as relevant to the area now as then.

The governing body and the county council of (old) Denbighshire had the foresight to establish the college with a wide stratification of land able to demonstrate shepherding of hill flocks at 1650 feet on the Clwyd hills, dealing with marginal land, and the management of rich lowland where breeding stocks of cattle and milking herds could be grazed, and quality crops grown.

We now run courses, not only for young people, but also for working farmers who need to keep abreast of modern technology; we teach farm management to suit the new I.T. culture and to comply with new government directives, in order that the farmer knows how to hold information on a computer so that all animals can be traced when moved, either for pedigree or for disease. The farmer has had to become his own farm manager and keep accurate records of stock and planting, as well as prices.

Education in agriculture as in other disciplines is politically driven and numbers attract financing. There has been a huge national reduction in recruitment to farming, not through lack of interest but because there is little opportunity to enter the industry from outside and secondly, because of low wages. Unless a farm is inherited, young people cannot afford to buy one. Even farmers' sons are forced to diversify by doing contract work on other farms or learning to repair farm machinery because their family farm is no longer as labour intensive as it used to be.

Llysfasi worked closely with the schools' careers service and we did a thorough survey of students and their ambitions, not only at our main supply school of Brynhyfyd, but at Rhyl and Connah's Quay, with a view to drawing our students from a wider area. We ourselves diversified and introduced plant biology (not horticulture, as that is covered by Northop College), and mechanics, and have formed links with Wrexham Training. Students who succeed — and 90% do — can go on to further, more academic training if they wish and gain degrees in agriculture. Given the marked gender split shown in our survey, we try to offer quality training, vocationally based and academically progressive.

Students working at Llysfasi during the 1920s.

Ten years ago we were a purely agricultural college with about 100 full-time students, some of whom boarded (we have accommodation for 62), and 400 part-time students. There are now part-time and full-time courses in our main subject, agriculture (taught in both English and Welsh), but also in: plant biology; small animal care; forestry and conservation; business management and I.T.; hair, beauty and holistic therapy; care and child care; food and drink; health and safety; engineering and welding; modern languages; as well as Welsh for adults.

The college is always mindful that it does not work in isolation, but must satisfy the needs of the community. Agriculture is still our core study and we are concerned to keep our farmers in touch with new ideas and technology, but we now think of ourselves as a community college and we provide a venue for activities such as the Young Farmers Club, the local Merched y Wawr and WI groups, the Beekeepers Society, and a patchwork and quilting group. There is a growing number of outreach centres in Ruthin, Bala, Llandudno, and surrounding villages, teaching Welsh, modern languages and I.T. Our lecturers take groups of students abroad (e.g. the Paris Agricultural Show, exchange visits with farms in Hungary) and we are proud to entertain overseas visitors here, as when we regularly have entries from Australasia for our annual sheep shearing competition. Llysfasi has a high profile for sheep breeding, shearing, handling and wrapping of wool.

We understand the need to retrench our agricultural teaching and practical training in farming skills, but realise the enormity of not meeting the future with a secure food production base to rely on when Europe becomes a greater entity, with the centre of gravity moving further east, when Poland, Slovakia and the Ukraine join the European Market and Wales is far out on the periphery. Coleg Llysfasi is well placed to be the centre to resource the training of this area's future farmers and, at the same time, serve the people of Clwyd and its hinterland.

Llysfasi College, 1990s.

Left: The original Elizabethan house as it looks today.

Below: Inside the new lecture theatre at Llysfasi.

In 2003 the future of Llysfasi as an agricultural college was in doubt, according to a report issued by ELWA. There had been a dramatic fall in the number of students entering for a national diploma course in agriculture, despite which Llysfasi has been getting 75 out of the 100 new entrants each year in Wales. This decline in new entrants throughout the country is thought to be because of the uncertainty of the future in farming and many farmers' sons are not opting to take over their fathers' holdings; preferring to go into higher salary high-tech jobs. Another reason given is the increasing burden of paperwork and bureaucracy in farm administration, not only from our own government but also from the EU.

In 2004, Coleg Llysfasi was chosen by ELWA as the sole college in north Wales tooffer full-time courses in agricultural training at the higher level . It already offered the widest range of NVQs in agriculture and related topics in the region and was able to continue to develop along these lines. This decisionwas taken on behalf of the Welsh Assembly Government following a far-reaching review and the evidence of the numbers of students already enrolled.

A.N.

Ruthin Animal Auction

A copy of the first accounts of the company in 1920/21 showed a profit of only £18 for the year, which was therefore a very poor year for the farmers. A loss was made almost every year until 1926 when an agreement was reached with Clough & Co to amalgamate the businesses. It was impractical to have two auction companies in town, especially during the 1920s. The company only managed to survive and no shares were paid out for about twenty years.

There were two animal markets in town; the oldest being the Lower Market which is over 100 years old. Before 1905 the land was owned by William Lloyd, Cefn Coch, Ruthin who rented the land to a man by the name of Byford to conduct auctions in the town to get the animals off the streets where they were previously sold. The site was bought by Fred Butler Clough in 1905 and Emlyn Maddocks and Bob Lloyd were his employees until he retired. The late Tom E. Lewis became the owner in 1951 until 1958, and then it was bought by Emlyn Maddocks and Bob Lloyd. Until 1926 Clough & Co held auctions in the Lower Market and the brothers T & W. Leathes owned the Upper Market and at this time Ruthin Farmers Auction Co. Ltd. was established and the first chairman was the late J. T. Lloyd, Plas Meredydd, Cyffylliog.

Over the years it was suggested that the two markets should be sited outside the town centre and during the 1980s there was a tremendous increase in the number of animals sold. There were traffic problems to the markets every Thursday and Friday on the busiest times of the

Yr Hen Marchnad Anifeiliad — a scene on the very last day of the auction market in Ruthin town. This is now the site of the Co-op supermarket.

The auction in progress in the old market.

The large annual sheep sale held in the fields of Castle Park..

The new auction market outside the twon of Ruthin.

year and it was unfair to expect farmers to wait for long periods to unload their stock on the morning of the sale. Buyers also experienced problems coming into the market to collect and load stock at the end of the day. Besides traffic problems, parking facilities for farmers also added to the company's problems and when Glyndŵr Council informed them that they were going to develop the site by the Ruthin Craft Centre it was obvious that the markets had to move or close down.

It was decided to try to place the market on a larger site, but to do this sufficient funds were needed. An application for grant towards the cost was submitted to the European Commission — but one of the conditions attached was that work had to commence before giving assurance that a grant would become available.

Although the financial situation of the company was satisfactory and money had been put aside for re-siting, it was obvious that the company had to expand before commencing the work as the building cost of the new market was very substantial. Many committee meetings and debates took place and three main factors were arrived at to proceed with the matter:

- resolution of the company shareholders to expand and sell more shares to fund the project.

- support of farmers over a wide area to buy shares to proceed with the design.

- support of Clough & Co of money received from the supermarket for the sale of the Lower Market.

The whole arrangement was prolonged and some farmers were concerned that the Lower Market had been sold before starting the new one, but finance was required before proceeding with the project. Sales were moved to Denbigh Market whilst transitions at Ruthin took place, which caused concern for both farmers and auctioneers, but the outlook was favourable.

The bell at the Lower Market — the Vale of Clwyd Market — was tolled for the last time by Robin Llwyd ap Owain, the Mayor of Ruthin on the 27th December 1991, before commencing the last livestock sale. The bell was later sited in the new market to call the farming fraternity together again. On the 30th December the sale of the buildings and market pens took place.

E. W. Lloyd

Yr Ocsiwn Anifeiliaid, Rhuthun

Blynyddoedd tlawd i'r amaethwyr oedd y dau ddegau y ganrif ddiwethaf fel y mae copi o gyfrifon cyntaf y cwmni (sef 1920/21) yn dangos elw o £18 yn unig am y flwyddyn. Bu colled bron bob blwyddyn hyd at 1926 a dyna pryd y gwnaed cytundeb a Clough & Co i ddod a'r ddau fusnes at ei gilydd. Ffolineb hollol oedd rhedeg dau gwmni o arwerthwyr yn y dref, yn arbennig felly yn y dau ddegau. Dim ond llwyddo i ddal dau ben llinyn ynghyd oedd hanes y cwmni am flynyddoedd ac ni thalwyd dim cyfrandal am tua ugain mlynedd.

Roedd dwy farchnad anifeillaid yn y dref — y farchnad hynaf o'r ddwy oedd y Farchnad Isaf. Mae'n siwr fod y farchnad hon dros gant oed. Perchen y tir cyn 1905 oedd gŵr o'r enw William Lloyd o Gefn Coch,

Yr hen farchnad anifeiliad ar y diwrnod olaf.
The old animal market on the last day.

Sêl fawr blynyddol yn caeuau Parc y Castell.
The large annual sheep sale in Castle Park fields.

Rhuthun a osododd y tir i ŵr o'r enw Byford i gynnal arwerthiant yn y dref er mwyn cael yr anifeiliaid oddi ar y strydoedd lle yr oeddynt yn cael eu gwerthu cyn hynny. Prynwyd y safle gan Fred Butler Clough yn 1905 a bu Emlyn Maddocks a Bob Lloyd yn ei wasanaeth hyd at ymddeoliad. Daeth y diweddar Tom E. Lewis yn berchen y safle yn 1951 hyd 1958 ac yna fe'i prynwyd gan Emlyn Maddocks a Bob Lloyd. Hyd at 1926 Clough & Co oedd yn cynnal arwerthiannau yn y Farchnad Isaf a'r brodyr T. & W. Leathes oedd perchenogion y Farchnad Uchaf. Dyna pryd y sefydlwyd y Ruthin Farmers Auction Co. Ltd. Cadeirydd cyntaf y cwmni oedd y diweddar J. T. Lloyd, Plas Meredydd, Cyffylliog.

Dros y blynyddoedd awgrymwyd y dylid lleoli y ddwy farchnad anifeiliaid allan o ganol y dref ac yn ystod yr wyth degau bu cynnydd aruthrol yn nifer yr anifeiliaid a werthwyd. Roedd trafnidiaeth i'r ddwy farchnad ar adegau prysuraf y flwyddyn, bob dydd Iau a dydd Gwener, yn achosi problemau ac annheg oedd disgwyl i ffermwyr aros am amser llawer rhy hir cyn gallu dadlwytho anifeiliaid ar fore marchnad. Roedd y prynwyr hefyd yn cael problem yn ceisio dod i mewn i'r farchnad i lwytho eu pryniant ar ddiwedd y dydd.

Ar wahân i broblemau trafnidiaeth roedd cael safle cyfleus i barcio yn peri mwy o ofid i'r cwmni, a phan gawsant eu hysbysu gan Gyngor Glyndŵr eu bod yn bwriadu datblygu'r safle ger y Ganolfan Grefftau roedd yn rhaid ail leoli'r farchnad neu, yn hwyr neu hwyrach, wynebu cau yn gyfan gwbl.

Penderfynwyd ceisio lleoli'r farchnad ar safle fwy ac i wneud hynny wrth gwrs roedd yn rhaid sicrhau cyllideb digonol. Yn gyntaf gwnaed cais am grant at Gymuned Ewropeaidd tuag at y gost — un o'r amodau oedd fod yn rhaid dechrau ar y gwaith cyn cael gwybodaeth os oedd y grant i'w chael neu peidio.

Er bod sefyllfa gyllidol y cwmni yn gryf, ac arian wedi ei roi i gadw ar gyfer ail leoli, roedd yn

Canolbwyntio! Mae'r cynnigio wedi dechrau.
Concentrate! The bidding is under way.

The new market — plenty of room for parking and for temporarily holding sheep in the fields at the front.

amlwg fod yn rhaid ehangu'r cwmni cyn mentro ymlaen gan fod costau adeiladu marchnad newydd yn sylweddol iawn. Bu llawer o ddyfalu a phwyllgora ond yn y diwedd digwyddodd tri pheth i'r cynllun fynd ymlaen:

- penderfyniad cyfranddalwyr y cwmni i ehangu a gwerthu mwy o gyfranddaliadau i ariannu'r fenter.

- cefnogaeth gan ffermwyr o gylch eang i brynu cyfranddaliadau er mwyn cael mynd ymlaen.

- cefnogaeth oddiwrth Clough & Co. o'r arian a gawsant a werthiant y Farchnad Isaf i gwmni'r archfarchnad.

Mae'n wir dweud fod yr holl drefniant wedi cymeryd amser hir, a rhaid oedd maddau i rai anwybodus a gyhyddodd y cwmni o gau y Farchnad Isaf cyn adeiladu'r farchnad newydd, ond rhaid oedd medru ariannu'r cynllun cyn cychwyn ar y gwaith. Symudwyd i Farchnad Dinbych dros dro a siwr bod hyn wedi peri poendod i rai ffermwyr ac i'r arwerthwyr ond braf oedd meddwl fod marchnad newydd ar y gweill.

Canwyd cloch y Farchnad Isaf, sef y Vale of Clwyd Mart, am y tro olaf gan faer y dref, sef Robin Llwyd ab Owain, cyn cychwyn yr arwerthiant anifeiliaid olaf ar Rhagfyr 27ain 1991. Ail osodwyd y gloch yn y farchnad newydd i alw'r teulu amaethyddol ynghyd unwaith eto. Ar Rhagfyr 30ain cynhaliwyd arwerthiant adeiladau a chorlannau'r farchnad.

E. W. Lloyd

Historical Notes

Pie Powder Court — was held up to the nineteenth century in Denbigh. 3yd. Flake was the space permitted by the guilds for each craftsman to exhibit his wares. A service was held in St. Hilary's Church before each market day and the incumbent was paid in oatmeal!

Muck Dinner — the council would celebrate on the income made from the muck scraped up after each market.

Pool Park

No history of Clocaenog would be complete without mention of Pool Park because, although the house itself was in the parish of Llanfwrog, the estate, which covered 17,550 acres, included the parish of Clocaenog and the many tenanted farmhouses and cottages of the area.

The house had been the home of the Salesbury family, descending from William Salesbury, of Bachymbyd, who had defended Denbigh Castle, when besieged in 1646 by Cromwell's troops, during the Civil War. Subsequently the estate passed, by the marriage of a Salesbury heiress, into the Bagot family of Shropshire; despite that, she is buried in St Marcella's Church, the parish church of Denbigh, where her monument says that she had a 'vast fortune fortune, honestly gotten, well bestowed and prudently managed'.

Two objects of great antiquity stood in front of the house; one was the Sepulchre Stone of Emlyn and the other was the stone chair which had been removed from Llys y Frenhines and was called Cadair y Frenhines (The Queen's Chair) — it has a resemblance to the Coronation Chair in Westminster Abbey and may well have served a similar purpose, as the ancient custom was to enthrone a new chieftain on a hill overlooking his kingdom.

There is an interesting story, written down by Peter H. Williams in the *Local History Broadsheet* of 1996, of a visit in 1827 by the Bagot family from Shropshire, one of whom was twelve-year old Eleanor Bagot, who kept a diary of the events during her stay. They arrived at Pool Park by horse-drawn coach, having passed through Mold and 'Agricola's Pass' to Ruthin where 'they received a gracious reception and Church Bells rang'. Alterations were in progress at the house [in 1828 Pool Park house was rebuilt in the Elizabethan style] so they stayed at Fir Grove and dined each evening in a tent at Pool Park, and throughout the evening a Welsh harpist played to them. They visited the new plantations and travelled through Bontuchel and Clocaenog; Eleanor thought the plantations very fine. During the week, she wrote of work being done by workmen and of how her Papa had given a dinner for 81 of the men. She noted how happy they looked, and with 'Hurrahs' called 'Lord Bagot forever!'

The Bagot family continued to own Pool Park until, one hundred years later, in 1928, when the estate was sold by public auction (see separate article). Pool Park House itself was sold to the North Wales Hospital for £2000 and was used to accommodate 100 of their more mobile psychiatric patients.

M.S.

Robert Thomas Roberts (2nd from left, front row) is thought to have been the Head Gamekeeper at Pool Park before joining the 1st Bn Welsh Guards in the 1914–18 war as Pte 2784. He was killed in action on 11 October 1918, at St. Vaast, near Cambrai, France. He originated from Telpin, Rhewl, but his home was at Bryn Awel, Clawddnewydd, where he left a wife, Ellen, six daughters and two sons.
This photograph was probably taken in 1913, outside the dog kennels, before a shoot. [Photograph and information sent by his grandson, Vernon Price of St, Neots, Cambs.]

From *The Carnarvon & Denbigh Herald*, August 23 1851

CLOCAENOG

MARRIAGE of HON. WILLIAM BAGOT M.P. of POOL PARK

A party was held in the village at the Cloion Tavern for nearly 60 people, presided over by the Rev. Thomas Hughes and a tea party for almost 50 children of the National School.
3 fat sheep were slaughtered and distributed to the poor of the parish, and a loaf of bread to each person in the parish.
Tea was served to about 60 females, and in the evening there were races for the males, with prizes for the winners of tea and tobacco, after which the numerous company peaceably retired.

The Auction of the Pool Park Estate

On Wednesday, 7 November, 1928, the sale was held of 17,550 acres of Pool Park Estate by the direction of Lord Bagot. This important Welsh estate extended from Rhewl to Llangwm, and north to the Ruthin/Denbigh main road, with a further 794 acres of sporting rights in the sale:

> The Pool Park Estate includes the well-appointed and moderate sized Mansion. The noted Grouse Moors, the Pheasant Shoot which is potentially the finest in the country, five or six miles of Salmon and Trout fishing in three rivers, the Petryal Trout Lake, Rich Farm Lands in the Vale of Clwyd, reputedly the Garden of Wales, Imported Sheep, Stock and Dairy Holdings … in the fascinating environment of some of the most beautiful scenery in North Wales.

For the purpose of the sale, the estate was divided into:

> a) the Pool Park Estate;
> b) the Hiraethog Estate;
> c) the Llanynys Estate;
> d) the Llangwm Sporting Estate;
> e) the Petryal Estate.

The Pool Park Estate group comprised the farms and smallholdings around Clocaenog. Many of the farms were made up of 50 acres or less, the exceptions being Plas Clocaenog, $136^{1}/_{2}$ acres; Parc, $243^{3}/_{4}$ acres; Pentre, $128^{1}/_{2}$ acres; and the Home Farm, 412 acres.

In addition to the sale of the farms, there was also the following stipulation on each property that 'the Standing Timber on this lot has been valued and is to be paid for in addition to the purchase price'. The timber on Pentre land was valued at £128 and Tyn y Celyn had .3 acres of woodland valued at £60. In many cases the value of a property (in the opinion of the auctioneers) was enhanced by its proximity to Derwen or Nantclwyd Station or another advantage to a property was as follows:

> It may be noted that the Birkenhead Corporation water main will pass near this lot (Ty'n y Celyn), and the proposed main to Clocaenog — brings the supply in such close proximity as to be of decided advantage to this property.

Mains water, which had first been applied for in 1925, was to come from the main supply pipe passing Bryn y Ffynnon, down one mile of pipetrack to the village, at a cost of £3,521 6s. 8d.; it would supply the school and the houses in the village. It was October 1928 before the work was successfully completed. Outlying farms would have to pay to be linked to this supply.

In the Pool Park Estate group there were 46 farms and smallholdings and, as now, sheep and cattle were the mainstay of these farms, but this group also contained 79 piggeries and, of additional interest, there were

25 bake-houses listed.

All the properties were noted with the acreages and rents; some examples of annual rents are:

Ty'n-y-Celyn £100

Cae Segwyn £105 8s.

These two properties did not sell on the day.

Nant y Celyn £87

Hen Blas £14 6s.

Clocaenog School: 50 square yards. Let on lease to Denbighshire Education Department for 99 years from 1905 at 5s. per annum.

Cloion Inn [now Tŷ Coch]: fully licensed. 24 acres. 'This property is prettily situated and could be developed as a summer hotel for ramblers.'

Paradwys was sold next day and ceased to be a shop.

It was rumoured that the estate had to be sold to cover debts of around £3,000, incurred by Lord Bagot — the auction brought in £3,200.

Pool Park House, itself, was sold exactly one hundred years after it was rebuilt in 1828. This sale was the big turning point in establishing the present basic pattern of the community of this parish. Many of these farm units have remained unchanged since 1928, only absorbing a few other smallholdings.

E. N.

Pool Park sale catalogue, 1928.

The Ty'n y Celyn Farm Sale

Held at the Brookhouse Mill, Denbigh at 6 P.M. On Thursday 1st May 2003.

FOR SALE BY PUBLIC AUCTION

6 Farmsteads and 7 Parcels of Accommodation Land, in all approximately 450 Acres.

The heading in the Denbighshire Free Press, April 10th, 2003 was

'FAMILY FORTUNE GOES BEGGING: State set to snap up proceeds of £1m estate.'

It then continues: 'A farming family's fortune is likely to be swallowed up by the state — because its last member has died without leaving a will.

The 450 acre estate, comprising six farmsteads in Clocaenog, was originally left by Roger Jones to his five children. But it is thought he had agreed a covenant that, if any of his children married, they would lose out on any inheritance from the estate. The children, none of whom married, included Mary Moss Jones, Eirlys Powell Jones, Iestyn Jones, Elizabeth Green Jones and John Roger Alfred Jones.

They all died between autumn 1997 and summer 1998, the last two within three days of each other, and so shared a joint funeral. It had always been understood that the family would will some of their money to the three churches, Clocaenog, Llanfwrog and Cyfylliog, but the final will was never written and so all the inheritance will pass to the Treasury.'

By kind permission of Mr. Syme, *Denbighshire Free Press*.

The sale of the 'Clocaenog Estate'

This sale was held on May 1st 2003, and like the Pool Park Estate sale in 1928 was the end of an era for Clocaenog. For so many years the Jones family of Ty'n y Celyn had control of much of the land surrounding the village, but for the last 30 years they had taken little part in village activities or helped to promote goodwill in the neighbourhood.

The family had originally come to live as tenant farmers at Graigwen but, when Roger married the village schoolmistress, they acquired Cae Segwyn which had been farmed by Thomas Davies prior to 1928, the time of the Pool Park Estate sale, but it did not sell at the auction and was bought later, in the early 1930s, by Roger Jones, with 116¾ acres. In 1928 Ty'n y Celyn also failed to sell and as David Davies, the sitting tenant, retired, the farm stood empty for some time. Then Roger also bought Ty'n y Celyn with 110 acres for £800 and the whole family went to live there. The Dy'Gwyl Domas Charity was persuaded that it was best to sell their properties in about 1930 because it was proving difficult to collect the rents from the tenants, as the tenants claimed there were repairs needing to be carried out. The Jones family took this opportunity to buy Graigwen. During the Second World War, Graigwen was requisitioned by the Ministry of Agriculture and a tenant installed so that the land could be better utilised for the war effort; the holding was returned to the Jones family after the war was over.

Time went on and the Jones family either bought or inherited more land. Their uncle, who had been living at Plas (but owning Henblas and Tŷ Isa, with additional land at Llanbedr), died in 1967, aged 97, and left these properties to the family at Ty'n y Celyn. No land was ever sold. Even when the village school needed a playing field, they refused to sell an acre and eventually the field next to the school was leased, under pressure, for the children's use, providing that the Jones' sheep could still graze it. [The football pitch was purchased for the school by the Denbighshire Education Committee prior to the 2003 auction.]

The family at Ty'n y Celyn in the 1930s consisted of Roger Jones and his wife Elizabeth Eleanor, who, before her marriage, had been a teacher in the village school. They had five children, Mary Moss (born 1910), Ellis (born 1912), Elizabeth Green (known as Bessie, born 1916), David Estyn (born 1920), and Alfred (born 1924). In her earlier years, Mary Moss had enjoyed dancing in the local 'hops'; Bessie Green was musical (she gained her L.R.A.M.), played for church services when she was younger, liked going to dances, had a good voice and sang in local *eisteddfodau*. Bessie was six years younger than Mary and was the only one ever to leave home while the parents were alive. She went to teach music at Rydal School, Colwyn Bay,

Plas, looking the worse for wear.

Henblas, before it was sold.

Below left: Old byre or cowshed at Plas, but sold with Henblas in 2003.

Below right: The byre had a centre walk-way to enable the farmer to feed the cattle in the loose boxes on either side. Recorded in Traditional Farm Buildings in North-East Wales, *by E. William, 1982.*

and lived-in for one term, but when she came home at Christmas, she never returned. Bessie is the one who was sent away to her mother's relatives in south Wales because she was pregnant. She came back to Ty'n y Celyn without the baby. Alfred, the youngest, loved shooting, particularly by moonlight, for rabbits and pheasants — and in fact died climbing a stile one night when carrying his gun; Estyn is the one I remember best because he had an ear operation and was only too pleased to show you the results of the surgery!

None of them ever married, probably because their parents formed them into a company to run the property, with the proviso that marriage would cause them to be disinherited. They lived a very enclosed life together, but Mary liked to drive big cars, and she and her sister would go abroad on holiday together in a caravanette.

Ultimately, when Bessie and Ellis died in August 1998, within four days of each other, but without a final will, the properties were left empty. After a lapse of five years, whilst a full search was made for possible beneficiaries, the sale of the farms (called, to everyone's surprise, the 'Clocaenog Estate') took place in 2003. The six properties went to auction and fetched £2,747,000.

In the 1930s, Roger Jones bought Ty'n y Celyn with 110 acres for £800. In 2003 the farm (listed 'E' by CADW) with approximately 50 acres, sold for £350,000 and land belonging to it, 110 acres, sold separately for a further £220,000. Another 19 acres advertised as being in the 'village centre', but outside the curtilage of the village, sold for building land and went under the hammer at £62,000. In 2004 the listed farmhouse was being refurbished and the outbuildings were being made into two more houses, all of which will eventually go for sale; other parcels of land have been sold off separately.

All the land has been fragmented and not one was sold as a viable farm unit:

Cae Segwyn was sold in 2003 with only $31^{1}/_{4}$ acres for £305,000, and another 19 acres auctioned at £62,000. The outbuildings round the farmyard have been converted into four separate dwellings.

Graigwen, was sold with $18^{3}/_{4}$ acres for £305,000 and a further 16 acres sold for £30,000. The farm was listed by CADW a fortnight after the 2003 sale and the new owner was unable to carry out renovations to CADW required standards and had to re-sell the property.

Ty Isa, a two-room cottage with pigsty, was sold, along with 8 acres of Henblas land, for £80,000. This has been transformed into a modern dwelling.

Henblas (listed 'D') and $45^{3}/_{4}$ acres and a barn sold for £350,000. Work on this is now finished and it is inhabited once more.

Plas Clocaenog (listed 'E') with 32 acres auctioned at £370,000 but the sale was not completed and Plas was sold again later. Land belonging to Plas sold separately, $14^{1}/_{2}$ acres for £38,000 and the 74 acres above the house for £205,000.

The $52^{1}/_{2}$ acres at Llanbedr auctioned at £355,000.

Plas, Henblas, Tŷ Isa and the Park Llanbedr land had been left to the family on the death of their relative in Plas 'for their lifetime' and after that was to go to the Church in Wales. The money from the sale of Ty'n y Celyn, Caesegwyn and Graigwen went to the Treasury. All the farms were fragmented and not one was sold as a viable farm unit.

The village community hopes that these properties, some of which have stood empty for up to 37 years, will again become homes for lively families who will be an asset to the village community.

The Jones Family

Plas
- John Jones — Died Feb. 1947 Aged 80
- Sarah Catherine Jones (sister) — Died 1957
- Hugh Jones (brother) — Died 1967 Aged 97

Ty'n y Celyn
- Elizabeth Eleanor Jones (mother--previously teacher) — Died 1955 Aged 72
- Roger Jones (father & brother of those at Plas) — Died 1959 Aged 89

- David Estyn Jones — Born 1920 — Died Dec. 1983 Aged 63
- J. R. Alfred Jones — Born 1924 — Died Oct. 1997 Aged 73
- Mary Moss Jones — Born 1910 — Died May 1998 Aged 88
- Elizabeth Green Jones (Bessie) — Born 1916 — Died Aug. 6 1998 Aged 82
- Ellis P. Jones — Born 1912 — Died August 10 1998 Aged 86

A.N.

Canolfan Cae Cymro

A major event of the 1990s was the building of the Community Centre at Clawddnewydd to serve the three villages of Clawddnewydd, Derwen and Clocaenog. Recreation facilities had been poor for many years, with Clocaenog and Derwen having to rely on the almost non-existent playing areas of their local schools and Clawddnewydd, as a growing community, having none at all. Consequently a joint meeting of the Community Councils was held to discuss future plans and it was agreed to hold an open meeting to present these proposals to everyone. The response was overwhelming with support shown from all areas.

The land (approximately four acres) was generously given by Arthur Williams of Allt y Celyn, and fund raising was started in 1995 with an 'Auction of Promises', held in Bryn Coch barn, which raised the considerable sum of about £9,000.

On the assurance of grants from Glyndŵr District Council, the Welsh Office and the National Lottery, work began in 1997. The architect, J. Bargiel, was engaged to draw up the design and Clwyd Builders were employed to carry out the construction.

Fund raising was continued by a willing group of dedicated local people and the building had its official opening on January 1st 1998. The following year in 1999 it won the Quayle Award for a new local building of outstanding appearance and interest and, due to the overall commitment of the inhabitants of the three villages, the building won a Certificate of Merit in the British Village of the Year Competition in 2001 and in 2003 was Calor Village of the Year, Denbighshire. In 2005, the three village communities won the Calor award for the whole of Wales.

In the last few years there has been much activity going on at the Canolfan. The following list of events indicates how well-used the centre is: public meetings, whist, aerobics, badminton, bowls, netball, football, Sunday lunches, concerts,

Above left: Fundraising at a local pub.

Above right: At the Auction of Promises in Bryn Coch barn.

Right: Some helpers for the ceremony of Cutting the First Turf.

The village shop (Siop y Fro) — an ideal meeting place for a gossip. Mair Jones and Myfi Owen.

Linda Price serving in the shop.

barbeques, quizzes, line-dancing, drama, children's parties, coffee mornings, craft fairs, wedding receptions, etc. With so much going on, it was decided to employ a caretaker and one was duly appointed.

Since opening in 1998, work has continued to improve the kitchen facilities, to provide a football pitch and a children's playground. The car park has been surfaced, and the general appearance has been much improved by landscaping and the planting of trees and shrubs. Also, there is a parking site with beautiful views and facilities, including water and power-points, for members of the Caravan Club to use.

A questionnaire was circulated to all the inhabitants to ascertain the needs and requirements in our rural community, particularly concerning the possibility of opening of a community shop and the loss of the Post Office in Clawddnewydd (Clocaenog is fortunate to still have a Post Office, run by Beryl Bailey in her own house). An encouraging number of replies indicated that a shop would be welcomed, and with promises to use these improvements. The shop eventually opened in February 2002 and has since become well used and returning a small profit — thanks to all the voluntary help given to staff it and also has a paid, full-time manager, Steve Ellis. Further developments have been the addition of a Post Office opening once a week and there is now a fortnightly police surgery held on the premises.

Canolfan Cae Cymro goes on from strength to strength.

A.N.

Cae Cymro, with Siop y Fro and the new delivery truck.

The mobile shop, with Gryff and John eager to serve you.

The Hall arranged for an evening of carpet bowling.

The Hall arranged for a concert.

Preparing the childrens' play area. Clawddnewydd Calvinistic Methodist Chapel, back left.

Management of Clocaenog Forest

Introduction

The Forestry Commission was established in 1919 with the main objective of establishing a strategic reserve of timber for the nation. This objective has governed the management of the Commission's woodlands (later run by Forest Enterprise) since that time. Clocaenog has been no different and has provided a high percentage of timber volume for Wales since its crops became productive. Over the last decade there has been a greater realisation of the environmental and conservation value of the forest with work being focussed on the Red Squirrel population and recently black grouse. Such diverse objectives cause tension, an example would be that red squirrels require a continuous tree cover yet black grouse require open ground and heather. The challenge of the future management of Clocaenog is to accommodate such diverse objectives as timber production, red squirrel management, recreation, local community objectives, archaeology and many others. The management document that shapes this future is the Forest Design Plan for Clocaenog. Before outlining the direction of that document it is important to provide some context for the future of forestry in Wales.

Woodlands for Wales

The twentieth century saw a major expansion of woodland in Wales from a low point of 5% to a level today of 14%. Many of these woodlands were plantations in the uplands to provide timber. Carwyn Jones (Minister for Rural Affairs, Wales Assembly Government) in his forward to the *Woodlands for Wales* document states that we now have the opportunity to place single purpose plantations firmly behind us and look for innovative ways in which to use our valuable woodland resource. The strategy is the first step towards fully integrating the role of woodlands into a wider environmental and economic policy for Wales.

The Woodlands for Wales strategy has a vision with a number of key principles. The vision is 'for the next 50 years that Wales will be known for its high quality woodlands that enhance the landscape, are appropriate to local conditions and have a diverse mixture of species and habitats. These will provide real social and community benefits both locally and nationally, support thriving woodland based industries and contribute to a better quality environment throughout Wales'.

The key principles that guide this vision are sustainability, social inclusion, quality, partnership and integration.

Finally the strategy sets out programmes for action against five strategic objectives,

- woodlands for people.

- a new emphasis on woodland management.

- Wales as a location for world class forest industries.

- a diverse and healthy environment.

- tourism, recreation and health.

A gateway into the forest.

A man-made lake in the forest to encourage wild life such as newts and frogs, and insects such as dragonflies.

In the forest, showing mature stands of conifers in the background and young growth in the foreground.

Implementation of the strategy is not something that can be achieved by the Wales Assembly Government alone, it requires involvement and commitment from everyone and herein lies the link to Clocaenog. Any future management in Clocaenog must seek to address these objectives in order to fulfil the Woodlands for Wales strategy.

Forest Design Plans

The Forest Design Plan (FDP) is the document that allows the Forest Enterprise to carry out its operations in an approved manner. The FDP addresses the need to improve landscape, better restructuring of the forest, smooth timber production flows, and to provide recreation, conservation, biodiversity and environmental benefits. The main tool by which we can manipulate the forest to achieve the above is through the felling of trees and one of the documents within the FDP is a felling plan. This outlines where we would propose to undertake felling operations in five year blocks over the life of the forest. The defined areas of felling are carefully designed so that they reflect and blend in with the landscape, rather than appear as geometric blocks. Current forestry practice is that following clear-felling, restocking will take place. Again the FDP has a plan that shows where particular species will be planted. Species are chosen to improve landscape, provide diversity, match species to sites and meet other objectives such as Norway spruce being the favoured species for red squirrels. It is important to point out that some areas remain as open space or are planted at lower densities such as adjacent to footpaths to improve views into and out of the forest.

This important document is approved by the following statutory consultees: Countryside Council for Wales, Environment Agency, Denbighshire CC and the Forestry Commission. We also treat local Community Councils within this category.

The Forest Design Plan is a detailed document and I could not give it justice in this short piece.

Clocaenog Future Priorities

1. Black Grouse

In Wales, the black grouse population has rapidly declined in the last 15years by 50%. It is therefore, considered as one of the highest national important species for prioritising to maintain the present population of approximately 200 lekking males, with an aim to reverse the rapid decline to a sustainable population.

The RSPB has acquired funding by European Union, and others to fund a three-year project to address the black grouse decline by monitoring the productivity and habits of black grouse and to manage designated key areas in Wales that hold 80% of the population.

One of these key areas is Clocaenog Forest, at Llanrwst Forest District. Historically, records of the black grouse population within Clocaenog Forest show that they utilise the open area of extensive clearfell and restock within the forest boundary. It is also one of a few forests that contain the population within the boundary. This has created a transient population that adopts the habitat suitability for a period approximately 10–15 years, until canopy closure. Creating a permanent, preferable habitat, within the forest such as Foel Frech, which already utilised, would stabilise the population in an area that we can manage permanently. It is also placed in a strategic position to utilise the transient habitat within the forest infrastructure, and also links other permanent open space of riparian, Craig Bron Bannog and Marial Gwyn SSSI.

Future management will expand the Foel Frech area to an ecological scale that can sustain a permanent population of black grouse, within a preferable habitat. The area would expand to link in other areas that are utilised by existing, black grouse population allowing movement to exploit transient habitat of clearfell and restock within the forest infrastructure. This project will be in partnership with the RSPB who will provide both funding and supervision

2. Red Squirrels

Clocaenog is home to Wales' largest red squirrel population. Felling and restocking proposals within the Forest Design Plan will consider their needs. The Forest Enterprise has recently commissioned research work within this area carried out by Sarah Cartmel. This work has shown that it is important to manage the forest in such a way as to produce a maximum food supply for the red squirrel without compromising the economics of the forest. At the same time, it is necessary to consider measures that would discourage the presence of grey squirrels. The following management guidelines will form the basis of our future work.

- Maintain present areas of Scots pine, Norway spruce and Japanese larch. Thin if necessary but no clear felling until new crops are at least 30 years old and producing cones.

- A minimum of 25% of the whole forest should consist of Scots pine, Norway spruce (and Japanese larch). Age groups:

    Pine and larch: 30%   0–15 years old,   30%   16–30 y.o.,   40% >30 y.o.

    Norway spruce: 30%   0–30 years old,   30%   31–45 y.o.,   40% >45 y.o.

One of the main criticisms often levelled at foresters is the public's dislike of clear-felling systems. As had been mentioned earlier the *Woodlands for Wales* document seeks to encourage a new emphasis on woodland management. One of the ways in which we can meet this objective whilst still fulfilling production needs and meeting red squirrel guidelines, is through greater use of thinning and other silvicultural systems that retain a tree cover. Research into the use of these new systems has become grouped under the heading of 'Low Impact Silvicultural Systems' and Clocaenog is one of three sites in Wales where research will be focussed.

4. Communities

The *Woodlands for Wales* document also places emphasis on woodlands for people. Whilst the Forest Enterprise has always provided recreational facilities we need to start thinking much wider. What do the local communities to Clocaenog want from their forest? In order to engage communities, the Forest Enterprise is in the process of restructuring, with proposed implementation of March 2002, though certain elements will be in place by January 2002. The restructuring will appoint a local area manager for the Clocaenog and Clwyd area; Mr Dave Liddy will become the local point of contact. The local area manager will engage communities to discover their aspirations and feed them back through the Forest Enterprises planning systems. It is hoped in this way that the Forest Enterprise can deliver real benefits to the people of Wales.

5. Archaeological

A recent survey has identified all archaeological sites within Clocaenog and management plans will be drawn up to conserve, manage and interpret these sites.

Conclusion

The Forest Enterprise operates the highest levels of management on its estate and this has recently been recognised with The Forestry Commission and Forest Enterprise having been presented with WWF's highest award for global conservation, the 'Gift of the Earth'. The award was made to acknowledge our work in forest certification and for good forest management. I hope that in the short narrative above I have been able to place into context and put across some of the important objectives for the future management of Clocaenog.

Jonathan Levell, MBA, M.Sc, B.A.(Hons), MICFor, FRGS. District Forester Planning Llanrwst Forest District

The Future of Clocaenog Forest

Woodlands for Wales, the official document of the National Assembly for Wales, sets out a 'vision for the next 50 years of the Welsh forests which will:

- provide real social and community benefits, both locally and nationally

- support thriving woodland-based industries

- contribute to a better environment throughout Wales.' How will this affect Clocaenog Forest? We will see changes (that have already begun) in woodland management. Far less clear-felling will be undertaken and there is a move to practise thinning of mature trees which will allow more light to filter through to the forest floor and permit natural regeneration to take place and yet maintain a continuous cover in the canopy. Modern machinery will enable sections of forest to be entered through firebreaks and trees cropped on either side with the minimum of disturbance. 'There is a strong case for moving away from single-aged plantations,' and at the same time 'low-impact silviculture protects the soil and retains a woodland appearance.' Manual planting of young trees should hardly be necessary. This envisaged woodland would be far more pleasant to walk through, would encourage more bird life and allow woodland creatures to survive in a better habitat than the dense, dark conifer forest we have had in the recent past.

Another factor will be the consideration of the forest in its environment and the landscape. During the First World War much clear felling took place and by 1919 a low point was reached when only 5% of Welsh land area was woodland and this crisis led to the formation of the Forestry Commission. They succeeded in planting acres of commercial coniferous woodland, and with the help of modem technology they 'drained wet-lands and established frees on nutrientpoor upland heath.' — 'The national forestry estate had been achieved, with the area of Wales under frees having risen to about 14% of the land area.'

At present 50% of the timber from Clocaenog Forest goes to BSW (British Soft Woods) at Newbridge on Wye, to be sawn and sold as structural joinery planks; 30% of smaller timber goes for fencing and pallet wood, some is sold to a sawmill at Chirk or to the local sawmill at Gwyddelwern and the rest to Clifford Jones, Ruthin and Corwen Forestry; and last year Christmas trees were sold from the forestry office at Clawddnewydd.

Now policies have changed we can expect to see Clocaenog Forest becoming a multi-purpose woodland managed for recreation, landscape and wildlife as well as for timber production. A mountain bike trail was established, but was taken over and ruined by motor bikers who had no right to use those tracks. Meetings were held to set up a recognised motor-cycle route away from habitations, hoping to minimise noise pollution and put a stop to wild riding, but this would have to be policed on a regular basis as is done in

Coed y Brenin. The scheme would need to attract finance to be viable; it could be an asset to the local tourist industry and prevent further damage in the forest. However, at the public meeting held to discuss these plans, the local opposition was so great that on the advice of Assembly Member and Sports Minister, Alan Pugh, the scheme was abandoned. Now we are still left with the problem of wild riding, but can attract no funding to police it.

The forestry is working closely with Denbighshire Archaeology to conserve all the known sites and clearings are being enlarged to prevent further root damage. It would be good to see exposition boards as have been placed at the Llyn Brenig sites.

We are fortunate to be hosts to the Przewalski horses and the viewing platform is very well positioned, as is the bird hide for seeing black grouse near Nilig, built with the co-operation of the RSPB. These are positive moves in the right direction.

This is a very long-term plan and nobody knows yet what the effects of global warming are going to be. There are bound to be influences on flora and fauna which will have to be considered as we proceed into the future and the plans for our woodland will need to be flexible.

The future felling areas and the tree species to be grown in the forest are shown in the design plans for Clocaenog Forest. The aims for the future of Clocaenog are stated in Programmes for Action as follows:

> 1. Woodlands for people
> 2. A new emphasis on woodland management
> 3. Wales as a location for world-class forest industries
> 4. A diverse and healthy environment
> 5. Tourism, recreation and health

With thanks to Dave Liddy, Local Area Manager of Clocaenog Forest, for reading, correcting and advising me, concerning this article.

Now, all these plans seem unlikely to come to fruition. The government has put pressure on the Welsh Assembly to find sites for the development of renewable energy. The Assembly has identified seven strategic areas throughout Wales which could become the key zones for major wind farms. In north Wales the area chosen is termed the Denbigh Moors, but in fact from maps it would appear that Clocaenog Forest and surrounding areas, including the popular Llyn Brenig and Llyn Alwen have been designated as sites for a series of wind farms to supply electricity to make up the shortfall in our electricity supplies, whose methods of production must look to be environmentally acceptable in this age of global warming.

The forest is easily bought land, not needing protracted negotiations with landowners, has access to roads for the transportation of equipment, and is only thinly populated. The fact that this is an unspoilt area of great beauty, with an extensive wild life which appeals to tourists, does not count, even when these qualities can never be recovered when wind farming becomes an uneconomic and outmoded system for energy creation. Windmills in themselves can look elegant— if not gigantic or too numerous — but the fear is also of the additional superstructures of substations and power lines they are bound to bring in their wake. Up to now, the Assembly has published a consultation draft of its Technical Advice Note 8 on renewable energy (known as 'Tan 8') to be taken into account whenever planning applications are made in these areas.

The harvester at work.

Politics will loom large in any decision-making, particularly as we approach an election. We can only wait and see.

A.N.

Red Squirrels

There are red and grey squirrels in Clocaenog Forest and because the former are an endangered species, and their population here is thought to be one of the largest in Wales, their protection is to be a key element in future forest planning. Clocaenog Forest has to be commercially feasible, but at the same time, the government and the Forestry Commission favour an approach which enables future schemes to include conservation of fauna and their forest habitats.

At the present time the numbers of red squirrels in Clocaenog Forest (estimated to be about 200) are only just above what is considered a viable population level. New, long-term improvements need to be implemented based not only on habitat but on the red squirrels' food supply. Squirrel numbers fluctuate in relation to food availability and breeding is dependent on good food sources. The main diet of squirrels is tree seed, and red squirrels have a preference for seeds from the cones of Norway spruce, Scots pine and Japanese larch. The main aim will be to try and ensure sufficient trees of these species that are of coning age. Stands of Norway spruce already growing will be managed by thinning, if necessary, to allow light through for regeneration to take place, but to leave a good canopy for the squirrels to travel through. Norway spruce trees are also favoured areas for squirrels to build their dreys and in the breeding season — April to October — forestry work should not be carried out nearby.

A big problem which needs to be taken into account is the age of the required trees; this is best explained by the chart below:

	First good crop	Maximum cone Production	No. of years between crops
Norway spruce	30–35 years	50–60 years	3–7 years
Scots pine	15–20 years	60–100 years	1–3 years
Japanese larch	15–20 years	40–60 years	3–6 years

At present (2004) Clocaenog Forest has only 7% Norway spruce of coning age, 2% of Seats pine and 5% of Japanese larch. The recommended age structure should be about

30% of trees	0–30 years old
30%	31–45 years old
40%	>45 years old

Scots pine and Japanese larch only provide food after 15 years growth and Norway spruce are particularly late to mature and do not cone well before 30 years of age. Into this equation there is also the consideration that there can be 3–7 years between crops, except for Scots pine which is the most consistent, producing mast crop most years in Clocaenog Forest — and squirrel colonies will only breed when there is a good food supply.

Only 17% of the forest consists of these favoured species and it has been recommended that more Norway spruce and Scots pine be planted to increase the proportion to over 20%. During the last three years clear felling has already given way to thinning in forest management so that self regeneration can take place naturally and result in stands of trees of differing age. In red squirrel areas this will eventually result in a continuous food supply of cone seeds. An insoluble problem will always be where wind damage creates open spaces. However, one idea is to keep the grey squirrels out by using the open spaces of surrounding farm land and by planting a border zone at the edges of the forest, at least 3 kms. deep, of Sitka spruce — not favoured by the grey squirrels as foraging areas.

The Red Squirrel.

The overall need is to create habitats for three or four colonies of red squirrels which have a continuous food supply, and with linked corridors of trees whose canopy will enable the red squirrels to travel between these colonies so that any one group does not become isolated. The gene flow needs to be facilitated and the recruitment of young stock made accessible so that the colonies can flourish without inbreeding.

A.N.

Przewalski Horse (*Equus Caballus Przewalski*)
Also known as Asiatic Wild Horse, Mongolian Wild Horse and Taki.

Twenty thousand years ago the ancestors of the Przewalski horse roamed the plains of Europe and Asia. These hardy 'horses' had become extremely scarce in the wild but a few were captured in the 1960s and sent to zoos where they thrived. They are now being re-introduced into the wild from the zoo population.

The Welsh Mountain Zoo (at Colwyn Bay) and Chester Zoo, in partnership with the Forestry Commission Wales, are using three Przewalski mares to graze a prehistoric site in Clocaenog Forest. The horses will prevent damage to the site by stopping the regeneration of trees whose roots could damage the remains of the early habitations — the archaeological area has not been dug and needs preserving. The horses' enclosure is best approached from the B5105 road at OR SJ 049518 (on the Ruthin to Cerrigydrudion road), and then a short walk along a forest track, following the signs, to a viewing platform at OR SJ 043524. [Ordnance Survey References]

Przewalski horses have placid temperaments and are comfortable in the presence of people. They are similar in size to the Welsh Mountain Ponies, and are very hardy, with a stocky build; they are reddish brown or dun coloured with a white muzzle, a stiff, dark brown mane which stops between their ears and is permanently erect (hence the Przewalski horse has no forelock). The tail is also different from the modern horse and more like the tail of an ass; whereas the long hairs of a horse's tail start right at the top, the Przewalski has short hairs on the dock, the long hairs only start lower down. Some authorities believe the Przewalski is a direct ancestor of the modern horse; others contend this is not possible as the Przewalski is a different species having 66 chromosomes, while the domestic horse has 64. The three mares in Clocaenog Forest still have an element of modern horse in them and so cannot be used in the breeding programme to produce pure Przewalski foals.

A Przewalski Horse.

Our prehistoric ancestors hunted them extensively as we see in the many cave paintings of 'horses' in France and Spain. In most of the caves, pictures of horses far outnumber pictures of any other species, therefore it is fair to assume that they were abundant. No knowledge of these horses was available until 1880 when Count Nikolai Przewalski, who made journeys of discovery into Central Asia by order of the Czar, announced that he had heard of wild horses still existing in Mongolia. By 1900 several horses had been captured and were to be distributed to various zoos in Europe and America; only 53 of these survived the long, rough journey from Mongolia, and they were dispersed to zoos and privately owned parks. All the captive Przewalski horses of today are the descendents of 13 of these animals. By 1969, no herds of wild horses were thought still to exist in south-west Mongolia, so something had to be done to save the wild horses from extinction in their ancient habitat. In 1990 a reintroduction project in Mongolia was started in a 24,000 acre area which has since become a national park. By 1998 some 60 horses were living on the steppes with some 1,450 Przewalkis spread over 135 zoos and private parks all over the world.

We are fortunate in Clocaenog to have the privilege of being host to these creatures whose ancestors may have grazed the very area of Clocaenog Forest where they are now enclosed.

By 2005 the breeding programme has been so successful that after being termed 'extinct' these horses have now been recommended by scientists at London Zoo to be classified as an 'endangered' species. In 1945 there were only 31 left alive and they were all in captivity — there were none in the wild; whereas now, 248 are roaming Mongolia, and the breeding programme continues.

E.N.

Black Grouse

The black grouse, or blackcock as the male is called, is a bird of mountain and moorland. These birds are a feature in Clocaenog Forest, partly because there has been a deliberate policy of forestry management in recent years to create suitable habitats for them, and their numbers have built up. Black grouse need a wide range of habitats to breed successfully; they prefer marginal farmland in the hills where the open spaces at the edge of woodland provide them with ideal places for lekking (displaying during courtship) and a variety of rowan, birch and hawthorn, as a source of food for the autumn and winter periods. Young plantations of conifers can offer good ground cover and protection in bad weather and in the spring the grouse will feed on larch buds. They also like wet areas where cotton grass flowers are an important food supply. Heather needs to be long — over 40 cms — to shelter and hide nestlings, and the birds feed all the year round on heather and bilberry shoots and berries; the chicks thrive best where the heather is managed and not too old and dense — mowing and burning can be beneficial.

In Wales, there had been a steady decline in grouse numbers to 1997 but sympathetic management of habitats showed a marked increase in lekking males by 2002. The males are handsome in their glossy black and white plumage and will lek for much of the year when encountering other males on short herbage by displaying spread wings and tail (the wings are really very dark brown) and the tail is lyre-shaped over a conspicuous white rump. The main lekking period is between about April 1st and May 15th when several

A Black Grouse.

males may gather at a traditional site at dawn or dusk and lek in the presence of the brown females. The female (the greyhen) is not drab but is grey-brown with striking barred plumage. Incubation of the eggs takes about four weeks and after hatching the hen will take her chicks to feed in wet areas in search of insects. Each brood will need up to 60 hectares of mixed habitat to survive and rear their chicks.

The forestry people, in conjunction with the RSPB, have built a special hide for watching the displays in spring time, near Nilig, on the road from Cyfilliog to Pentre-llyn-cymmer, in the valley between Foel Frech and Foel Gasnach.

A.N.

Ideal ground for Black Grouse to lek.

Fauna in Clocaenog

Birds
Goldfinch   Nuthatch   Blue tit   Great tit   Coal tit   Long-tailed tit
Goldcrest   Spotted flycatcher   Pied flycatcher   Redpoll   Siskin
Song thrush   Wren   Robin   Blackbird   Song thrush   Wood pigeon
Crossbill   Tawny owl   Barn owl   Goshawk   Redstart   Raven
Buzzard   Sparrowhawk   Curlew   Redwing   Fieldfare   Sea gull
Green woodpecker   Great spotted woodpecker   Yellowhammer
Swallow   Lesser spotted woodpecker   Blackcap   Chiffchaff   Swift
House martin   Tree pipit   Heron   Chaffinch   Pied wagtail
Whitethroat   Sedge warbler   Black grouse   Garden warbler   Jay
Grey wagtail   House martin   Collared dove   Dunnock   Snipe
Willow Warbler   House sparrow   Canada goose   Greenfinch
Bullfinch   Crow   Jackdaw   Magpie   Starling
Redstart   Brambling   Mallard   Dipper   Kestrel
Crossbill   Wood warbler   Bittern   Treecreeper
Lapwing   Dipper   Pheasant   Pochard.

Mammals
Fox   Rabbit   Mole   Bats   Field mouse   Hedgehog
Dormouse   Common shrew   Grey squirrel   Red squirrel   Hare   Bank vole   Water vole   Badger
Water rat   Polecat   Weasel   Stoat.

Amphibians and Reptiles
Adder   Slow worm   Toad   Frog   Newts.

and many different butterflies, dragonflies and damselflies.

Right, top–bottom: Buzzard.

Adder.

Common Toad.

Dragonfly.

Below left: Fly Agaric [Amanita muscaria] a poisonous toadstool common in coniferous woods.

A.N.
Plants of Clocaenog Parish

There is so much enjoyment to be had from finding, looking at and absorbing the beauty of all wild flowers and plants. My aim is to show what beautiful specimens can be found in the parish of Clocaenog, on the hills, in the valleys, forest and hedgerows.

Here, they are in chronological order according to their approximate time of flowering in spring, summer, autumn and winter. Each plant has its Welsh name (often a local name), its English name, botanical name, as well as the name of the family to which it belongs.

The photographs of a few of those plants were taken as I saw them in their natural habitat, on walks through this lovely countryside. Hopefully, you will gain pleasure from finding them too.

Planhigion Plwyf Clocaenog

Mae llawer o bleser i'w gael wrth ddod o hyd i flodau gwyllt, a mwynhau eu harddwch. Fy mwriad yw tynnu sylw at rai o'r enghreifftiau arbennig sydd i'w cael ym mhlwyf Clocaenog, ar y bryniau, yn y cymoedd, yn y goedwig ac ar y cloddiau.

Dyma restr ohonynt yn ôl eu tymor blodeuo yn ystod y gwanwyn, yr haf, yr hydref â'r gaeaf. Rhoddir yr enw Cymraeg i bob un (enw lleol ambell dro), yn ogystal â'r enw Saesneg, yr enw Lladin ac enw'r teulu.

Tynwyd y lluniau o'r planhigion yn eu cynefin, wrth i mi ddod ar eu traws tra'n crwydro'r ardal hyfryd hon. Gobeithio y cewch chwithau yr un pleser wrth dod o hyd iddynt.

M.L.

SPRING

Llygad Ebrill, Lesser Celandine [Ranunculus ficaris RANUNCULACEAE).

Blodyn llefrith, Cuckooflower (Cardamine pratensis CRUCIFERAE).

Cam yr Ebol, Colt's-foot (Tussilago farfara COMPOSITAE).

221

Had Dant y Llew, Dandelion clock/seed head.

*Gwernen, Alder catkins (male)
(Alnus glutinosa BETULACEAE)*

*Briallen, Primrose
(Primula vulgaris
PRIMULACEAE)*

*Dant y Llew, Dandelion
(Taraxacum sp. COMPOSITAE)*

*Pidyn y Gog, Lords-and-Ladies
(Arum maculatum ARACEAE)*

*Perfagl fach, Lesser Periwinkle
(Vinca minor APOCYNACEAE)*

Blodyn y gwynt, Wood Anemone (*Anemone nemorosa* RANUNCULACEAE)

Draenen Ddu, Blackthorn (*Prunus spinosa* ROSACEAE)

Llwyn coeg-fefus, Barren Strawberry (*Potentilla sterilis* ROSACEAE)

Llusen, Bilberry (*Vaccinium myrtillus* ERICACEAE)

Serenllys mawr – local name *Botwm crys*, Greater Stitchwort (*Stellaria holostea* CARYOPHYLLACEAE)

Llwyn mwyar duon, Bramble (*Rubus sp.* ROSACEAE)

Castanwydden y meirch, Horse-chestnut (*Aesculus hippocastanum* HIPPOCASTANACEAE)

Craf y geifr, Ramsons (*Allium ursinum* LILIACEAE)

*Gwyddfid, Honeysuckle
(Lonicera periclymenum
CAPRIFOLIACEAE)*

*Pig-yr-aran loywddail,
Shining Crane's-bill
(Geranium lucidum
GERANIACEAE)*

SUMMER

*Draenen wen, Hawthorn
(Crataegus monogyna
ROSACAE)*

*Rhosyn gwyllt, Dog-rose
(Rosa Canina ROSACAE)*

*Lloer-redynen, Moonwort
(Botrychiun lunaria
OPHIOGLOSSACEAE)*

*Eithinen Ffrengig, Gorse
(Ulex europaeus
LEGUMINOSAE)*

Ffacbysen y berth, Tufted vetch (*Vicia cracca* LEGUMINOSAE)

Clychlys dail danadl, Nettle-leaved Bellflower (*Campanula trachelium* CAMPANULACEAE)

Carpiog y gors, Ragged-robbin (*Lychnis flos-cuculi* CARPPHYLLACEAE)

Banhadlen, Broom (*Cytisus scoparius* LEGUMINOSAE)

Glesyn y coed, Bugle (*Ajuga reptans* LABIATAE)

AUTUMN

Efal y derwen, Oak apple gall *(Biorrhiza pallida on derwen oak Quercus* sp.*)*

Collen (cnau), Hazel (nuts) *(Corylus avellana* CORYLACEAE*)*

Gwyddfid, Honeysuckle *(Lonicera periclymenum* CAPRIFOLIACEAE*)*

Derwen mes caoesynnog, Pedunculate oak *(Quercus robur* FAGACEAE*) Leaf with unidentified galls.*

Eiddew, Ivy *(Hedera helix* ARALIACEAE*)*

Llwyn mawr duon, Bramble *(Rubus* sp. ROSACAE*)*

226

Pidyn y gog, Lords-and-Ladies (*Arum maculatum* ARACEAE)

Llin y llyffant, Common toadflax (*Linaria vulgaris* SCROPHULARIACEAE)

Bysedd y Cwn, Foxglove (*Digitalis purpurea* SCROPHULARIACEAE)

Clychau'r eos, Harebell (*Campanula rotundifolia* CAMPANULACEAE)

Castanwydden y meirch, Horse-chestnut (*Aesculus hippocastanum* HIPPOCASTANACEAE)

Ffawydden, Beech *Fagus sylvatica* FAGACEAE

WINTER

Eiddew, Ivy (berries) Hedera helix ARALIACEAE)

Eirlys, Snowdrop (Galanthus sp. LILIACEAE)

Celynnen, Holly (Ilex aquilfolium AQUIFOLIACEAE)

Collen, Hazel (Crylus avellana CORYLACEAE)

A Brief History of Clocaenog W.I.

Clocaenog W. I. was formed on December 7th 1927, when 20 ladies from the village met in the schoolroom and heard Mrs. Jones-Bateman speaking about the aims of the Womens' Institutes: the meetings were to be non-party political, non-sectarian, and based on the spiritual ideals of friendship, truth, tolerance and justice. It was advocated that women should work together to improve and develop the conditions of rural life.

At that first meeting officers were elected including Mrs. Hopkin-Jones (the Rectory), as President, Mrs. M. E. Francis (the Post Office) as Secretary, and the schoolmistress, Miss A. M. Davies, Pentre — later known to many of us as Mrs. A. M. Jones — to act as treasurer. A further meeting was planned for January 11th at 3.30 p.m. when there was a demonstration of basket-making which was so appreciated that another demonstration was held a fortnight later on January 25th. Dr. Mary Watson was asked to give a talk on Health Matters in the February meeting and the varied programme of WI sessions was under way. It was at this next meeting that the chore of tea hostesses was inaugurated 'at a small charge', and the meetings were moved to 5.30 p.m.

In June the committee resolved to have an outing to Loggerheads; the fare was to be 2/3 (two shillings and three pence) and tea would be ordered at 1/- (one shilling) per head. No meetings would be held in August — no change there — 'owing to harvest work'.

Up to then everything was planned from one meeting to the next, but on September the committee drew up a programme for the coming months. On the following evening only the President and Secretary were present because it was a busy time with the corn harvest. The W.I. ladies relied heavily on their own skills for demonstrations, but also employed the expertise of speakers from Llysfasi College. They set up fortnightly sewing classes with a grant from the Denbighshire Education Authority, and held them in the Sunday School at Clawddnewydd. 'Outings' included trips by char-ã-banc to the Horseshoe Pass, Llangollen, Wrexham and Chester; Liverpool and Southport; New Brighton (on the Wirral) and Llandudno Royal Welsh Show.

In 1931, on December 23, they gave the first tea party for the school children, in 1932 tea and sports was started in October with 22 members present to help. In 1983 a coffee morning was held to contribute towards funds for those children taking part in the Urdd Eisteddfod in south Wales.

For many years we have entertained some of the patients from Pool Park Hospital to a Christmas Party, taken fresh farm eggs to the hospital at Easter and played whist with the patients on other occasions. Now the hospital has closed.

After the Flint and Denbigh Show in held at Rhyl in September, Clocaenog W.I. gained 10 first prizes, 3 seconds and numerous thirds for their entries in jam, marmalade, chutney, brown and white eggs, butter and unsalted butter, with prizes distributed at

Above left: An early W.I. trip.

Left: A W.I. picnic to Foel Fawr 'mountain'.

Mrs M. E. Francis, the first W.I. secretary, and her family outside the old Post Office.

the October meeting. They had a choir and a drama group and moved to the Church Hall and paid 1/- per meeting. A Sale of Work and a Garden Fête were held, and there were whist drives, socials and concerts, the proceeds of which went partly to their W.I. funds and partly towards paying half towards members' trips. Another event was a picnic in a field at Voel Cilcen, Clawddnewydd, which was very much enjoyed, especially the competition for the best bunch of wild flowers gathered on the day.

After the war started, a note of realistic self-help becomes even more apparent. Meetings were held on 'How to make slippers out of old felt hats', 'How to make rugs out of old stockings' there were talks on National Savings, the Salvage of Waste Materials, demonstrations of cutting out overalls, and a very challenging one was 'Common Sense in Air raids — How to deal with unexploded bombs'. They had demonstrations of War Time Cookery and how to spin out the rations. Then they joined the Fruit Preservation Scheme and bought a canning machine, after joining with other W.I.s and arranging a centre for its use; it was sold in 1957. What a lively, enterprising group they were.

We have produced two county chairpersons, Mrs. A. M. Jones and our present member, Anne Richards, has risen to the position. Since the beginning, Clocaenog W.I. has always had a name for being friendly and has drawn its members from quite a wide area, not just from the village as when it started; but without the initiative of the founding members we would not be holding our W.I. meetings here in 2004.

A.N.

Memories of Clocaenog W.I.

Ceinwen Roberts
Cartref, Clawddnewydd

One of my first recollections of the Women's Institute is when my mother became a member after Mrs. Idwal Evans, Tan y Llan, persuaded her to join. Mrs. Evans said 'You can't come to the WI without make-up', so my mother went to her home before the meeting so that she could look respectable for the occasion. I think they both enjoyed it because they were members for quite a few years.

I asked my sister, Buddug, what she remembered about the WI and she said 'Country dancing, the Christmas party, evening classes and the lovely trips we had'.

The Christmas party was a very big occasion with every member inviting a friend, and the hall was beautifully decorated for the occasion - the tables always looked gorgeous. Mrs. Gwen Evans was one of the women in charge and was an excellent member, like many others, walking all the way from Ty'n y Mynydd whatever the weather to attend the meetings. She always brought Mrs. Blodwen Hughes, Plas Newydd, with her to the party so that she could have company to walk home as it was quite late when the party finished because of all the games we played. In her later years, Gwen Evans came to live at Paradwys and prepared the hall for the meetings

Clocaenog School Sports Day, c.1954.

Clocaenog W.I. 21st Anniversary Party, 1948.

Below right: W.I. members having tea with Mr Llew Roberts, headmaster, after the Sports Day, 1936.

Below left: Schoolchildren's tea party in the school yard (provided by the W.I.), 1936.

with Jinny, Bryn Fedwen, helping her. It is now Mrs. Beryl Jones who does this work and we are very thankful to her.

My sister and I also remember the classes we had with the W.I. including needlework and glovemaking, taken by Mrs. Jones from Llansannan; there was also stool making and Mrs. Ross Thomas came to help us with the dancing.

When Mrs. H. F. Jones, the wife of the new headmaster, came to live at Henblas, she joined the W.I. and was a very talented member, helping with the drama, singing and dancing and, later, became president. There was also Mrs. Hughes, Isfryn, who helped by making costumes for the dramas, and Mrs. Davies, from the Forestry House (her husband was the Forester) who became a president and was a very helpful and useful member — now retired, she lives in Cannock.

Mrs. Rhoda Hughes, Pen y Coed Uchaf, and Mrs. Ella Roberts, Tŷ Isa Cefn, both from Pwllglas, walked a long way to be at the meetings. We can't think of faithful members of Clocaenog W.I. without remembering the late Mrs. A. M. Jones (Maes Gwyn), Mrs. Williams (Foel Fawr), Mrs. Williams (Allt y Celyn), Mrs. Francis and Gwyneth from Clocaenog Post Office, all of whom were always ready to help with every occasion.

After praising the good work of the oldest members who by now have left us, let us not forget the new members who have come along and are carrying on the good work.

I now wish the WI all the best for future years.

Elsa Jones
Parc Bach, Troed-y-Rhiw, Ruthin, talking about her time as a member of Clocaenog Womens' Institute, when she resided at Pool Park Farm.

I joined as a member of the W.I. in 1950 when meetings were held in the Church Hall kitchen with about 12 members present. I used to walk three-quarters of a mile along the lane through the fields to meet Mrs. Edmunds, Penymaes, and we both walked another three-quarters of a mile along the Ruthin to Clocaenog

Clocaenog W.I. in 1956 with 28 members present.

road to reach the Church Hall. Several women from Clocaenog were members but there were not many houses in the village itself as the Council Estate had not been built at this time; quite a few members came from Clawddnewydd, a few from Pwllglas and one or two from Cyffylliog.

We were fortunate to get very good speakers and demonstrators showing handiwork, cookery and other interesting subjects. A Welsh night took place annually in March when the food served had a Welsh flavour with *Bara Brith*, and Welsh cakes. The meeting would be conducted in Welsh and I believe the minutes were also written in the Welsh language, but that ceased many years ago. In our October meeting we elected new officials for the following year and during December we enjoyed an excellent Christmas Party. In the other months we had film shows or someone talking about their holidays abroad and we enjoyed interesting evenings throughout the year.

We had an annual full day trip to start with, when many members had to walk quite a distance to meet the coach but then it became a half day and in later years an evening trip was arranged. I remember travelling to Swansea for the Welsh Annual Meeting and other members would travel to London for the Annual General Meeting which was a very good trip.

We would be invited to Pool Park Hospital for an evening whist drive and were made very welcome, with a supper prepared for us; our members would enjoy supper in one room and the residents in a separate room and then we would get together to play cards, with very good prizes for the winners. Another evening, in December, Pool Park Hospital residents were invited to our Church Hall for a Christmas party. Seven o'clock was the official time for them to arrive but they were so eager that they would be there by half past six when we had not finished preparing their supper! They would eat the meal as if they had not been fed for weeks, but we knew they were well cared for at Pool Park. After the supper we all enjoyed an evening of games, before they were transported back in their mini bus.

Every member could invite one person to the W.I. Christmas Party at the Church Hall. The evening commenced with supper which was prepared and donated by the members, followed by games when everyone joined in the fun. Robert Jones, Maesgwyn, (Mrs. A. M. Jones' husband) and Gwilym Williams, Maestyddyn, were a great help on these evenings.

Two members from nearby institutes were invited — Cyffylliog, and Pwllglas when a branch there was established. I remember one year when we had a fall of snow on the evening of the party and two young women from Cyffylliog travelled by car through the forest and 'over the mountain', as we called it, with spades in the boot in case they had problems on the return journey. They must have arrived home safely because I saw them several times afterwards. Two excellent Christmas parties, our own and that of Pool Park folk that are well worth remembering. I feel that in the past we had many activities to look forward to and to look back upon.

To raise funds to meet WI expenditure we held activities, one being the annual whist drive every November which was very popular and well attended. On one occasion when the hall was full we had to set up tables in the kitchen and even used the top of the piano. As cars became more common, parking became a problem and numbers attending were less, but now the W.I. holds this annual event at Cae Cymro, Clawddnewydd. Another form of fund raising was to sell surplus food brought in by members and sometimes we had a sales table. Later on one of the members would invite us to her home for either a coffee morning or afternoon tea and, by charging, a very good profit could be made. We needed the extra money to pay the rent for the hall as we had outgrown the kitchen, due to the increase in membership.

We prepared tea for the children and staff from the village school in July, before they closed for the summer holidays, but had to make sure the date did not clash with the Welsh Show. The childrens' sports commenced after lunch and two members would go to the field with ice cream, which was well received if it was a hot day. Tea was prepared in the hall; jelly used to be popular but now the children seem to prefer sandwiches and crisps. Afterwards, prizes were presented to the winners but every child went home with a small amount of money. This was a pleasing day for members and children alike and the practice still goes on.

I served as president for one year and enjoyed the experience, mostly because everyone was so helpful. I was also treasurer one year but found this rather difficult because I am not very good at mathematics although anyone else would probably find it quite easy. I must admit I found it more relaxing and enjoyable when I was not an official.

One of the members I particularly remember was Miss Higgins who came here after the war from Devizes, Wiltshire, to work in the Agricultural Offices in Ruthin. She lived in a caravan a short distance from my home and I gave her lifts to the meetings. Miss Higgins was a bit eccentric and, although she was always clean, she dressed quite differently from everyone else. Mrs. A. M. Jones, Maesgwyn, was a faithful and conscientious member and the backbone of Clocaenog W.I. She went on to hold the posts of county secretary and county chairman and so could share valuable knowledge with members and officials. Miss Gwen Evans was a very good cook and one year she won a Gold Star at the Denbigh and Flint Show. Members did well when they competed in the local shows in the cookery, handicraft and floral sections.

In 1953 I boarded the train at Rhyl for the journey to Denman College and on the train I met some other women from Anglesey, Llansannan and Bala with whom I have kept in touch. The train took us to Oxford where a coach met us to take us to the college. I was allocated a single room so was not fortunate enough to stay in the 'Denbighshire room' which accommodates three people. Each county is responsible for one bedroom that will often contains quilts and pictures made by members; my bedroom had been furnished by Huntingdonshire. We attended lectures morning, afternoon and evening but they were quite light-hearted subjects; one demonstrator talked about vacuum cleaners which had recently come on the market but I did not possess one till many years later. The lectures took place in ex-army huts from wartime. Everyone enjoyed herself while attending these courses and I felt it was a privilege to have been to Denman.

I was a member of Clocaenog W.I. for 45 years, and remember the monthly meetings held on the second Monday of the month with pleasure as there were few other functions and they were a good opportunity to socialise and make new friends.

Interview by Gwyneth Roberts

Elsa Jones
Parc Bach, Troed-y-Rhiw, Rhuthun, yn son am y cyfnod pan oedd yn aelod o Sefydliad y Merched, Clocaenog, a hithau yn byw yn Fferm Pool Parc yr adeg honno.

Yn y flwyddyn 1950 wnes i ymuno a'r sefydliad, ac yn cyfarfod yn y gegin yn Neuadd yr Eglwys a tua deuddeg aelod yn bresennol.

Cerdded tri-chwarter milltir ar hyd y lôn i fyny y caeau a cyfarfod Mrs Edmunds, Penymaes, ac yna cerdded tri-chwarter milltir arall ar hyd y ffordd sydd yn arwain o Rhuthun i Clocaenog, i gyrraedd Neuadd yr Eglwys. Byddai dipyn o aelodau o Clocaenog, ond ychydig o dai oedd yn y pentref ei hun gan nad oedd y tai cyngor wedi cael ei hadeiladu yr adeg honno, amryw o aelodau o Clawddnewydd, dipyn o Pwllglas ac un neu ddwy o Cyffylliog.

Yr oeddem bob amser yn cael siaradwyr da iawn, yn dangos gwahanol bethau, gwaith llaw, coginio ac amryw o bethau eraill diddorol. Noson Gymraeg oedd cyfarfod mis Mawrth, gyda bwydydd Cymreig, megis cacennau cri a bara brith, ac yr oedd y drafodaeth yn Gymraeg hefyd, ac yr wyf yn credu bod y cofnodion yn cael eu ysgrifennu yn yr un iaith ond mae yr arferiad yma wedi peidio a bod er llawer blwyddyn. Yn ystod mis Rhagfyr cael parti Nadolig rhagorol ac yn mis Hydref byddem yn ethol pwyllgor a swyddogion am y flwyddyn ganlynol. Yn ystod y misoedd eraill deuai rywun i ddangos ffilmiau neu i son am eu gwyliau dramor, nosweithiau difyr iawn a rhaglen dda bob blwyddyn.

Byddem yn cael trip bob blwyddyn. Trip trwy y dydd am ychydig o flynyddoedd ac yr oedd yn rhaid i amryw o'r aelodau gerdded yn reit bell i gyfarfod y bws i fynd i ffwrdd am y diwrnod. Yn ddiweddarach trip hanner diwrnod byddem yn gael ac yna yn mhen blynyddoedd aeth yn drip gyda'r nos. Byddai Cyfarfod Cymraeg Blynyddol yn cael ei gynnal ac 'rwyn cofio mynd i Abertawe i'r cyfarfod yma a byddai rhai yn mynd i Lundain i'r Cyfarfod Blynyddol ac yr oedd hwnnw yn drip rhagorol.

Byddem yn cael ein gwahodd i Ysbyty Pool Parc i gael gêm o Chwist efo'r trigolion a cael croeso bendigedig yno, swper a gwobrwyon da; byddai aelodau y sefydliad yn bwyta mewn un ystafell a hwythau mewn ystafell arall, ac yna pawb yn ymuno wedyn a cael noson ddifyr iawn yn eu cwmni. Yr oeddem yn cael llawer o bethau i'n diddori ac yn cael hwyl da iawn a rhywbeth i edrych ymlaen ac i edrych yn ôl arno. Byddem yn gwahodd trigolion Ysbyty Pool Parc atom am noson ac yn paratoi swper iddynt. Saith o'r gloch oeddent i fod i gyrraedd ond gan eu bod yn edrych ymlaen gymaint am y noson byddent wedi cyrraedd am hanner awr wedi chwech, a'r merched heb orffen paratoi y bwyd. Wedi eistedd i lawr wrth y byrddau byddent yn bwyta fel pe baent heb gael bwyd ers wythnosau, a ninnau yn gwybod yn iawn eu bod yn cael y gofal gorau yn Pool Park. Mi 'roeddent yn mwynhau a ninnau yn mwynhau y noson gyda nhw a cael gemau cyn iddynt droi am adref yn y bws bach.

Noson hwyliog oedd y parti Nadolig pan fyddai pob aelod yn cael gwahodd gŵr neu ffrind, neu rhywun oeddent yn dymuno; swper iawn i ddechrau a'r bwyd wedi cael ei roi ai baratoi gan yr aelodau, a noson o gemau i ddilyn, gyda pawb yn ymuno yn yr hwyl, a neb yn swil. Byddai Robert Jones, Maesgwyn (gwr Mrs A. M. Jones), a Gwilym Williams, Maestyddyn, yn helpu llawer gyda'r adloniant. Byddai dwy aelod o ganghennau cyfagos yn cael gwahoddiad, sef Pwllglas, pan agorwyd cangen yno, a Cyffylliog. Yr wyf yn cofio un flwyddyn mi ddaeth i fwrw eira noson y parti ac fe ddaeth dwy wraig ifanc o Gyffylliog mewn car dros y mynydd fel yr oeddem yn ei alw, a thrwy y fforest gyda rhawiau yn y car rhag ofn iddynt fynd i drafferthion ar y siwrnau gartref ond bu y ddwy yn y parti nes iddo orffen ac mae yn rhaid eu bod wedi cyrraedd adref yn ddiogel gan i mi eu gweld lawer gwaith ar ôl hynny. Yn y gorffennol teimlaf fod gennym gymaint o weithgareddau i edrych ymlaen atynt at i edrych yn ôl arnynt.

I godi arian i'r mudiad cael Gyrfa Chwist bob Tachwedd, a rheini yn ei bri yr adeg honno. Yr ydwyf yn cofio rhyw flwyddyn bod y neuadd yn llawn a rhaid oedd gosod byrddau yn y gegin a rhai yn gorfod chwarae cardiau ar ben y piano. Fel y daeth ceir yn fwy poblogaidd yr oedd anhawster gyda parcio a'r nifer yn dod yn lleihau ac erbyn hyn mae'r mudiad yn eu cynnal yn flynyddol yn Cae Cymro, Clawddnewydd. Byddai pawb yn rhoi bwyd at y swper yr oeddem yn ei gael ar derfyn y cyfarfodydd misol ac yna gwerthu y gweddill i godi arian. Cynnal 'dewch a phrynwch' ambell dro, pawb yn rhoi rhywbeth oedd ganddynt i sbario a hynny yn dod a dipyn o bres i mewn. Yn nes ymlaen byddem yn cael bore, neu noson goffi yn gartref un o'r aelodau o bryd i'w gilydd a cael elw reit dda. Yr oedd angen pres i gadw y mudiad ar fynd gan fod eisiau talu rhent am y neuadd gan ein bod erbyn hyn wedi symud o'r gegin gan fod nifer yr aelodau wedi cynyddu.

Byddem yn gwneud tê i'r plant a'r athrawon ac y mae y mudiad yn dal i wneud hynny hyd heddiw. Yn mis Gorffennaf byddai hyn yn cymeryd lle ychydig o ddyddiau cyn i'r ysgol gau am wyliau yr haf, ond yr oedd yn rhaid gwneud yn siwr nad oedd yn digwydd ar ddiwrnod Sioe Frenhinol Cymru. Cael y mabolgampau ar ôl cinio a byddai dwy aelod yn mynd a hufen iâ i'r plant i'r cae, a hwythau yn ddiolchgar ohono pan oedd yn ddiwnod poeth iawn. Yn y neuadd byddai yr aelodau eraill yn paratoi y tê a hwnnw yn dê rhagorol; jeli oeddent yn gael ers talwm ond tydi plant ddim amdano rŵan ac yn well ganddynt gael brechdannau a creision. Ar ôl tê byddai yr ennillwyr yn y mabolgampau yn cael pres a rhai oedd heb ennill yn cael pres dipyn llai na'r lleill wrth gwrs. Byddai y plant yn edrych ymlaen yn fawr am y diwrnod yma. Yr oedd y merched yn edrych ymlaen i gael roi y tê ar plant yn edrych ymlaen am ei gael.

Bum yn llywydd am flwyddyn a mwynhau y profiad yn fawr iawn gan fod pawb mor barod i helpu efo naill beth ar llall. Mi fum yn drysorydd rhyw dro hefyd and yr oedd y gwaith yma dros fy mhen i gan nad oeddwn yn dda iawn gyda ffigyrau, ac felly wnes i ddim mwynhau y cyfnod yna. Fum i ddim mewn swydd

Mrs Elsa Jones

arall a rhaid i mi gyfaddef fy mod yn mwynhau fy hun yn well yn eistedd yn y gynulleidfa.

Yr wyf yn cofio un aelod oedd yn byw ar draws y cae lle yr oeddwn yn byw, sef Miss Higgins a ddaeth i'r ardal yma o Devizes yn Wiltshire a byddai yn cael ei chario yn ôl ac ymlaen yn y car efo mi; yr oedd yn gweithio yn swyddfa y 'War Ag' yn Rhuthun ar ôl y rhyfel a byddai yn gwisgo yn wahanol i bawb arall ond yn berffaith lân ac yn byw mewn carafan a bu yn aelod am flynyddoedd lawer. Yr oedd Mrs A. M. Jones, Maesgwyn, yn aelod eithriadol o ffyddlon, hi oedd asgwrn cefn y mudiad yn Clocaenog ac os oeddech eisiau unryw wybodaeth, dim ond gofyn iddi hi. Bu yn ysgrifennydd sirol ac yn gadeirydd y sir ac yn llawn gwybodaeth a bu yn gefn mawr i ni. Yr oedd Miss Gwen Evans yn un dda iawn am goginio ac ennillodd 'Seren Aur' un flwyddyn yn sioe Dinbych a Fflint. Byddai yr aelodau yn gwneud yn dda iawn pan yn cystadlu yn y sioeau yn adrannau coginio, gwaith llaw a gosod blodau.

Yn y flwyddyn 1953 mynd i Rhyl i gyfarfod y tren i fynd i Denman. Cyfarfod merched eraill nad oeddwn wedi eu gweld o'r blaen ond yn dal mewn cysylltiad a hwy byth ers hynny. Un eneth ieuanc o Sir Fôn, dipyn iau na fi, un arall o Llansannan ac un o'r Bala ac yr ydym yn ffrindiau ac yn gweld ein gilydd o bryd i'w gilydd. Mynd efor tren i Oxford, a bws yn ein cyfarfod i'n cludo i Denman. Fe gefais i ystafell sengl ac felly ddim digon ffodus i gael aros yn ystafell Sir Ddinbych gan fod honno yn addas i dri person. Fe gefais i aros yn ystafell 'Huntingdonshire' ac mae yr enwau wedi cael ei rhoi ar ôl y siroedd oedd yn gyfrifol am y costau i'w dodrefnu.

Cael darlithoedd bore, prynhawn a gyda'r hwyr, ond yr oeddynt yn wersi ysgafn ac yr wyf yn cofio un ddynes yn son am '*vacuum cleaners*' oedd newydd ddod ar y farchnad a hithau yn egluro i ni sut i'w defnyddio, a hynny yn 1953, ond chefais i yr un am flynyddoedd lawer ond yr wyf yn cofio y wers yma yn dda iawn. Cael y gwersi yn yr '*Army Huts*' lle yr oedd y sowldiwrs yn aros adeg y rhyfel. Byddai pawb yn mwynhau eu hunain ar y cyrsiau yma, ac yr wyf yn teimlo ei bod yn anrhydedd i mi gael y cyfle i fynd i Denman. Bu ambell i aelod arall yno hefyd a hwythau yn cael amser da yno. Bum yn aelod o'r sefydliad yn Clocaenog am 45 o flynyddoedd, a chofio y cyfarfodydd misol a gynhaliwyd ar yr ail nos Lun bob mis gyda phleser mawr gan nad oedd ddim llawer o gymdeithasau eraill i'w cael flynyddoedd yn ôl a'r noson yma yn amser da i gymdeithasu a gwneud ffrindiau newydd.

Sgwrs gyda Gwyneth Roberts

Clocaenog WI in 2006

Our members, 22 at present, are fully involved in all aspects of the WI. We meet on the second Monday of the month at the Church Hall and have a varied programme of speakers and activities. The Group, Federation and National Meetings are attended, and many members compete successfully in the Ruthin, the Flint and Denbigh,

Clocaenog W.I. 50th Anniversary Party, 1977.

Clocaenog Women's Institute Band,

and the Royal Welsh Shows. Clocaenog WI came second in the Federation Public Speaking Competition.

One of the highlights of the year had been the Christmas party that we held for the inmates of Pool Park Hospital but unfortunately the hospital was closed in 1990. We continue to provide a tea party for the Clocaenog School children after their annual sports. Whist drives are always popular, but are now held at the Canolfan, Clawddnewydd because of the better parking there, as everyone arrives by car these days. Our members participated in the 'Village of the Year' competition and were runners up to Betws yn Rhos, the winners. In the autumn of 2004, ten members will be attending week-end courses at the WI Denman College, Oxfordshire.

Our members were fully committed to the 'Pathway to the 21st Century' initiative in 2000. One of the projects was the co-operative effort to make the Village Embroidery, undertaken by several people, some of whom had never embroidered before. Following on from this success, a group now meet regularly at Enid Jones' house, Bod Angharad, to work on individual pieces of embroidery, again under Pat Edward's' guidance. The present book will be the culmination of our efforts and, resulting from this, we hope to organise a walking group to enjoy and become more acquainted with our locality.

Many members have come and gone, both English and Welsh speakers, and women with a wide variety of backgrounds and

Oriental evening, 1998. Some of the members dressed for the occasion! Deirdre Lund, Marie Salters and Margaret Read.

Oriental evening, 1998. The display being judged by Pauline Linley and Freda Crawford.

experiences are still joining. Considering that we live in a thinly populated rural area we are fortunate to maintain our membership, and of these only six live in the village, other members coming from Llanfwrog, Galltegfa, Ruthin and Clawdd-newydd. The commitment of the WI which 'offers opportunities for all women to enjoy friendship, to learn, to widen their horizons and together to influence local, national and international affairs' still rings true for Clocaenog WI members.

G.J.D.

Clocaenog Womens' Institute, 2004.

Bibliography

The Celts, Christiane Eleure
The Atlantic Celts, Simon James
A Short History of Wales, A. H. Dodd
When Was Wales?, Gwyn A. Williams
A Social History of England, Asa Briggs
The Church and the Welsh Border in the Tenth and the Eleventh Centuries, Christopher Brooke
The Holy Wells of Wales, Francis Jones
Sacred Places, North Wales Borderlands Tourism booklet
Enjoy Mediaeval Denbighshire, North Wales Borderlands Tourism booklet.
The Archaeology of Clwyd, Ed. by J. Manley, S. Grenter and F. Gail.
Archaeology Cymru Journals
The Prehistoric and Roman Remains of Denbighshire by E. Davies
The Romano-British Period by Kevin Blockley
The Dark Ages by Nancy Edwards
Medieval Settlement by Glanville Jones
The Drovers' Roads of Wales, Godwin & Toulson
Pilgrimage, Terry Johns and Nona Rees
Discovering Horse-drawn Farm Machinery, D. J. Smith
Turnpike Roads, Geoffrey N. Wright
Home-made Homes, Eurwyn William
Archaeologia Cambrensis
Ale and Hearty, Alan Wykes
The Taming of the Dragon, W. B. Bartlett
History Today (various issues)
Transactions of the Denbighshire Historical Society (various articles) viz:
    R. R. Davies, 'Lordship and Society in the Marches of Wales'
    R. A. Roberts, 'The Court Rolls of the Lordship Dyffryn Clwyd'
    R. I. Jack, 'Mediaeval Charters of Ruthin Borough'
Woodlands for Wales — The National Assembly for Wales Strategy for Trees and Woodlands
Leaflets from the Forestry Commission
Leaflets from The Foundation for the Protection and Preservation of the Przewatski
Cyfres Enwau Creaduriad a Phlanhigion: 2. Phlanhigion Blodeuol, Conwydd a Rhedyn, Cymdeithas Edward Llwyd
English Names of Wild Flowers, J. G. Dony, *et al*
The Wild Flowers of Britain and Northern Europe, R. Fitter, *et al*
British Trees in Colour, C. Hart, *et al*
Wild Flowers of Britain, R. Phillips
New Flora of the British Isles, C. Stace
Flora of Flintshire, G. Wynne

Clocaenog Parish Past and Present

Parish boundaries have been superseded by Community Council administrative areas.

This parish which was from seven to eight miles in length by about two and a half miles in breadth, was roughly 6,400 acres. It had the following townships: Bryn y gwrgi, Maen ar ei gilydd, Meastyddyn, Llanerch Gron, Clocaenog Isaf and Clocaenog Uchaf. The boundaries of the parish were altered from time to time as properties (and their inhabitants) were exchanged with neighbouring parishes.

The sketch map aims to show the maximum spread of Clocaenog Parish, reaching from the Afon Alwen in the east to Llanerch Gron in the west, and the modern extent of Clocaenog Community Council authority.

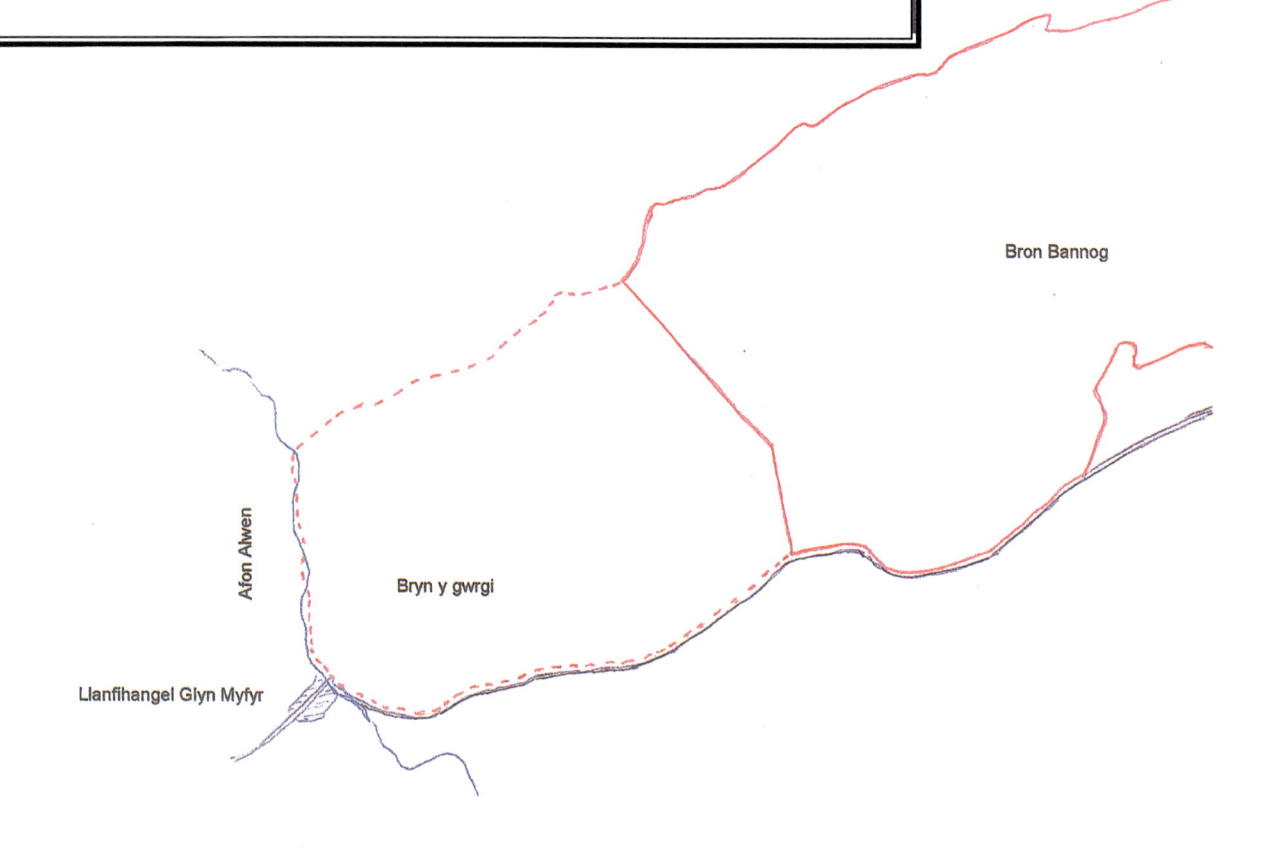

239

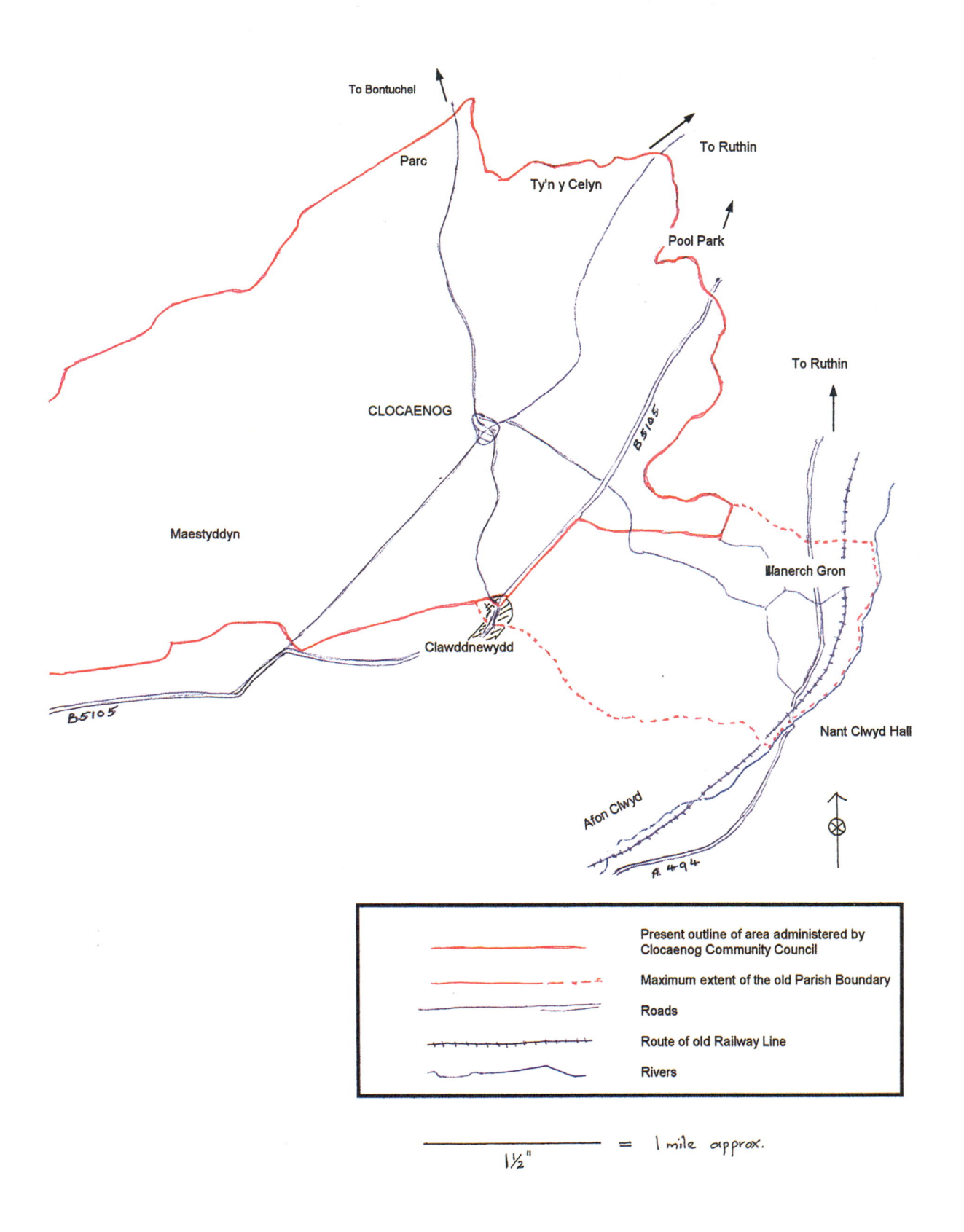